The Rise of Christian Democracy in Europe

The Wilder House Series in Politics, History, and Culture

The Wilder House Series is published in association with the Wilder House Board of Editors and the University of Chicago.

A complete list of titles appears at the end of this book.

THE RISE OF CHRISTIAN DEMOCRACY IN EUROPE

Stathis N. Kalyvas

Cornell University Press

Ithaca and London

First published 1996 by Cornell University Press.

Printed in the United States of America

Library of Congress Cataloging-in-Publication Data

Kalyvas, Stathis N., 1964–
The rise of Christian Democracy in Europe / Stathis N. Kalyvas.
p. cm. — (The Wilder House series in politics, history, and culture)
Originally presented as the author's thesis (Ph.D.)—University of Chicago, 1993, under the title: Religious mobilization and party formation.
Includes bibliographical references and index.
ISBN 978-0-8014-8320-2 (pbk. : alk. paper)
1. Christian democratic parties—Europe—History. I. Title. II. Series.
JN94.A979K35 1996
324.2′182′094—dc20

96-5600

Cornell University Press strives to use environmentally responsible suppliers and materials to the fullest extent possible in the publishing of its books. Such materials include vegetable-based, low-VOC inks and acid-free papers that are recycled, totally chlorine-free, or partly composed of non-wood fibers. For further information, visit our website at www.cornellpress.cornell.edu.

Paperback printing 10 9 8 7 6 5 4

To my parents

For Anna

Contents

Acknowledgments ix

Introduction: The Christian Democratic Phenomenon 1

1. Actors and Preferences 21

2. Strategies and Outcomes 58

3. The Puzzle of Nonformation: The Case of France 114

4. The Formation of Confessional Parties in Historical Context 167

   Belgium 187, *The Netherlands* 192,
   Austria 196, *Germany* 203, *Italy* 215

5. After the Formation: The Confessional Dilemma and the Construction of a Catholic Political Identity 222

Conclusion: Toward a Theory of Christian Democracy 257

References 265

Subject Index 291

Author Index 297

Acknowledgments

Publishing this book in the Wilder House Series makes me particularly happy because it was at Wilder House that I became a social scientist. Through five years of participation in the Comparative Politics and Historical Sociology workshop, which met every Wednesday evening at this rather odd-looking building, I learned how to read, analyze, criticize, and discuss work in a wide range of disciplines and approaches. As a part of the University of Chicago, Wilder House acquired the qualities of its institutional setting: interest in important questions; commitment to theory; search for original and innovative explanations; concern about interdisciplinary approaches; and, above all, deep attachment to open intellectual debate.

My interest in confessional parties was not the result of some preexisting concern about Christian Democracy but rather the product of the confluence of substantive and theoretical concerns fostered at Chicago. I was initially interested in the Right as a political phenomenon. In most of Europe, the Right has tended to be Christian Democratic; I found this as puzzling as the odd religious connotation of this political movement. Religious fundamentalism is widely considered the major enemy of the post–Cold War democratic world, and yet the politics of this democratic world were partly based on religious foundations. I also became interested in related theoretical issues. How are parties formed? How do they interact with society? Where do political identities come from? How can one explain unintended outcomes? How can agency be combined with structure, micro-level with macro-level analysis, rationality with contingency, history with theory? The strange (to me) world of Christian Democracy was also the perfect ground for the exploration of these wider issues.

Two books and their authors had a profound influence on this work: *Paperstones: A History of Electoral Socialism* and *Hegemony and Culture: Politics and Religious Change among the Yoruba*. Both books raised questions

I have sought to answer in my own work. The authors of these books, Adam Przeworski and David Laitin, together with Bernard Manin, guided and encouraged me. They taught me how to think analytically and helped me keep in mind that asking interesting, theoretically significant, and politically important questions is what matters most. In short, they taught me how to do social science. While at Chicago, I benefited particularly from my interaction with Daniel Verdier, who was always willing to read and comment on my work and remained a continuous source of questions and ideas, and François Furet, a unique source of intellectual stimulation. I thank them all. A third book shaped my thinking: *Stillborn Republic: Social Coalitions and Party Strategies in Greece, 1922–1936*. After introducing me to political science at the University of Athens, its author, George Th. Mavrogordatos, kept in touch, encouraged me, and discussed with me a variety of issues, always with remarkable insight. Finally, I thank the manuscript's two anonymous reviewers and the dozens of historians whose work made mine both possible and enjoyable. Unless otherwise indicated, all translations are mine.

Four Chicago friends read my manuscript: Camile Busette, Ivan Ermakoff, Akis Hadjisotiriou, and Guy Stuart. I am indebted to all four. Our ongoing discussions give sense to my everyday work. I also thank Judy Kullberg and Kevin O'Brien for fruitful discussions at the Department of Political Science of Ohio State University, and Marcus Kreuzer and Carolyn Warner for insightful comments on the manuscript. Finally, many thanks are due to my colleagues at the Department of Politics of New York University, where Russell Hardin is bringing together people who share common interests and a common language despite their divergent substantive concerns. In addition to Russell, I thank Youssef Cohen, Mike Gilligan, Anna Harvey, Gabriella Montinola, and Alex Schuessler for great (and ongoing) discussions about our work, social science, and life in general—especially in Japanese restaurants and during late hours in the department!

Outside the world of political science it was to friends that I turned for support and inspiration. I especially thank Nikos Argyropoulos. Even though we are separated by thousands of miles, Nikos is always close and available. I also thank my fellow travelers on this long intellectual journey: Mary Adamaki and Dimitris Mavroudis, Platon Chaldeos, Panos Giannakopoulos, Yannis Zervas, and especially Angeliki Louvi. My brother Andreas helped me considerably with his presence and insights. Needless to say, it is my parents who made all this possible. I am grateful to them because they raised me in an environment filled with books and ideas, where I was able to develop both an eagerness to learn and the ability to satisfy this curiosity. This book is dedicated to them, as well as to Anna Psarrea, whose presence was invaluable.

S. N. K.

New York City

The Rise of Christian Democracy in Europe

I N T R O D U C T I O N

The Christian Democratic Phenomenon

Traditional historians just say someone ordered something and it happened. Well yes, but how?

—Carlo Ginzburg

What is Christian Democracy? Christian Democratic parties have dominated the politics of Western Europe for more than a century, yet we have little understanding of what makes them distinctive.[1] These parties have a fuzzy identity and do not fit in clear-cut categories. On the one hand, they are secular rather than religious. Although they are products of past state-church conflicts and retain traces of a religious identity, they do not carry the baggage of aliberalism, intolerance, and dependence on the church supposedly carried by politicized religion. Rather, they engage in a political discourse and practice that is secular by nature. On the other hand, these parties do not fit into the conservative slot. Their mass organization, their

[1] Deschouwer 1995; van Kersbergen 1994. I use the terms "Catholic party," "confessional party," and "Christian Democratic party" in an interchangeable and generic way. With the exception of the Dutch Calvinist parties, all other notable nineteenth-century confessional parties were Catholic, and "Catholicness" was central to their identity. Christian Democracy was associated in the past with a particular ideological component of the Catholic movement, but today the term has acquired a more generic significance. When I refer to Christian Democracy as this particular ideology or movement, I use quotation marks. I do not enter into the interminable normative debates about the ideology and interpretation of Christian Democracy that dominate the literature (see, for instance Jadoulle 1990, Zsigmond 1970, and Maier 1969). Also I avoid the debates on terminological issues such as the difference between "social Catholicism," "Christian Socialism," and Christian Democracy. Such debates quickly evolve into charting endless and almost imperceptible nuances. They also tend to be irrelevant with respect to party formation. The overwhelming attention paid to ideological issues comes at the cost of disregarding the actual party formation process. As Nipperdey (1992:187) acknowledges, these "political theologies did not mark durably the concrete reality of the parties actually formed." They were an inspiration, he adds, but became "relativized" within the new parties as the representation of the interests of the church and the Catholic population took precedence over ideological concerns.

ties to trade unions, and their concern with welfare and social policies clearly set them apart from traditional Conservative parties.[2] Furthermore, most still carry the Christian label and maintain a connection, however loose, with the church. Christian Democratic parties therefore are very different from Conservative ones such as Britain's Tories (*Economist,* 17 March 1990).

Despite their hard-to-define identity, the political significance of Christian Democratic parties poses no problems: their importance cannot be overstated. These parties are frequently in power in five major European countries (where the main nonsocialist party *is* a Christian Democratic party),[3] while the European Popular party (the European federation of Christian Democratic parties), together with the Socialists, dominates the European parliament.[4] In short, Christian Democracy is rightly considered the most successful western European political movement since 1945 (*Economist,* 17 March 1990).

The Christian Democratic phenomenon raises several puzzles: the contradiction between these parties' religious roots and their enduring success in the heart of one of the most secular social environments in the world, western Europe; the success of religion in structuring impressively successful political parties at a time of general secularization and decline of the institutional power of the church; the translation of religion, a supposedly premodern cleavage, into mass parties, the modern political weapon par excellence; the emergence of confessional parties in some countries but not in others; the domination (and often monopolization) of the bourgeois political space by confessional parties; the integration into liberal democratic regimes of initially aliberal social movements; and the self-promoted secularization of these parties with the simultaneous retention of a religious label and traces of a confessional identity.

Solving these puzzles requires a theory of Christian Democracy. Such a theory should specify the conditions under which parties that appeal to voters

[2] In the early 1990s, Christian Democratic parties still had a mass membership and a highly elaborate organization with numerous ancillary organizations (Caciagli 1992; de Winter 1992; Katz et al. 1992). These parties were central in building the European welfare states (Maier 1969; Stephens 1979; Wilenski 1981; Esping-Andersen 1990; Huber et al. 1993; Boswell 1993; van Kersbergen 1995). On the relationship between Christian Democracy and unionization see Misra and Hicks 1994 and Ebbinghaus 1992.

[3] Germany, Austria, Belgium, the Netherlands, and, until recently, Italy. From 1946 to 1983, cabinets based, in part or as a whole, on Christian Democratic parties had a total tenure ranging from 256 months in Germany to 292 months in Austria, 397 in Belgium, and 456 in the Netherlands and Italy (von Beyme 1985:333). Even in Italy today, successor parties play an important pivotal role.

[4] There were 199 Socialist deputies and 162 Christian Democrats in the 1994 567-seat European parliament (for a history of the European Popular party see de Brouwer 1992). Christian Democrats were the driving force behind the creation of the European Community.

on religious grounds form and succeed; account for the failure of such parties to emerge in seemingly favorable environments; and determine the impact of confessional parties on the politics of the societies in which they operate and the ways in which they shape the relationship of religion and politics.

The starting point of such a theory is the theoretical understanding of the origins of Christian Democratic parties. Hence this book is a study of how political identities and parties are formed.[5] On a substantive level, this book explores the origins, evolution, and shifting identity of confessional parties in Catholic Europe during the late nineteenth and early twentieth centuries.[6] On a theoretical level, it examines how a democratic arena shapes politicization of religion, how that politicization affects democratic development, and how basic units of analysis of much of political science—political identities and parties—are formed. This book is based on evidence from five countries where a successful confessional party formed—Belgium, the Netherlands, Austria, Germany, and Italy—and one country where it did not—France.[7]

The synthetic literature on confessional parties (synthetic in that it offers a general and comprehensive account of their origins and formation) contains, usually implicitly rather than explicitly, two causal explanations of the emergence of these parties in nineteenth-century Europe. A first explanation, rooted in historical sociology, views these parties as creations of the Catholic church in the face of the combined rise of anticlericalism and mass politics (the classic statement is Lipset and Rokkan 1967:103). For example, Edward Lynch (1993:24) points out that "Christian Democracy was born of the determination of the Catholic popes that lay Catholics get involved in the political process." This approach posits that the conscious creation by

[5] A group of politicians becomes institutionalized, i.e., merits recognition as an established political party, when they create a crosslocal organization to contest elections nationwide; they nominate candidates to fight national elections; and they continue to nominate candidates at successive elections (Rose and Mackie 1988:535).

[6] It is not my purpose here to uncover the causes of the dissimilar political behavior displayed by Catholic societies (where confessional parties were formed) and Protestant ones (with no such parties, with the exception of the Netherlands). Explanations focus on the subordinate character of the Protestant churches with regard to the state, their institutional weakness as a result of fragmentation into multiple denominations and decentralization, and their focus on individualism (Hatfield 1981b; Martin 1978:38; Lipset and Rokkan 1967:15). The dissimilar political behavior of Catholics and Protestants does not appear to be culturally driven: when challenged by anticlerical legislation, Protestants in the Netherlands reacted the same way Catholics did, whereas when no anticlerical attack took place, Irish Catholics did not organize politically on the basis of religion.

[7] With the recent exception of Italy, these are the countries with the largest Christian Democratic parties today. Confessional parties emerged in some other countries as well: Spain (including Catalonia), Switzerland, Poland, Lithuania, Slovakia, Slovenia, and Croatia. But they were usually small, and most of the countries in which they were formed soon entered into protracted periods of authoritarianism. As a result, these parties often left no trace.

the church of a distinct Catholic identity in the political realm and of a confessional party as its direct and unequivocal expression was the obvious, inevitable, and automatic reflection of the conflicts that erupted between liberal state-building elites (and later Socialist parties) and the Catholic church. A strong extension of this argument is that these parties are the church's political arm. In its most extreme version, this approach descends into crude instrumentalism: Giovanni Miccoli (1973:189) points out that the Italian Catholic party (PPI) was "a tool of the Holy See, at least in the sense that it was part of a broad strategic plan for the political and religious reconquest of society." This argument mirrors the traditional anticlerical view of confessional parties as *polichinelles entre les mains du clergé* (puppets in the clergy's hands), a typical comment of Belgian Liberals about the members of the Catholic party.[8] (Mélot 1935:43). A weak extension of this argument is that these parties are part of the Catholic culture and institutional context (Misra and Hicks 1994). A general implication is to collapse church and Catholic people into one category (Whyte 1981:72; Houska 1985).

A second explanation, rooted in political science, emphasizes the role of conservative political elites in appropriating religion and Catholic social doctrine to build mass parties and fight the rise of socialism. This approach downplays the religious and emphasizes the conservative aspect of confessional parties, ultimately denying the distinctiveness of the Christian Democratic phenomenon (Lane and Ersson 1991:108; Broughton 1988:195; Layton-Henry 1982:17). For example, Maurice Duverger claims (1966:412–13) that the Catholic parties of Belgium, the Netherlands, and Austria are "purely and simply conservative parties that changed name." This point is persuasively undermined by recent research which shows that Christian Democratic parties affect their political and social environment very differently from Conservative parties (van Kersbergen 1995; Misra and Hicks 1994; Huber, Ragin, and Stephens 1993; Esping-Andersen 1990). An instrumentalist distortion of this approach sees political elites as purposefully building political organizations on the basis of religion to use and control mass mobilization (Witte and Craeybeckx 1987).

The failure of this approach to recognize and account for the specificity of Christian Democracy is partly rooted in the lack of what Alessandro Pizzorno (1970:57) calls a "historical reconstruction." Christian Democratic parties are usually assumed to be an exclusively postwar phenomenon disconnected from the confessional parties that preceded them (Leonardi and Wertman 1989; Broughton 1988:222; Lyon 1967:69). Yet it is as unthinkable to disre-

[8] In Anderson's (1981:6) words: "The Catholic Church appears on the historian's stage just long enough to be unmasked as an instrument of social control; its benighted adherents, a third of the population of the German Empire, are written off as 'marionettes.' "

gard prewar confessional parties as it would be to ignore prewar Social Democracy in the study of Social Democratic parties. Indeed, there is a remarkable continuity between prewar "Catholic" parties and postwar Christian Democratic ones in organization, personnel, ideology, and even strategy.[9] Clearly, a theory of Christian Democracy presupposes a theoretical understanding of its origins.

The Italian socialist newspaper *Avanti* combined both approaches in an original way. In a cartoon published in its issue of 20 May 1920, it depicted the Capital and the Jesuits manipulating a puppet pope who in turn manipulated Luigi Sturzo, the leader of the Catholic party PPI and hence the party itself[10] (Molony 1977:82).

Within these broad approaches, additional isolated variables are often stressed, such as exogenous events and leadership. For instance, John Molony (1977:47) underlines the causal implications of World War I. The personality of several popes (Hanson 1987:50; Lynch 1993:3; Diamant 1960:10) or political figures (Zeender 1976:5) is also assumed to have been instrumental in the formation of confessional parties. For example, William Bosworth (1962:17) stresses "how the personality of the Pope is an important factor in the political impact of the Church," and Piero Zerbi (1961) goes so far as to structure his entire history of the Italian Catholic movement around the tenure of various pontiffs. R. E. M. Irving (1973:35) argues that the Catholic workers' movement in France did not result in a Christian Democratic movement or

[9] For a powerful argument about the links between postwar Christian Democratic and prewar confessional parties see Mayeur (1980). For evidence on the continuity between prewar and postwar Social Democracy see Przeworski and Sprague (1986).

[10] A few interpretations question the role of the church, but they remain incomplete and atheoretical. Gramsci saw past the contention that confessional parties were deliberately created by the church. According to Fulton (1987:213), "The initial growth of a Catholic party, farming cooperatives, and workers organizations was, as Gramsci pointed out, by no means deliberately fomented from the clerical center. It was the spontaneous action of a Catholic population excluded from political life but seeking to solve its economic difficulties at the local level without direct political intervention from the center." Gramsci failed to follow up on this point and build systematically upon it. Likewise, Billiet and Gerard (1985:105) have emphasized the element of contingency in the process of party formation: "The results of the actions taken by the various actors in this arena (the episcopate, the clergy, the laymen engaged in social action, and the politicians) are never the direct extension of one or another group." This insightful observation is left hanging, however. Finally, Baum and Coleman (1987:xix) stress the role of lay Catholics in the context of "Christian Democratic" movements: "From the nineteenth century on, Christian political parties were creations of lay people who wanted to protect their Catholic identity and at the same time were open to the emerging democratic ideals. The Church tended to be afraid of these christian democratic movements. In most instances these movements, while firmly Catholic, were not interested in protecting the institutional privileges of the Church. . . . For these reasons, then, the christian democratic movements lived in some tension with the Church and occasionally were suppressed altogether." The point is well taken, but it is not developed further.

political party "partly due to the fact that Albert de Mun and Léon Harmel did not get on well together. . . . Harmel also lacked the personality of a great leader." Likewise, Jean-Dominique Durand (1995:188) underlines the fact that in France "no personality was capable of playing the role of a Windthorst or a Sturzo."

My account of confessional party formation goes against both approaches. Its central thesis is that the formation of confessional parties was the contingent outcome of decisions made by political actors. More specifically, it was the unplanned, unintended, and unwanted by-product of the strategic steps taken by the Catholic church in response to Liberal anticlerical attacks. Very simply, the existing political situation and the preferences of the prominent actors involved when these attacks began were not conducive to the formation of such parties, but the process set in motion in response to these attacks led to the creation of a new political identity among lay Catholics and the formation of confessional parties.

In short, confessional parties were formed in spite of and not, as is usually assumed, because of the church's intentions and actions. Nor was their formation intended by Conservative political elites. In fact, both sets of actors who initiated the process that led to their formation had a compatible set of preferences that excluded the creation of these parties. The outcome, however, surprised both the church and Conservative political leaders. This outcome became firmly established and structured the organization of politics and future choices in unanticipated ways.

Why did the literature fail so spectacularly to capture the most crucial aspects of the confessional party formation process? To begin with, this is an underdeveloped literature.[11] The propensity of social scientists to study the Left more than the Right was noted by Seymour M. Lipset (1981/1961) a long time ago—and the point is still valid (Kitschelt 1994:1). Despite its intriguing characteristics and political relevance, there is a general consensus that the Christian Democratic phenomenon has been overlooked, especially compared to Socialist parties (Hanley 1994:1; Anderson 1991:707; Delbreil 1990:7; Vecchio 1979b:53; Irving 1973:7). Even among non-Socialist parties, Conservative ones have received more attention than Christian Democratic ones (Misra and Hicks 1994:320). Despite a recent revival of the study of Catholicism, the literature remains underdeveloped, particularly in its theoretical and comparative dimensions.[12] Indeed, the study of confessional par-

[11] Fogarty (1957) and Irving (1979) remain the major comparative political studies on the formation and development of Christian Democratic parties. The main historical comparative works are Lönne (1986), Mayeur (1980), Whyte (1981), and Vecchio (1979a).

[12] A revival of the study of Catholicism in its political and cultural dimensions has been recently taking place in history and sociology (Noiret 1994:105; Ford 1993; Anderson 1991:682).

ties, like that of the Catholic church during the same historical period, remains in "a historiographical ghetto" (Blackbourn 1991:778–79). The cause is to be found in an intellectual and political tradition that sees religion as a premodern (and therefore irrelevant) cleavage. Social science has consistently downgraded, even ignored, the religious cleavage in favor of the class cleavage[13] (Castles 1994:19–20; Spohn 1991:109; Sartori 1990/1968:171; Hanf 1984:268). Even Lipset and Stein Rokkan (1967), who brought attention to nonclass cleavages, dubbed them preindustrial. Commenting on the state of research on confessional politics in Germany, Karl Schmitt (1990:180) points out that "even when it is accepted that confessional conflicts are real and legitimate, they are often treated as a transitional stage." Thus these parties have generally been viewed as relics of preindustrial conflicts. Such approaches predicted that religiously oriented parties were bound to disappear because they represented only a transitional stage in political and social evolution. As Antonio Gramsci pointed out in 1919, the Italian *popolari* (the members of the Italian Catholic party) were to socialists what Kerensky was to Lenin (Giovannini 1981a:151).

The result was to view confessional parties as a political and historical anomaly, an "error of history" (Schmitt 1990:180). From Bismarck, who denounced the Zentrum as an "unnatural" party (Evans 1981:56), to the French socialist leader Guy Molet for whom the Mouvement républicain populaire (MRP) was *"ce parti qui ne devrait pas exister"* (this party which should not exist)(Mayeur 1980:6), anticlerical politicians and intellectuals alike consistently denied the political legitimacy of confessional parties (Anderson 1991:707; Anderson 1988:378; Zeender: 1984:428).

Besides its underdevelopment (and because of it), the literature on confessional parties suffers from five major problems: functionalism, essentialism, the assumption away of the problem of collective action, the exogenization of mobilization and organization, and exceptionalism.

The literature on confessional parties is functionalist. Causes are accounted for by outcomes, and the historical origin of confessional parties is derived from an interpretation of their purported utility. This is also an instrumental-

---

Unfortunately, though sophisticated and devoid of the earlier ideological and doctrinal preoccupations, this research often tends to be descriptive and noncomparative.

[13] This error has been replicated in the study of developing countries. According to Haynes (1994:6), in both the modernization and dependency paradigms "religion and other cultural phenomena were depicted as epiphenomena. They were regarded as remnants of a tradition which would inevitably and invariably decline in significance as cultural rationality and national integration development." In predicting the waning of religion in developing countries, modernization theory ignored the presence and significance of political Catholicism in European political development.

ist and teleological perspective that views confessional parties as predetermined and automatic responses to a variety of exogenous forces ranging from industrialization to liberalism, including secularization, the French Revolution, socialism, and modernity. As Margot Lyon (1967:69) points out, "Christianity *was obliged* to adapt itself to the new social and political situation," and as Val Lorwin (1971:149) argues, "With industrialization, urbanization, and geographic mobility . . . the churches became concerned about risks to the faith of the masses. If isolation could no longer protect the faithful from exposure to influences corrosive to their faith, special institutions *had* to encapsulate them." Likewise, Hans Maier (1969:17) asserts that "in a society where the liberties of the church are no longer a matter of course but depend on the activities of its members (above all, the laymen), Catholicism *had* to develop political forms. Hence, political Catholicism is the natural child of Catholicism per se" (emphasis added; for similar views see Durand 1995:25; Nipperdey 1992:179; De Kwaasteniet 1990:69; LaPalombara and Weiner 1990:28; Neitzel 1987:9; Irving 1979:1; von Beyme 1985:81; Mendershausen 1973:1; Rhodes 1973:14; Rommen 1950:608). In its extreme version, this perspective views confessional parties as a product of historical necessity (De Rosa in Magleri 1969:xiii). The teleological element inherent in this approach has been aptly criticized by Blackbourn (1991:786).

Needless to say, functionalist approaches ignore choices, alternative possibilities, conflicts, and their consequences; they hence overlook actors and their preferences and strategies.[14]

The second problem of this literature is its essentialism. Two related assumptions are made. First, religious identity always exists in a crystallized fashion as a primordial, that is, naturally strong and dominant, collective sentiment. Second, primordial identities are assumed to emerge inevitably in the realm of politics, usually through a vehement eruption. In other words, the transfer of religion into politics (i.e., the transformation of religion into a politicized cleavage) and the simultaneous transformation of religion from a social into a political identity are considered unproblematic, both individually and collectively. As C. Bauer (cited in Maier 1969:17) points out, political Catholicism is nothing more than "a manifestation of Catholic religiosity within politics." Likewise, Maier (1969:13) argues, "The easiest way to understand Christian Democratic unity, however, is to understand it from the ideological viewpoint: as a community of people who have

[14] The ignorance of actors and strategy is hardly a phenomenon restricted to accounts of party formation. DeNardo has recorded a similar phenomenon in the study of revolutions: "The ironic result," he notes (1985:9–10), "is that some of the most influential studies of revolution devote hardly a word to revolutionary groups or to their strategies, while few of them accord to them more than a secondary role in the larger historical drama."

taken the path of politics because of certain earlier pre-political convictions." In short, the literature posits the organization of politics on the basis of confession as something natural and inevitable. Hence the widespread conceptual anachronism of referring to "Catholic politicians" even when discussing the period that preceded the emergence of the religious cleavage.[15]

Religious faith does not always constitute a primordial identity, however, even less the basis for a politicized cleavage. As David Laitin (1986:146) notes, "Myths of solidarity are based on blood ties *combined with* a social idea about which blood ties are real." And even then, Laitin (1986:136) points out, "primordial identities need not translate into politicized cleavages." Catholicism remained during the nineteenth century a strong religious and social identity. It also still carried significant political implications, a legacy of its past. But the collective social and political meaning it was going to assume in the context of modernity and mass politics was far from obvious. Even as an existing social identity, Catholicism was quite heterogeneous. As a prominent student of Catholicism, Emile Poulat, has pointed out (1977:198), religious education inculcates a "habitus" that creates social predispositions but does not condition behavior mechanically. In fact, there is no necessary overlap between a religious Catholic identity and a political one, between what André Siegfried (1913/1964) has dubbed Catholicism and clericalism.[16] Indeed, more often than not, Catholics were, as they still are, divided along class or ethnic lines. Pace (1995:29) refers to the political unity of Catholics as a "collective myth" and points out (1995:31) that among Italian Catholics, "the diversity of the position is the norm, the dialectic is the rule; unity is the exception." The power of a myth, he concludes (1995:48), is that it succeeds in passing as united what is divided. Likewise, Bosworth (1962:309) reports about contemporary France that "outside of a narrow dogma, Catholics disagree among themselves on practically everything relating to social and temporal life." The same author adds (1962:28) that "it is always difficult to bring all Catholics together for a common political purpose." To paraphrase Adam Przeworski and John Sprague (1985:54, 182), solidarity among Catholics is not a mechanical consequence of their common religious creed.

Thus the assumption that social identities automatically and inevitably

[15] Nipperdey (1992:178) and Mayeur (1980:27), refer to the presence of a "Catholic party" or of "Catholic parliamentarians" in Belgium during the 1830s-40s. Yet Mayeur adds (1980:27) that it "would be imprecise and anachronistic to imagine at that time the opposition of a Catholic and a Liberal bloc."

[16] In his classic work, Siegfried (1964/1913:392) defined Catholicism as "simply religion" and clericalism as "a political frame of mind and system." Catholicism, he argued, makes a distinction between the citizen and the faithful man, but clericalism does not.

become political ones is flawed. The transition from a Catholic *social* identity to a Catholic *political* identity has to be accounted for. The presence of large Catholic populations in a country is analytically and empirically insufficient for predicting the emergence of a common Catholic identity in politics, even less the formation of a confessional party. Indeed, religion does not necessarily structure politics even in religiously divided societies (Laitin 1986), and historical evidence indicates that rarely did religion constitute the basis for parliamentary or mass political action before the emergence of a religious cleavage even in the countries where confessional parties were later formed (Anderson 1993; Kossmann 1978; Lebas 1960). The political organization of individuals on the basis of their religious faith was neither obvious nor inevitable because, as Pierre Bourdieu (1987:11) has pointed out, "the sense of the social world does not assert itself in a univocal and universal fashion." It was not obvious, as Adrien Dansette (v.1 1961:238) has noted: "If the idea of a Catholic party worried the clergy, it seemed even more extraordinary to laymen." And it was not inevitable as the case of France indicates: despite the presence of the right structural conditions no confessional party emerged.

If a religious cleavage and confessional parties were neither obvious nor inevitable, then how did they emerge in most countries of nineteenth-century Catholic Europe? As Laitin (1986:159–60) argues, primordial identities are forged politically; only once forged do they become commonsensically real. The process of cleavage and identity formation is linked to mobilization and organization and, in turn, to the choices and decisions about mobilization and organization made by political actors. In the terms used by the early socialists, what matters are *liens de volonté* (ties of will) rather than *liens de nécessité* (ties of necessity)(Pizzorno 1970:46). According to Przeworski and Sprague (1986:7):

> Class, religion, ethnicity, race, or nation do not happen spontaneously as reflections of objective conditions in the psyches of individuals. Collective identity, group solidarity, and political commitment are continually transformed—shaped, destroyed, and molded anew—as a result of conflicts in the course of which political parties, schools, unions, churches, newspapers, armies, and corporations strive to impose a particular form of organization upon the life of society. The relation between places occupied by individuals in society and their acts is a contingent historical outcome of struggles that confront interests and images, that involve preferences and strategies, that bring victories and defeats. The political behavior of individuals can be understood only in concrete historical articulation with these conflicts—particular traits become causes of individual acts when they are embedded within a definite structure that has been imposed upon political relations at a given moment in history.

Recent research has highlighted the importance of political actors in shaping cleavages, identities, and politics.[17] This action leads to the politicization of certain cleavages and the concomitant politicization of certain identities, in certain ways, places, and periods and not others. Hence a theory of Christian Democracy will have to account for the construction of a Catholic political identity. In other words, such a theory should endogenize political identity and specify how Catholics reach the equivalent of what Ira Katznelson (1986:17–19) has identified as the third and fourth levels of class formation: the formation of a group sharing dispositions that "map the terrain of lived experience and define the boundaries between the probable and improbable" and "the realization of collective action through movements and organizations." In sum, the emergence of a Catholic political identity is, in Margaret Somers's terms (1994:630), "an *empirical* rather than a presuppositional question."

The third problem of the literature lies in its assumption away of the problem of collective action through the positing of a direct and automatic leap from common interests to organization and action. For instance, George Windell (1954:11) argues that "in Prussia there was a combination of circumstances which made a formal Catholic party useful. The Hohenzollern kingdom was predominantly Protestant; therefore, Catholics as the largest religious minority, had special interests to defend." Likewise, Heinrich Rommen (1950:608) argues that the growth of political Catholicism was "necessary wherever the political groups that controlled the 'neutral' state showed an outspoken enmity against the Church." We know, however (Olson 1971; Hardin 1982), that the existence of a group of individuals with common interests does not necessarily produce collective action on behalf of this interest. Therefore, the leap from common interests to collective action has to be accounted for.

Fourth, this literature assumes that political actors (such as the church or the Conservative political elites) had both the incentive and the interest to mobilize the masses on the basis of a religious appeal, first into permanent mass organizations and then into confessional parties. This literature thus echoes the widespread tendency in the traditional study of political mobilization and organization building to focus exclusively on the masses to be

[17] Przeworski and Sprague (1986) have shown how the electoral strategies of Social Democratic parties affected the saliency of class as a cleavage. Laitin (1986) has shown how the strategies of the British colonizers made religion irrelevant as a political cleavage among the religiously divided Yoruba of Nigeria; Biagini and Reid (1991:15) have stressed that "the form eventually taken by popular politics will depend on the relative success of appeals from rival parties and programmes"; Rosenstone and Hansen (1993) have shown that political mobilization depends on the strategic choices of political actors, which, in turn, reinforce collective identities. As Bartolini and Mair (1990:217) put it, "It is only through the historical process of mobilisation, politicisation, and democratisation that any specific cleavage acquires its distinctive normative profile and organisational network."

organized. The decisions and choices of political actors are ignored; mobilization and organization are taken for granted and assumed away. Political entrepreneurs are seen as always having an interest in mobilizing and organizing people and as always doing so. Indeed, the creation of lay mass organizations by the church is generally seen as a costless choice with only positive returns (McLeod 1986). But as Steven Rosenstone and John Hansen (1993:30) point out, this assumption is wrong: "Mobilization is not a universal or a constant occurrence. Political leaders do not try to mobilize everybody, and they do not try to mobilize all the time. Mobilization, after all, is not their real goal. . . . Mobilization is one strategy they may use, but it is neither the only one nor, always, the best one." In this perspective organizations and parties are "endogenous institutions" (Aldrich 1995:4). Politicians do not always seek to achieve their goals through parties because they can turn to other arrangements such as interest groups, issue networks, or personal electoral coalitions (Aldrich 1995:26). Likewise, Michael Wallerstein (1989) points out that recruitment of workers by unions is a function of its costs and that the level of unionization is a function of strategic decisions made by unions under constraints.

In short, mobilization and the formation of mass organizations and political parties do not happen always and automatically. They are a function of the costs they induce and the benefits they confer to political actors. Therefore, mobilization and organization have to be accounted for; a theory of party formation has to endogenize them.

Finally, with the exception of a few comparative studies (which tend to be mere juxtapositions of cases), the great majority of works are case studies. Their authors routinely claim that their object of study is unique. For example, the opening statement of Herman Bakvis's book (1981:1) is that "the Catholic party in the Netherlands is unique." Similarly, Henri Carton de Wiatr (in Guyot de Mishaegen 1946:i) claims that the Belgian Catholic party "is, anyway, a specific Belgian phenomenon," while for the German historian Golo Mann (1968:212) the Zentrum is "a strange product of German history." The lack of comparative perspective is a major source of flawed insights. For instance, Philippe Boutry and Alain-René Michel (1992:674) argue that the claim the French Action libérale populaire (ALP) and its successor parties made about not being confessional parties "is evidently explained by the political context particular to France." A similar claim was made by confessional parties in all five countries. In like fashion, Caroline Ford (1987:240) argues that "one can perhaps attribute the relative cohesiveness and longevity of the Center party in Germany [compared to the failure of the French ALP] to the fact that Catholicism was a minority religion in the Empire." In Belgium, Italy, and Austria, however, confessional parties were cohesive and lasted for a long time even though Catholicism was not a minority religion.

This book represents a step away from the approaches outlined above. Contrary to the literature, the account that follows is comparative and endogenizes political identity, mobilization, and organization into the process of party formation. In so doing, it supplies some of the micro-foundations of Lipset and Rokkan's theory and delineates its applicability.

To unpack the party formation process, I examine the way social and political actors make decisions based on their own self-interest under conditions that constrain their choices and the information available to them. I seek to understand the causal dynamics of the party formation process and uncover the reasons why religion was important in molding political identities and voting behavior in some countries but not in others, during some periods but not in others, in some ways but not in others. I ask *how, why,* and *by whom* the confessional parties were formed. What were the preferences of the main actors, the strategies chosen by them, and their effects? I reconstruct the structure of choices and dilemmas the actors faced, define and elaborate the set of strategies at their disposal, describe the tensions that arose between them, examine the nature of the conflicts provoked by these tensions, and spell out the mechanisms that explain when and how political conflict led to party formation. The result is a model of party formation that accounts for both outcomes of formation and nonformation. At the same time, I show how choices made by political actors under constraints can lead to outcomes that have been unplanned and unforeseen by those actors, are unwanted by them, yet become firmly established and, in turn, shape the organization of politics and the structure of future opportunities and choices for individual and collective actors.

The traditional (mostly functionalist) sociological literature on organization building (see, for example, Stinchcombe 1965) is too general to be of much help; in fact, it often reads as description on an abstract level. As Theda Skocpol (1979:34) points out about similar work on revolution, such theories "are framed in such general conceptual terms, [that] it is very difficult to tell if they ever *do not* apply to a given case." Organization is treated as an outcome of general social processes, while political actors and their strategic choices are absent from the analysis. The same is true about party formation. Kjell Eliassen and Lars Svaasand (1975:96) point out that the vast literature on political parties is "fairly rich in describing the *phases* of development and also the kinds of parties that develop, but offer[s] little in the way of the analysis of *conditions* for organizational formation as such." The macrohistorical theory of Lipset and Rokkan (1967) remains the most powerful theoretical account of party formation in Europe, but it suffers from shortcomings. According to this approach, conflicts (in the form of crucial junctures) produce cleavages, which are articulated by political parties; the emergence of a religious cleavage and the subsequent formation of confessional parties is therefore seen as the automatic consequence of the conflict between state and church; likewise, mass mobilization is seen as ineluctably leading to party formation. But conflicts and cleavages, even mass mobilization, need not translate into parties, and the organization of politics in terms of confession is not inevitable. Furthermore, this approach "blackboxes" the process of party formation, ignores its micro-foundations, loses track of agency, and does not specify how and by whom parties are formed. Finally, it fails to account for a case in which the conditions set by the theory were present yet the predicted outcome did not obtain: in spite of a very intense state-church conflict, no confessional party was formed in France.[18]

Yet very few studies have attempted to generate an analytical framework specifically geared toward the study of party formation. As Peter Mair (1993:121) points out, "Very little may have been proposed in order to qualify Rokkan's understanding of the origin and early development of mass politics in Western Europe." Most such studies are very vague (Hauss and Rayside 1978; Eliassen and Svaasand 1975), while others (Pinard 1971, on the rise of the Social Credit party in Canada, and Kitschelt 1989, on the formation of Green parties in Belgium and West Germany) have a more limited scope because they focus on party formation in already crystallized party systems, which vastly differs from contexts of total party system fluidity.

This study is comparative and analytical. It is based on the premise that social science should be looking "for a single set of variables and logically consistent causal connections that make sense of a broad range of national experiences rather than a collection of nation-specific explanations" (Luebbert 1991:5). Obviously, this set of variables should explain both cases of success and failure in party formation. I, therefore, rely on the comparative method (Lijphart 1971; Skocpol and Somers 1980). Using multiple cases provides variation on the dependent variable while controlling for independent variables. For example, no confessional party emerged in France although the state-church conflict is present across all cases. One can eliminate variables that vary across cases with the same outcome, such as the personality of leaders, and variables that remain constant across cases with different outcomes, such as exogenous events like the war. For example, Molony (1977:47) underlines the causal implications of war: "The main contributing historical factor to the formation of the PPI was undoubtedly the First World War. After a conflict in which Catholics had fought and died for their country it was not possible to deny them a role in its peace." This claim is undermined by a focus on France, where a similar process produced exactly the opposite

[18] Structuralist approaches are often methodologically inconsistent: ad hoc, personalistic, and incidental factors abound when it comes to explaining the failure of the emergence of confessional parties; as a result, one is faced with approaches that simultaneously explain emergence by structural factors and failure by personalistic or incidental ones.

result: the war fostered fraternity among the French and contributed to the integration of Catholicism into the Republic, but it pushed French Catholics away from politics and into individual piety (Bosworth 1962:31). Likewise, Jonathan Sperber's argument (1980:390; 1982:305–18) that the success of political Catholicism in the Rhineland and Westphalia regions of Germany was caused by a religious revival that took place after 1850 is undermined by the failure of a similar popular religious revival in France to lead to the emergence of a confessional party.

By establishing analytic equivalence it is possible to treat all cases in a complementary fashion. First, the cases under study are contiguous (Sewell 1992). Second, even though the individual confessional parties and the exact way they were created differ on several points, the pattern and underpinning of the dynamic process that led to their formation is fundamentally the same—a point emphasized by Roger Aubert (1982:191).[19] The formation of confessional parties took place in the same period (1870–1920) in several European countries facing similar challenges: industrialization, democratization, rise of working-class movements, and strong Catholic churches attacked by Liberal governments. The preferences of the main actors were similar or very close, particularly those of the Catholic church, which was a centralized, hierarchical, and supranational institution.

Using the comparative method alone is not sufficient, however. A focus on mechanisms is necessary because the comparative method can establish associations but not causality. As Laitin (1995:6) warns:

> The identification of plausible connections between independent and dependent variables only suggests association, but not cause. The empirical relationships become powerful if they are part of a deductively driven "story" which provides a rationale as to how and why the situation on the independent variable leads to specified outcomes on the dependent variables. This story should suggest mechanisms that drive the variations in the predicted directions. The stronger the theory (its assumptions are reasonable; the number of independent variables is few; its applications to other cases are wide; its account of the cases at hand are plausible), the more confident one is that the empirical association has causal properties.

This enterprise is therefore an attempt to tell a deductively driven and theoretically generated "compelling tale" (Przeworski and Sprague

[19] Individual confessional parties were more conservative, like the Belgian and Dutch parties, more centrist, like the German party, more progressive, like the Italian party, and more radical, like the anti-Semitic Austrian party. Despite their differences, however, these parties shared a crucial characteristic: their formation and identity were based on a primarily religious and antiliberal appeal.

1986:181) about the formation of confessional parties and its impact on politics, stressing "intuitively plausible causal links" (Rogowski 1995:469–70), and to assess its validity against historical evidence. This amounts to an "explanation by mechanisms"[20] (Elster 1989:1). To unpack the process of party formation and to uncover and study its mechanisms, I use an analytical approach based on rational choice theory. The formation of confessional parties is analyzed as a process. The analysis focuses particularly on the transition from one strategic situation, or choice point (node), to the next and is path-dependent because it stresses the binding quality of choices at one node for action at the next one. I study political actors embedded in concrete historical situations and their strategies, interests, perceptions, possibilities, and choices. Objective factors and economic and social structures are seen not as determining outcomes but as constituting at most constraints on that which is possible in a concrete historical situation (Przeworski 1986:47, 48). Political actors have preferences that are specified and interact by selecting strategies that maximize their fundamental utility within given constraints (Levi 1991:131). I use the "thin" definition of rationality: actors are seen as rational in the sense that they choose a course of action that is likely to produce the best outcome for them (Elster 1989:22). Following Raymond Boudon (1982:9; 1995:105), I see actors as having "limited" or "cognitive rationality": an actor is intentional, "endowed with a set of preferences, seeking acceptable ways of realizing his objectives, more or less conscious of the degree of control that he has over the elements of the situation in which he finds himself (conscious in other words of the structural constraints that limit his possibilities of action), acting in the light of limited information and in a situation of uncertainty."

Because outcomes are a function of the choices actors make under constraints and in interaction with the choices of other actors, they can fall outside the actors' preference sets and expectations.

While structuralist approaches disregard process, most rational choice approaches, beginning with the Downsian treatment of party competition, treat actors and preferences as given and exogenous to the political process, in fact assuming them away (Koelble 1995; Taylor 1993:94; Thelen and Steinmo 1992:8). This often leads to simplistic and unrealistic assumptions about

[20] According to Elster (1993:3), "A mechanism is a specific causal pattern that can be recognized after the event but rarely foreseen." I follow Elster in his assertions that "by concentrating on mechanisms, one captures the dynamic aspect of scientific explanation: the urge to produce explanations of ever finer grain" (1989:7) and that "for explanatory purposes the mechanism is what matters. It provides understanding" (1989:10). As Elster (1993:5) has argued, "The distinctive feature of a mechanism is not that it can be universally applied to predict and control social events, but that it embodies a causal chain that is sufficiently general and precise to enable us to locate it in widely different settings."

actors and their preferences and, consequently, to fundamentally misspecified models (Przeworski 1990:23–26). In fact, such assumptions come with a blatant ignorance of the historical, social, and political context within which strategic interaction takes place. As James DeNardo (1985:28) warns, "Strategies are constrained by political circumstances, and a fundamental problem in a theory of strategy is to understand the interaction between strategic choice and the political environment." Finally, rational choice arguments often fail to take into account the internal dynamics of collective actors (Koelble 1991:28; Kitschelt 1989:46). I, therefore, follow here what Boudon (1982:177) has dubbed a "paradigm of Tocquevillean type" in which preferences are not disregarded but have to be explained and accounted for.

Telling a deductive story without pitting it against evidence would be incomplete and unsatisfactory. Where does the evidence come from? Fortunately, besides the synthetic literature on Christian Democracy there exists a large body of mostly traditional historiographic monographs. This literature is made up of case studies that tend to be purely descriptive and are clogged with an incredible amount of detail. It emphasizes normative, doctrinal, or ideological issues and often ignores questions of political organization and particularly of political strategy.[21]

Still, this body of literature is far more realistic than the synthetic literature. Lacking grand theoretical pretensions, this work describes, often in minute historical detail, the nonlinear process of party formation in all its complexity and identifies the conflicts and confrontations that took place during this process—conflicts marginalized or totally ignored by grand histories and synthetic studies. Even though this literature fails to analyze the party formation process in a systematic way, swamps the significance of these conflicts, and ignores their implications, it remains an invaluable empirical source on which to build and against which to check deductive models and theories.[22]

To restate the central substantive argument of this book: the formation of

[21] In a recent bibliographical essay, Noiret (1994:100) describes the historical work on political parties in nineteenth-century Belgium as follows: "Few genuinely historical studies offer a global discussion of the history of the party as institution; most content themselves with a traditional descriptive approach, covering the political and ideological positions of parliamentary leaders or taking in account only a partial chronological or regional split. They fail to concentrate upon the nature of the party as an institution, its internal functioning and, as a consequence, its relationship with the other components of the political system. . . . Only recently has the sociological school taken an interest in the nineteenth century." Excellent French historical regional studies are the exception since they combine meticulous attention to historical detail with a strong sociological quality.

[22] Many authors assume that these conflicts ultimately were irrelevant because confessional parties were finally formed (see, for instance, Whyte [1981:69]; Aubert [1982:192]). As a result, their point about the church's hostility to the new forms of action and organization remains irrelevant and peripheral in their account.

confessional parties was the contingent outcome of the conflict between church and liberals. Confessional parties were formed in spite of and not, as is often assumed, because of the church's intentions and actions. They emerged as an unplanned, unwanted, and ultimately detrimental by-product of the strategic choices the church made under constraints. Nor did Conservative political elites intend that confessional parties be formed. In fact, both sets of actors who initiated the process that led to the formation of confessional parties had a compatible set of preferences that excluded the creation of these parties. The outcome, however, surprised both the church and Conservative political leaders. It became firmly established and in many ways ended up being damaging for both. Paradoxical as this might appear, it was fully justified from the point of view of the actors' rationality. The conflicts that took place during the emergence of the Catholic movements were not necessary birth pains with a purely historical significance. By shaping the structure of future choices, these conflicts had a tremendous significance for the development of politics in Europe and tell an important story about the twin processes of the construction of political identities and the emergence of political organizations.

As will become apparent, the formation and action of the Catholic movement created a Catholic political identity rather than the other way around —a point made by Francesco Traniello (1981:46): "At this point is born . . . the 'Catholic world' as a distinct reality endowed with a specific physiognomy of its own and, in many ways, with an ideological system of its own. The 'Catholics,' or as their adversaries define them . . . the 'clericals,' are born unmistakably qualified not only on the religious or devotional plan, but as [a] complex and diffuse reality of [an] association in a phase of extension in all the dimensions of civil society."

Once formed, Catholic organizations shaped and maintained this identity by enforcing the collective discipline necessary to overcome class or ethnic divisions among Catholics. As Ludwig Windthorst, the leader of the German Zentrum, used to say, *"extra centrum nulla salus"* (no salvation outside the Zentrum).

Confessional parties, far from being a dependable instrument of the church, were antagonistic to it, first, by competing with the church for the right to represent the same constituency, lay Catholics; second, by deemphasizing the salience of religion in politics to appeal to broader categories of voters and strike alliances with other political forces; and third, by altering their religious identity to ensure their independence and autonomy of action from the church. I show that, as a result, confessional parties from their inception detached themselves from the church. I argue that these parties may even have provoked increasing rates of disaffection among the faithful, thus reducing in subtle but important ways the importance of religion in their respective societies. In a parallel fashion, the emergence of confessional parties ended up being damaging for the Conservative political elites that were involved in the formation process. The autonomy of their action was reduced, they were eventually replaced by leaders of Catholic mass organizations, and they saw the objectives of the new parties, which now dominated the Conservative space, move in more radical directions. To summarize, the organization of politics on the basis of religion was the unintended (and, also, the perverse) outcome of the strategies chosen by political actors under the constraints generated by the state-church conflict.

I proceed as follows: Chapters 1 and 2 lay out the theoretical framework of the analysis. In Chapter 1, the preferences and strategies of the actors are reconstructed and examined in detail. In Chapter 2, party formation is analyzed as a dynamic process. The outcome, the formation of a Catholic political identity and confessional parties, is accounted for as a result of this process. Chapter 3 introduces variation on the dependent variable and accounts for the failure of confessional party formation in France. Chapter 4 contains the five case studies that constitute the rest of the historical evidence on which the model is based. Finally, Chapter 5 looks at the implications of the formation of confessional parties for politics and society and the evolution of the Catholic political identity. It proposes an argument that explains the secularization of confessional parties as a process endogenous to these parties.

Some preliminary qualifications are necessary. This book stresses the common path followed by the emergent confessional parties. This is not to say that there were no differences between these parties; but an accurate understanding of these differences presupposes a theory of their formation. Moreover, the book's stress on political action and strategy rather than ideology is not meant to deny the importance of ideas; rather, it is intended to reestablish a balance that has been upset by an almost exclusive focus on ideology. I define as confessional those parties that use (or have used when formed) religion (or issues related to religion or the church) as a primary issue for political mobilization and the construction of political identities.[23] It does not matter if religion might have eventually acted as a proxy for other issues or cleavages or if activists and followers might not have had exclusively religious motivations. What is important is that the church and religion were

[23] Definitions of confessional parties vary. For Boutry and Michel (1992:673) a confessional party is "a political organization with a recruitment, an electorate, a program, and goals which depend on a confession." Irving (1973:7) defines Christian Democracy as "organized political action by Catholic democrats." Alzaga's (1973) more restrictive definition requires the presence of the use in its label of terms such as "Christian," "Catholic," or derivatives; inspiration from the doctrine of the church; submission to the directives of the hierarchy; and the profession of the Catholic religion as a prerequisite for membership.

central elements in the process of emergence of these organizations. This fact defined the character of confessional political organizations in an unequivocal way, both for supporters and opponents. The term "church" means the Catholic church because confessional parties were (with one exception) Catholic parties. My time frame is the period that begins from roughly 1860 and goes up to 1920: this is the period of the development of mass politics. Although full-fledged parliamentary democracies were not yet operating in all the countries under examination, they were anticipated as inevitable by all actors.[24] This is also the period of the formation of party systems all over Europe. It is a crucial period because, according to Lipset and Rokkan's (1967) well-known "freezing hypothesis," the outcomes that were reached then still determine contemporary party configurations in Europe.[25]

[24] During the process of party formation, two countries (Germany and Austria) had yet to reach parliamentary sovereignty while in four countries (Belgium, the Netherlands, Austria, and Italy) the right to vote was still restricted.

[25] Bartolini and Mair (1990) and Mair (1993) have shown how stable the European electorates have remained in the last hundred years and how persistent still are the parties created then.

CHAPTER I

Actors and Preferences

In the Vatican there is an absolute aversion that a party of Catholics either exists or appears to exist.

—Dino Secco Suardo

The parliamentary, Catholic, and liberal Right was rejecting the idea of an organized, centralized, and confessional party.

—Jean-Luc Soete

This chapter begins with a preview of the story of the emergence of confessional parties. Its purpose, to use Barrington Moore's (1966:xx) phrase, is to "sketch in very broad strokes the main findings in order to give the reader a preliminary map of the terrain we shall explore together." I then introduce a simple model of party formation, which includes the preferences of the two main actors and maps their options by reviewing the range of strategic alternatives available to them and their cost. Finally, from this model I derive some hypotheses about the formation of confessional parties and discuss them.

Scattered attempts by political entrepreneurs to create political parties based on a religious appeal before the 1860s consistently failed. These attempts were ignored by both the church and the faithful Catholics among the electorate. Most practicing Catholics thought of themselves as Conservatives or Monarchists, often even as Liberals. Their political behavior was consistent with these identities. Among parties, existing Conservative factions were usually concerned about the protection of the church's rights and privileges, but this was not always their first or overarching priority.

The church behaved politically in a pragmatic way, dealing directly with both Conservative and Liberal governments (through concordats among others), much like an interest group.[1] "The logical end of such a strategy was

[1] Means of church influence in Catholic states included hand-picked confessors for kings and ministers and pressure on ministers and high functionaries formed in Catholic colleges. In non-Catholic states, the action of the pope's diplomatic agents, nuncios and ambassadors, was central (Aubert 1982:192).

ecclesiastical quietism on political issues in exchange for Conservative and government protection of the church's confessional interests" (Anderson 1981:194). The "discreet lobbying of ministers on specific concessions to the Church" (Blackbourn 1975:846) was preferred over mobilization by lay Catholics, which was rejected. In fact, the church firmly opposed the spontaneous mobilization of its members in its support. Carl Schorske (1967:363) reports that the "rowdy mass demonstrations" of the Viennese Christian Socials were "as shocking to the old-guard Catholic hierarchy as they were alarming to the liberals," and Anita May (1973:82) recounts that during a minor conflict over education in France during the 1840s, "The bishops believed that the church could best be represented in peaceful negotiations among themselves, the king, and the minister of worship. They resented the fact that the Catholic press mobilized the lower clergy and the faithful without consulting the bishops on the prudent path of action. Several bishops were particularly alarmed when *L'Univers* organized petitions for freedom of education in May and June 1844."

The political weight of lay Catholics thus was minimal, a situation consistent with the doctrine and organization of the church: "Lay people had assuredly an important role," Aubert (1982:192) points out, "but as members of the *Establishment,* to the extent that they were part of the top of the ruling class."

The preferences of voters, the concerns of party elites, and the strategy of the church did not suggest that viable and strong confessional parties would come into existence. On the contrary, party systems all over Europe appeared to develop along the familiar Conservative/Liberal dichotomy. From the 1860s on, however, centralizing, state-building governments began launching attacks against the church, seeking to deprive it of much of its control over education and family. In Germany and Italy, these attacks were also connected with movements of national unification. As expected, the church perceived anticlerical attacks as being of tremendous consequence for its future. Increasingly deprived of its traditional privileged access to governments, the church had to devise new strategies. This forced break with its past strategy led it along a path that induced two crucial choices and set in motion a process that resulted in the unplanned formation of confessional parties.

Initially the church faced the choice of whether to seek compromise with the Liberals or to go for an all-out fight against them based on the formation of mass organizations. The strategy of outright resistance, which I call organizational strategy, consisted of the exclusive use of the church's resources in the fight against anticlerical measures. This struggle would be waged outside the electoral and legislative process and by the church alone. The fundamental element of this strategy was the creation of mass organizations, which were conceived as the starting point for a countersociety that would grow to swallow the Liberal state and reestablish the church in its former glory. The organizational strategy was preferred over compromise in five out of the six countries examined in this book. Liberals, however, were not deterred and escalated their attacks against the church.

The church now faced a new choice: whether to remain outside the political process or enter it. Both choices included high risks. The church reluctantly opted for the second, participation strategy. To avoid being transformed into a political party, the church put together electoral coalitions based on existing Conservative factions. These coalitions fought electoral campaigns that emphasized the defense of the church and aimed to revoke the anticlerical reforms. Contrary to the former practice of unsystematic support of Conservative candidates, this strategy entailed coordinated electoral action, particularly by the newly formed Catholic mass organizations. Such support necessitated the transformation of these organizations into increasingly politicized and electorally oriented organizations that would help get the Conservative coalitions in power and, once there, pressure them to implement the pro-church program. In essence, this strategy was based on a reciprocal contracting out of undesirable but necessary activities between the church and Conservative politicians: the church would contract out to Conservative political elites the political struggle against anticlerical reforms, and Conservative politicians would contract out mass organization to the church.

Still, the church had no intention of politicizing Catholic organizations on a permanent basis, nor was there any plan to fuse Catholic mass organizations and Conservative factions within a single organizational frame. There was, in other words, neither intention nor plan to create confessional parties. Such parties were unwanted by the church because they would end its monopoly of the representation of lay Catholics and undermine its universalistic claims. The church intended to keep Catholic mass organizations under its strict control and depoliticize them after this struggle ended. As a result, the church obstructed all attempts by Catholic activists to increase the autonomy and independence of these organizations, as well as their attempts to create confessional parties. Likewise, Conservative political elites had no desire or plan for the formation of confessional parties. To them, confessional parties were detrimental for two reasons: their association with religion would restrict their issue space; and their connection to the church, a force beyond their control, would restrict their autonomy of action and threaten their political survival. Moreover, the formation of confessional parties was inefficient for both actors because it induced higher costs but only marginal improvements (if any) compared to the participation strategy. Historical evidence indicates that even in the darkest moments of the anticlerical attack, both actors had no intention of creating confessional parties. Nevertheless, confessional parties based on Catholic mass organizations emerged in five out of the six countries under study. They succeeded in establishing themselves as *the* Catholic parties, came to dominate the Conservative political space, and became increasingly independent from the church. How was such an unintended and inefficient outcome reached?

The answer, I argue, is that the strategies implemented by the church had unintended yet important political consequences, resulting in the formation of new identities and organizations. These strategies mobilized politically and electorally, for the first time, lay Catholics *qua Catholics,* creating a Catholic political (as opposed to religious or social) identity. The transition from the participation strategy to the formation of confessional parties (or the translation of the new political identity into a new party) was made possible by the large and unexpected electoral success of the defense of the church coalitions. Electoral success proved a unique opportunity to two sets of, up to then, secondary actors: low clergy and lay Catholic activists. By providing them with a new source of power and legitimation, electoral success allowed these actors to transform these ephemeral and loose coalitions into political parties against the wishes of both church and Conservative politicians. Table 1 provides a chronological guide to the process of party formation in the countries under study.

The church fell victim to the success of its own strategy: it could not transform itself into a political party so as to control these developments because to do so would sacrifice its universalistic claims. But the church could not freeze the process and prevent its mass organizations from evolving into political parties because it was extremely costly to bring Catholic activists back into the fold. Having newly acquired political power, these activists were no longer willing to accept being relegated to the margins of political life as passive spectators subject to the control of the church hierarchy. Although the church realized that these emerging confessional parties were amputating a big part of its organization and membership, it had no choice but to recognize them. By creating a new political class, the strategy of the church affected the other side as well. The Conservative politicians who led the electoral coalitions of the participation strategy were swept away by the leaders of the Catholic mass organizations.

The process of party formation had important political consequences. One was the crystallization of the association between conservatism and religion on a partisan level and the monopolization of the Conservative political space by confessional parties. Confessional parties, however, were different from traditional Conservative parties. They could not shed their confessional character because religion had become the basis of the political identity of their electorate and the cement that held their heterogeneous social basis together.

Table 1. The formation of confessional parties

	Belgium	Netherlands	Austria	Germany	Italy
Church support for Liberals	1830–1847	1850–1864	N/A	1860s	N/A
First threats	1850–1860	1857–1878	1866	1866–1870	1850–1861
First National Catholic Congress	1864	1883	1874	1871	1874
Organizational strategy	1864–1878	1868–1878	1868–1874	1867–1870	1874–1913
Anticlerical attack	1878	1878	1867–1874	1870–1878	1861–1890
Participation strategy	1878–1884	1878–1888	1887–1890	1870–1871	1913–1919
Electoral success	1884	1888	1887	1870; 1871	1913; 1919
Participation in government	1884	1888	1880s (Vienna)	N/A	1916
Formation	1884	1879,[a] 1888[b]	1890	1871	1919
Institutionalization centralization of party	1910s	1926	1906	1880s	1919

Notes:
Church support for Liberals: periods during which pro-church politicians support Liberal governments.
First threats: first Liberal moves against the church.
Organizational strategy: church fights alone and outside the political system.
Anticlerical attack: full-fledged anticlerical attack, through legislative or other means.
Participation strategy: church fights with political allies inside the political system.
Electoral success: first success in elections.
Formation: official formation of a Catholic party.
Institutionalization/centralization of party: creation of local branches throughout the country controlled by a central office.

[a] Formation of the Calvinist party.
[b] Formation of the Catholic party.

As a result, these parties had to retain links to the church and religion. But they succeeded in declericalizing, in fact secularizing, themselves. They redefined the meaning of Catholicism for politics, increased their distance from the church, and became autonomous political organizations. I show, in the fifth chapter, how the declericalization of confessional parties is related to the process of party formation. Finally, and paradoxically, the politicization of religion had beneficial effects for democratic development. By integrating newly enfranchised masses and by turning themselves from opponents into supporters of parliamentary democracy, confessional parties contributed to the consolidation of democratic regimes. I submit that this outcome hinged, to a great extent, on the process of party formation as well.

A Model of Party Formation

The process of party formation took place in three time periods, starting with the first attacks against church rights by the Liberals. In the beginning of the process (t_1) there were three actors: the church, Conservative politicians, and Liberal politicians. In this section I sketch the preferences and strategies of the church and Conservative politicians. Like Conservative politicians, Liberal ones aim for reelection, and their strategy remains constant throughout the process (anticlerical attack). Strategies are associated with costs and benefits, that is, they yield specific payoffs. I follow Margaret Levi (1991:132) in deducing one "fundamental utility" for each actor.

The church is a self-interested actor.[2] As Grey Chapman (1962:153) puts it: "The Church—it could scarcely do otherwise—thought in terms of what was good for itself." Gramsci underlined the "tendency for the church to resolve political conflicts in favor of its perception as to what was best for its own integral existence"[3] (Fulton 1987:212). The church maximizes power, generally conceived as its ability to shape or influence society.[4] In doctrinal terms, the church has been charged "to preserve and extend the kingdom of heaven wanted by Jesus Christ" and "penetrate all mankind" (Simon 1966:9). A significant indicator of power is church rights and privileges, such as control over some sectors of society and the concomitant exclusive or preferential provision of certain societal services, particularly education. The Liberal attack against the church during the second half of the nineteenth century challenged the church's influence and neutralized its privileged access to decision-making centers.

In looking for new means of political action to preserve its influence, the church faces costs. The church seeks to maximize (or preserve) its influence *(i)* without suffering unacceptably high costs. These costs, as I show below, are mostly of organizational nature *(oc)*. At t_1, when the first signs (first threats) of an anticlerical attack become clear, the church has a choice between two strategies: it can adopt a conciliatory stance and not fight, seeking a compromise *(C)*, or it can fight by creating mass organizations (organization or *O*). There initially exists a range of intermediate actions, such as a campaign of civil disobedience, but all eventually require mass organization to be effective. At t_2, assuming that the church has chosen organization in

[2] All claims made here about the church apply only to the late nineteenth-century Catholic church and with regard to major strategic decisions related to issues relevant to this study.

[3] Likewise, for Max Weber (1963:235–36), "the goal of the Catholic Church is to salvage its ecclesiastical power interests, which have increasingly become objectified into a doctrine of the fundamental interests of the church, by the employment of the same modern instruments of power employed by secular institutions."

[4] Studies that treat the church as a rational actor include Gill (1994) and Iannaccone (1991).

the previous node and the Liberals escalate their attack, the church faces three choices: it can stick to organization and remain outside the political process *(O)*, enter the political process directly by organizing electoral coalitions and fully backing them (participation, or *P*), or create a confessional party (*CP*).[5] These strategies produce payoffs that are a function of the expected influence to be gained (or preserved) and the costs to be incurred.

Conservative politicians are members of loose parliamentary factions. They enter the process at t_2. Generally, they seek to further their political careers; to do so, they maximize their probability of being reelected[6] (Aldrich 1995; Geddes 1991; Schlesinger 1984). It is true that parties, particularly in their early stages of development, often appeared to shun vote maximization, engaging instead in debates about the desirability of wooing public opinion in the first place (Kreuzer 1995). As will become apparent, the constraints imposed by mass politics made purely electoral considerations a priority, even among the most jaded Conservative notables. Reelection entails costs that can threaten their chances of political survival. Thus Conservative politicians maximize their probability of being reelected *(r)* subject to the costs of reelection *(rc)*. At t_2, Conservatives choose between three strategies: ask/accept only unsystematic support from the church *(U)*, ask/accept for systematic support from the church through the participation strategy of the church *(P)*, or create a confessional party (*CP*).

The model yields the following hypotheses:

1. At t_1 the church will choose to adopt the organizational strategy over compromise only when the payoffs of the former exceed the payoffs of the latter. Since the cost of the organizational strategy exceeds the cost of not fighting ($c_O > c_C$—I show below why this is the case), the choice hinges on the values of i_C and i_O. In other words, the church will choose organization over compromise when the influence generated (or preserved) by the former significantly exceeds the influence generated by the latter. This will depend on the severity and efficacy of the anticlerical attack, the availability of alternative means of defense, and the expected positive impact of mass organizations on influence.

2. At t_2 the church will choose to enter the political process (participation) over remaining outside of it only when the payoffs of the former exceed the payoffs of the latter. The participation strategy induces additional (again mostly organizational) costs on top of the cost of the organizational strategy.

[5] In theory, strategies *P* and *CP* are available at t_1, but they are so costly as to be practically out of question. Both (effective) participation in the electoral process and the organization of a new party require mass organization, which does not exist at t_1.

[6] Of course, Conservative politicians have policy preferences as well, but their implementation entails reelection. Reelection, however, does not necessarily require them to compromise these policy preferences.

Thus $c_P > c_O$; hence the choice depends again on the values of i_P and i_O: the church will select mass organization over not fighting if its influence continues to decline significantly between t_1 and t_2. This is the case when the anticlerical attack is severe and no alternative action is available: Conservative allies are politically weak, the regime solid, and extraparliamentary means of action (such as a military coup) unavailable. Under these conditions, the church will accept some loss of control and fight by entering the political process.

3. At t_2, the church will form a confessional party only when its payoffs from party formation exceed those of participation. The formation of a confessional party induces new costs—below I explain why the costs are cumulative. Since $c_{CP} > c_P$ the gains in influence from party formation (i_{CP}) must significantly exceed the gains produced by participation (i_P).

4. Conservative political elites will opt to follow the participation strategy of the church when the payoffs of this strategy exceed those derived from unsystematic support from the church. Since $r_P > r_U$, Conservative politicians will opt for participation when the cost of reelection generated by the participation strategy (rc_P) is not heavy.

5. Finally, Conservative political elites will opt for the formation of confessional parties over sticking to participation when the payoffs of party formation exceed those of participation. Since $rc_{CP} > rc_P$, Conservative politicians will opt for the formation of confessional parties only if the probability of reelection under party formation r_{CP} significantly exceeds the equivalent probability produced by the participation strategy r_P.

To determine the value of the various parameters, I now turn to a detailed examination of the actors, starting with their preferences.

The Preferences of the Church

Rights and privileges are both an expression of the church's influence and a requirement for its reproduction and expansion. The anticlerical attack led to the decline of the church's main strategic instrument, its independent and direct lobbying capacity and access to government, and the neutralization, if not destruction, of the "altar and throne" alliance. At the same time, a new factor surfaced: the masses. The ability of the church to maximize its influence gradually came to depend on the degree of its direct influence over the masses. Thus membership size became a crucial concern. While always an important consideration for the church (as attested to by its missionary activity), membership size now acquired a more direct and instrumental dimension. Contrary to the past, membership had to be mobilized to replace (at least provisionally) the church's lost lobbying capacity. Mass mobilization entailed the creation of a new organizational structure, mass organization, which carried important costs that the church was a priori unwilling to undertake. The main cost of mass organization was related to the weakening of hierarchical control.

Organizational costs are mostly, although not exclusively, related to control. Control is a central concern for the Catholic church. The nineteenth-century Catholic church was a firmly hierarchical, rigidly stratified, and highly centralized organization with a pyramidal structure that could best control its members when it had exclusivity over their loyalties and could better keep track of its potential constituency through an institutional monopoly over its representation. Traditionally, the church achieved control over its members through the twin mechanisms of hierarchy and centralization.

Since its inception "the Catholic church has moved gradually from grass-roots democracy and collegial authority to a vast concentration of power and authority in the hands of the clergy and the hierarchy"[7] (Hanson 1987:27). Because Catholicism is, as Poulat (1977:96) emphasizes, a "religion of authority," "a regime of authority" even, the church was governed by an "authoritarian leadership" (Vaillancourt 1980:3), exercising its authority *"quasi-dittatoria"* (Simon 1961:3) within a system of "authoritarian centralism" (Lill 1977:78). In such a system, the concept of obedience is central (Rahner et al. 1968).

Catholic ecclesiology strikingly contrasts church and secular government both in origin and, by implication, in significance: contrary to social contract societies, the church was divinely created and the authority of its hierarchy was vested in divine power, similar to that of absolutist kings. This implies that "the authority established in the church holds commission from above, not from below. . . . The church's pastors govern and direct the flock committed to them by virtue of jurisdiction conferred upon them by the Christ" (Joyce 1913:754–55). The Belgian archbishop Cardinal Désiré-Joseph Mercier (quoted in Dondeyne 1964:43) left no doubt when he pointed out, in 1919, that "the Pope and the bishops are the external organs of divine vocation."

The structure of the church is rigidly stratified. Ecclesiastical authority is clearly "hierarchical, based on the absolute power of bishops over priests and priests over laymen" (Gabbert 1978:643). At the top is the Vatican and just below the episcopates of the national churches. The lower clergy are subject to strict supervision from the hierarchy, and the priest's task is to aid his bishop "in the exercise of his pastoral functions" (Dondeyne 1964:46). As the French bishop Marie Dominique Auguste Sibour (quoted in Gabbert 1978:654) pointed out, "[In every diocese] the clergy and the bishop form a

[7] This shift took place during the late eleventh century under Pope Gregory VII (1073–1085)(Berman 1983:221) and remains in force today.

family of which the bishop is the father; placed vis à vis the bishop in a relationship of necessary subordination and dependence . . . without which the constitution of the church would perish, priests are everywhere associated with his ministry." During the second half of the nineteenth century, these characteristics were decisively reinforced (Blackbourn 1991:780; Yonke 1990:208), and the church was turned into a "unified and powerful bureaucratic organization" (Vaillancourt 1980:2).

At the bottom of the church structure are the lay Catholics. The distance between laymen and clergy is even greater than the distance between episcopate and lower clergy, reflecting the sharp distinction between the religious order and the ordinary people. Church rules excluded lay Catholics from any governmental power within the church (Congar and Varillon 1947:24). Indeed, lay Catholics came to be canonically defined in negative terms as "those who lack any participation in power of jurisdiction, and especially of order [in the church]" (Gambasin 1969:14; Vermeersch and Creusen, quoted in Congar and Varillon 1947:8). In fact, the analogy between the position of the layman in the church and of the subject in an absolute monarchy emerged in the theological canonistic language during the eighteenth century, a period when the subordination of laymen was reinforced (Gambasin 1969:13). Religion became more clerical, stressing "the virtues of authority and the values of obedience, [and] diffusing a vertical image of the religious society where the lay were confined to the lower level" (Mayeur 1973:141). As Pope Pius X (quoted in Aubert 1975:155) reminded Catholics in his 1906 encyclical *Vehementer Nos,* "The church is by nature an unequal society; it is composed of two categories of people: the pastors and the flock. Only the hierarchy moves and manages. . . . The duty of the mass is to accept to being governed and to follow with submission the commands of those who lead it." Arguing that the administration of the church should be entrusted to laymen or that the proper exercise of episcopal authority depends on the consent or participation of laymen or priests is, in fact, a heresy, laicism. The archbishop of Rouen (quoted in Dansette v.1 1961:236) put it bluntly: "Laymen have no function to perform in church affairs."

Hierarchy and control are organizational rather than ideological attributes. Jean Vaillancourt (1980:15) notes that even today "religious ideology has increasingly become subordinated to organizational imperatives. Among these internal and external organizational imperatives, organizational control of lay elites seems to have become a major preoccupation and necessity for Church authorities." As a result, control was emphasized and enforced by all bishops, whatever their personal ideological preferences. As the "liberal" French bishop Sibour (quoted in Gabbert 1978:653) pointed out, the authority to govern the church was given by God to the episcopacy and lay "neither in the community of priests nor in the community of the faithful." Conversely, control was implemented because of its organizational rather than just its ideological implications. Pius X (quoted in Aubert 1982:198–99) made clear to a group of Belgian "Christian Democrats" that submission prevailed over ideological conformity. Contrary to Italy, he asserted, where Christian Democrats agitated for autonomy, "in Belgium, you have good democrats: Conservatives and democrats, you all obey your bishops."

An organization such as the Catholic church has little incentive to create mass organizations. Indeed, the creation of mass organizations by already established, centralized, and rigidly stratified organizations such as the church produces negative externalities for them, primarily because it reduces the level of control they can exercise over their members.[8] This situation derives largely, as I argue below, from the fact that more than the active recruitment of members, mass organization requires the formation of a totally new organizational structure and logic of action. In addition, the entry of these mass organizations into party politics further reduces the level of church control. Grasping the full significance of these points presupposes a discussion of the church as an actor.

The church is run by the hierarchy or episcopate. This body charts the course of the church and determines its strategy.[9] Given the church's pyramidal structure and its extreme centralization and hierarchy, the following claims can be made: first, the leadership of the church can be treated as *the* church; second, the church can be treated as a unitary actor;[10] and third, the church can be equated with the Vatican (or Roman Curia).

Although the period under study was a time of territorial losses and limitation of rights, it was also one of major reinforcement of the papal authority over national churches. The 1846–1958 period is considered to be the most disciplined and homogeneous period in Catholic history (Altermatt 1991). As Blackbourn (1991:780) points out, "In a period of centralization and

[8] Recent research on transaction costs and the theory of the firm stresses the importance of control for a firm in its relationship with agents. "In a world of transaction costs and incomplete contracts, ex post residual rights of control will be important because, through their influence on asset usage, they will affect ex post bargaining power and the division of ex post surplus in a relationship" (Hart 1989:1766).

[9] The episcopate acts as a unified body (usually the college of bishops), meeting regularly to formulate policies (the exception to this rule was France). The role of the archbishop was often decisive in expressing this unity of action, as indicated by the cases of Cardinal Rauscher in Austria, Cardinal Sterckx in Belgium, and the popes in Italy.

[10] The leadership of the church is, implicitly or explicitly, treated as *the* church in many studies (Blasco González and Dios González-Anleo 1993; Vaillancourt 1980). As has been pointed out (Agócs 1988:11), "The study of the intentions and directives of leaders is especially relevant in connection with religious hierarchies such as the leadership of the catholic church, for in such institutions directives from above have an unusual salience." Still this is not equivalent to saying that the fundamental preferences of the church vary substantively with changes in the *person* of the leader.

bureaucratization, the church followed the same road as the state and business. This was especially true of papal power." This reinforcement culminated in the introduction of the dogma of papal infallibility in 1870 and the transformation of the pope into an object of unprecedented worship for millions of Catholics. National churches were short-circuited by the growing use of the concordat, the implementation of new canon law codifications, the reintroduction of Peter's Pence in the 1860s to aid Vatican finances, more summonses to Rome, and more papal feast days (Blackbourn 1991:780). The increasing acceptance by the national churches of Rome's preeminence over them became known as ultramontanism, a term suggesting the newfound tendency of the churches to look for inspiration "beyond the mountains" to Rome (McLeod 1981:47). The reinforcement of papal authority reverberated back to the national churches, where it resulted in a parallel reinforcement of the national episcopates over lower clergy and laymen (Faury 1980:226). Thus, though the church replicated the process of centralization undertaken by states, it diverged from another fundamental trend of the times, democratization.

It is generally problematic (although hardly unusual) to treat collective actors as if they were individual ones because collective desires or beliefs do not exist[11] (Elster 1986:3–4). The nineteenth-century Catholic church is probably one of the very few exceptions to the rule, given its use of a dictatorial procedure for aggregating individual into group preferences. Still, three empirical objections can be raised against treating the church as a unitary actor.

First, in a few cases, decisions taken by national churches diverged from Vatican directives.[12] However, the rule was congruence between national

[11] This is why the analysis of intraorganizational politics is extremely important (Koelble 1992; Kitschelt 1989). For Tsebelis (1990:21), collective actors, or "informal social aggregates," can be considered rational. The problem, according to him, is rather that "their very existence remains unexplained in terms of rationality." In fact, political science studies often use collective actors such as states, social classes, and unions (Lalman, Oppenheimer, and Swistak 1993:80–81; an example is Wallerstein 1988).

[12] The case of Belgium, where the church supported an alliance with the Liberals despite the directives of the Vatican is a clear, if isolated, example. The papal secretary of state (quoted in Shelley 1990:53–54) declared in 1829 that the Holy See "understands deeply that the monstrous alliance presently concluded between Catholics and Liberals—unless it is broken as soon as possible—will have the most disastrous consequences, whether it fails or succeeds." Yet the Belgian church ignored these directives. The dissension between the Austrian church and the Vatican over the Christian Socials is also well established (Boyer 1981). Dansette (v. 2 1961:96) notes that, "although since the triumph of ultramontanism, a bishop or a parish priest could not openly oppose a papal policy, he could adopt an attitude of passive opposition, overlooking it or slowing down its application. The episcopal and priestly functions conferred some protection against any abuse of power by Rome." Still, open and active resistance to the Vatican and disregarding fundamental directives were unthinkable.

churches and the Vatican. In cases of disagreement on crucial matters, Rome's opinion prevailed—a fact that allowed the Liberals to accuse the church of unpatriotism and treason.[13] Moreover, the Vatican was extremely skillful in exploiting divisions among bishops and tensions between higher and lower clergy to enforce its decisions (Vismara Chiappa 1982:225; Dansette v.1 1961:137).

Second, bishops often disagreed with each other and emphasized different goals. Dissension within the episcopate, as well as internal conflicts and power struggles, were not uncommon (Anderson 1981; Gadille 1967; Dansette 1961). Yet when it came to crucial decisions such as the response to anticlerical legislation or the building of mass organizations, the episcopate acted as a single body. When the bishops still remained divided over questions of grand strategy, as was often the case in France (Arnal 1985; Chapman 1962), the Vatican intervened decisively and neutralized internal division (Hilaire v.1 1977:343; Mayeur 1966:107). When, finally, a decision was made at the top, all bishops had to follow in a fashion anticipating communist democratic centralism. The most telling example is the Ralliement in France (see Chapter 3).

Third, despite the severe control exercised over them, lower clergy and lay Catholics did voice dissenting opinions and even acted in ways that were not authorized by the episcopate. When their action was perceived as threatening, however, the episcopate eagerly repressed them. Still, there is one deviation to this pattern: in the case of confessional party formation, members of the lower clergy and lay Catholics succeeded in imposing their own preferences upon the church. This unique instance of breakdown of control, the object of this study, does not contradict the assertion that the church was a unitary actor during the process of party formation. This breakdown took place only at the very end of this process. Up to that point (and following it) the church acted in a unitary fashion.

In short, the church can be realistically treated as a unitary actor. As the bishop of Versailles Charles Gibier (quoted in Bessières 1924:9) remarked in 1924, "The general organization of the Catholic church is reduced to this: the faithful are one with their priests, the priests are one with their bishops, the bishops are one with the Pope, who in turn is one with Jesus Christ whose vicar he is."

[13] Dansette (v.2 1961:45) provides the following striking example from the papal attempt to institute a compromise between French church and government in 1880: "Told by the Bishop of Nîmes what the Pope wanted, Père d'Alzon, the superior of the Assumptionists, broke down. 'This will mean a breach with the whole of my past and turning my back on the tradition I share with my friends,' he said. 'But since the Pope wants it that way, I shall obey.' And the old man went down on his knees to sign the declaration."

Religion and Politics: The Calculus of the Church

Much as individuals participate in politics based on the political choices and incentives they are offered, political actors decide to mobilize and organize people on the basis of a calculus of incentives and constraints. Jean-Marie Donegani (1993:18–19) points out that religion and politics interact on two levels. At the first level are the relations between the church and its societal environment; the second level encompasses the relations between the church and its members. Decisions concerning the first level are particularly sensitive to considerations about the second level. Hence the creation of mass organizations, participation in the political process, and the formation of confessional parties were choices contemplated both in light of the benefits they provided for maximizing influence (first level) and the (mostly internal) costs they generated (second level). Yet only the first level is usually considered, and the creation of lay mass organizations by the church is seen as a costless choice with only positive returns. This is not surprising inasmuch as "sociology has neglected the study of religious bureaucracies, their leaders, and the control mechanisms that they use to protect their authority" (Vaillancourt 1980:3). Below I discuss the costs of the various options of the church.

Organizational strength can be thought as having two dimensions: a quantitative one, size (an indicator of which is expanding membership), and a qualitative one, intensity of the members' loyalty and faith. While expansion and appeal to society at large increases the church's legitimacy, the loyalty of members makes church action more efficient and helps sustain hierarchical control. The church often manipulated these dimensions, both symbolically and materially. According to Gramsci (1995:106): "The sophism is clear: when it finds it convenient, the Church is identified with society itself (at least 99 per cent of it), and when not convenient, the Church is solely the ecclesiastical organization or even just the person of the pope." But unconstrained manipulation is not always possible. There is usually some trade-off between wide appeal (which leads to overextension—a large but weak church) and control (which leads to sectarianism—a solid but smaller church).[14] This outcome is hardly unique to the church. For instance, the explosion of the Italian Communist party's membership at the end of World War II "made it

[14] In a different formulation the trade-off is between "the position of the Hierarchy with regard to . . . social life" and the "Hierarchy's leadership within . . . Catholicism" (Bosworth 1962:99). The development of Catholic Action groups, Bosworth argues, strengthens the former but weakens the latter. Likewise, O'Gara (1962:12) argues that "while clericalism seems to guard the strength of the Church in the face of attack, it in fact weakens it and reduces the area of the Church's influence."

far more difficult for the [party] to exercise effective organizational control"[15] (Tarrow 1975:599).

Although the church is willing to sacrifice a measure of its control in order to expand (or retain) its influence in society, it is unwilling to sacrifice too much control. Accordingly, it usually emphasizes individual loyalty over expansion: as Zerbi (1961:72) puts it, the church used "extreme firmness in the defense of its most precious treasure, the repository of faith"; and as E. E. Y. Hales (1958:114) recounts, "The Church . . . having flatly contradicted the confident sophistries of an age of superficial progress, having condemned its easygoing optimisms and denounced its crude secularism, would have lost the good will of many, but would have saved her own soul, would have renewed her strength, and would have girded herself for the battles of a new age." In fact, the church never hesitated to decrease the size of its membership when faced with a steep decline of its control. In 1871, for example, the German church excommunicated more than one thousand Catholics who opposed the Vatican Council's decision about papal infallibility and the hierarchy's authority to decide alone on such matters (Yonke 1990:220–21). The Belgian church did not hesitate in 1879 to refuse sacraments to parents who sent their children to public schools, thus provoking an enormous decrease in rates of religious practice—one which was to last. Of these, only half returned to the church after the revocation of its measure, making this a case of "clerically induced dechristianization" (Laury 1964). As the French author Hippolyte Taine pointed out in 1891 (quoted in Gibson 1989:231), "Faith is increasing in the restricted group and declining in the large group." Thus maximizing membership size is by no means the church's first and only consideration, even during anticlerical attacks.[16]

The a priori preference of the church for control flows from two sources. First, it is the result of reflexes connected with the traumas of the Reformation and past heresies (Pirenne in Tash 1991:37). Second, it is an organizational attribute of highly structured and hierarchical organizations such as centralized firms (Hart 1989) or mass parties, particularly in periods of crisis. Communist parties often had to face this trade-off and make similar hard

[15] A similar trade-off affects other organizations, including political parties. Kircheimer (1966:184) suggests that parties face a trade-off between "effectiveness in depth" (which requires "intellectual and moral *encadrement* of the masses") and appeals to a "wider audience." Sferza (1991:19–20) contrasts vertical extension, a party's capacity to increase its appeal among groups that constitute its traditional electorate, and horizontal extension, its capacity to capture the electoral support of groups that neither the party itself nor its allies had in the past been able to influence. These problems were faced particularly by Communist parties.

[16] Thus it would be wrong to argue (in the context of this study) that what the church maximizes is the number of the faithful, an argument made by Gill (1994) about the Catholic church in contemporary Latin America.

choices. They were often reluctant to increase their membership "because it would be difficult to incorporate [a big number of new members] without weakening Party discipline and diluting the ideology" (Godson and Haseler 1978:28). In emphasizing control, Communist parties followed the Leninist precept "that strength lies in discipline and discipline is found in a devoted cadre of pure revolutionaries" (Tarrow 1975:606). The practice of the purge, whereby organizations intentionally chose to reduce their size to spur participation and reinforce control, constitutes the most striking instance of this trade-off (Pizzorno 1970:44) and is a characteristic shared by Communist parties and the church.[17]

The Costs of the Organizational Strategy

Organizing lay Catholics into mass organizations was totally alien to the doctrine and experience of the church. Furthermore, it was widely perceived within the church that such a development would weaken, and could even eradicate, the asymmetrical relationship between the church leadership, the lower clergy, and the mass of lay Catholics. It is an indication of the church's apprehension about mass organization that the role of laymen in the action of the church was officially recognized with a lag of about sixty years (in the 1922 encyclical *Urbi Arcano Dei*), and the political dimension of mass organization was never recognized. The creation of mass organizations generates organizational dynamics that spawn several detrimental effects for a centralized and hierarchical organization such as the church.

Mass organizations (and other institutions, such as the Catholic press)[18] require their own separate and mostly lay hierarchies. For all the control exercised upon them by the church, they represent a potential threat by leading to what Gabriele De Rosa (quoted in Scoppola 1977:107) has dubbed *deformazione laicistica dell'organismo ecclesiastico* (lay deformation of the ecclesiastical organism). These parallel hierarchies represent a threat, first because they require a new and active role from lay Catholics, and second because they are an unprecedented new power center within the church, cracking its monolithic structure. In the most extreme case they even seek to

[17] White (1992:244) reports that "Soviet governments, pre-1990, have been strikingly similar to the Catholic Church in underlying architecture of control," and Vaillancourt (1980:15) compares the Vatican to the Bolshevik party. In fact, the church often implemented purges to eliminate (or prevent the rise of) heresies, much as did Communist parties (White 1992:244).

[18] In France, for instance, "when the church began to employ [the press], it opened the door to both structural and ideological change—first, by allowing the lay journalist, who had no consecrated hierarchical position, a role in the decision-making functions of the Church, and secondly, by respecting and appealing to public opinion" (May 1973:79).

reform the church. In Italy, for instance, lay Catholic activists argued that from the womb of the new Catholic organizations "a renewed church would be born which would unite clergy and laity in a common work of all society" (Molony 1977:14). Charles Molette (1968:478–79) succinctly describes the church's reasoning during the creation of the Association Catholique de la jeunesse française (ACJF). The "fundamental question" about the ACJF within the episcopate was, "Wouldn't the structure of the ACJF risk appearing as a parallel hierarchy?" Furthermore, "What was this kind of lay hierarchy? Even if it is a carbon copy of the organization of the church of France, wasn't it going to duplicate the ecclesiastical hierarchy? Didn't it depend on election, a way of designating [leaders] that fails to remind that in the church power comes from the top?" A public attack against the ACJF in 1906 (quoted in Molette 1968:513–14) made this point even clearer:

> On the religious field chosen by the ACJF, it is not election that must provide us with those "leaders who know to command." We have no other leaders than our legitimate pastors: the priest, the bishop, the pope. What is the meaning of this hierarchy on the side, of these presidents named by some young Catholics only, members of a given association, who believe that they have the right to speak in the name of the whole Catholic youth? . . . It is impossible to have these lay lieutenants imposed upon the Catholic hierarchy, and the formation itself of the ACJF is real nonsense.

Besides the creation of parallel hierarchies, the presence of multiple organizations within the same institutional frame can lead to dilution of members' loyalty because allegiance to more than one organization is required. Moreover, the creation of mass organizations undermines the church's exclusivity over its members' loyalties and its institutional monopoly over their representation. A tight subculture and web of organizations might strengthen the allegiance of individuals to Catholicism as an abstract concept and might even create and reinforce a sense of community (particularly in countries where Catholics are an economically backward minority). But it can also weaken their allegiance to the dominant institution within this web, either spreading it around multiple organizations or transferring it to another organization within the same subculture.[19]

A situation is created in which a variety of lay organizations (from mutual aid organizations and newspapers to trade unions and parties) pursue their

[19] This is what in fact happened. Billiet and Dobellaere (1985) have shown how the "pillars," as the web of these organizations became known in Belgium and the Netherlands, have remained externally intact but the influence of the church within them has waned while the influence of unions, parties, or other organizations has expanded.

proper agenda, compete with the church for privileged access to the same constituency, and demand priority of loyalty from this constituency. They undercut the up to then privileged and exclusive relationship between the church and its members and can even lead the latter to "rebellion" (Suardo 1962:135) against the church. More practically, but just as important, they make competing demands on their members' time and efforts. Joseph Houska (1985:19) has pointed out that cooperation between subcultural organizations is problematic because "the elites in whose action subcultural unity depends are also the leaders of the organizations whose particular interests may diverge from those of the subculture." They may diverge, he adds (1985:21), because "the strength of [subcultural] organizations allows and even encourages elites to pursue the functional or ideological interests of the organization at the expense of the larger subculture. Thus the organizations that begin as the strength of the subculture become potential sources of weakness by giving their leadership an independent position from which to base opposition to the subculture as a whole." As Gramsci (1995:108) pointed out, "To the extent that every national Catholic Action grows and becomes a mass organization, it tends to become a real and proper party, whose orientations are dictated by the internal necessities of the organization." A particularly pernicious negative externality of organizational proliferation can be the decrease of religiosity: "Overorganization may have greater dangers for religious life than underorganization," remarks Lorwin (1971:168).[20] Thus, even when they remain apolitical, lay organizations represent a threat for the church. Bosworth (1962:99) notes: "Although in certain respects Catholic Action [the main Catholic organization] has strengthened the position of the Hierarchy with regard to French social life it seems to have affected some of the Hierarchy's leadership within French Catholicism. The local Catholic Action group rather than the parish, the national group rather than the diocese, have become for many Frenchmen the real centers of moral and spiritual principles."

The church was aware of this danger because in the past it had faced the lesser threat of lay confraternities. Often, these lay associations came into existence, developed, and endured in the margins of the official church.

[20] According to Lorwin (1971:168), "Critics of segmented pluralism argue that the complex of confessional social and political organizations tends to diminish the spiritual character of the church and hamper its true mission. What once appeared to be the organizational means to a Christian life in society risk becoming ends in themselves. Overorganization may have greater dangers for religious life than underorganization. Associations taking in every aspect of social life but employment (and often that, too) envelop the masses in a 'sociological Christianity' likely to foster a religious practice of social conformity than religious devotion. At the expense of the aims of the lay apostolate, they risk inducing in the elites a concern with the organizational and instrumental."

Some remained quasi-independent from the church and many became tightly controlled by it, but all faced episcopal attacks because they were seen as "siphoning off the adherence of local inhabitants" from the parish (Henderson 1986:69–83). As a result, they were often condemned.[21] The bishop of the French town of Montpellier found them, in 1837, "purely and simply scum" (Gibson 1989:57), and the church vigorously reasserted its control over them during the nineteenth century.

Catholic organizations provide individual lay Catholics with a new collective identity which is reflected in a set of new priorities and influences imposed upon them. As A.C. Jemolo (1960:61) points out, they "imbu[e] the mass of believers with new sensibilities." The result is a new breed of Catholics: Catholic activists (as opposed to the Catholic faithful). These Catholics, drawing a sharp distinction between the church's field of action and theirs, tend to pursue political objectives that reflect their own priorities, to select strategies of action based on their own preferences, and to adopt "theories of political action . . . differ[ing] from those favored by the prevailing tradition of Catholic thought" (Webster 1960:95). These activists often openly antagonize the church, while their leaders demand, as in 1903 in Italy, "the greatest possible distance from the sacristy" (Giuseppe Sacchetti, quoted by De Rosa 1972:218), and publicly claim, as did the German priest Eduard Cronenberg in 1871, that "the interests of the Catholic people extend further than the interests of the Catholic church" (quoted in Brose 1985:47). Obviously, the church abhorred such a prospect. The title of a French bishop's newspaper article is telling: *"Servir l'Eglise et non pas s'en servir"* (to serve the church rather than use it)(Durand 1995:105).

The creation of mass organizations in which clergy and lay coexist subverts their asymmetrical relationship. Within the church, the hierarchical prominence of the clergy over the lay is a matter beyond question, but their coexistence within a mass organization does not necessarily imply the replication of this relationship. Even when they are oligarchic, mass organizations allow a degree of mobility and inclusion that is nonexistent within the church. The notion of hierarchical supervision is lost because the creation of modern bureaucratic organizational structures provides lay Catholics with both the incentive for seeking access to higher positions and the opportunity for mobility within the new organization, hence, also, with the incentive of competition with the clergy when both coexist within the organization. The link between the church and its members is weakened not only within the

[21] This is illustrated by the decision of the 1517 synod of the Florentine church (quoted in Henderson 1986:82): "A great abuse had developed among these fraternities of laymen, so that, gathered together on those festive days, they abandoned the main churches at that hour when mass was sung in them, to open their synagogues and sing their Offices to the people, so that the majority of people was withdrawn from the church."

Catholic organization but within the church itself, as this subverted relationship reverberates back to the latter. Indeed, bishops sometimes found themselves receiving orders from lay Catholic activists. Zerbi (1961:78) reports that within the Italian organization Opera, lay leaders ended up "giving directives to bishops, provoking frequent complaints from the episcopate." The Belgian archbishop Victor Dechamps (quoted in Lamberts 1984:73) complained to the pope about two prominent and politically active lay Catholics who "both are fervent and good soldiers, but they want to command within the church." The utterance of an Italian bishop (quoted in Zerbi 1961:79) is striking: "I hope that the time of bishops with round hats has finally come to an end!"

Such problems exist even when the clergy is absent from Catholic mass organizations. The substitution of a lay leadership for clerical leadership and of lay personnel for clerical personnel has similar consequences. Catholics cease to be supervised by a clerical hierarchy. In addition, the concept of supervision shifts from rigid hierarchical control to more flexible secular bureaucratic relations that allow for mobility within the organization and even permit a degree of dissent unheard-of within the church.

The link between the church and its members is also affected by the deterioration of the relations between low clergy and episcopate. The creation of mass organizations pushes priests to become increasingly active in political action, a domain that lies outside the realm of their traditional duties. As a result, priests grow increasingly independent of their hierarchical superiors. They dare "to transfer institutions with a secular political aura into the realm of ecclesiastical authority" (Boyer 1995:303), and even use their new role as mass organizers to rebel against the episcopate—a trend referred to as presbyterianism (Mayeur 1968:216) and often equated with heresy.[22] Examples abound. In many countries, priests organized clerical congresses apart from their bishops, and in some cases they even set up unions. For instance, the priest Josef Scheicher, who played a key role in Christian Social politics in Austria, helped organize a general congress of the Austrian clergy in Vienna in which he declared that the "bishops must cease to act autocratically." Both the congress and Scheicher's speech "caused a sensation" and were seen as "a direct challenge to the Austrian episcopate" (Boyer 1995:302).

[22] The episcopate resented even the most innocuous expression of independence by the lower clergy. When members of the lower clergy tried to organize a congress of their own in France during the 1890s, the bishop of Annecy accused its main organizer, the abbé Lemire, of "spreading the germs of a new schism" and creating "hierarchical encroachment." He denounced this initiative as "a mortal threat for religious authority" (Rémond 1964:27). Cardinal Richard (quoted in Rémond 1964:111) was milder when he argued that "the idea of these gatherings of priests, which are not presided by the natural leaders of the Hierarchy, the Bishops, seems dangerous to me."

The Italian priest and journalist Davide Albertario often publicly attacked the bishop of Milan (Webster 1960:7). In 1873, the bishop of the German town of Trier complained that his clergy were combining in a clique to monitor his activities (Anderson 1986:109). The year before, a resolution of the Catholic organization (Volksverein) of Ebermannstadt called on the bishop of Passau to step down from his office; the instigator of this resolution was Friedrich Mahr, the founder of the organization, a priest, leading political activist, and Landtag deputy (Southern 1977:302–4).

An additional but hardly negligible aspect of this situation is that because it took place at the expense of the priests' central professional obligation, the (universalistic) religious service, the priests' organizational and political activity hampered the primary objective of the church and circumscribed its appeal. It was not rare for bishops to forbid the political activity of priests both because they disliked their politics and because priests neglected their priestly duties (Southern 1977:294). As John Boyer (1981:181) puts it, "The more the priests became politicians, the less they could sustain the pretense of service to all society."

Thus the organizational dynamics unleashed by the creation of mass organizations produce negative externalities for the church. The creation of mass organizations produces divisions within the church. Two consequences flow. First, action is inefficient and outcomes are suboptimal for the church. Second, the hierarchical structure of the church is undermined. By becoming activists in mass organizations, lay Catholics and lower clerics grow more independent from the episcopate. They agitate for power within the church and demand organizational autonomy. To use Albert Hirschman's (1970) famous formulation, when the church is unwilling to grant voice to anyone besides the bishops, exit becomes the only alternative for activists.

The creation of mass organizations produces additional costs beyond those induced by organizational dynamics, including the cost of organization building, the fear of heresy, and psychological costs.

Organization building does not come naturally or automatically to political actors. It is a difficult, time-consuming, costly, and often risky enterprise. For instance, Gregory Luebbert (1991:9) found that working-class entrepreneurs "never preferred" organization building if hegemonic allies were available because comprehensive, coherent organization was a slow, arduous, and tedious strategy." The church faced similar costs. For example, the formation of mass organizations had a negative effect on its infrastructure because it absorbed all its energy: the decision of the Belgian church to form mass organizations forced it to neglect the development of parishes in the region of Brussels, an important failure because this was precisely the time of the city's demographic explosion (Houtart 1953:704).

The church associates organization building with traditional reflexes of heretical danger. The Belgian historian Henri Pirenne (cited in Tash 1991:37) notes that the church saw religious sects as doubly perilous; not only did they represent a danger to orthodoxy and dogma but they also failed to lend themselves to hierarchical control. The medieval history of the church includes numerous instances of reformist lay movements *(tiers-ordres séculiers)* that eventually were either clericalized or separated from the church (Molette 1968:5). As Vaillancourt (1980:2) points out, radical organizational reform "had always been forced to take its course outside the Catholic fold, and pressure for change within the Church had nearly always been suppressed by ecclesiastical officials." In the course of the Catholic church's long history there was never until the nineteenth century much space for parallel lay organizations.[23]

Besides the tangible cost of the organizational strategy, the church faced psychological costs. As a deeply conservative institution, both ideologically and organizationally, the church was extremely uncomfortable about radical organizational innovation. First, the church felt it "imprudent" to abandon its traditional way of doing things (Suardo 1962:135). The bishops "from time immemorial . . . had expressed the wishes of Catholics to the government and looked to the government for satisfaction. . . . They remained wedded to their view that only by direct negotiation with the authorities could the church's situation be improved" (Dansette v.1 1961:236). Second, organization building was totally alien to the church, being the most modern weapon and one closer to radical politics than religion. As the bishop of Cremona argued in 1892 (quoted in Vecchio 1987:49), "A bishop . . . is not an economist, a politician, [or] a legal reformer; he must attend to his ministry, which is sacred, interpret only the Bible and not abandon the moral and religious domain, where only persuasion has power."

It should be clear by now that the organizational strategy entailed impressively higher costs for the church than did a strategy of compromise; to use the notation of the model, $c_O > c_C$. This point is clearly made by Aubert (1982:192):

> While many laymen and young priests quickly realized that [mass organization] was the way of the future, the ecclesiastical authorities kept for a long time the nostalgia of the old regime of diplomatic bargains at the top. . . . [In some countries], particularly in France, the bishops proved on the whole reluctant and sometimes downright hostile; and in the Vatican, where people thought that they detected in the new tactic *"the spirit of revolution,"* they did not hide their anxiety, at least initially, and preferred in more

[23] The confraternities of late medieval Europe are not an exception because they were far smaller than the mass phenomenon of nineteenth-century organized Catholicism.

than one instance to pursue direct bargains with the governments through diplomatic means, ending in agreements antithetical to those demanded by the pressure groups of the base.

The Costs of the Participation Strategy

Despite its high cost, the church decided in five out of six cases to implement the organizational strategy (see Chapter 2). This meant adopting a new means of political action which was fundamentally unpleasant to the church. At this point (t_2) the church faced a new hard choice related to the prospect of participating in the political process. In addition to the costs of organization, the costs of participation include organizational dynamics, loss of organizing advantage, and retaliation.

Participation in the political process further weakens the link between the church and its members. The impact of organizational dynamics can be contained more easily when Catholic organizations have a restricted field of action. The degree of control that the church exercises on its actively politicized members diminishes substantially as the source of power and legitimation for Catholic activists shifts from the church to the voters. Participation in democratic politics opens up a new arena, outside and beyond the realm of the church, on both the individual level (for the members of Catholic organizations) and the collective level (for Catholic organizations). This produces three effects. First, important payoffs unconnected to the church are available in this arena; personal and collective success is now more the outcome of active participation and less the outcome of passive obedience; more the outcome of independent and autonomous action and less the outcome of deference to the hierarchy. Thus political participation in a representative parliamentary regime creates "means of both clerical and lay activism removed from direct episcopal supervision" (Gellott 1987:68). Second, participation in democratic politics impregnates the Catholic world of obedience and divinely rooted hierarchy with the secular democratic values of individual autonomy and equality. Third, participation leads Catholic activists to push for more autonomy of action and further participation in the political process because it gives them, for the first time, a sense of the potential that politics holds for the advancement of their cause. The church foresaw these trends and tried to prevent them. Leo XIII argued in a series of encyclicals, letters, and press briefs published between 1883 and 1890 that "no group acting within the temporal sphere should attempt to impose the pursuit of its temporal ends, however lofty, upon the ecclesiastical power. The Pope and the bishops rule the Church, not ecclesiastical journalists or pious laymen, and it is 'an abuse of religion' to 'attach the Church to a party or to try to use it as an auxiliary to defeat opponents' " (McManners 1972:70).

Using an analogy from political economy, we can think of the church as a rent-seeking concentrated interest. Daniel Verdier (1994:17–20) has shown that the advantage these interests enjoy compared to diffuse interests is the ability to overcome free-riding. Yet this advantage is canceled when issues are seized by parties and become part of partisan politics. Moreover, concentrated interests lose their exclusive access to lawmaking. Finally, organizing a large coalition and politicizing a particular issue increases the cost of rent seeking for three reasons: first, it requires field expenses, such as mobilization and organization; second, the set of feasible policy alternatives decreases because the specific issue has to be turned into a general issue to attract public support; and third, the risk of shirking on the part of the political agents becomes greater.

The fear of retaliation is a real one for the church because politicizing religion raises the risks of harm for both Catholics as individuals and the church as an institution. The church feared that the formation of highly visible and politicized Catholic organizations would be interpreted as a provocation and produce a backlash. Indeed, a spiraling process often took place, whereby Liberals became increasingly anticlerical after the first interventions of the clergy in the elections (Windell 1954:184). The bishop of the French town of Valence (quoted in McManners 1972:174) pointed out that "if Catholics made specific demands on candidates for favour to their Church, they could not complain if others made specific demands against it." As Michel Darbon (1953:51) describes the situation in France during the middle of the nineteenth century: "The episcopate often accepted with difficulty that laymen, through their initiatives, appeared to lead religious protests. [The bishops] thought that laymen left their position and, this has to be admitted as well, they feared that this compromised, besides their official dignity, their tranquillity as well, because they anticipated that it would lead to conflicts with the government."

The Costs of Confessional Party Formation

Finally, the prospect of the formation of a confessional party carried even higher costs than the participation strategy, including organizational dynamics, association with unpopular political causes, and ideological preoccupations.

Under the participation strategy, the source of power and legitimation for Catholic activists shifts from the church to the voters. This shift becomes even more pronounced when a confessional party is formed. A party activist tends to be less controlled by and less connected with the church. Being popularly elected is critical and becomes a catalyst for independence, pushing the members of the church further away from it and transforming the role of Catholic laity by substituting a new active function for its traditional passive fidelity (De Rosa 1972:183). When the elected Italian Catholic communal and provincial councilmen met in 1907 to formulate a program of action, a lively discussion took place in which the prospect of openly affirming the "plain responsibility of laymen in the electoral struggles" was put forth and some of the participants even suggested that they explicitly rule out the intervention of the hierarchy[24] (Belardinelli 1979:162). When the leader of the German Zentrum, Ludwig Windthorst, refused to follow the pope's order to support Bismarck's military budget, he made this point crystal clear: "The Center party," he uttered in his famous Gürzenich speech, "subsists simply and solely on the confidence of the people: no other support stands at its command, and it is . . . required, therefore, more than any other fraction, to heed the pulsebeat of the people" (quoted in Anderson 1986:112). Priests acted in a parallel fashion. After the formation of the Zentrum, priests participated in politics "motivated less by theological concepts and canon law than by a kind of broad socio-political approach. Instead of shaping their policies around the tenets of the church, the *Volksverein's* clergy plunged ahead on the Centrum's program unmindful of the teachings and guidelines laid down by the hierarchy" (Ross 1976:64). When the priest and Zentrum deputy Theodor Wacker asserted in 1914 that the hierarchy had no voice in the party's affairs, he was speaking "as a practical politician, not as a priest or theologian" (Ross 1976:62).

Furthermore, the formation of a confessional party subverts traditional relations within the church. A Catholic develops a different relationship with a bishop as a party leader than as a simple layman or priest. Within a confessional party a lay Catholic parliamentarian commands more power than a secretary of a local organization who happens to be a priest. This situation undermines the relationship Catholics have with the clergy within the church and weakens the control the church exercises over its members. The Parisian newspaper *Le Temps* reported in 1881 a dispute between the Monarchist and Catholic politician Albert de Mun and the bishop of Vannes over the organization of a political campaign for the defense of religion as follows: "Here is a lay bishop who undertakes, following the orders of Mr. the count Chambord, a political campaign, and who finds nothing better than to address the authentic bishop like a master" (quoted in Gadille v.2 1967:181). Likewise, in

[24] In the end, an "autonomist" motion was passed, but as Belardinelli (1979:162) reports, to avoid "heavy censure," the Catholic leaders had to alter it so as to make clear that the hierarchy retained its influence.

a letter to the papal nuncio, the Belgian archbishop Victor Dechamps (quoted in Becqué v.2 1956:269) declared that "my consciousness obliges me to add that the Belgian episcopate, always faithful and ardently devoted to the Holy See . . . does not deserve the humiliation of seeing itself lectured by brave manufacturers and soldiers."[25] The reaction of a Jesuit to Windthorst's expression of opinion about papal infallibility is a perfect illustration of these developments: " 'Here alone lies the wound of our times, a wound from which regrettably your high-placed Catholic . . . seems also to suffer!' the Jesuit exclaimed. 'People no longer want to hear authority, but rather to parlamentize freely and . . . to write and give speeches and even act according to however their own subjective opinion thinks best' " (quoted in Anderson 1981:124–25).

The reduction of hierarchical control becomes more pronounced after the electoral weight of religious issues subsides. Thus Felix Porsch, a leader of the Zentrum, warned Cardinal Kopp during the 1893 crisis over Bismarck's military bill that since the tension generated by the Kulturkampf had declined, "the Centre men now weighed matters up very carefully, where once they had followed blindly" (Blackbourn 1975:824). Because the church needs to control its members so it can act autonomously and efficiently, the growing independence of a large segment of its members, who now claim that *they* represent Catholics and tend to take decisions on their own, constitutes an important blow. In short, the encounter between democracy and ecclesiastical hierarchy proves fatally dangerous for the latter: "The princes of the church could not consider laymen—particularly non-noble laymen, whose authority rested on their election by the masses—as partners" (Anderson 1981:279). This is why autonomy quickly became a "dirty word" and was identified with modernism and heresy (Agócs 1988:169).

Besides the reduction of control over its members and the subversion of its hierarchical structure, the formation of a confessional party can have a negative impact on church influence. First it diminishes its negotiating capability because undivided political direction of Catholicism is necessary for effective negotiations with other actors such as the state. Second, it reduces the political saliency of its concerns because, as Josef Wackernell, the leader of the Tyrolian Conservatives, complained in 1903 about the Austrian Christian Social party (quoted in Boyer 1995:95), these parties value "only the will

[25] Similarly in 1897, abbé Letourneau (quoted in Mayeur 1962:191) accused a "Christian Democrat" journalist, as follows: "A little composed layman, M. Mouthon, settled doctrinal questions, corresponded directly with bishops and archbishops . . . Isn't that a stunning victory for laicism?" Belgian bishops took an even stronger position against the lay ultramontane paper *La Croix.* They argued that the directors of this paper "elevated themselves in doctors of the Church and even in judges of the bishops who seemed to them gallicans" and decided "that the newspaper had to disappear" (Becqué v.2 1956:266).

of the people, not ecclesiastical authority." As the Italian Catholic Filippo Meda (quoted in De Rosa 1972:272) argued in 1904, "The Pope's protest [against the Italian state] will be diminished by the presence in the Parliament of one or more Catholic deputies, because these [deputies] as every deputy, do not receive their mandate from the Holy See, but from their electors." What is more, with simple priests like Luigi Sturzo or Herman Shaepman, commanding as much power, and even more, than their hierarchical superiors, political participation decisively threatens the hierarchical structure of the church. Since the consequences of participation in democratic politics include autonomy and independence for the members of the church, the hierarchical structure of the Catholic church is broken when it comes in contact with politics. A process of "ideological and programmatic dislocation" (Traniello 1981:48) is taking place.

The church considers itself a *Weltanschauungsgemeinschaft*, a community with a worldview (Boyer 1995:210). Its entry into politics can lead at best to the trivialization of religion and at worst to its irreparable harm. By becoming explicitly politicized, religion is exposed to the vagaries of ephemeral political passions.[26] This association circumscribes its universalistic appeal. While political Catholicism strengthens the church's hold on certain sections of society, it alienates others (McLeod 1986:439). In the Netherlands, one of the arguments against the creation of a Catholic party was that such a move would endanger the future of Catholics. The Dutch church leaders reasoned (Bakvis 1981:60) that "the awareness by the general public of the existence of a Catholic electoral organization would place our fellow Catholics in jeopardy." The power of Catholics, the argument went, was in their civil position, and the creation of a party would lead to hostility against them (Beaufays 1973:374).

Both the church and religion run the risk of being associated, at best, with the everyday political routine—religion being trivialized and degraded from a spiritual duty to a mere electoral choice—and, at worst, with political disasters or unpopular political movements not necessarily related to it. A Catholic government, for instance, that fails in the economy while intensely emphasizing its Catholicness (increasingly so, to recoup its losses) will hurt religion as an ideal and the church as an institution. For instance, the Austrian Social Democrat leader Victor Adler did not fail to denounce "the spectacle

[26] This argument was made by Tocqueville in *Democracy in America* (1988/1835:298): "When a religion chooses to rely on the interests of this world, it becomes almost as fragile as all earthy powers. Alone, it may hope for immortality; linked to ephemeral powers, it follows their fortunes and often falls together with the passions of a day sustaining them. Hence any alliance with any political power whatsoever is bound to be burdensome for religion. It does not need their support in order to live, and in serving them it may die." On Tocqueville's point see also Chaves and Cann 1992.

of degradation of religion into mere sloganeering" (Boyer 1995:276). The archbishop of Algiers, Cardinal Charles Martial Lavigerie (quoted in McManners 1972:56–57) clearly expressed the disadvantages of open political action: "There are two methods. The first: to address unbelievers individually to bring them to believe in God and his Son. If you win them, you transform their society. The second: to address the national community (which has forsaken Christianity) and to teach that Christ ought to reign over it. If you fail, you are inevitably cast out."

In addition, the close association of the church with one side of the political spectrum can be extremely dangerous. A French bishop (quoted in McManners 1972:56) remarked that "it is our duty to ensure that the altar does not go down with the throne," the implication being that "the pastoral function was not given to priests for supporting always fragile thrones, but for leading souls to God" (Gadille v.1 1967:218; about France). This is why Pius IX (quoted in Mélot 1935:8) argued that "religion must never be in the service of a party to avoid diminishment." A Catholic author, Albert Bessières (1924:128), turned the danger of retaliation into the main argument against politicization: "Want it or not, with all the national or international spiritual interests it represents, the Church will be made solidary of the votes, the interventions, and the mistakes of the representatives. And if Caesar judges, rightly or wrongly, that the men of the church did not give him what belonged to him, he will be forced, as a measure of reprisal, to refuse to the church what belongs to it." A. Simon (1958:50) pinpoints this factor to explain why the Belgian church for a long time "avoided provoking the formation of a party," while Bismarck attacked the church partly to destroy the Catholic party (Boyer 1981:28).

The church proceeded to give a doctrinal dimension to this argument. It argued against the formation of a confessional party on the grounds that "a 'Catholic' party or union was not admissible in terms of theory and practice, because Catholicism is a universal doctrine and embraces all those who believe in the apostolical symbol, while a party is a faction and is subjected to the law of the conflict and the logic of the divergence of parts" (Gambasin 1969:25). The universalistic argument that "the church cannot become a party because it is common to everyone" was included in the 1890 papal encyclical *Sapientiae Christianae*.

Finally, because the church was ideologically opposed to democracy and "the modern liberties," it viewed with profound skepticism the organization of a party, the very instrument of democracy. In fact, the formation of confessional parties would mean an implicit acceptance of democracy and modernity. Leo XIII (quoted in De Rosa 1972:134) often remarked that elections were not a means in which he believed.

It is clear that the costs of the participation strategy exceed those of the organizational strategy ($c_P > c_O$). Hence the church disliked participating in the political process. It is easy to understand why Leo XIII argued, first, that Christian resistance to anticlerical legislation in France was desirable "provided it does not become a party instrument" *(un instrument de parti)*, and second, that the "civic consciousness" of Catholics should be awakened "without doing politics" *(sans faire de politique)* (quoted in Gadille v.2 1967:216).

Although the costs generated by the formation of a confessional party far outweigh the costs of the participation strategy ($c_{CP} > c_P$), the gains in influence from party formation are, at best, minimal. In terms of pure influence, it makes little positive difference for the church if the party in power is its political subcontractor depending on its support for reelection or if it is a confessional party made up of politicians from the ranks of Catholic mass organizations. Short of the transformation of the church into a party, however, a lay confessional party will be difficult to control because of principal-agent problems connected to the factors discussed above. As a result, such a party will not necessarily be a better political agent of the church than a Conservative party acting as the church's political subcontractor and depending on its mass organizations. In fact, since mass Catholic organizations are incorporated into a confessional party and placed under the direction of its lay leaders rather than the church, such a party will probably prove a worse agent of the church than Conservative political elites.[27] As Jean-Marie Mayeur (1980:8) points out, "Between the creation of interest-group kinds of organizations and political parties, the church clearly preferred the first option."

Thus the formation of a confessional party is an inefficient outcome for the church, and the model's main prediction is that the formation of confessional parties is not rational for the church.[28] Figure 1 illustrates this point.

The extension of religion into the (democratic) political realm through the creation of confessional parties was invariably opposed by the church. "Not

[27] The threat by the church to withdraw support from Conservatives can appear incredible given the anticlerical Liberal alternative. But because Conservative parties are loose alliances of notables, the church can play various Conservative factions against each other. It can also appeal to Conservative factions of Liberal parties (as it did in Italy in 1913). True, the church can also pressure confessional parties by appealing directly to the faithful through the pulpit, but this is difficult and costly given the superior resources of mass Catholic organizations (compared to Conservative parties), including the loyalty of huge numbers of believers to confessional parties.

[28] In this respect, the parallels between the Catholic church and trade unions are striking. As Luebbert (1991:17) reports about Britain, "the unions were generally content to have labor interests represented by sympathetic Liberal (or in some instances Tory) MPs and were especially loathe to have to sponsor independent working-class candidates." For similar evidence about American trade unions see Shefter 1986.

Figure 1. Costs and benefits of the church's strategies (t_2)

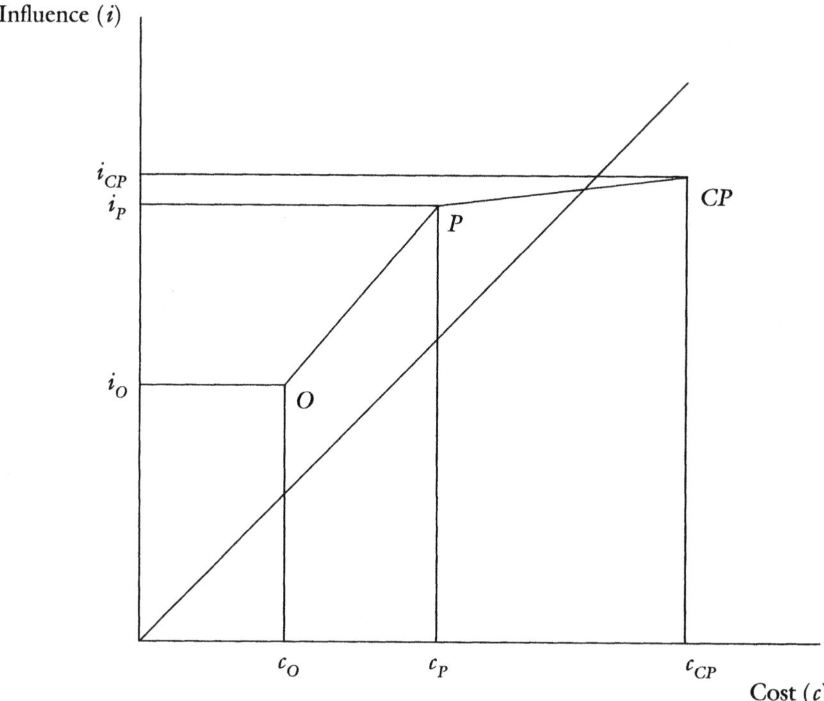

Strategies	O : Organizational strategy
	P : Participation strategy
	CP : Formation of a confessional party
Costs	c_O : cost of O
	c_P : cost of P
	c_{CP} : cost of CP
Influence	i_C : influence generated by O
	i_P : influence generated by P
	i_{CP} : influence generated by CP

only did the church forbid the formation of a true and proper political party, it did not even concede a minimum degree of autonomy in the electoral field," points out De Rosa (1972:284) about Italy; and Webster (1960:97) adds, "It was clear that the political autonomy of Catholics was deeply resented by the pope. Italian Catholics, considered as a political force, should evidently be a compact mass at the disposition of the Holy See." Benito Mussolini best captured the feeling of wariness that prevailed within the church with respect to the Catholic party when, in 1922, he pointed out in one of his editorials that "in high Vatican circles the question is asked whether the birth of the Popular Party will not cause a fearful harm to the church"[29] (Einaudi and Goguel 1952:21). The bishop of Genoa (quoted in Molony 1977:86) summed it all by warning the faithful in a 1920 pastoral letter "of the danger the PPI posed to the church by confusing Italian catholics, breaking them away from ecclesiastical authority and not leading them along the 'true path to follow in public political life.' "

The evidence presented in Chapter 4 leaves no doubt about the position of the church with respect to confessional party formation. It is, therefore, impossible to take at face value accounts that view the formation of confessional parties both as the automatic and desired outcome of the church's action.

The Preferences of Conservative Political Elites

Liberals, strong among the rising industrial and urban bourgeoisie, stood for state rationalization and centralization and fought against local particularisms and privileged bodies such as monarchies, established churches, and hereditary aristocracies. They favored governments responsible to elected parliaments. They supported religious equality, the abolition of political censorship, freedom of speech and association, market forces, and international free trade. Conservatives, in contrast, were mostly associated with the old order. Stronger among the aristocracy and, often, the peasantry, they fought for the preservation of local particularisms and ancient respected institutions, such as the church, and against state centralization and democratization.

Conservative factions were decentralized and loose associations that allowed their members almost total autonomy of action. Nevertheless, their members shared the same fundamental concerns, and when making critical decisions, they acted as a unified body. Generally, politicians maximize their probability of reelection, and Conservatives were no exception. In the 1860s, Conservative factions were lagging behind the Liberals in organizational development (De Trannoy 1905:238). As Liberals were organizing, winning elections, and controlling governments, Conservatives increasingly found themselves in opposition. As a result, they were in a state of intense demoralization that bordered on inertia.[30] Right-wing newspapers accused the Con-

[29] Traniello (1981:52) comments that "in this sense Mussolini was proven historically right: as a mere party of the church the PPI presented a balance of little significance."

[30] Rivet (1979:511, 519) sees the Right as being "paralyzed immobility." He refers to the "passivity of the Right" and its "lethargy and discouragement." In Belgium, the Conservative leader Jules Malou kept calling for organization but was consistently ignored. In 1861, he recognized that "the attempt at organization failed" (De Trannoy 1905:447). De Trannoy (1905:387) concludes that these were "years of political inertia for Catholics."

servatives of "doing nothing" compared to their adversaries (Rivet 1979:511). The recollections of a Belgian Conservative were particularly dramatic in tone: "Our beginnings were extremely painful. . . . We were fighting desperately, without resources, without support, against an enemy relentlessly seeking the destruction of our religious faith and political rights" (quoted in Hendrickx 1969:52). De Trannoy (1905:237, 380) concludes that the Conservative camp suffered from lack of unity of action, absence of cohesion, absence of organization, and sometimes even penury of candidates.

Conservatives were unwilling to generate political mobilization through mass organization building that would allow them to face the Liberals successfully. This unwillingness constituted for them a central and insoluble problem. Conservatives were mostly aristocrats who resisted the formation of grass-roots organizations both by temperament and self-interest. On a symbolic level, mass organization put each member on an equal footing, while on a political level it prevented the use of patronage. To top it all, mass organization unequivocally threatened their political survival even if it assured their reelection because it led to the emergence of a new professional political class[31] (Pizzorno 1970:35). William Irvine (1989b:17) summarizes the dilemma of the Right:

> Conservatives recognized that, to survive, they had to appeal directly to constituents whose subservient support had heretofore been taken for granted. Everywhere there were calls for organized, mass-based, popular conservative parties which might attract the newly emancipated masses and insulate them from subversive new political forces. Yet such calls were rarely answered precisely because mass-based parties ran against the grain for most *notables, notabile,* or *Honoratioren.* Hostile toward and suspicious of the lower classes, conservatives could not—and usually did not want to—emulate the political style of their democratic challengers.

The consequences of such an attitude were predictable. The Conservative

[31] Resistance of notables to mass organization was, and is, a universal phenomenon. Shefter (1994:32–34) argues "that the more 'external' the circumstances of the party's origins—the fewer the allies it had within the preexisting regime." Irvine (1989b:68) reports that "fear of losing power and autonomy to a committee, especially a committee whose composition was uncomfortably 'democratic,' was a commonplace among Conservative politicians during the [French] Third Republic and invariably hampered efforts at political organization." Mavrogordatos (1983:74) found that in interwar Greece "the relationship between local factions and partisan associations was in general extremely antagonistic. As a rule, the development of the latter was inversely related to the strength and resilience of the former. Established politicians would normally view associations as a Trojan Horse of ambitious aspiring competitors (which was often an accurate perception) and would strenuously oppose or boycott them accordingly."

electoral committees, "formed hastily on the elections' eve" (De Trannoy 1905:384), were totally ineffective. The secretary of such a committee in France (quoted in Irvine 1989a:44) remarked that "royalist committees were full of lethargic *notables,* more adept at finding reasons for sitting out an electoral campaign than at generating plausible candidates." As a result, Conservatives failed to mobilize lay Catholics, who, to make things more difficult, were divided both politically and by class, with the nobility looking down on the bourgeoisie.[32] The few attempts by Conservatives to mobilize and unite lay Catholics met with failure (Leblicq 1978:241).

Because they were unwilling to create mass organizations, Conservative politicians had only one way to survive as significant political players. They sought organizational resources elsewhere. As a general rule, politicians prefer to mobilize people indirectly rather than directly. That is, they prefer to mobilize people through social networks rather than building their own organizations because social networks assume the costs of mobilization and relieve politicians of the need to provide people with selective incentives (Rosenstone and Hansen 1993:27–30).

Since political issues are necessary to achieve mobilization (Rosenstone and Hansen 1993:34) and politicians who are permanent losers in electoral politics seek to introduce new dimensions of competition (Riker 1986), Conservative politicians were also looking for issues that would help them get back in power, but they had considerable difficulty finding any. The 1852 "Conservative appeal" of Jules Malou in Belgium, failed miserably to mobilize Belgians: "Malou expected a surge but the masses remained inert" (Guyot de Mishaegen 1946:105). Belgian Conservatives complained bitterly. One of them, Barthélemy Dumortier, pointed out: "Nobody wants to fight . . . you have no idea how much our party has fallen into a political lethargy" (quoted in Guyot de Mishaegen 1946:105). Malou (quoted in Guyot de Mishaegen 1946:121) argued: "We need to create a powerful diversion, to inflame, for example, the opinion with economic reforms, tax reductions. But where is the Robert Peel of this bold campaign? If he appeared would he be understood and followed?" Before the advent of anticlerical attacks, religion was seen as an ineffective mobilizational tool and was dismissed by most Conservative politicians: "According to one of my oldest convictions, confirmed by experience, we will continue to flounder and to receive blows as long as party competition remains in the field of the moral and religious interests," declared the Belgian Conservative leader Jules Malou in 1864 (quoted in Guyot de Mishaegen 1946:121). Moreover, Conservatives disliked

[32] In 1863, Fréderic Delmer, a member of the Brussels chapter of the Association conservatrice (quoted in Leblicq 1978:229) called Catholics of every class to practice "the great rules of the Christian fraternity."

religion because, contrary to other cleavages, it depended on another power, the church. Nationalism was out of question because of its association with the French Revolution and its requirement for political centralization.[33] In fact, nationalism was used by the Liberals, particularly in Germany and Italy. Attempts to use constitutional issues for purposes of political mobilization failed in Austria (Bled 1988:226). In Prussia during the 1860s Conservative Catholic politicians tried to make an issue out of the preservation of the old economic regime (guild laws and the like), but "these efforts, were, in general unsuccessful. The clerical politicians did not strike a responsive chord among the voters in their campaign for the preservation of the economic old regime" (Sperber 1980:226). Anti-Semitism seems to have been an effective appeal, but it was restricted to the relatively few places with a substantive presence of Jews (especially cities such as Vienna and Berlin); its use was also more or less restricted to independent political entrepreneurs and fringe politicians: most traditional politicians balked at the prospect of using this issue.

The advent of the Liberal attack against the church caused many changes. Conservatives realized that for the first time religion appeared to have the potential for mobilization across class and region and to promise electoral victories. The Austrian Conservative Count Leo Thun (quoted in France 1975:99) expressed this point with exceptional clarity in 1868: "[It] is a great profit for the general political struggle of today that the church question has been stepped so decisively into the foreground. That [question] alone promises to help the masses of the conservative population to a correct understanding of contemporary issues and to the realization of where their enemies and where their friends are to be found. It is nearly the only issue which offers the ground for drawing together conservative efforts in all parts of the Reich, since it transcends provincial and national interests."[34]

Once the anticlerical attack was launched, Conservative politicians for the first time had a new issue at hand that appeared to translate into mass political support, and they were eager to exploit it. Even though they resented what a French Monarchist dubbed "the spirit of association" introduced by Cath-

[33] In France, for instance, patriotic nationalism as promoted by General Boulanger in the 1880s "terrified royalists who, still traumatized by the Paris Commune, equated foreign war with social revolution" (Irvine 1989a:31). Rémond (1982:150) points out that in France nationalism was "a totally unforeseen phenomenon in the political context of the nineteenth century which transferred from left to right a group of notions and values that were until then considered part of radicalism. This was a decisive mutation which dates, as we know, from the period 1887–1899."

[34] That Conservatives wanted to use religion as a political issue does not imply that they wanted to build a religious party, as France (1975:99–100) seems to imply from this quotation, in the same fashion as the discovery of the electoral potential of the free-trade issue did not imply the formation of parties exclusively based on and identified with that cleavage.

olics (Denis 1977), they were eager to tap the huge reserve of voters who were influenced by the church and seemed sensitive to religious issues—especially after the implementation of the organizational strategy led thousands of people to become members of Catholic organizations. The defense of the church presented two related advantages: first, a great appeal, both in broadness and intensity, especially to just enfranchised or soon to be enfranchised masses, and second, the direct access it provided to the organizational resources of the church. The second advantage was particularly important because it solved for the Right, in a relatively inexpensive and convenient way, the burning problem of mass organization. Since Conservatives rejected the prospect of mass organization building, contracting out electoral campaigns to Catholic organizations, and hence mass organization, to the church was an extremely attractive solution. The attractiveness of the alliance with the church was reinforced by a mutual indifference about most political priorities of the two sides. Though genuinely concerned about the church's fate, Conservatives were usually indifferent about the religious issues that preoccupied the most devout Catholics. At the same time, the church was indifferent about a range of policy issues that were crucial in everyday party politics. This mutual indifference greatly facilitated the political relationship between the church and Conservative politicians.[35]

Yet this was not naked manipulation of religion, as was often claimed by the Liberals. Conservatives expected a situation that would allow them to exploit the issue of religion without having to identify too closely with it. While they wanted to protect the church, they were also animated, as Simon (1955:47) notes, by "political realism." Together with the church, they preferred a situation that would allow them to be Catholic parliamentarians beholden, like the German Windthorst, "neither to party nor to confession" (Anderson 1981:139), rather than parliamentary Catholics, permanently constrained by the representation of a confessionally defined constituency and the defense of religion and of the church.[36] They wanted access to organizational resources at low cost, rather than dependence on the church and its mass organizations; they sought a temporary marriage of convenience, not a permanent and structural association with the church and religion. As a

[35] According to Jemolo (1960:89), "The sort of conciliation which came to be regarded as more and more possible of achievement was a conciliation rooted in indifference. The two sides were impelled to accept this idea by the necessity of facing together a number of very real dangers, of being able to count on each other's support in the battles which those dangers would make inevitable—in short, of building up confidence in each other's reliability as an ally in case of need. But Catholics and Conservatives alike displayed a marked indifference to all that was unrelated to the purpose of the alliance.

[36] Windthorst had openly stated his preference for the creation of a broad nonconfessional Conservative party rather than the Catholic Zentrum (Zeender 1976:9).

result, Conservatives viewed favorably, albeit suspiciously, the formation of mass Catholic organizations closely controlled by the church and safely removed from politics. But they rejected the idea of the formation of confessional parties for two reasons.

First, they wanted to avoid turning religion into a recurring and central feature of politics, and they were totally opposed to being permanently associated with the church. They understood that religion, an electoral magnet, was as Kees van Kersbergen (1994:35) observes, very much like a real magnet, with the simultaneous faculty to attract and repel. They also understood that the creation of confessional parties with religion as their banner would restrict their autonomy and hamper their flexibility in picking issues and selecting policies. It would also make them extremely vulnerable to pressure from the church. The Right, as Auguste Rivet (1979:519) points out, saw the clergy not only as an ally but as a rival.

Second, Catholic activists represented a threat for Conservatives through both their radicalism and their potential to control the new confessional parties. Catholic activists made their intentions clear by pressing for an imperative mandate and openly advocating the need for a truly Catholic party[37] They often claimed, as in 1877 in Belgium, that "an opposition exists between the Right of the Chamber and the Senate and the Catholic nation" (Soete 1984:200). Conservative politicians were good Catholics, but they did not want the bishops and the petit-bourgeois lay Catholics to boss them around in their own preserve. Even in France, where the French Revolution had associated Catholicism and the Right in an unprecedented fashion, "the majority of Catholic parliamentarians, called upon to face the various problems of a Christian restoration, were not much attracted by the outlook of the [Catholic] extremists" (Dansette v.1 1961:328). In fact, when in power, Conservatives had often displayed a great deal of paternalism toward the church by exercising a high degree of control and imposing multiple restrictions on it (Whyte 1981:34).

Thus the political calculus of Conservatives was straightforward. For them the participation strategy of the church was preferable to unsystematic support from the church because it boosted their probability of reelection ($r_U < r_P$) while carrying relatively low costs since the church guaranteed that its mass organizations would remain aloof from politics. The participation strategy was clearly preferable to the formation of a confessional party because such a party did not increase their probability of reelection but threatened their political survival. The model predicts that Conservative political elites

[37] In Belgium, Catholic activists demanded that since the "Catholic people" are on the side of its representatives, "those must represent their desires and aspirations" (Guyot de Mishaegen 1946:177).

will not find it rational to form a confessional party. To use the remarkably appropriate Italian terms (used by the pope), pro-church politicians were to be *cattolici deputati* rather than *deputati cattolici.*[38] The nuance might seem subtle, but it illustrates, in its very simplicity, the gap between the intentions of both church and Conservatives and a Catholic political identity. Indeed, one can draw here a linguistic metaphor: Catholicism became a political identity when it made the transition in the political language from adjective to noun or, in other words, from attribute to object.

To conclude, in the interaction between the church and Conservatives the participation strategy constitutes a stable equilibrium. It is an equilibrium based on the mutual contracting out of undesirable but necessary activities: political struggle against anticlerical reforms for the church and mass organization for Conservative political elites. It is a stable equilibrium because no side has, at this point, the incentive to defect unilaterally. Nevertheless, confessional parties were formed in five out of six cases. To account for this outcome (and for the surprising collapse of this equilibrium), I turn in the next chapter to an examination of the strategies selected by the two actors.

[38] In 1904, the pope permitted a few Catholics to run for seats in the Chamber, but under the condition that they would sit in the parliament as *cattolici deputati* rather than as *deputati cattolici* (Webster 1960:14).

CHAPTER 2

Strategies and Outcomes

In the thought of their creators, Catholic Action organizations were supposed to maintain a clerical structure. But they gave voice to laymen who escaped from the authority meant to control them.

—Jean Delumeau

The model outlined in the previous chapter predicts that the two main actors, church and Conservative politicians, will not find it rational to form confessional parties. Yet these parties were formed in five countries. To account for this outcome, I discuss the strategies chosen by the actors and the ways these strategies shaped the process of party formation.

The Strategy of Conservative Political Elites

The calculus of Conservative politicians led them to a straightforward choice: participation. This strategy was based on a pact with the church whereby Conservatives would make the defense of the church their central electoral issue in exchange for Catholic electoral support. As I pointed out in the first chapter, it was not rational for them to strive for the formation of permanent and centralized parties built around religion. What they wanted was a situation in which they could, as the Italian prime minister Giovanni Giolitti did in 1913, *"acquistare a buon mercato"* (purchase cheaply) the Catholic votes (De Rosa 1972:352). This choice was perfectly compatible with the participation strategy of the church. This compatibility is best encapsulated in De Rosa's (1972:266) comment about the 1904 elections in Italy: *"I moderati entravano solo come eletti ed i cattolici solo come elettori"* (The moderates [Conservatives] entered only as elected and the Catholics only as voters).

Conservative politicians resisted the formation of confessional parties. Their alliance with the church was not intended to be a permanent and structural association. Political issues come and go, and religion was no exception. Conservatives expected instead to retain the loyalty of Catholics and absorb them as individual voters. They rejected the use of confessional labels to avoid becoming identified with religion and the church and described themselves as Conservatives (Zeender 1976:9; Jenks 1965:123). Margaret Anderson (1981:138) describes a striking scene from Germany: "When a priest suggested they call themselves the Catholic Fraction, and Peter Reichensperger had boomed down from the other end of the table, 'that would be a great misfortune for us Catholics!' Windthorst had joined him in warning against a confessional designation. . . . Windthorst said later he had wanted to assure himself that the Zentrum would not be a confessional party."

The Belgian case illustrates how the parliamentary Right viewed its association with religion and the defense of the church. Conservative leaders viewed religious mobilization and mass organization with great suspicion. They were skeptical about the organization of Catholic congresses, which were organized by lay Catholic activists, and most prominent Conservatives were conspicuously absent from the first Catholic congress of Malines. Their leader, Jules Malou, confessed that he understood neither the object nor the utility of this congress (Guyot de Mishaegen 1946:97). But above all Conservatives rejected the formation of a confessional party. Conservatives welcomed the electoral intervention of the clergy in their favor, but they insisted that politics should not be mixed with religion and rejected the exclusive political identification of their party with the church and religion. They were opposed as well to the adoption of a religiously oriented political program, which they thought would restrict their independence (Mélot 1935:7). The Conservative appeal launched by Malou in 1852 did not contain the word "Catholic." The 1858 statutes of the Conservative Association emphasized its conservative character and called for the defense of the "religious character of the populations" rather than the church (De Trannoy 1905:388–92). Adolphe Dechamps, a prominent Conservative, argued that "the constitution of a Catholic party is a peril, a misfortune for everyone, and particularly for religion" (quoted in Soete 1986:201). During a parliamentary debate in 1863, the Conservative deputy Kervyn de Lettenhove bluntly refused the label "Catholic" for his party. He declared that the Right was the Conservative party *(parti conservateur)* and argued that the association of the Right and religion benefited the Left (Erba 1967:230). Conservative politicians also warned that political agitation with religious overtones would be harmful to the party (Guyot de Mishaegen 1946:128). In 1878, the parliamentary Right went so far as to call for Vatican intervention against the anticonstitutional agitation provoked by Catholic organizations. Some Conservative deputies even called for "full and entire independence from the clergy" (Mélot 1935:44). In short, Conservatives made clear that they rejected the use of religion as their central and primary organizing political principle.

Yet the Conservatives' decision to climb on the bandwagon of religion after the anticlerical attack is consistent with their preferences. They knew what the preferences of the church were and based their choice on the expectation that the church would keep Catholic organizations on a leash. Their mistake was to underestimate the potential for autonomy of Catholic organizations. They did not anticipate how tremendously successful the political use of religion was going to be and hence how constraining and destructive it would be both of the church's control over Catholic organizations and of their own control over the Conservative political space.

The Strategy of the Church

Compared to the Conservatives' decisions, the choices of the church appear puzzling. I pointed out in the previous chapter that both the organizational and the participation strategies carried extremely high costs for the church, and I showed that the church was well aware of these dangers. Why, then, did it decide (in five out of six cases) to implement these two strategies? How did confessional parties emerge and why did the church accept their existence? It is doubtful if confessional parties could have survived, particularly at their early stages, without the legitimacy provided by an implicit or explicit endorsement from the church. As Auguste Mélot (1935:44) remarks about the church: "No one can defend such a power without its recognition and authorization."

To unravel this puzzle it is necessary to consider the options available to the church. When faced with the Liberal attack, the church had two initial choices. It could either use mild forms of resistance and compromise with the Liberals or fight back and create mass organizations. Both choices carried costs. By not resisting, the church ran the risk of sending a signal of weakness that could lead to worse attacks, besides absorbing the losses of influence induced by the anticlerical attack. By fighting back, the church would assume the costs associated with the organizational strategy. The church's decision hinged on the severity of the anticlerical attack, the availability of alternative ways of protecting its influence, and the expected positive impact of mass organization on its influence.

Given the cost of the organizational strategy, the church preferred to avoid a fight. In fact, the church made numerous attempts to negotiate with the Liberals, sometimes even accepting an important part of the anticlerical legislation.[1] In Austria, for instance, the bishops initially supported a "realistic"

[1] Compromise was even justified in a theological fashion through the famous thesis-hypothesis postulate, according to which the unrelenting principles of the church never cease to be taught (thesis), but in practice concessions made necessary or advisable by circumstances can take place (hypothesis).

attempt to work within the state of affairs established by the anticlerical laws (Boyer 1981:28). Soon, however, it became clear that such action would have no effect. Liberals were bent on implementing their anticlerical program and went ahead with their legislation, in part because they felt they were following the tide of history. Indeed, the Austrian church's attempt failed because "several of the Liberal ministers were opposed in principle to the continuation of negotiations [with the church] on any terms" (France 1975:137). As an Austrian Liberal commentator proclaimed in 1867 (quoted in France 1975:13), "the free constitutional citizens of Austria do not have any desire to make pacts with the papal curia, to ask for their own laws back." This attitude certainly reinforced the hard-liners within the church: "The successors of the apostles, not the rulers of the world are the ones to decide whether the union between man and wife is really a true marriage," declared the Archbishop of Vienna Joseph Rauscher (quoted in France 1975:88).

The church attempted as well to block the parliamentary process through direct petition to the head of state or appeals to the people. As soon as anticlerical educational legislation was introduced in Bavaria in 1868, the church submitted a petition to the king asking for "careful and unbiased consideration" of the bill before any irrevocable steps were taken (Windell 1954:176). The Belgian church, in anticipation of the imminent voting on educational reform legislation in 1879, issued a pastoral letter expressing its hope that no law would be passed (Simon 1955:120). This failed to produce results, reflecting the transfer of power from palace to parliament.

The Liberals' intentions left the church with the choice of either resisting or absorbing this loss of power without budging—and the reduction of power was substantial. Education, which traditionally belonged to the sphere of influence of the church together with health care and poor relief, was the field where the power of the church was most visible and where the church seemed to be most vulnerable to state attacks. Education and family were the "institutions to which the transmission of culture from generation to generation was (and is) charged" (France 1975:31). Education in particular was, according to Langlois (1980:403), "the last institution in which Catholicism was coextensive of the social body." Education reform laws asserted the right of the state to control education and ranged from the outward imposition of a state monopoly over education to the termination of state support for confessional schools with a parallel rise in the standards and costs of education. The anticlerical legislation, which mainly affected education but also family law and diplomatic relations with the Vatican, was perceived almost as a reenactment of the French Revolution and was labeled by Catholics accordingly: *loi de malheur* in Belgium (Mélot 1935:35), *loi scélérate* and *loi maudite* in France (Ozouf 1963:82; Hilaire 1977:697), *decretum horribile* in the Netherlands (Verkade 1965:41). In Austria it was described as "a worse setback for the country than the military defeats of Marengo, Austerlitz, and

Königgrätz" (Bled 1988:120) and in France as "a disaster worst than Sédan" (Gadille v.2 1967:204). In a nutshell, there was a growing perception within the church that if "one takes away the Church's right to bring up the children, one takes away her future" (Anderson 1981:61). In addition, the uncompromising stance of the Liberals reinforced the perception within the church that this legislation was only the beginning of a wider offensive and thus the first and decisive step that would inexorably lead to dechristianization and the destruction of the church.

More than just hurting the church, measures touching on education and family affected all Catholics in a way that was both direct and easy to grasp: "The school question was far more important in arousing political interests among Catholic laymen than the former struggle over the bestowal of church offices had been. . . . The question of the schools touched the average man in a way the other issue did not" (Windell 1954:21). The rumor spread that the "godless" state schools would dechristianize children and slowly but inevitably strangle the church and religion. Joseph Edmund Jörg, the leader of the pro-church Bavarian Patriot party succinctly expressed this fear in 1864: "If [modern Liberalism] succeeds only in separating completely the schools from the church, then the existence of the latter will cause little concern in the future. The church will then be a building with four walls, whose interior, as the liberals count on, will become emptier with every decade"[2] (quoted in Windell 1954:17). The Catholic press used stronger language: "If the program of that [Progressive] party is carried out," warned a Prussian Catholic newspaper, "then we will be on the edge of that abyss against which the watchman of the Throne of Peter has time and again warned us" (Sperber 1980:223–24). Lay Catholics were truly alarmed: "They are not going to have it, the beautiful soul of children," sang the Flemish peasants (Mélot 1935:40).

To make things worse, the church (in five out of the six countries examined here) lacked alternative ways of protecting its influence. The church examined all possible actions, including nonparliamentary ones. As Gramsci (1995:45) put it, "For this defense no holds are barred for the Church: neither armed insurrection, nor attempts on the life of individuals, nor appeals to

[2] Many Liberals had such intentions. The French Republican prime minister Jules Ferry declared in 1892 that the school reform was "the bigger social reform and the most serious and durable political reform. . . . When all the French youth would have been educated and would have grown under this triple star of *gratuité*, *obligation* and *laicité*, we will have nothing to fear from a return to the past, because we will have in our defense . . . the spirit of all new generations, of these young and innumerable reserves of republican democracy, trained at the school of science and reason, who will oppose the retrograde spirit, the insurmountable obstacle of the free intelligence, and the disfranchised consciousness" (quoted in Mayeur 1973:112–13).

foreign invasions." But, the options of the church were very restricted. Emperors and kings in Belgium, the Netherlands, Austria, Prussia, and Bavaria were willing to let the Liberals proceed with their plans. Liberal governments were strong, but the parliamentary Right was weak and divided—and pro-Catholic forces had often been militarily defeated, as in Germany and Italy. The Austrian Conservative politician Leo Thun (quoted in Zeps 1979:114) expressed this feeling of impotence in 1877: "The conclusion, therefore, according to my conviction, is that the salvation of the Christian school as well as the whole Christian order, the maintenance of which determines the existence of Austria, cannot be won through the Reichsrat but rather through its downfall." Resources for nonparliamentary action were not available, however, because national armies were controlled by centralizing elites and no country was willing to engage in war to protect the church.

Given the Liberal unwillingness to compromise, the severity of the anticlerical attack, and the lack of alternative means of defense, the church decided to fight ($O > C$). This decision was based on a rational calculus: the church accepted the high cost of fighting because less costly ways to protect itself were unavailable. As Gramsci (1995:34) observed, "It is no longer the Church that determines the battlefield and weapons; it has instead to accept the terrain imposed on it by the adversaries. . . . The Church, in other words, is on the defensive, has lost its autonomy of movement and initiative." But how to fight? When the church rejected compromise, the "era of illusions" gave way to a new tactic of confrontation, which included three means of action: first, the clear and open denunciation of anticlerical legislation by the episcopate; second, a campaign of civil disobedience and the use of religious sanctions (such as refusing sacraments to parents who sent their children to public schools and the excommunication of Liberal politicians); and third, and most important, the creation of mass organizations.

First Step: The Organizational Strategy

The essence of the organizational strategy was that the church fought against the anticlerical attack alone and outside the political process, a point stressed by Lipset and Rokkan (1967:40): "The Church felt impelled to defend its position through its own resources." Some help was requested from individual Conservative politicians; appeals were made for the election of candidates friendly to the church, and priests even suggested the "right" electoral choice to their parishioners. But these elements were peripheral to this strategy. The church backed no electoral crusade or organized political struggle. No political force fighting for the defense of the church was formed.

Indeed, the decision to fight was often taken without prior consultation with the parliamentary Right and surprised it (Terlinden 1929:146).

The organizational strategy was accompanied by the reinforcement of the church's position against democracy and the development of an alarmist ideological discourse, which rejected the foundations of political modernity, representative democracy and the modern liberties. The main elements of this ideological program, which Angelo Gambasin (1969:159–92) aptly dubs *pastorale difensiva,* were contained in the papal encyclical *Quanta Cura* and its annex *Syllabus Errorum.*[3] In fact, the Catholic movement was built around these encyclicals rather than the later famous social encyclical *Rerum Novarum.*[4]

The cornerstone of this strategy was the creation of mass organizations. The first Catholic associations were formed in the wake of the initial anticlerical attacks, usually by lay Catholics, in an unsystematic and decentralized way. The raw material for these associations was an already existing but loose and decentralized church network including parishes, reflection clubs, confraternities, and other devotional societies of Catholics most of which developed after the end of the French Revolution (Mayeur 1980:20). The church's decision to implement the organizational strategy amounted to a takeover of these disparate Catholic groups, their expansion, centralization, and coordination into a centralized network of lay associations, the tightening of its control over them, and the shifting of their members' focus from private to public life. Catholic organizations were now officially sponsored by the church, their structure duplicated the church's by following the parochial and diocesan levels, and they lost whatever autonomy of action they previously had: the Catholic movement was born.

There is evidence suggesting that in its initial stages, the organizational

[3] The *Syllabus,* "the most coherent model of the intransigent Catholic ideology ever formulated" (Ravitch 1990:82), was published in 1864. It denounced concepts such as freedom of speech, freedom of the press, freedom of conscience and religion, the doctrine of progress, Liberalism, and the modern conception of civilization. Condemned also were the sovereignty of the people, the assertion of the right of civil society to interfere in religious matters, the separation of church and state, and the denial of the right of Catholicism to be recognized as the sole state religion and of the church's right to educate youth. It ended with a condemnation of the idea that the Holy Roman pontiff can and ought to reconcile himself to what is called progress, liberty, and modern civilization. This alarmist discourse was popularized and propagated by Catholic newspapers and church bodies such as diocesan synods.

[4] The encyclical *Rerum Novarum,* often credited with a central role in the formation of confessional parties, was issued in 1891, after the formation of most parties. Moreover, besides its well-known social message it did not call for the formation of Catholic parties. As Sturzo (quoted in De Rosa 1972:251) noted in 1902, "The *Rerum Novarum* is not a manifest, nor does it create parties. . . . The encyclical suggests solutions, encourages initiatives that could solve the workers' problem on the basis of a Christian-oriented society, [but] it does not impose forms of organization and political directions."

strategy was conceived as an emergency measure and that it lacked a long-term perspective,[5] as is reflected in the fact that lay Catholic activity acquired doctrinal justification and canonic institutionalization only in 1922.[6] "In no way" would the new organizations affect "the fundamental, canonical and hierarchical organization of the church, which was divinely instituted by the Christ," declared the French bishop Charles Gibier (quoted in Bessières 1924:9). In his detailed examination of the decisions of diocesan synods in Italy, Gambasin (1969:192) found that a feeling of perplexity with regard to the new organizations, reflected in "cautious and uncertain" language, developed within the church. Catholic associations were initially interpreted as a new expression of the old devotional societies of men. In fact, as Aubert (1982:192) points out, "While many laymen and young priests quickly realized that [mass organization] was the way of the future, the ecclesiastical authorities kept for a long time the nostalgia of the old regime of diplomatic bargains at the top."

Yet, although initially conceived as an emergency measure in the face of the Liberal attack (Zeps 1979:132; Gambasin 1969:65), the creation of mass organizations took such dimensions that a historian would later claim that "the history of the Catholic Church since the middle of the nineteenth century is partially, at least in Europe, a history of Catholic associations" (Köhler 1981:212). In fact, the Germans developed a term to describe the phenomenon of mass organized Catholicism: *Vereins-* or *Verbandskatholizismus* (McLeod 1986:411).

The development of a network of confessional schools and the organization of petition drives against the anticlerical laws generated a first wave of

[5] An analysis of articles published in the Jesuit Italian newspaper *Civiltà cattolica* points to an initial short-term conception of the Catholic movement as "the totality of Catholics' actions aiming at reestablishing the pontiff's freedom, into which was included the territorial question" (Traniello 1982:38). No thought was given to what would happen to these organizations beyond this goal. Moreover, attention was initially given to practical (as opposed to political) considerations such as the financial support of the church's alternative educational network, which required a vast organization (Soete 1980). For Delfosse and Frognier (1988:76) the creation by the church of an associational network was a sign of its "inadaption" to the Liberal state, which unintentionally produced positive electoral results.

[6] Lay Catholic activity was justified theologically in 1922 in the papal encyclical *Urbi Arcano Dei*, which downplayed it into a transition of the laymen's apostolical mission from the private to the public level (Congar and Varillon 1947:35). It now became known as Catholic Action and was defined in very restrictive terms as "the participation of the lay in the hierarchical apostolate under the special impulse, direction and control of the hierarchy" (Congar 1967:13; Congar and Varillon 1947:42). The laymen's mission was "an auxiliary one to the salvific work of the priest" (Molony 1977:20), while collaboration between the hierarchy and the lay could "only be a dependent collaboration from the layman's point of view"; this collaboration was based on "communication, which, on the upper side takes the form of advice, and on the lower side the form of suggestion" (Congar and Varillon 1947:61–62).

mobilization and introduced the faithful masses to public life. Such movements took giant dimensions. In the Netherlands during 1878, the signatures collected against these laws added up to three times the number of the electorate (Daalder 1960:201); the same was true in Belgium, where the petition against the 1879 law was signed by 317,000 people at a time when the electorate hovered around 100,000. In Prussia, during 1868 and 1869, "tens of thousands of signatures were gathered in defense of confessionally-bound public education and in support of the beleaguered position of the pope" (Sperber 1980:266). In Austria, thousands of signatures were collected and sent to the emperor in 1867 to protest the new anticlerical laws (France 1975:83), as was done in Bavaria in 1872 (Southern 1977:64). In France, a petition against the law of 1879 gathered an impressive 1,775,000 signatures (Boulard and Cholvy 1992:25). These petition drives were an indicator of the political potential of religious mobilization. In the Netherlands, "every observant political analyst saw plainly what a magnificent reservoir of voters those men possessed. . . . It gave a sort of preview as to what would happen when those thousands would be able to go into effective political action" (Vanden Berg 1960:94). For reasons specified below, however, this signal was ignored, particularly by the Liberals, who did not alter their course of action.

As mass mobilization and organization building proceeded, a political project emerged, formulated mostly by ultramontane lay Catholics.[7] This project saw mass organization not as a simple means of church defense against a particular anticlerical attack but as an all-out struggle against secular-liberal society and modernity, the "polemical confrontation with the lay and secularized society"[8] (Vecchio 1987:100). The Austrian Catholic Con-

[7] Initially, lay Catholics were divided about the role of organizations. In the first congress of Belgian Catholics in 1863, lay Catholics proposed two contradictory positions with regard to organization. Liberal Catholics supported the idea of autonomous lay organizations, which were to be part of society rather than the church; they argued for detaching laymen from the sacristy. Intransigent Catholics advocated the isolation of laymen from society and the reorganization of the temporal order "according to God" through the mediation of ecclesiastical institutions (Gambasin 1969:16). The church opted for the second alternative, and lay Catholics followed.

[8] The provost Claessen of the Aachen Cathedral, asking for permission to form a new Catholic brotherhood in the city, spelled out the logic of the organizational strategy: "Now, as is well known, the brotherhoods (associations) stand legally under the control of the episcopate. . . . Consequently, with an hierarchical reinforcement through the appropriate control by the bishops, the brotherhoods could become an incomparable means to encourage pious behavior and bring the faithful closer to the church. This seems to me to be all the more important, as nowadays the swindlers with their slogans of humanity believe they can use their godless associations to thrust religion from the stage" (quoted in Sperber 1980:97). Although made in 1834, well before the organizational strategy was implemented, and being more "wishful thinking than a realistic portrayal" of the situation (Sperber 1980:97), this statement encapsulates the logic of the organizational strategy. According to Traniello (1981:46), the creation of the Catholic movement resulted from the "anti-Christian revolution which de-

gress of 1877 called for the creation of Catholic organizations to fight dechristianization (Zeps 1979:132), while the Italian Catholics called for organizations to fight irreligion and Liberalism and for "defense against the enemies of the church and the civil society" (Gambasin 1969:65–66). *"All'Associazione del male l'Associazione del bene"* (Against the Association of evil, the Association of good), proclaimed the first congress of Italian Catholics. "Why shouldn't these [Liberal] associations of hell now being formed, be countered by truly Christian ones?" asked a German priest (Sperber 1980:97). Gradually the movement acquired a wider societal objective, moving from defense to offense, from negative to positive action, and from a narrow interest group mentality to a wider political vision.

The focus of the organizational strategy was society rather than the state and the political process. In this context Catholics promoted the distinction between *legal* country (meaning the Liberal state) and *real* country (their own network of associations)(Tramontin 1981a:337; van Isacker 1955). This was a utopian project of a counterculture and a countersociety hostile to and separate from the Liberal state and society (Aubert 1982:213), a "sort of residue of Israel immersed within a reality considered hostile and apostate" (Traniello 1981:46). The objective was isolation rather than participation in the political process in a fashion greatly resembling early communitarian socialists: "To build a society within society . . . in complete independence of the bourgeois world" (Przeworski 1985:7). The Dutch Calvinists' motto "in isolation lies our strength" (Coleman 1978:40) embodied the deeper meaning of this strategy, and indeed "in every city Catholics went into voluntary isolation, constituting separate communities which boycotted schools and clubs . . . and as soon as economic circumstances permitted, even formed self-contained economic units" (Jemolo 1960:58). By isolating and entrenching Catholics, the church hoped to shield them—and itself—from anticlerical legislation and secularization. The expectation was that isolation would eventually translate into the reconquest of society from below and the "reconstruction and the development of a globally Catholic order which would recognize a general function of guide to the hierarchically structured church"[9] (Traniello 1981:47).

---

stroyed the Christian state, the Christian law, the Christian power" and was equivalent to the "organizational structuration" of the "Catholic society and the Christian people."

[9] Von Beyme (1985:159) has pointed out that for Marxist and Christian parties "organization was often an anticipation on a sub-system level of the society the party wanted to see in the future." This was even more the case for the mass movements that preceded confessional parties. As a Dutch Protestant leader (quoted in Houska 1985:15) put it, the Christian Protestant movement was the "instrument for the propagation of God's kingdom in the realm of the state."

Besides protecting the church, the creation of an entrenched and self-sufficient Catholic world provided two side benefits. First, it placed Catholics under the exclusive control of the church and thus mitigated the negative effects of mass organization; second, it minimized the church's dependence on political brokers and preserved its control over the struggle. The bishops, who "had been in the habit of regarding themselves as interpreters to the government of Catholic opinion" (Dansette, v.1 1961:236), made clear that the church was to act alone, without any interference, and that its defense was not to be left in the hands of the lay Catholics, the low clergy, or the Conservative politicians. "The defense of the Catholic interests is the business of the bishops," proclaimed the leader of the Austrian church, Cardinal Rauscher (Bled 1988:121).

As the radically novel nature of mass organizations began to become apparent, the hierarchical synods reacted vigorously against their political aspirations and spirit of autonomy. The initial apprehension about the fact that these organizations appealed directly to the pope and seemed to bypass traditional hierarchical channels gradually gave way to increasing clericalization. The church asserted the rights of priests and bishops within these organizations, proclaimed their diocesan and hierarchical character, and pressed for their disciplining (Gambasin 1969:203–29). The first article of the statutes of the Italian Opera (quoted in Gambasin 1969:4) reflected the anxiety of the church. It stated that the goals of the organization were to "assemble and reorganize the Catholics and the Catholic associations of all Italy in a common and concord action for the defense and the support of all the religious sacrosanct rights of the church and the papacy, and the religious and social interests of the Italians, in accordance with the wishes of the highest pontiff and under the escort of the episcopate and the clergy."

The church immediately attempted to mitigate the deleterious effects of mass organization in three ways. The first was to limit the development of mass organization and keep open communication channels with the Liberal governments.[10] The second was to restrict the scope of the organizations' action by keeping them away from electoral and political action. The third way involved the adoption of preventive measures to reinforce control over

[10] The coexistence of militancy (both ideological intransigence and organization building) and pragmatism (secret negotiations with the government) was not as contradictory as it might appear. Both entailed the use of the church's own resources only. One useful by-product of this simultaneous use of seemingly contradictory tactics was that it worked both ways against the formation of a confessional party. When the church advocated pragmatism it could, indirectly, undercut the intransigent Catholics who promoted the cause of a confessional party. In addition, the church's support for militancy and the promotion of a struggle outside the political process had the advantage of lending support to its position against democracy and, therefore, party formation.

both laymen and priests, such as communion for children, confirmation at the age of seven, and the recommendation of frequent, even daily, communion for both lay and clergy[11] (Jemolo 1960:112). Instructions given to priests about annual confession and Easter communion demanded closer supervision of the laity (Jones and Swart 1976:218). Under Pius X, a general streamlining took place, including the reform of the papal administration and the canon law (Aubert 1981). The church also institutionalized popular forms of piety, previously deemed as superstition by the clergy, "in order to control them" (Ford 1993:166). In some cases, as in the Netherlands in 1904, "the bishops ordered that an association of reform-minded priests and lay Catholics be disbanded on the grounds that priests and laymen could not consort with each other in a common society" (Bakvis 1981:23). The 1907 papal encyclical *Pascendi* institutionalized such practices by, among other means, placing "severe, almost draconian restrictions on clerical congresses organized by priests" (Boyer 1995:303).

Catholic organizations acquired a structure replicating that of the church and became "strongly centralized and hierarchized" (Gambasin 1969:5). The position of lay Catholics within these organizations was expected to be an exact replication of their position within the church. This emphasis on control was articulated from the very beginning and in a entirely open way. The church underlined that "the ultimate foundation of Catholic activism was the sacramental and juridical belonging of the Christian to the church" (Gambasin 1969:202). Obedience to the hierarchy was assiduously emphasized. In 1867, the Austrian lay leader Heinrich Clam-Martinic refused to introduce a procedure in the Catholic organization he was heading whereby members could approve the decisions of the episcopate because that would imply that they would also be able to reject them (Bled 1988:97). The affirmation that the organizations "depended directly" on the church followed always and in an almost automatic fashion any public mention of them by the church (Suardo 1962:62; Bessières 1924). Statements stressing the "spirit of unlimited adhesion and obedience to the pontiff and the bishops" were included in every declaration of the new organizations (Belardinelli 1981:4). In an archetypal fashion, the Catholic Congress of 1875 in Florence called for "solemn declarations of absolute submission to every teaching of the church." The congress also stated that it did not pretend to substitute its

[11] The papal recommendation for frequent communion was made in 1905 in the face of strong theological resistance (Aubert 1975:136). Communion for children was received with considerable reluctance by both clergy and lay. For example, in the French department of the Isère it was "as everywhere else . . . a decision which was not expected" and provoked "a somewhat keen emotion." The local bishop, Mgr. Henry (quoted in Barral 1962:251) commented: "The pope spoke; we have to look not toward the past with sadness, but toward the future with joy."

action for that of the ecclesiastical authority which it intended to support "with humility and subordination" *(Preliminari Avvertenze del Comitato Promotore* in *Colloquio sul movimento cattolico italiano* 1976:38). The Sicilian bishops did not use nuance when they pointed out that the Catholic associations were to be "under the total and absolute dependence of the respective bishops" (D'Andrea 1980:256).

The "fundamental norms of the Catholic diocesan action" spelled out by the papal secretary of state Rafael Merry del Val in 1906 codified certain basic rules. The objective, according to the first article of the norms, was "to promote, regulate and coordinate local Catholic action, in conformity with the teachings and the institutions of the Holy See." The activity of the Catholics in every diocese was explicitly placed under the "high dependence of the bishop" (De Rosa 1972:310). As Merry del Val (quoted in De Rosa 1972:314) reminded the president of a Catholic organization in 1909, "the soul and life of any Catholic movement is the supreme ecclesiastical authority."[12]

Finally, the church made clear that membership in Catholic organizations could in no way substitute for traditional church activity: as proclaimed in the Catholic Congress of Florence in 1875, "The Congress is convinced that every correct action would be completely vain and dangerous, if some could pretend that the action of a Congress of laymen can substitute, compensate, or exempt from the piety, discipline, private fervor and example of the Catholic life, and from . . . these practices of humility, modesty and charitable activity that form the life of the Catholic in his parish (the fundamental and principal center of the Catholic life)" *(Preliminari Avvertenze del Comitato Promotore* in *Colloquio sul movimento cattolico italiano* 1976:38).

The church successfully obstructed the emergence of Catholic organizations that did not follow this model. As Dansette (v.2 1961:96) points out, the "lay leaders' position depended on the goodwill of the clerics. If their zeal was thought to be misdirected, their only resort was to retire from the scene." Justifying his decision to dissolve the Italian Opera in 1904, the pope put it bluntly: "Those who care about the real progress and the results of the Opera dei Congressi, in all its manifestations, always remember the following sentence: 'it is preferable that a work *[opera]* is not carried on at all, rather than it be done without or against the will of the bishop' " (quoted in De

[12] This model was replicated everywhere. In the Bavarian province of Swabia, the statutes of the Catholic associations stressed reliance on episcopal leadership (Southern 1977:236). In France, the formative declaration of the Catholic youth (ACJF)(quoted in Molette 1968:70) stressed the "absolute obedience to the sovereign and infallible authority of our Holy Mother the Catholic church, visible and living authority within the august person of the reigning sovereign pontiff and, below him, within the persons of the bishops who are united with him and whom the Holy Spirit has placed to govern the Christian people."

Rosa 1972:259). Likewise, the bishop of the Belgian town of Liège vehemently rejected organizational plans related to the Catholic school network which were presented to him by the Conservative leader Jules Malou. He remarked that "the leadership that belongs to the bishop by divine right is reduced [by these plans] to simple support." The bishop's counterplans were nothing more than a replica of the church's structure: "the priest in his parish, . . . the bishop in his diocese, surrounded by devoted laymen" (quoted in Boulange 1986:310–11). Malou saw in the church's refusal to accept his plans an attempt to impose "a totally ecclesiastical form of organization" in which "the bishop alone is legislator [while] the layman must . . . provide him with all the necessary consent" (Boulange 1986:311). Despite their reservations, Belgian laymen had to accept the church's verdict: the Belgian Catholic leader Charles Woeste commented in his memoirs (1927:198) that "following these events the free educational system was organized on an episcopal basis."

Organization was to be implemented outside the political sphere narrowly defined, in particular outside electoral politics. Together with control by the church, the official exclusion of politics from the action of these new organizations was the defining element of the organizational strategy. "Let's create Catholic associations that will take care of only the matters that concern God and the church, but rigorously excluding politics to avoid any tension," argued the archbishop of Vienna, Rauscher (quoted in Bled 1988:122). Rauscher declared repeatedly that the Catholic associations should never be allowed to become political associations (France 1975:223). The Italian priest Bartolomeo Sandri argued in 1891 that the organization must at any cost act in such a way as "to make it impossible for it to enter at all either liberal society, parliamentarism, or elections" (quoted in Gambasin 1969:85).

Catholic organizations emphasized religious and social activities and professed explicitly in their statutes that they had no political aims. In Germany, "almost universally their charters contained provisions which specifically forbade discussion of political questions in their meetings" (Windell 1954:33), while the Belgian Catholic Congress of Malines forbade in its statutes "any participation in electoral matters and in party conflicts" (Plavsic 1968:215). The same was true with the statutes of French Catholic organizations (Bessières 1924). According to the statutes of the Gesellverein, the German Catholic organization of journeymen, individual members and local clubs could be expelled for political activity (Neitzel 1987:88). To the contrary, their purpose "was specifically religious in that it concerned itself with dogmatic instruction, ecclesiastical ceremonies, spiritual retreats and the diffusion of edifying literature" (Molony 1977:20; Italy). In the same spirit, don Francesco Ogliati (quoted in Vecchio 1987:98) proclaimed that the goals of the Unione giovani cattolici milanesi, formed in 1907, were "catechism, frequent communions, weekly and daily, closed spiritual exercises and days of retirement, hours of devotion and nightly devotion, ardent love, obedience to the pope and the bishops, purity, Christian courage, apostolical activity, mortification, necessity to carry a Christian soul even in public, economic, and, social life."[13]

Although statutory provisions excluding politics from the activity of Catholic organizations also had the purpose of deterring state attacks, they were not empty words. They were often enforced, as in Italy, where a series of diocesan synods during the 1880s condemned the "political party infiltrations" in Catholic associations (Gambasin 1969:192) and where constant attempts to depoliticize Catholic mass organizations were "consistently carried out by the popes" (Horner 1983:34). True, political discussions often took place within Catholic associations, but electoral participation and direct and open political agitation were absent. Furthermore, the initial emphasis of Catholic organizations on piety "tended to lead the faithful away from any kind of political action" (Sperber 1980:104).

Catholic mass organizations gradually began to change and evolved into hybrid organizations that combined elements of religious associations and interest groups.[14] Although they were far from being political parties, they played an important role in the formation of a distinct Catholic political identity. For instance, the local Catholic committees in Belgium "contributed in bringing Catholics out of their lethargy," by creating fora for "informal meetings and public manifestations" (Soete 1990:81); the German Gesellverein contributed to the political socialization of its members (Neitzel 1987); the Italian Opera led to the "maturation of the Catholic laity" (Zerbi 1961:80) and became "an element of great importance for making Catholics conscious of their responsibility in the civil life of the country" (Gherardi 1967:47); and the Bavarian Catholic Vereine, "aside from the representation of certain interests, grievances, or viewpoints . . . contributed in a major way to the politicization of the Bavarian Catholic populace" (Southern 1977:319). To use Katznelson's terminology, the organizational strategy of the church

[13] Likewise, the Italian Associazione della gioventú cattolica was created with the intention of being "a purely religious Catholic society categorically excluding any ambition of political character" (De Rosa 1972:50). Indeed, the Catholic youth remained for a long time "on a level of religious or strictly papal activity" (De Rosa 1972:54). When some of its members argued in favor of political action they were rebuffed by older members, who contended that the purpose of the organizations was fulfilled by teaching the "religious feeling" and the "devotion to the pope" to the youth (Vecchio 1987:93). An examination of statutes of Italian Catholic union locals found that only 4 out of 198 specifically excluded religious orientation (Chiri quoted in Agócs 1988:171).

[14] For instance, Zerbi (1961:77) terms the Italian Opera a sui generis political party because it displayed political concerns (such as opposition to liberalism) but did not participate in the elections and remained mostly a religious movement dependent on the church.

led Catholics to the third level of identity formation, at which Catholics began to share a common social identity.[15]

Because it permitted the creation of mass organizations, democracy (short of participation in elections) was viewed only as a means for the struggle. "We shall continue our fight by constitutional means, in order to drive you from power, to demolish these criminal laws, and thus to make the Republic livable," asserted the French intransigent Catholic journalist Eugène Veuillot (quoted in Barbier v.2 1923:272), echoing a similar point made in the program of the Catholic Congress of Florence in 1875: "As Catholics and as citizens we will use all the legal means that have been permitted to gradually, firmly and constantly oppose and defend ourselves from such a flood of evil"[16] (De Rosa 1972:84). Still, the adoption of weapons made available by Liberalism did not imply the acceptance of democracy. As the lay Catholic activist Giuseppe Saccheti (quoted in De Rosa 1972:85) put it, *"la legalità non era che un modo di guerra, nuovo forse nel nome, ma non più che nel nome"* (legality is just a mode of war; the name may be new, but nothing more besides the name).[17]

Throughout this strategy, the church made clear that a Catholic party was not an option. Leo XIII, a supporter of the participation strategy, made a clear distinction between, on the one hand, individual political participation of Catholics in the political life of their country and, on the other, the formation of confessional parties. He pushed for the former and rejected the latter (Durand 1995:63). As De Rosa (1972:309) points out, from the lecture of the statutes of the Unione (an Italian Catholic organization) emerges "the will of the Holy See to have a disciplined and submissive laity divided in determined branches of work, with no vain ambitions of any sort to form a party. Any idea concerning the possibility of organizing a true and proper Catholic party was completely strange to the report." Likewise, Jean Beau-

[15] This common identity did not yet imply collective action. According to Katznelson (1986:19–20), "Groups of people sharing motivational constructs ('disposition to behave') may or may not act collectively to transform disposition to behavior. Even where workers have close contact at work and in their residential communities; even if this interaction promotes strong collective identities; and even if the workers share common systems of meaning that incline them to act in class ways, they may not necessarily act together to produce collective action."

[16] The congress was prompt to delineate the limits of such action: "Among the means that we could use there is none that has been declared by the supreme leader of the church to be forbidden or inadequate" (De Rosa 1972:84).

[17] De Rosa (1972:85) notes that "the Opera adopted the freedom of the revolution only as a means of better fighting the revolution." The Belgian journalist A. Delmer (quoted in Preneel 1982:120) similarly argued in 1863 that "universal suffrage in the hands of people, whose great majority is Catholic, will help us defend religion, family and property against the liberalism of today and the socialism of tomorrow."

fays (1973:57) notes about Belgium that "the church found inopportune the undertaking by a political party of the responsibility of dealing with the ecclesiastical interests with the state." Moreover, the church aimed at excluding those who, in the words of the papal secretary of state in 1906 (quoted in De Rosa 1972:311), "would want to use the Catholic cause for their own objectives and with party aims." (See Chapter 4 for further evidence.)

Once formed, Catholic organizations became increasingly militant. As the Liberals stepped up their attacks, priests and lay activists increasingly agitated for political participation. They did so because they sensed that by participating in politics they could better defend the church and themselves as Catholics; and they sensed so because they were finding out that the organizational strategy had reached its limits. Indeed, although the church would at times call its members to vote for friendly candidates, this was done in a decentralized, vague, unorganized, and eventually ineffective way. Candidates would obtain church support by putting forward their individual religiosity, without committing themselves to specific action. There was no political subcontracting, and the defense of the church was essentially left to the goodwill of individual politicians. The lack of a clear candidate choice and of a common organizational frame in the elections divided and confused the pro-church electorate: in Prussia, "the clergy was divided on whom to support; lay activists could not always count on clerical cooperation" (Sperber 1980:249). Pro-church candidates either failed to provide the services expected from them[18] or scattered within various parliamentary factions, making any effective action on behalf of the church all but impossible. For example, ten of the Catholic representatives elected in Rhineland in the 1867 elections joined the Free Conservatives, one the National Liberals, six the old Prussian Left, and six were unaffiliated (Windell 1954:61). Not surprisingly, this tactic produced electoral and legislative ineffectiveness: "Each Catholic deputy customarily voted according to his own convictions, or according to the convictions of the party with which he was at the time associated. Even on questions involving the status of the church they were divided, at least on the method of reaching the goal" (Windell 1954:80).

The organizational strategy had no effect on policy because it failed to provide a way of overthrowing Liberal governments. Reconquest of the society from below proved a very long shot, not to say utopian, prospect. Quite the contrary, the organizational strategy proved counterproductive because it provoked intensified attacks by Liberals, who interpreted the church-sponsored organization of the masses as a challenge to the very core of the regime. Indeed, the biggest anticlerical attacks were launched in Belgium, the

[18] The case of the Malou cabinet in Belgium (1870–1878) is the most typical of a Conservative government that failed to satisfy the demands of the church.

Netherlands, and Germany after the implementation of the organizational strategy, while in Italy and Austria anticlerical Socialist parties were on the rise. Thus anticlerical legislation continued to be passed, the influence of the church continued to decline, and "clerical conservatives were forced to recognize their impotence in the face of the overwhelming Liberal parliamentary majority"[19] (France 1975:142; Austria). Additionally, the new networks of Catholic schools were facing tremendous financial problems, making the need for state subsidies imperative (Boulange 1986:336). In sum, not only did a new Christian society fail to materialize but the church found itself in a more precarious position.

The failure of the organizational strategy is not an indicator of the church's irrationality in adopting this strategy. The formation of mass organizations was the best possible strategy under the circumstances at t_1 and was implemented as a self-contained strategy that intended to shield the church and its flock from further Liberal attacks. The church was not alone in believing that liberal democracy would not sustain itself in the long term: early socialists had similar expectations and projects (Przeworski and Sprague 1986). As a result, when forming mass organizations (at t_1), the church had a limited time horizon, expecting the process to end at t_2, and did not anticipate future direct participation in elections or other electoral implications.

The failure of the organizational strategy provided the mechanism of transition to the participation strategy. This failure was expressed in the escalation of anticlerical attacks and the realization that the available Conservative parties were not able, through the use of their own resources and the unsystematic support they were receiving from the church, to bring about significant policy change. The new wave of anticlericalism further curtailed the influence of the church, while the pressure that the low clergy and lay Catholics were applying on the church for political participation through the mass organizations increased and certainly helped (but did not provoke) the strategy shift. The church realized that the problem called for a different reaction and decided to implement a new strategy to reverse anticlerical legislation and thwart future attacks—one it wished it could have avoided. As E. E. Schattschneider (1960:40) has pointed out, the losers of previous conflicts attempt to turn their grievances into partisan politics: "It is the weak who want to socialize conflict, i.e., to involve more and more people in the conflict until the balance of forces is changed." The new strategy was based on a direct alliance with Conservatives. Coalitions in politics are often like consor-

[19] Even in the few cases where Conservatives remained in power in the presence of a strong anticlerical opposition, they were tempted to strike deals that ignored church interests. In Austria, where the Liberals were overthrown in 1879, they were not replaced by forces that would decisively shift policies in favor of the church; the educational reform laws were not reversed, and an amendment that was eventually passed was extremely mild (Papanek 1962:29).

tia in business: they are formed by those who have lost (*Economist,* 2 April 1994).

Second Step: Participation Strategy

The participation strategy implied the discovery of the overriding significance of legislative action and hence the discovery of electoral politics: "It is not blood that must daunt the church, it is the legislators," argued a French bishop (quoted in de Montclos 1965:527). Democracy had to be used all the way down to elections—short of the creation of a confessional party. In this sense, the participation strategy represented a recognition by the church of the utopian character of the Christian society project. This strategy was also a new trade-off for the church. Faced with further erosion of its influence, it decided to assume the costs of political participation.

The fundamental difference between the organizational and the participation strategies was their scope. The participation strategy consisted of fighting against anticlericalism with allies and within the political sphere. It was a break with the previous practice of unsystematic support for independent individual Catholics or divided Conservative factions. Now the church sought the specification of a platform (the equivalent of a contract) as the basis for the formation of a political alliance with antiliberal political forces. The relationship between the church and its allies would take the form of a mutual subcontracting, whereby the political allies would conduct the political fight for the defense of the church in the name of Catholicism (although not as the official representatives of the church), and in exchange the church would support them electorally by mobilizing its members and using its full organizational resources. In other words, the two actors would contract out the activities that were unacceptably costly for them: the church would contract out to Conservatives political and legislative action, while the Conservatives would contract out to the church mass organization. The term "contract" was occasionally used explicitly and publicly. For example, a local electoral agreement between Conservatives and Catholics in Italy in 1895 produced a common list of candidates called *lista contrattuale,* and delegates from both sides signed a *dichiarazione di contratto* (Suardo 1962:103–4). Likewise, in 1928 a Catholic journalist openly praised the Federation nationale catholique (FNC) for imposing a *contrat* to candidates as "the price of its electoral support" (Viance 1930:146). To describe the relationship between the church and its allies in Belgium, Mélot (1935:45) uses the following metaphor: "[Their relationship] is somewhat similar to that of a lawyer vis-à-vis his client. The client of the Catholic party is the church. [The church] sets out its views and its lawyer tells it until what point he thinks he can support them, with what means, using what tactic and the two sides agree more or less easily."[20]

The electoral alliance between church and Conservatives took a variety of forms, ranging from the explicit seven-point Gentiloni pact struck between representatives of Catholic organizations (controlled by the church) and Conservative deputies in the 1913 elections in Italy, to more complex coalitions. These could be looser, as in 1887 in Austria (United Christians), or tighter as in 1879 in Belgium (Fédération). Two basic forms can be discerned: first, a pact between the church and antiliberal forces (Netherlands, Italy). Such pacts explicitly excluded organizational implications. Abraham Kuyper, the leader of the Dutch Calvinist party, clearly defined the terms of his alliance with the Catholics in a series of articles published in the newspaper *Standaard* in 1879 (quoted in Vanden Berg 1960:167): "No fusion or amalgamation with Rome; . . . . each party must retain its own organization, unfurl its own banner, be perfectly independent as to the other, but the two parties must cooperate or not in each specific case that arises, each party to decide in every particular instance which party it would support." Second is a coalition between Catholic organizations and antiliberal forces (Belgium, Austria, Germany). These coalitions took a tripartite form. As Jean Stengers (1981:68) notes, the struggle "was fought under the joint direction of the episcopate . . . , the political leaders, and the Catholic notables [i.e., the leaders of Catholic mass organizations]." Table 2 maps the various forms of the participation strategy.

The church preferred pacts because they were more discreet (they could even be secret) and minimized the probability of loss of control over Catholic organizations. But pacts were difficult to achieve because they presupposed the availability of a strong Conservative party (such as the Giolittian Liberals in Italy or the Calvinists in the Netherlands). This was rarely the case. Contrary to pacts, coalitions implied some sort of organizational collaboration during and after the elections, although not in the context of a unified confessional party.[21]

[20] Who the client is, however, depends on the observer's perspective. Mélot, using the angle of legislative action, sees the church as the client of the party. Viewed from a different angle, that of electoral competition, the party is the client of the church.

[21] The choice between pact and coalition was often discussed openly. In France, such a discussion took place in 1909, and the two options were pitted against each other. The pact option, called the Toulouse pact, was advocated by Mgr. Germain of Toulouse and supported by the newspaper *L'Univers.* It advocated providing Catholic votes to candidates who signed a declaration in favor of issues important to the church. The coalition option, labeled the Nancy project, was advocated by Mgr. Turinaz of Nancy and supported by the newspaper *La Croix.* It advocated the formation of a vast opposition party, though not a confessional one, with Catholics forming its central core (McManners 1972:171). Neither of these options was put into practice.

Table 2. The forms of the participation strategy

Country	Type of strategy	Name	Date
Belgium	Coalition	Fédération-Association coalition	1879
Netherlands	Pact	Catholic-Calvinist (ARP) alliance	1888
Austria	Coalition	United Christians coalition	1887
Germany	Coalition	Soest program	1870
Italy	Pact	Gentiloni pact	1913
France I	Pact	Droite Constitutionnelle	1890
France II	Mixed	Fédération Electorale	1894
France III	Coalition	Alliance Libérale Populaire	1901

Type of Strategy
Coalition: alliance of antiliberal forces based on the creation of a common organizational structure.
Pact: alliance of antiliberal forces based on an explicit pact with no organizational implications.

Although the form of alliance varied, the bargain struck did not. The church would actively help elect its political allies, who, in turn, would repeal the anticlerical legislation and support the church. Contrary to the previous practice of pro-Catholic representatives dispersing in various parliamentary factions, the expectation was that there would be concerted and systematic action after the elections as well.[22] The church took an active part in the electoral process by "using the maximum of its spiritual weapons" (Stengers 1981:62) and by intervening openly, massively, and directly in favor of its political allies. In the past church interventions in elections were not uncommon, but this intervention was far greater in intensity and size. For example, the political activity of the Belgian bishops reached its peak in the years 1879–1884 (Van Isacker, cited by Whyte 1981:60), precisely the years of the participation strategy (see Table 1). Yet for all its importance, the activity of the church was only one element of this strategy. A more crucial one was the political mobilization of the masses achieved through the introduction of a major change in the role of Catholic organizations. By giving its mass organizations a clear political objective—the mobilization for the election of a pro-Catholic Conservative coalition—the church transformed them into

[22] The church wanted to avoid the postelectoral defection of Conservatives which previously often happened. For example, under the 1904 Bonomi-Tittoni agreements in Bergamo (Italy), Catholic organizations mobilized and succeeded in electing moderate Liberal candidates in both the 1904 and 1909 elections. The Vatican gave its silent approval to this transaction because of the fear generated by the general strike of 1904. Catholic support was unconditional, and the result was that the deputies elected with Catholic votes ignored the demands of Catholic organizations. Subsequently the frustrated leaders of the Catholic organizations asked to present their own candidates in the elections (De Rosa 1972:347–48).

political organizations. This was a decisive innovation that was to prove particularly successful in elections.

The participation strategy introduced Catholic organizations into electoral politics and gradually transformed them into the foundation of the yet unformed confessional parties. Thus the implementation of this strategy crucially affected the nature and the future of these organizations. Furthermore, it had important identity consequences for Catholics. By inducing political participation, and thus collective action, this strategy led Catholics to the fourth level of identity formation, turning them into a group "organized and act[ing] through movements and organizations to affect society and the position of the [group] within it" (Katznelson 1986:20). The participation strategy reinforced and gave a political dimension to the Catholic identity that first emerged through the organizational strategy. As Pizzorno (1970:45) points out about class, "Class consciousness promotes political participation, and in its turn, political participation increases class consciousness."

The implementation of the participation strategy reduced the church's control over Catholic organizations. Although the church decided to undergo the costs of the participation strategy to protect its influence from further erosion, it tried to mitigate them by reinforcing its control over Catholic organizations and by planning to remove them from politics after the elections. The alliance with Conservatives was intended to be temporary. As with every contract, partners were not permanently bound. This was a marriage of convenience and a short-term one. The church dreaded the prospect of its political allies undermining its control over lay Catholics and using religion to promote their own interests at its expense. As in France, there was a permanent fear that these allies "would push the Church down to ruin simply to raise up hatred against the Republic" (McManners 1972:58). The church still opposed the formation of permanent and autonomous Catholic political organizations or confessional political parties (Mayeur 1980:56). Consequently, it blocked every attempt create a Catholic party during the period of implementation of this strategy (see Chapter 4 for evidence). The purpose and expected outcome of its strategy was only to reverse anticlerical reforms and replace them with a new domestic concordat. The logical end of the church's participation strategy was, according to Anderson (1981:194),

> a subtraction of the Catholic factor from [their countries'] political life. Catholics would of course have continued to vote and to serve in parliament; but the [party] itself under such a domestic "concordat" must inevitably have withered away. . . . The subtraction of confessional issues from party debate—either by the continued protection of Catholic interests by the Conservatives and government, or by the competition between conservative and liberal parties for the Catholic vote—would soon have caused a re-

grouping of the Catholic constituency (admittedly smaller because less mobilized) among other parties.

Thus the ultimate objective of the participation strategy was a return to the past rather than the institutionalization of political Catholicism. The church planned to depoliticize Catholic organizations and transform them to voluntary semireligious associations.[23] The church expected that the electoral coalitions it put together would then cease to be exclusively identified with it. As Gramsci pointed out in his analysis of the Catholic movement, the church expected Catholic trade unions and parties "normally to perform a *conjunctural* or occasional role, dispensable should the necessity arise" (Fulton 1987:212).

The Conservative politicians who participated in the enterprise had the same intention. They viewed their identification with the church and the promotion of religion as the central political issue as a temporary strategy. As Ludwig Windthorst (quoted in Anderson 1981:217) declared in 1872, "If the burning complaints of Catholics are finally settled . . . the Zentrum will be glad to dissolve." The temporary aspect of these alliances was often stressed openly. A local electoral agreement between Conservatives and Catholics in Italy in 1895 stated that the common list of candidates was to be *occasionale,* that is, temporary and with no future implications (Suardo 1962:103–4). In the Netherlands, a similar pact was viewed as a "temporary truce" (Verschave 1910:242). The temporary character of these alliances was underscored by the numerous problems and antagonisms that occurred because their composing parts had very different, often antithetical, priorities. In Belgium, the attempt by Catholic organizations to impose a precise, strict, and binding Catholic program upon the Right, which became known as *programmisme,* provoked forceful reactions from the latter. Conservatives insistently argued against imperative mandate (Soete 1986:53; Preneel 1982:124).

But the expectations of both the church and Conservatives were thwarted because participation in politics, even if incomplete, can create an unanticipated dynamic. For all the reinforcement of the church's control, the sheer logistic needs of electoral mobilization allowed a small degree of independent lay Catholic participation. In Italy, local Catholic electoral committees some-

[23] The case of the Austrian Katholikenverein, which was transformed into a philanthropic organization as soon as the danger of the 1848 revolution disappeared and absolutism was reestablished, is a textbook example of the eagerness and ability of the church to destroy Catholic political organizations by turning them into religious ones when it did not need them anymore. Similarly the German Piusverein was turned into a charitable organization after 1848. The papal encyclical *Urbi Arcano Dei,* issued in 1922, confirmed this perspective by recognizing only apostolical duties for laymen within the structure of nonpolitical organizations, tightly controlled by the church.

times took part on in the deal-making process of the Gentiloni pact and drafted local political programs following a national blueprint set up by the church (De Rosa 1972:339). Guido Formigoni (1988:28) argues that the drafting of political programs was a "decisive moment" of "desacralization" of politics and "insertion" of Catholics in modern democratic politics. Some Catholic activists ran as candidates for parliamentary seats, although on an individual basis. In some cases (particularly in Austria), the degree of independent activity and autonomous initiative that Catholic activists were able to grab from the church was more significant. In short, as Sturzo pointed out a few months before the formation of the Italian Partito popolare, "there existed already [within the Catholic organizations] almost a 'substructure of the party,' brought about by a series of events. . . . These events have allowed us to distinguish, to cast out, the political functions from the specifically religious activity." The only thing still missing, he added, was "the political consciousness of a national party operating from the one end of Italy to the other, [but] not through the organizations of Azione cattolica"(quoted in De Rosa 1969:8). Thus the participation strategy, to use De Rosa's terms (1972:338), "foreshadowed, was a premonition of the necessity for the Catholic people to have a party."

Still, the participation strategy was not equivalent to the formation of confessional parties. On the contrary, it was specifically designed to exclude such a prospect. Permanent politicization and autonomy of action for lay Catholic organizations were still rejected by the church. For all the small windows of opportunity that opened, the church reserved to the members of Catholic organizations a purely passive role. Lay Catholics did not enter the political process as active participants. They were expected only to mobilize and deliver the votes, to be what Sturzo (quoted in De Rosa 1972:282) dubbed "a convenient electoral mass." The church aimed at keeping the Catholic movement under tight control and expected to take all decisions alone. The Italian lay Catholic Giovanni Maria Longinotti (quoted in De Rosa 1972:343) encapsulated this logic in 1912, remarking during the preparation of the Gentiloni pact that "the truth is, there is by now not one person not knowing that His Sanctity is also the effective president of the electoral action." The participation strategy was a step of critical significance for the formation of confessional parties, but it did not produce them. The church was still in control of the process and had both the intention and the capacity to prevent a derailment of the participation strategy into a confessional party.

How, then, did the "long walk of Catholics toward a role of plain responsibility in public life" (Belardinelli 1979:162) reach its target? How did the Catholic movement manage to "get out of the sacristy?" (De Rosa, in Malgeri 1969:xii). How was the participation strategy transformed into actual party formation?

From Catholic Organizations to Catholic Party: The Unraveling of the Church's Strategy

The participation strategy unraveled and led to the creation of confessional parties after the pro-church coalitions obtained unexpected and spectacular electoral successes. This electoral success provided the mechanism of transition and was engineered by two new political actors who emerged as a by-product of the strategy of the church. They originated from the church but were distinct from its leadership: they were the members of mass Catholic organizations, priests and lay Catholic activists.[24] They took organizational initiatives that were independent from the hierarchy and not a part of its strategy. They created confessional parties despite the church's plans and intentions. Although these actors became relevant through the organizational strategy and were empowered by the participation strategy, their independent and autonomous initiatives were successful only because of the electoral success of pro-church coalitions.

The lower clergy played a crucial role in the creation of mass organizations and the formation of confessional parties. Priests were vital in the formation of mass Catholic organizations and, later, in the conversion of church associations into party organizations.

As a general rule, the lower clergy were far more militant and politically active than the bishops. Priests took initiatives that were often autonomous and independent from the church leadership; in some cases they were even contrary to the orders of their hierarchical superiors. The Belgian episcopate often blamed its subordinates for their "intemperance" (Simon 1958:55). Catholic trade unions in the Netherlands were formed in clear opposition to the church leadership by priests, who called for the creation of sincerely Catholic rather than church organizations (Bakvis 1981:41). Priests such as the Dutch Catholic L. T. J. Poell proved to be "the most resolute adversaries

[24] In a few cases, certain bishops took the independent initiative of creating mass organizations as did, for example, Archbishop Andrea Carolo Ferrari of Milan, who helped formed a youth Catholic organization in Milan (Vecchio 1987:87), or Cardinal Rudigier of Linz in Austria, who led "a wave of episcopal anarchism" (Boyer 1981:31; Bled 1988:213). Some other bishops, such as Radini Tedeschi of Bergamo, Luigi Pellizzo of Padova, and the bishop of Regensburg in Bavaria showed a more tolerant stance toward independent-minded lay activists (De Rosa 1972:314; Southern 1977:231). This tolerance was either linked to regionalist movements, was the effect of internal infighting, or was simply a result of personal sympathy toward individual Catholic activists; it was never intended to promote lay autonomy and political participation (Vecchio 1987:101). The action of these local bishops was generally marginal and facilitated the independent action of Catholics rather than generating it. Furthermore, the church made serious efforts to crack down on independent activity by bishops. As early as 1840, Pope Pius IX told the Belgian ambassador that he was "firmly determined to discipline any Belgian bishop who would let himself to be dragged along in the field of political battles" (Mélot 1935:8).

of clericalism" (Brachin and Rogier 1974:145). The lower clergy were instrumental in the formation of the Christian Social party in Austria despite the church's desire to the contrary (Boyer 1981:123). In Bavaria, the parish priests participated in popular mobilization on behalf of the Patriotenpartei "despite pressure from the bishops" (Windell 1954:180) and created Catholic associations often against the explicit will of their bishops (Southern 1977:230–31). The German lower clergy intervened in electoral campaigns, following their own initiative and ignoring or purposefully misinterpreting the pastoral letter of their archbishop (Sperber 1980:247; Windell 1954:126). Similar activity took place in Italy, where church control over priests was particularly strict. Numerous young priests participated in failed attempts to create a Catholic party (De Rosa 1972:290), and "the most vociferous rebels were priests" (Jemolo 1960:119). Although the Partito popolare went into its first elections "without the direct support of the Vatican," it did enjoy "private clerical support" (Molony 1977:66). The political activity of priests took such proportions that the Prussian ambassador in Munich pointed out that the lower and middle clergy were the most dangerous enemy (Windell 1954:126), an opinion reflected by the prefect of the department of Aisne in France (quoted in McManners 1972:26) in 1879: "Under the influence of ultramontane newspapers the greater part of the lower clergy has become fanatical and intractable. As you go higher in the hierarchy, you find more sense of proportion and reasonableness . . . the bishop is incontestably the most conciliatory of the priests of the diocese."

Why did the lower clergy take such initiatives even though the church's doctrine placed them under the strict obligation to obey their hierarchical superiors? The causes of this singular activity are to be found in a combination of political, professional, and institutional factors.

First, the Liberal attack against the church was perceived by both clergy and lay as an event of tremendous significance. To the extent that there was a genuine popular concern, priests, being closer to the people than bishops, were better able to translate it into action (Simon 1958:54). Moreover, their persecution by Liberal governments contributed to the political radicalization of many previously apolitical priests (Lamberti 1986:80).

Second, priests had a big stake in maintaining the structure of education as it was. They stood to lose a lot, both materially and in status, if religion was dropped as a discipline from the schools' curriculum, if they were replaced by lay teachers, and if the schools where they were teaching were closed down. As Boyer (1981:151) points out, "On no other issue did the fortunes of religion as a system of belief and the subjective occupational interests of the clergy coincide so much as they did on the school issue."

Third, the militant activity of the priests was reinforced by two cleavages within the church: a generational cleavage because many of the activist priests were young (Yonke 1990:241; Aubert 1982:193; Southern 1977:206; Mayeur 1968:396) and a social cleavage because the episcopate was usually of higher social status than the lower clergy (Southern 1977:311–12). The second cleavage was captured by the term *proletariato di chiesa* (church proletariat) used by the Italian Left to refer to priests but eagerly adopted by the latter[25] (Erba 1990). These cleavages reinforced rather than created the autonomous militant activity of the lower clergy.

Fourth, the trend toward independence was often facilitated by exogenous factors. In Italy, for example, the poverty experienced by the lower clergy during World War I led them to depend on the support of their congregations, thereby loosening their ties to the church leadership and increasing their political independence (Howard 1957:133). Obviously, such factors would have produced no effect without the Catholic organizations, which provided the outlet for the political expression of this independence. The lower clergy found the new structures being created to be a medium to voice their professional concerns and Catholic identity and as a way to acquire some leverage in their relationship with the hierarchy.

Fifth, and most important, the participation strategy increasingly allowed priests to disregard directives from above. The transformation of Catholic associations into political organizations required the political action of priests, giving them more room for action. Often, the bishops encouraged lower clergy to participate in politics but, as in 1876 in Austria, "on an individual and purely non-partisan format" (Boyer 1981:164). Likewise, the leaders of the Conservative parties encouraged the political action of the clergy, whom they viewed as perfect political agitators. The Bavarian Patriot leader Jörg (quoted in Windell 1954:185), himself a priest, put it crudely: "The Bavarian clergy in the present generation can, whatever it wishes, support and advance, either directly or indirectly, no other policies than the instinctive one of the real people or the well-thought-out one of their uncompromising enemy."

The decision of priests to agitate politically and ignore the directives of the church was never an easy one—certainly not initially. Mayeur (1968:609) aptly refers to the "tragedy of priests engaged in politics." In a typical instance, a Bavarian journal published in 1869 contained a letter from a priest who admitted that he had undergone a terrible inner conflict about partici-

[25] Priests even engaged in quasi-union activity to better their lot. Examples include the congresses organized by French, Austrian, and Czech priests at the end of the nineteenth century and the Italian FACI (Federazione tra le Associazioni del Clero Italiano), created in 1917. According to Carillo (1992:137), "The efforts of the clergy to improve their status through organization aroused the suspicions of the Roman Curia, who feared that the concept of a union was being introduced into the ecclesiastical order. In the end FACI became an appendage of the episcopacy."

pating in politics. He argued against participation because the church was not of this world and the form of the state was of no matter to him as a clergyman (Windell 1954:184). Priests realized that their activity could create antagonisms between their two functions and force them to make painful choices. Klemens Von Klemperer (1972:15) reports that the more the Austrian Christian Social leader Ignaz Seipel "threw himself into politics . . . the more the priest and the politician clashed." Sturzo's decision to enter politics was dramatic. Following the meeting at which the decision to form the PPI was taken, he went to pray in a church, realizing that now "he would give himself entirely to politics" and accepting the leadership of the PPI "with bitterness in the heart, but as a sacrifice" (Mayeur 1968:609). Once the decision to participate was taken, the decision to place politics over religion was never far behind. For instance, Jules Auguste Lemire, one of the few French priests to be elected to parliament, opted to exercise plainly what was a political, not a religious, mandate; such decisions were often dubbed a "liberal heresy" that consisted of the "separation of the political from the religious mandate" by priests who were parliamentarians (Mayeur 1968:396). Often priests justified their action in interesting doctrinal ways. Ignaz Seipel (quoted in von Klemperer 1972:14) wrote in his diary that "ideally, at least, politics was an indirect pastoral function."

If so many priests crossed this threshold, it was because there were powerful arguments and incentives in favor of participation. Modern mass politics demanded a new kind of action, as priests had realized early. In 1867, members of the Bavarian lower clergy, in a letter sent to the bishop of Augsburg, requested the convocation of a public assembly of all the members of the clergy to decide on "the legal means of defense and on their immediate use." They argued (quoted in Goyau v.4 1909:187) that

> in principle the defense of the interests of religion and the clergy is undoubtedly the exclusive business of the episcopate; but in modern states, where the helm has been entrusted to political parties no consideration is paid to the *jus divinum* of the episcopate. . . . The clergy must adapt to this situation. As long as a party government is authorized to see the clergy as an inert political mass, it will have few qualms in treating it as such, despite, unfortunately, the complaints of the episcopate; but if life enters this mass, if it spreads among thousands of people who stand for their rights with one voice . . . then the party government will start counting. It will get a just idea of the degree of influence that suits the clergy.

Participation in elections constituted a *prise de conscience* for the priests. They discovered the power they wielded in politics, and this discovery had far-reaching consequences: in Bavaria, for example, "before the campaign [of

1869] ended, a large number of rural clerics did abandon their traditional conservatism and disregarded the strictures of the bishops" (Windell 1954:185). Although it strained their own relationship with the episcopate, the action of the priests strengthened their position within their flock and reinforced the position of Catholic organizations vis-à-vis the church.

After a certain point, the episcopate found it extremely difficult to control this trend. The most successful mass crackdown on priests was probably made in Italy. The promulgation of the *Codex* by Pius X included the introduction of a charter on the possibility of dismissal of parish priests by decree of their bishops (Jemolo 1960:112). The papal encyclical *Il fermo proposito,* issued in 1905, stated that "the priest, raised above all men in order to accomplish the mission he has from God, must also remain above all human interests, all conflicts, all classes of society" (quoted in Agócs 1988:100). Likewise, the Belgian church forbade religious associations from engaging in secular activity and segregated the associations led by priests from charities and organizations of social relief run by laymen (Billiet and Gerard 1985:90). These measures, however, were often not applied in a rigorous manner, and the rule seems to have been closer to toleration of these activities (Mayeur 1968). The church could repress the clerics who went too far but could not easily discipline at low cost the hundreds of priests who entered politics in the name of the defense of the church. The task of suppression was made more difficult because the political action of priests was useful to the church in countering the anticlerical attack. Furthermore, the political action of the lower clergy enjoyed a legitimacy provided by the *Syllabus,* which was interpreted as condoning a strategy of confrontation with the Liberals by any means. Describing the situation in Bavaria, Gilbert Southern (1977:315) summarizes the attitude of the church toward the growing independence of the lower clergy: "Apparently even most of the bishops who were unfriendly towards political agitation preferred to avoid direct action against clergymen who were politically active, as long as their activity did not cross over into extremism or cause a public scandal. These bishops undoubtedly took every opportunity to make known their displeasure over such activities, but the active priests would have been prepared to ignore this displeasure, while also taking care to avoid a stance which might bring actual disciplinary measures."

The most decisive new actor was forged out of the up to then silent mass of the faithful. Even though Catholic mass organizations were tightly controlled by the hierarchy, they increasingly depended on lay Catholics. Without their contribution, as Traniello (1982:34) points out, the Catholic movement would not exist.

Until the formation of Catholic organizations, lay Catholics were not involved in politics *qua* Catholics—*"Cattolici in quanto tali"* (Pace 1995:29). Most were not involved in politics at all. Following the "Christian tradition of respect for the constituted authority" (Suardo 1962:41), they "had traditionally viewed the state as confessional and therefore as a buttress of the church and themselves as passive subjects of the state" (France 1975:194). They were used to following the commands of the church without questioning, and this fostered an attitude of passivity and retreat described by the maxim "the kingdom of Christ is not of this world" (Anderson 1974:170). Their behavior was found to "indicate a habit of secular subordination from which [they] could not depart. [Lay Catholics] have always been expecting the impetus to come from the ecclesiastical authorities" (Cordewiener 1970:43). As a result, they were in a situation of "torpor" (Boulange 1986:335; Aubert 1952:134). In 1880, the Italian priest Sandri (quoted in Gambasin 1969:66) implored Catholics to "wake up from the lethargy and the inertia and to proceed to action." Likewise, the preparatory commission of the 1887 All-Austrian Catholic Congress (quoted in Schorske 1967:362) argued in a message to the pope that "there is no dearth of peoples loyal to the faith in our lands, but many of the most upright Catholics lack a clear understanding of the situation, knowledge of the methods of combat necessary under the new conditions, and above all the requisite organization. Always accustomed to being ruled in a Christian spirit by our Catholic monarch and the trustworthy men freely chosen by him, the great majority of Catholic laymen no longer know how to orient themselves."

These reports about torpor, inertia, and lack of orientation recognized the absence of a Catholic political identity. The organizational strategy of the church radically altered this situation because it endowed lay Catholics with a common political identity and an organizational infrastructure that generated an impetus for action. For Catholic lay activists everywhere, the fight against anticlerical reforms became equated with a quest for autonomy and a demand for political participation. This is not to say that the desire to participate in politics and form a political party came easily to them. On the contrary, it came gradually and painfully. They accepted the doctrine of the church which rejected liberal democracy.[26] As a result, most developed a gut dislike for democracy and even politics. In the Netherlands, for example, "many Christian leaders were mortally afraid of, and even abhorred the idea of, political parties" (Vanden Berg 1960:71). Paul Verschave (1910:66) points out that the Dutch Protestant leader Abraham Kuyper "never loved the parliamentary milieu. It appeared that he had difficulty adapting to this atmosphere." Likewise, Mayeur (1968:401) reports "the usual distrust that French

[26] Even today, "Catholicism's doctrinal exigencies with respect to politics" are "simultaneously imperious and indeterminate," points out Borne (1965:21): "A Catholic, if he knows his texts too well, does never know if to participate in politics is to collaborate with the devil or give himself to a virtuous work of devotion and charity."

Catholics felt for the political sphere, willingly imputed with every defect." Lay leaders went to great lengths to convince fellow Christians that political participation was the right course of action. For all his dislike of parliamentarism, Kuyper declared in 1869 (quoted in Vanden Berg 1960:53) that "politicophobia is not Calvinistic, is not Christian, is not ethical." In his 1906 piece, *Il programma politico della democrazia cristiana*, the Italian lay leader Filippo Meda had to develop intricate and complex doctrinal arguments as to why the representative system was not contrary to the teachings of the church and why universal suffrage was necessary (Formigoni 1988:34).

As it had been for priests, the anticlerical attack proved to be the best argument in favor of political participation. "Let's depend on ourselves and they will count on us," declared the Austrian Catholic Gustav Blome[27] (quoted in Bled 1988:119). Similar arguments were used by Conservative politicians such as the French Jacques Piou (quoted in Molette 1968:365), who appealed for political participation in a congress of French Catholic youth in 1903: "Should young faithful people like you only bend their head and decline to participate by saying: 'We do not do politics'? When the government exchanges its role of impartial arbiter for that of wild aggressor, when it turns itself into a syndicate of persecution, politics and religion become so closely mixed that we do not know where the one ends and the other starts. . . . When religious hatred becomes the soul of politics, the duty is to struggle everywhere and always, at any price."

And indeed, this message was successful. Although the Dutch Calvinist A. F. de Savornin Lohman "had no taste for politics and no inclination in that direction, he yet in 1879 [a year after the anticlerical attack], and for the first time, went to Parliament, but solely to obtain justice for the nonstate elementary schools. It was the beginning of a distinguished career of more than forty years in national politics" (Vanden Berg 1960:162). Similarly, Windthorst went to great lengths to convince the professor of philosophy Georg Hertling to enter politics in 1875, "on the ground that a Catholic must bear testimony to his Church in evil days of persecution" (Epstein 1971:42). Hertling initially hesitated but ended up becoming a prominent Zentrum political figure.

It was through the organizational strategy that lay Catholics discovered that their role could be different, both within the church and in society at large: they "grasped eagerly the fundamental concept whereby the laity as such were given a task to play in the world, complementary but not essentially subordinate to the church's salvific work in the spiritual order" (Mo-

[27] Even in England, lay Catholics argued that too many Catholics stood aloof, "watching the battle between the priests and the enemies of the Church, whereas the layman should have his part in the fray" (quoted in Doyle 1986:463).

lony 1977:22). In Gambasin's (1969:25) lyrical terms, lay Catholics saw their organizations as "a point of encounter between the universal principles of Christianity and the particular events, and they favored a process of osmosis between the transcendent and the imminent."

Political awakening was only a step away. When in 1878, a Belgian lay activist appealed for the explicit politicization of Catholic organizations, he formulated his claim in the following terms: "The question is not to create *cercles catholiques* in order to form societies of discussion [*agrément*]; the most important is to turn them into centers of action and struggle" (quoted in Guyot de Mishaegen 1946:145). This exultant feeling of possibility and power about the "great Catholic movement" was best expressed in 1877 by the Italian Catholic activist Sacchetti (quoted in Tramontin 1981a:338): "We are not anymore soldiers who fight in dribs and drabs like flying bands in guerrilla warfare, but legionnaires of a single army which moves forward in a compact and uniform way, full of discipline and ardor no longer ready just for poor skirmishes, but for the hard day instead."

As Catholic organizations grew, young outspoken activists emerged. As Aubert (1982:198) puts it, the layman subordinated to the clergy gave place to a layman increasingly conscious of his autonomy regarding his engagement in temporal matters. Sándor Agócs (1988:167) describes this process:

> During the papacy of Leo XIII, laymen began to play a new role in Italian Catholic Action. Perhaps the Vatican did not fully realize where this new development would lead. Whatever the reason, there came about a degree of independence on the part of Catholic activists. Old-style conservatives like Medolago were hesitant to make a move without checking with church authorities. Typically, he submitted for the pope's inspection not only major policy statements but apparently all the circulars he was to issue as the president of the Unione Economico Sociale. Just as typically, Guido Miglioli, representing the new lay activists, proceeded to do what he thought had to be done even after some high-ranking churchmen strongly criticized it. The young generation of activists were more courageous in the sense that they were willing to risk censure by acting on their own.

These activists quickly became impatient with the strategy followed by the hierarchy and increasingly outspoken against it.[28] They were dismayed by the bishops' aversion to an active Catholic intervention in politics. They started

[28] The questions of autonomy, confessionalism, and political participation preoccupied intensely Catholic activists rather than Catholic lay people in general (Vecchio 1987:64). But to the extent that Catholic activists increasingly came to control Catholic organizations, they influenced rank-and-file Catholics.

realizing that to let the bishops run the struggle against the Liberals would have a demobilizing effect because the church was always eager to seek diplomatic solutions that ignored the demands of activists. "Our bishops are mute," declared one of them in 1874 in Austria (Bled 1988:123). Even clerics "found the bishops' strategy of slow negotiations tiresome and sterile" (Boyer 1981:153). Some activists went so far as to accuse their bishops of betrayal and sabotage because of their attempts to reach a compromise with the Liberal government: "This willingness [of activists to act autonomously] was in part the consequence of the generally conservative attitude of the church hierarchy. The activists knew their bishops often sought to prevent them from performing tasks that, from the point of view of those who were attuned to reality, were long overdue. This explains why the activists pressed for independence from church authorities" (Agócs 1988:167).

More than anything else, Catholic activists resented the backroom deals that the hierarchy made with Conservative parties in the context of the participation strategy. They openly denounced them as a prostitution of their vote (Canavero 1981:289). Part of the reason for this assessment was that Catholic activists mistrusted Conservative politicians, whom they perceived as opportunists, not really committed to religion. They were suspicious as well of the Conservatives' tendency to exploit religious issues and use Catholic organizations for their own objectives (Viance 1930:66). Catholic activists particularly resented the use of Catholic organizations by the church without prior consultation and for purposes they disapproved. Italian lay activists openly complained in 1906: "Who gave you—we ask the bishops—such authority to deal with other parties in the name of Catholics, without asking them first? Why abuse your position and your ecclesiastical authority for personal and political objectives?" (quoted in De Rosa 1972:301).

Consequently, lay activists started pressing, timidly at first and more aggressively later, for political participation and autonomy of action. The advent of electoral competition, initiated through the participation strategy, reinforced this trend by creating what Dino Suardo (1962:126–27) calls a "feeling for action in the masses." According to Suardo (1962:127), "The drive to win, the pride in achieved victory, generated a growing patriotism of party that every new occasion served to mobilize and reinforce with always more profound effects on the solidarity of the groups of Catholics."

Demands for independence were raised everywhere. In Belgium, after first "humbly" asking the bishops for permission "to work in order to modify the actual composition of the parliamentary Right" (Simon 1958:152), lay Catholics decided to enter the political arena "with, sometimes, a frankness and independence that might have displeased the bishops" (Simon 1958:17). Participation soon developed into an open critique of the action of the bishops. In 1875 the Belgian bishops were forced to demand the pontiff's help. They complained in a collective letter about the activities of militant lay activists who agitated for an antiliberal revision of the country's constitution. They claimed (quoted in Lamberts 1984:64) that these lay activists "overstepped their competence" by publishing a religious journal "dealing with sensitive questions such as . . . the participation in the elections and the direct authority of the pope." They added that these "simple lay people, instead of behaving as devoted faithful, spoke like doctors and gave themselves the mission to teach the bishops." In a comparable fashion, Victor Jacobs, a prominent lay activist (quoted in Guyot de Mishaegen 1946:125), openly argued in the 1867 Catholic Congress of Malines "against the direction of [Catholic] newspapers . . . by the clergy"; he added that "the episcopate has nothing to win from interfering with political life."

In Austria, the cleavage between supporters and opponents of political action ran almost perfectly between lay and clerical activists on the one hand and higher clergy on the other (Bled 1988:37). The Austrian Eduard Stillfried (quoted in Bled 1988:123) summarized the point of view of Catholic lay activists:

> Not only we, the laity, do not receive help from our bishop, but we even face obstacles in our action with Catholic associations, an action which cannot be separated from political action. While our opponents use politics to harm the church, we, as Catholics, [are told] not to get involved in politics, nor do anything to advance our cause. The reason [for this] is to be found in the conviction that religion must not be used for political purposes, an intention that the Cardinal thinks that he sees in the activities of lay Catholics. . . . By acting in this way, by exercising his influence in the opposite way, he provokes a disastrous effect upon those who wish to work for the Catholic interests within the legislative frame, or hope to achieve an improvement of the way things are through the electoral way.

In Germany the issues raised by Catholic organizations regarding the role of the laity "had not been answered" (Yonke 1990:186). Matthias Aulike, the director of the Prussian Division of Catholic Affairs and an active lay Catholic, complained about this situation in 1857 (quoted in Yonke 1990:186): "Most of our bishops maintain that they want everything handled exclusively by the clergy and push the well-intentioned laity in the background. Every true Catholic layman recognizes his place in the church and demands nothing beyond that which the clergy grants him. There is a middle way, however, that would spare the laity from feeling superfluous, except merely for donations, and perceive its interests as actual cooperation. The time and the circumstances in which we live today enjoin us to pursue this course."

In 1869, lay Catholics from the town of Koblenz drafted a petition demanding fuller participation in church life (Yonke 1990:209–10). In Bavaria, pamphlets published in 1872 attacked the bishop of Passau for his opposition to Catholic lay organizations (Southern 1977:141). Gradually the centrifugal forces represented by Catholic organizations began to overcome the centripetal force of the hierarchy (Yonke 1994; Nipperdey 1988).

In Italy, Catholic activists began pressing for autonomy early. Gambasin (1969:89–102) reports that Italian Catholic activists argued that parish priests should not interfere in the work of local Catholic committees, that the presidents of these committees should be laymen and command significant power, and that diocesan committees should not be under the jurisdiction of bishops on the grounds that dependence creates confusion rather than unity. They managed to obtain permission for the creation of regional committees (a level between the national leadership and diocesan committees) which were based on a geographical rather than an ecclesiastical division. Still, it was "regret and ill-concealed impatience with which so many Catholics viewed their inability to enter into the political struggle" (Jemolo 1960:109–10). "We cannot in all sincerity uphold official Catholic policy," declared the lay leader Tomaso Gallarati Scotti in 1906 (quoted in Jemolo 1960:119). The push toward political participation by most lay militants generated intense conflicts within the Opera dei Congressi: "We are divided," wrote a Catholic journalist in 1903 (quoted in De Rosa 1972:218), "over the fundamental concept of Catholic action; some want it essentially religious and social, while others social and political; therefore so, from one part [is expected] full obedience and deference to the bishops and the clergy, while from the other independence of local organizations and the biggest distance from the sacristy." The participation of Catholic organizations in the 1913 elections on behalf of Conservative candidates was critical in that it made clear to them that "if the Catholics constituted an organized political body, they could have profoundly and decisively affected national life" (Tramontin 1981c:393). Nobody, perhaps, argued for politicization more eloquently than Meda, the vice-president of the Opera's youth section, in 1890 (quoted in Vecchio 1987:82–83):

> All of us are perfectly convinced that the practices of piety and charity, the protests, the pilgrimages, especially when they take a character of public manifestation, are acts that should not be missing from the program of a Catholic association; but we believe that it would be harmful not to go a step forward and that it is necessary to constitute an efficient and practical Catholic action: we have to get out from the churches and get in the public places, we have to infiltrate every part of society, we have to learn from [our] adversaries the use of the new weapons which, I repeat, are basically two—voice and press—we overall have to become educated and educate public

life if we want to persist without dishonoring our character. We have, in a word, to do politics.[29]

Even in France, the few existing Catholic organizations agitated for political participation. When the Catholic youth (ACJF) decided to take an active part in the elections of 1897, its president (quoted in Molette 1968:235) declared: "From now on, Catholics are not electoral dust anymore, they are an organized force."

Still, the formation of a confessional party was out of question. Despite all the calls for autonomous political participation, the church was still in control: it could easily repress (as it did) most attempts for autonomy that went too far. Gramsci pointed out that Catholic organizations would demand autonomy from the church but remarked (quoted in Poggi 1967:165) that "this development can never become organic because of the Holy See's intervention." The participation strategy could not in itself enable lay Catholics to get their demands accepted. More was needed to overcome the plans of the church and Conservatives.

In 1922, three years after the Italian Catholic party was formed, its friendly review *La Politica Nazionale* argued that the party was born of a "beneficial crisis" in Catholic organizations (Vecchio 1988:101). What was this crisis and how exactly did it lead to party formation?

Third Step: The Surprising Electoral Success

The transition from the participation strategy to the formation of confessional parties was made possible by the surprising electoral success of the pro-church coalitions. The success of the participation strategy contained the seeds of its own demise. Because it exceeded all expectations of success, political participation produced binding outcomes that were unplanned and undesired by the church. Besides producing momentum (Bartels 1988), electoral success was proof to Catholic activists and political entrepreneurs alike that religion was a powerful political issue with a potential for tapping huge forces. Indeed, together with Socialist parties, although before them, Catholic movements were the winners of mass politics. Electoral success was also the proof to Catholic activists that they had the power to intervene decisively in politics and that they could at last become autonomous and independent

[29] Meda's point provoked "reactions and polemics" both from the archbishop of Milan and the president of the Opera, Paganuzzi. Because of the spirit of independence that developed within the youth section, the relations between the youth and the Opera leadership grew tense. The youth used their clerical radicalism to protect themselves. They remained intransigent and argued against a Conservative-Catholic coalition (Vecchio 1987:83–84).

from the church. In Italy, after the 1913 elections "it was understood for the first time that, had they constituted an organized force, Catholics could have influenced in a profound and decisive way the public life of the country" (De Rosa 1972:351). This success provided Catholic activists with the concrete opportunity to play a direct and major role in the politics of their societies after the participation strategy had opened a new and vast source of power and legitimation that could replace the church: voters. Electoral success was thus the turning point in the process of formation of confessional parties. It is impossible to stress the importance of electoral success more than a contemporary Belgian did: "Until 1884 [the party] was called the 'conservative party.' From then on it is called the 'Catholic party' " (Carton de Wiart in Guyot de Mishaegen 1946:iii; 1884 was the year of the Catholic victory). This was a far more consequential development than just a change of labels. The electoral success of the coalitions that fought in defense of the church is indeed remarkable (see Table 3). As the Belgian historian Henri Pirenne (1932:234) points out, "It had never been seen before: the people, harassed in their consciousness, provided the [Liberal] agitators with the naive and brutal response of their mass."

In two cases—Belgium 1884 and the Netherlands 1888—these coalitions won resoundingly: in Belgium, the 1884 elections were pronounced a "rout for the liberals" (Pirenne v.7 1932:241), "a day of absolute triumph for the right" (Collin 1961–63:252), and a Catholic "tidal wave" (Laury 1979:801). The leader of the Belgian Liberals, Walther Frère-Orban (quoted in Luykx 1969:179), remarked that "this is not a defeat, this is a disaster."

Even when they did not get the majority of votes, these coalitions made an impressive entry into party politics. In Germany, there were warning signs: the 1868 Zollverein elections produced "startling" results for pro-church forces in the main Catholic regions (France 1975:143), and the 1870 Prussian Landtag elections "produced a massive realignment of Catholic voters" (Anderson 1986:89). But it was the crucial 1871 Reichstag elections that really made a difference: "In one massive step political Catholicism emerged as the major dominant force in the [predominantly Catholic] two western provinces of Prussia" (Sperber 1980:274–75). As Luebbert (1991:90) remarks, the Zentrum obtained "a stunning success for such a new party and one that no doubt explains the frightened reaction of the liberals to it." In Austria, the newly formed Catholic-Conservative coalitions achieved "resounding electoral successes" in local elections during the 1880s (Gulick 1948:26), and the 1895 municipal elections led to the conquest of the city of Vienna by the Christian Socials. According to Boyer (1995:1), this victory "represent[ed] perhaps the most extraordinary shift in voter loyalties ever experienced in a major Central European city before the First World War." Finally, in Italy,

Table 3. Breakthrough elections for antiliberal coalitions

Country	Year	Results
Belgium	1884	Catholics: 86 seats Liberals: 52 seats
Netherlands	1888	Catholics and Calvinists: 54 seats Liberals: 44 seats
Austria	1887	[Local Viennese elections]
	1895	[Municipal elections, Vienna]
Germany	1871	Catholics: 61 seats Liberals: 125 seats
Italy	1913	Gentiloni pact (228 out of 310 Liberals elected with Catholic votes)
	1919	Catholics: 100 seats Various Liberal groups: 197 seats Socialists: 156 seats

the 1913 pact between moderates and Catholics led to the election of 228 conservative Liberals with Catholic votes. The few independent Catholic candidates were successful, but government ministers failed (De Rosa 1972:357). Ronald Cunsolo (1993:42–43) reports that in Rome the electoral returns constituted "astounding triumphs" for the Catholics and that "Liberal opinion was that universal manhood suffrage, the Gentiloni Pact, and Nationalist-Clerical Moderate solidarity, as in Rome, had left the Liberal party in ruins." The 1919 elections were such a big success for the first showing of the PPI that, right after the elections, Sturzo (quoted in Molony 1977:77) remarked that "he personally was appalled to see so many successful candidates at their first attempt at an election." As Gramsci (1990:335) remarked in 1920, "In Italy we have seen a powerful party of the rural class, the Popular Party, arising virtually from nothing in the space of two years." These successes reverberated abroad. The French Catholics saw the electoral performance of Catholics in Belgium, Austria, and Germany as "a striking political success" (Martin 1978:58) and were inspired by it.

In fact, what mattered was not just the absolute electoral score—the percentage of votes obtained or number of seats won. The percentages obtained by Catholic coalitions in Germany or Italy were certainly not high in absolute terms. The Zentrum obtained 18.7 percent of the votes cast in 1871, and the PPI got 20.5 percent in 1919. What mattered, instead, was the *perception* of a Catholic electoral success by *all* participants, Conservatives, Catholics, and Liberals. This perception obtained because the electoral performance of Catholic coalitions surpassed all expectations. Three reasons explain this perception. First, the relative ranking of Catholic parties was high. Both the

Zentrum and the PPI emerged as the second single largest parties in their countries. Second, the losses they imposed on Liberals were impressive.[30] Third, this was the first showing of organized openly Catholic forces defending the church. Despite their lack of experience and preparation (underscored by their failure to nominate candidates in some districts), Catholic coalitions did extremely well, and unknown outsiders managed to beat famous Liberal politicians. As a result, even when not always high in absolute terms, the electoral performance of Catholic coalitions was viewed as an indicator of their future potential. These coalitions were seen as the wave of the future, the only ones able to compete with Socialist parties (Salvemini, in Molony 1977:72). Anderson (1986:95–96) reports that even though the Zentrum was able, in 1871, to mount electoral campaigns in only six of Upper Silesia's twelve districts (obtaining just 27 percent of the votes), the perception of the future potential of the party "spread so quickly" that the Zentrum's lone success in one district "excited attention and anxiety far out of proportion to its numerical significance." Likewise, the outcome of the 1919 elections—the first in which Catholics participated under the flag of the Partito popolare—is clearly perceived to have been a "great," even a "formidable," success for the party (Lynch 1993:34; Agócs 1988:14; Fonzi 1950:141). After the results of the elections became known, the consensus was that "by any estimate the PPI had gained a resounding victory, both symbolic and factual"[31] (Molony 1977:67). The pro-PPI review *Conquista Popolare* argued in 1920 that the 1919 elections "have created perhaps more surprise for the election of 100 *popolari* than for that of 156 socialists" (Vecchio 1988:166). As a result, "the old liberal elements in Italian life were deeply displeased at this young, refractory party, the Socialists were angered at the appeal it made to the catholic working masses while in the Vatican there was concern and

[30] In Italy, Conservative, Liberal, and democratic groups got 36 percent of the suffrage in the 1919 elections, down from 61 percent in the previous ones. In the Netherlands, the number of Conservative seats in the lower house declined with tremendous speed, going from nineteen to one between 1869 and 1888, while in the same years the Calvinist party increased its number of seats from seven to twenty-seven. Similarly, in Germany, all twenty-five Catholic deputies from predominantly Catholic districts whose allegiance had been to anticlerical parties lost their seats in the 1871 elections. According to Anderson (1993:1458), "The share of seats belonging to those parties whose victory the government actively promoted began with a modest 57 percent in 1871, a figure that is even less impressive when one remembers that the polling took place the very day after peace was signed in a hugely successful war." The presence of the Zentrum was a central cause of these losses: according to Reinerman (1993:762), the Zentrum's performance in 1871 was "a clear defeat for Bismarck."

[31] Contrast this judgment with the assessment of the performance of the French ALP in 1906 (when it got about 40 percent of the votes): "the ALP suffered a serious reverse"; "the ALP sustained a major setback"; "the disaster of 1906" (Martin 1978:200, 203). Even the 49 percent share of votes obtained by the ALP in the 1902 elections was perceived by all participating actors as a defeat because the Right obtained far fewer seats than everyone expected.

some degree of awe at the success of the organized Catholic laity" (Molony 1977:67).

The electoral success of these coalitions resulted from what I call religious mobilization: the unprecedented political mobilization of voters in favor of the defense of the church. This mobilization changed the way elections were fought and can be accounted by four factors: the anticlerical attack, the action of the church, and the twin innovations introduced by the participation strategy: the participation of Conservative parliamentarians and, especially, the role of Catholic organizations.

Religious mobilization was triggered by the decision of the church to confront the Liberals. As Sperber (1980:392) points out, "The bitter struggle [between state and church] was certainly a tremendous mobilizing element. The persecutory actions of the ministry helped convince waverers and skeptics that religion really was in danger." Education became the focal point, first in the mobilization to defend the church and then in the electoral campaigns.[32] By translating a complex issue into a sharp dichotomy, it made religion a clear-cut issue for voters. More than other issues related to the church (such as church property), educational reforms were seen as forced dechristianization through the indoctrination of children in public schools; as a result, they generated powerful emotions that could be channeled into political mobilization once the church took the decision to fight. The struggle over education was labeled in ways that reflected the passion it generated: school war *(Guerre scolaire)* in Belgium or school conflict *(Schoolstrijd)* in the Netherlands. In Germany, "the question of the schools . . . involved local interests directly and thus served to introduce many Catholics more or less painlessly to the complexities of political action" (Windell 1954:21). As Southern (1977:49–50) reports, the Bavarian electoral campaigns of 1869 were notable for "the savagery of temper, propaganda, and oratory with which they were fought." The atmosphere in the meetings of the Belgian Fédération des cercles catholiques, reports G. Guyot de Mishaegen (1946:139), was dominated by "activity, fervor even." A clergyman who was in Belgium at the time, recounts in his memoirs that "the generosity and the ardor of the catholics surpassed everything imaginable" (Mgr. Ferrata, quoted in De Moreau 1929:520). Franz Eichart, an Austrian Catholic activist (quoted in Boyer 1981:119), described the atmosphere at the meetings of a Catholic association in Vienna in the late 1880s: "Almost every Catholic meeting which I attended at that time so energetically was a fiery furnace for the souls, from which a torrent of sparks and flames of holy enthusiasm was generated; a powerful

[32] There were certainly other issues that were activated by the pro-Catholic coalitions and helped them defeat the Liberals such as taxation, agricultural tariffs, military service, and regional autonomy, but the issue of education towered over all others.

forge, in which the armaments were hardened for a battle for the Cross now threatened from all sides."

In the context of the participation strategy, the church took an active part in the electoral process by intervening openly, massively, and directly in favor of its political allies, using all its available resources. As P. M. Jones (1985:233) argues "The very scale of democratic politics placed a premium on organization and the institution that best responded to this challenge most incisively and effectively was the catholic church." The militant lower clergy constituted one of the two major strategic advantages of the pro-Catholic coalitions over competing parties. Indeed, the mobilization of faithful Catholics during elections was achieved, especially in rural areas, by parish priests.[33] The influence of priests overcame class barriers. Priests convinced Bavarian peasants to vote against the wishes of their landlords, Rhineland workers to ignore the recommendations of their bosses, and Upper Silesian peasants to vote down the local Junkers (Windell 1954:127; Sperber 1980:295; Anderson 1986:95–103). In fact, priests were the initial group of agitators who solved the collective action problem for Catholics during the first crucial years. Their activity was often contrasted to the torpor and moderation of Conservative parliamentarians: "With the exception of the clergy do you know what the Catholic party is? It is the party of cowards!" exclaimed the Belgian Conservative leader Barthélemy Dumortier (quoted in Guyot de Mishaegen 1946:105).

Yet the church alone could have not have achieved such resounding successes. They cannot be explained by simple reference to clerical action, as the Liberals arrogantly wanted to believe. The church had mobilized in the past with less success, although it did so on a smaller scale and in a less systematic way. Clerical mobilization had definite limits. Ultimately, the action of priests was circumscribed by their subordination to the hierarchy. For all their autonomous political agitation, priests faced limits in their action, which generated intense internal frictions that compromised their effectiveness. According to Southern (1977:329):

> In this respect political Catholicism in Bavaria faced a dilemma which political Catholicism, and particularly activist priests, faced in any country with a party system. A spiritual allegiance to Catholicism entailed a basic acceptance of the institutions—and the power of the hierarchy—which supported and

[33] The Bavarian Liberal Friedrich Graf von Luxburg (quoted in Southern 1977:82) accounted for the Catholic electoral victories: "In all *secret direct* elections the Catholic priests are absolute masters over the votes of almost all rural communities with a Catholic population since, through the confessional, they have exact knowledge of every allegedly secret election outcome and thereby perpetrate an unlimited terrorism." Likewise, Kossmann (1978:243) reports that "year after year the electors from the Flemish villages were seen to be conducted in groups by their local priest to the polling stations in the main towns."

> spread the doctrine. However obedience to this hierarchy might be modified in practice, such modification could not take place without much soul-searching and the expenditure of much energy and effort in avoiding occasions for the open enforcement of obedience in curbing political activity. This kind of effort, in any case, however much it contributed to the reduction of overt conflict between bishop and activist priest, seems to have played a major role in reducing the effectiveness of the Patriotic Party in Bavaria.

The growth of urban centers where the influence of the church was declining, the rise of mass organizations of the Left, and the increasing competitiveness and cost of mass politics were all circumscribing the impact of the church's action. In addition, the church concentrated its action in the regions where it was the strongest, neglecting the rest of the country (Rivet 1979:315). As Jones (1985:294) points out, "by the end of the century piety alone could not win elections."

The participation of Conservative politicians proved to be a moderating factor that toned down the external image of a religious crusade. Conservative politicians had a sense of political realism and strongly disliked the fanatical religious activists. The element of moderation brought by Conservatives succeeded in attracting (or avoided repelling) crucial segments of voters. These voters, especially in cities, were opposed to the attacks against the church but scared by religious fanaticism. Belgian, German, and Italian coalitions ran with political programs that underscored the need to protect the church but downplayed confessionalism and avoided mentioning any theocratic project. In Germany, the Soest program was a moderate version of far more confessional drafts (Sperber 1980:270). In Belgium, the Catholic-Conservative coalition that fought and won the crucial 1884 elections in Brussels, a Liberal stronghold, was named the Federation of Independents (Falter 1986:43). A contemporary Catholic observer (Carton de Wiart 1948:13) noted that this was a title "chosen ingeniously by the tacticians of the Right, with the objective of obtaining the support of a floating bourgeois mass which probably would have been frightened at the time by a label of confessional character." This way Catholics managed to win crucial moderate votes in critical constituencies and the cities. In short, the participation strategy was effective because the alliance between church and Conservatives produced a diversified mode of electoral appeal adapted to the particular characteristics of different constituencies.

The most decisive innovation of the participation strategy was the new political role of Catholic organizations. Very simply, these organizations were transformed into electoral machines that proved to be a powerful political weapon. Parties require an organizational apparatus and infrastructure if they are to be effective (Luebbert 1991:162). As Mair (1984:180) remarks, organizational effectiveness hinges on the connection of a party with a "broader political and social *movement* of which the party is part." Empirical cross-national research indicates that organizational membership has been more important in accounting for political participation than social status, political information, political attention, and political efficacy (Houska 1985:34–35). In addition, an abundance of empirical evidence points to the crucial role of organizations and social networks in mobilizing citizens (Rosenstone and Hansen 1993) and to the importance of subcultural organizations in determining the voting behavior of individuals (Houska 1985).

There is also considerable historical evidence that underlines the importance of Catholic organizations in mobilizing voters and leading the pro-church coalitions to electoral victories. According to Simon (1958:110), the action of the politicized Catholic organizations in Belgium made a tremendous difference in elections. These organizations became, under the participation strategy, "true civil agencies of electoral propaganda" (Delfosse and Frognier 1988:76), leading to "a remarkable mobilization of the electorate which contributed to the Catholic victory" (Soete 1986:67). In the Netherlands, organization was crucial in leading to electoral victories (Verhoef 1974:207), as it was in Austria (Boyer 1981). In Bavaria, Catholic organizations "were instrumental in the Patriotic victories in the Landtag elections of 1869" (Southern 1977:128). The practical result of Catholic organization was that "Liberals could in no way match this massive effort" (Sperber 1980:241). When the Liberal mayor of the Rhenish town of Erkelenz (quoted in Yonke 1990:238) attended a local Catholic meeting in 1872, he was so impressed that he concluded: "More than ever, therefore, future elections are unfortunately assured for this party." In Italy, Catholic organizations introduced techniques associated with modern electioneering as early as 1913, when they campaigned for Conservative candidates: "Fund raising, distribution of position papers, posting of banners, extensive use of radio and public address systems, monster rallies, and free transportation to the polls. These imaginative efforts did not go unrewarded" (Cunsolo 1993:42).

The electoral performance of confessional coalitions strongly correlated with the density of the networks of Catholic organizations. In Italy, the PPI was most successful in 1919 in the regions where the Catholic movement was the strongest and where Catholic organizations had been able to recruit farmers and workers into unions (Malgeri 1981:354–55). According to Mario Einaudi and François Goguel (1952:14), "The [Popular] Party's greatest strength was in the North, and especially in industrial cities, and was the result of the long work of schools, study clubs, of workers' associations, of the activities, in brief, of some of the more 'politically conscious' sections of the electorate." The density of these networks did not necessarily overlap with the strength of the Catholic church. In southern Italy and Prussian Silesia the church was strong but Catholic organizations weak. As a result, the electoral performance of the Catholic coalitions was mediocre in these regions.[34] Organization was crucial even under conditions of growing but still restricted franchise because of the increased weight of each new vote. In Belgium, for example, the number of registered voters in the 1884 elections grew "remarkably," a development attributed to the action of Catholic organizations that mobilized eligible but previously inactive voters. Moreover, Catholic organizations prepared the ground for mass politics. Recent electoral research suggests that the pro-Catholic coalitions, through the action of Catholic organizations, managed to conquer the biggest part of the newly enfranchised electorate (Falter 1986:43; Soete 1986:67, 194). It was, then, the action of Catholic organizations rather than the church alone that produced the electoral successes of the pro-Catholic coalitions.[35] How were these organizations able to achieve such levels of mobilization?

First, Catholic organizations were the first and, for a crucial period, the only mass organizations in their respective countries. Trade unions and Socialist parties were still young and underdeveloped when not repressed by the state.

Second, these organizations were able to reach voters whom the church and its priests alone could reach only with difficulty, if at all. As Rivet (1979:337) points out about post-1906 France (when Catholic organizations had started to develop), "From now on, the instructions and the examples of the Church are not just spread from the top of the dominical pulpit, in the assemblies of pious women or in the residential visits of the priest, but

[34] The difficulty of the Catholic movement in penetrating the Mezzogiorno is explained by the position of the clergy within the southern class structure (Gramsci 1978:456) or the general feudal social structure of the region (D'Andrea 1980:250–57).

[35] Sperber (1980, 1982) argues that the 1870 Catholic victory in Prussia was attributable to the religious revival that took place in Rhineland and Westphalia after 1850 as a response to the socioeconomic crisis of the time. This revival stopped the disintegrating tendencies of Catholic religiosity. This new "clerically centered religiosity seal[ed] off Catholic masses from the Catholic notables and made the clergy the masters of political life at the local level" when universal suffrage was introduced. According to this argument, "among the Catholic electorate, the Center party already existed in 1867; it only remained for the clerical politicians to create it" (1980:318). Besides analytical problems (e.g., the translation of a potential into a real party is not specified), the argument suffers from an absence of comparative insight. A similar religious revival took place in France between 1850 and 1870 (Cholvy and Hilaire 1985; Dansette v.2 1961:9). During the 1870s, "spectacular pilgrimages" were organized in France similar to the pilgrimages of Trier or Kevelaer in Germany (Dansette v.1 1961:334). Yet no confessional party formed. Conversely, although the nineteenth century was for the Catholic church a "great age of religious revival" all over Europe (McLeod 1981:v); in the Netherlands, Austria, and Italy the explosion of piety and devotion seems to have been less pronounced than in Germany or France. For a historical critique of Sperber's argument see also Anderson (1991:683–86).

also in every occasion of gatherings or encounters that are offered or created through job, leisure and vicinity."

In fact, the influence of mass Catholic organizations exceeded the traditional influence of the church, even in rural areas. A study of the department of Isère in France (Barral 1962:265) shows that in some parishes Catholic mass organizations created in 1924 exceeded in membership Easter mass attendance. Moreover, Catholic organizations were particularly effective in penetrating regions where the church was weak because of the perverse effects of the hierarchy's fundamental dislike of organizations: the strongest regions of implantation of the Jeunesse agricole catholique (JAC), created in France in 1929, "were not necessarily those which were the most Catholic for, in such regions, the novelty of the JAC met with some hostility from the church hierarchy"[36] (Cleary 1989:89–90).

Catholic organizations made a big difference in urban areas. This was very important in cases of restricted franchise, where the electoral weight of cities tended to exceed that of the countryside. The most sophisticated Catholic organizational infrastructure was to be found in urban areas (Mendershausen 1973:49) and easily translated into electoral performance. Massia Gruman (1964:169) stresses the importance of the Catholic organizations, particularly youth associations, in securing the Catholic victory in Brussels, up to then a Liberal city. Sperber (1980:274) notes that in Germany "one new element in the [1870] election was the energetic action of the Catholic political clubs in the big cities." These clubs attracted people the church had a difficult time reaching. According to a report of the Bavarian Ministry of the Interior (cited in Southern 1977:208), Catholic organization meetings included "many who had been known before as Progressives." Workers often proved receptive to the call of new Catholic working-class organizations—even those who had previously voted for Socialist parties. Electoral data from the Düsseldorf area show an important swing of workers from Socialist parties to the Zentrum between 1867 and 1871 (Hunley 1974:144–45). This swing was attributable to a very large extent to Catholic organizations.[37] The Division of the Interior in Düsseldorf reported in 1874 the presence of 389 Catholic associations in the entire region and warned that "the network spreads over all and has ensnared the populace" (quoted in Yonke 1990:241).

[36] Likewise in postwar Italy, Catholic Action organizations were stronger in northern Italy, even though the south was far more religious, scoring higher than the north on a composite index of religiosity. See Putnam (1993:107–9).

[37] Although religious devotion reignited by the Kulturkampf might account for this shift, the role of Catholic working-class organizations cannot be underestimated. When the Catholic workers' organization of the Essen region disagreed with the Zentrum over the social content of its program, it ran its own candidate in the 1877 elections against the official candidate of the party. This candidate won the contest and subsequently joined the Zentrum, which supported him in the following elections (Hunley 1974:146). This example indicates the loyalty these organizations inspired in their members.

Third, Catholic organizations were disciplined, an extremely important element for successful electoral mobilization. A decree of the Amberg city government in Bavaria described the local Catholic association as "monolithic" (Southern 1977:223). The Division of the Interior in Düsseldorf reported that the Catholic network's "strands respond to the lightest pressure from above" (quoted in Yonke 1990:241).

Fourth, Catholic organizations educated seasoned and experienced activists. The Catholic electoral victories were won by activists who, according to Boyer (1995:1), "had little or no formal experience in regional politics *or* in public administration" and whom Guyot de Mishaegen (1946:180) dubs "outsiders." But these activists enjoyed high local visibility and had acquired substantial experience through their organizational activity. As Suardo (1963:178) remarks about Italy, "In 1919 the men whom the PPI presented to the nation were, in their very great majority, exposed for the first time to parliamentary life, but they were not new to politics." Besides their skills in mass mobilization, these men brought with them the added advantage that they were far more attractive to voters as candidates than the traditional notables who ran the Conservative parties.

Finally, contrary to the traditional electoral committees of notables, which were active only during electoral campaigns, Catholic organizations kept up a high and constant level of political activity between electoral campaigns.[38] (Southern 1977:38–39; Beaufays 1973:60). The result of all this was that many people became socialized and began to participate actively in politics, for the first time, *as* Catholics.

Not only was electoral success, striking, but it came as a surprise. The element of surprise was recorded in all cases. The Belgian Liberal prime minister Frère-Orban in a parliamentary speech after the June 1884 Liberal defeat (quoted in *Le Patriote,* 8 August 1884) declared that "no one could have predicted our downfall." The Belgian Catholic leader Charles Woeste reports in his memoirs (1927:216) that the Conservative leaders did not expect to win the 1884 elections. Likewise, the Belgian historian Pirenne (1932:297–98) points out that the victory of the Right was "unexpected" and adds that "the Catholics' resounding triumph in 1884 was a surprise for everyone. The most informed politicians expected only a reduction of the [Liberal] majority." In the Netherlands "the unprecedented Antirevolutionary progress at the polls startled the Liberals and the Conservatives" (Vanden Berg 1960:99). In Vienna, the implementation, during the 1880s, of the alliance between Catholics and Conservatives led to the election of the first non-Liberal candi-

[38] As a Conservative newspaper of the Haute-Loire pointed out in 1894, "During electoral periods, Conservatives disseminate lots of pamphlets in our countryside, imitating their adversaries. But they imitate them too late. Propaganda must be continuous to be effective" (quoted in Rivet 1979:524).

dates, "to the astonishment of Scheicher [the Conservative leader] and the Catholics, who had been trying for years (with no success) to break down liberal power in provincial Lower Austria" (Boyer 1981:218). The series of elections that took place from 1868 to 1870 in various German states produced results that consistently surpassed all expectations. According to Alan France (1975:143), the results of the 1868 elections in southern Germany were a "surprising success." As Anderson (1981:114–15) puts it, "In Bavaria, where particularists controlled only a tenth of the votes in the lower house, no one expected these rustics to pick up more than a handful of seats [in the 1868 elections]." The Prussian ambassador in Munich (quoted in Windell 1954:127) described the electoral results of the 1868 elections as "astounding" and "surprising." Anderson (1981:116) reports that following these elections "astonishment at the particularists' victory was as great among the winners as among the losers. Catholic leaders had never advocated manhood suffrage. Suddenly they realized the vast potential of political Catholicism in an age of mass politics." For reasons laid out below, the results of these German regional elections were ignored and the elections of 1871 produced new and more impressive results. In these elections, "the concerted action of these various political leaders, plus the labors of the clergy, produced results which surprised even some of those who had worked hardest to bring them about" (Windell 1954:282). Anderson (1993:1458) adds that given the effectiveness of Germany's authoritarian institutions, the results of these elections "should come as something of a surprise." In Italy, the publication by the newspapers of the list of the Conservative deputies elected in the 1913 elections by Catholic votes "provoked a big clamor," both because of the collaboration between Liberals and Catholics and because of the size of the Catholic vote (De Rosa 1972:351). The electoral returns of the 1919 elections "were superior to the most optimistic predictions" and "exceeded the expectations" of the leaders of the Partito popolare (Malgeri 1981:115;356), who expected at most sixty seats and got one hundred. Suardo (1962:195) points to the PPI's "resounding electoral success, much superior to the expectations." This point is confirmed by Stefano Jacini (in Vecchio 1979b:55), Alfredo Canavero (1981:290), and Richard Wolff (1979:2).

The electoral results were unexpected not only in aggregate national terms but also on an individual basis. Anderson (1986:93) reports that in the Krefeld district of Prussia, "the incumbent, Ludwig Friedrich Seyfardt, a National Liberal and a Protestant, had been unexpectedly unseated by August Reichensperger, a Catholic and an outsider, by an astonishing 4,000 vote margin." Similarly the election in 1871 of the Zentrum candidate Father Eduard Müller in a district of Upper Silesia over a Free Conservative Catholic aristocratic landowner—the "astonishing victory of a nobody," as Anderson (1986:95–6) puts it—led the National Liberal deputy Eduard Lasker to "express the shock of the entire chamber that a distinguished Catholic deputy, only recently the head of a delegation to the Vatican, had been suddenly 'pushed out' of Pless-Rybnic by a complete unknown, running for the Center Party. The eminent incumbent had been 'driven out of his district in the name of the Catholic religion,' Lasker complained, 'by . . . a man whose merits may be extraordinarily great, only the world knows little of them, and still less the district in which he has been elected.' "

That electoral success took everyone by surprise is crucial. It indicates that neither the church nor the Conservatives anticipated the degree to which the participation strategy would succeed; it therefore indicates both the church's and the Liberals' tremendous miscalculation and underestimation of the power of religion as an issue and of the power of Catholic organizations as an agent of mass mobilization. The expectations of both the church and the Liberals as to the electoral potential of the pro-Catholic coalitions ranged from mediocre to satisfactory. They expected them to do well but not to win big. A decent result would have satisfied the church because it would have scared the Liberals into moderating their anticlericalism. It would also have allowed the church to depoliticize Catholic organizations. It is the failure to anticipate these electoral successes that accounts for the church's underestimation of the probability of losing its control over Catholic organizations and, as a consequence, of the probability of the formation of confessional parties.

How do we account for this myopia? It is particularly puzzling since the electoral potential of religion had manifested itself with numerous signs: mass petitions, elections in other countries, previous elections in the same country (such as the 1913 elections in Italy), and regional elections in the same country (such as the 1868 elections in various German states).

First, the electoral potential of religion as the dominant political issue, especially after the advent of the anticlerical attack, had not been gauged. Mass petitions were widely rejected as electoral indicators (France 1975:154). The same was true of regional elections or by-elections (because of their strong local character) and elections held under special circumstances such as the 1913 elections in Italy (where electoral pacts made it difficult clearly to estimate the size of the Catholic vote).

Second, this was an age of transition to the new political era of mass politics. Nobody knew exactly what the power of mass organization, or even the effects of extended or universal male franchise, would turn out to be. Their advent represented "a staggering leap in the dark" (Jones 1985:233). As Anderson (1993:1448) says about Germany, "Bismarck's revolutionary new franchise was a 'leap in the dark.' What would happen was anyone's guess." This confusion and uncertainty were best expressed by a French parliamentary candidate just before the 1848 elections—the first fought under universal male suffrage after the French Revolution: "Chance will decide the election; the ignorant voters, and there are a lot of them, will throw in the ballot box the ballot that will first come to their fingertips" (Jones 1985:233). Democracy and uncertainty go hand in hand. As Przeworski (1986:58) has pointed out, democracy is the "institutionalization of uncertainty": "Outcomes that are unlikely can and do occur."

What is in retrospect particularly surprising is the degree of the Liberals' myopia since they ended up the big losers. As Southern (1977:319) notes, "Not only the campaign against Catholicism but also the prevailing attitude of Bavarian Liberals toward the Catholic masses clearly aided the politicization process in a way of which few Liberals were aware." To quote Anderson's (1981:115) excellent observation, "Manhood suffrage proved an acid that picked out the lines of a previously hidden political landscape, one whose unfamiliar terrain was peopled with countrymen who bore little resemblance to the Liberals' ideal." As France (1975:94) notes about Austria, "That the clericals might put themselves forward as leaders of the new 'political consciousness,' the 'politically active spirit,' was a danger rarely perceived by liberal spokesmen." Likewise, the Italian Liberals "refused to consider and underestimated not only religious life, but all the confessional political activity" (Suardo 1962:12). As a result, the success of the PPI "came as a painful surprise" to them (Einaudi and Goguel 1952:15). This myopia, caused by the Liberals' blind belief in secular progress and their elitist underestimation of the power of the masses coupled with a complete unfamiliarity with rural reality, proved crucial in bringing about the Catholic victories.[39] In Germany, the National Liberal daily *Wilhelm Wehrenpfennig* attributed the Zentrum victory in the Bavarian district of Bamberg, to the "dumbness" of the population[40] (Anderson 1986:93). The Austrian Liberal minister of justice failed to grasp the message of the thousands of signatures that accompanied the petitions for the repeal of the anticlerical legislation. In 1868, he declared in the parliament (quoted in France 1975:154) that "no other than those belonging to legally elected organs are entitled to speak in their name. . . . What good are the petitions which emanate from an anonymous mass whom no one knows, compared with those from legally elected representatives of the com-

[39] Liberal parties were "perfectly adapted to the urban electorate" (Witte 1973:377), but they totally lacked an understanding of the political dynamics shaping the countryside and the power that the village priests commanded (Anderson 1981:115).

[40] In Cologne, "the political activity of the Catholic masses excited the indignation of the 'greatest part of the educated and patriotic portions of the population,' as one group of protesters modestly described themselves" (Anderson 1986:95). Similarly, in 1848 in France, the Republican observers of the elections in the Haute-Loire (quoted in Jones 1985:234) reported back to Paris that "what we see every day would almost make us desire that these inhabitants of the countryside of the Haute-Loire be disinherited of a right which they do not understand and which, we fear, they might use badly, since they are being excited by the priests."

munes and districts?" The Austrian Liberal historian Richard Charmatz (quoted in France 1975:94) is a perfect example of this spirit of condescension toward popular masses. He noted in 1909 that "the mass of the population of the Reich was too apathetic and too little elevated culturally to be able properly to appreciate the civil freedom . . . granted by the constitution." Even Giolitti, famous for his political flair and ability more than for his attachment to doctrinal Liberalism, fails to mention in his autobiography (published in 1922) both Catholics and the Catholic organizations (Suardo 1962:12).

An additional question concerns the issue of diffusion of information across countries. With Liberal defeats and Catholic victories across Europe, how did this myopia still prevail? There are three answers. First, as observed by Sidney Tarrow (1994:194), social movements (and information about the rise of such movements) spread far slower in the past than they do today, mainly because of the state of global communications and the lack of a universal "repertoire of collective action." Second, the European political landscape looked fuzzy. The case of France, where the anticlerical Republicans kept attacking the church and defeating the pro-Catholic Conservatives from 1879 to 1919, loomed large and biased the visible sample. For instance, the victory of the Republicans in the French elections of 1879 was interpreted by the Belgian Liberals as a great victory of Liberalism and reinforced their conviction that attacking the church was the right path to follow (Laury 1979:678–79). Conversely, other cases were often interpreted as idiosyncratic and not prone to generalization. For example, the fact that the first Catholic victories were recorded in Germany was often attributed to the minority status of Catholics. As a result, the pro-Catholic Austrian newspaper *Das Vaterland* did not exploit the 1868 electoral successes of southern German Catholics beyond simply mentioning them (France 1975:94).

Thus electoral success provided the mechanism of transition from mass organization to party formation. The pro-Catholic coalitions had the potential to become confessional political parties, but they made this step only after their stunning electoral victory. In Belgium, the Netherlands, and Austria the confessional party was formally established after the crucial elections. But even when confessional parties had been formed before the elections (the German Zentrum and the Italian PPI), they survived and became established only because of their electoral success. An electoral defeat for the Zentrum in 1870 would have been fatal. The PPI had more chance to survive a 1919 defeat because of the 1913 elections and the Catholic collaboration in the cabinet of 1916. Still, a defeat would have had devastating results for its future: witness the case of the French ALP, formed before elections but disappearing after two electoral defeats (a case examined in Chapter 3).

Electoral success was important in two respects. First, it proved the political potential of religion and provided Catholic activists with the alternative source of support and legitimation they needed to assert their autonomy from the church. Second, it produced an important practical consequence: the need for organizational consolidation and institutionalization. To preserve the spoils brought by their victories, these coalitions had to be transformed into permanent structured organizations, in other words, into political parties.[41] Traditional Conservative politicians and Catholic organizations merged into what gradually became the new Catholic parties. Still, mass organizations remained crucial after these initial victories. As Rudolf Lill (1977:78) points out about Germany, "[It was] the support of the Catholic associations [that] made possible the formation and the quick consolidation of the Catholic parties . . . the power of these parties, still with small organization, and the relative stability of their electorate was based on the Catholic organizations." Although the process of consolidation and institutionalization of the new parties was often slow, arduous, and conflictual, it is obvious that the crucial point was the electoral success. As Simon (1958:111) points out about Belgium, "Maybe more than anything else, this [1884 electoral] success established the Catholic party. From now on there will be unity between the parliamentary Right and the religious and electoral associations."

The Unintended Consequences of Choices

The process of confessional party formation can now be stated in full. The formation of confessional parties was achieved in three steps. First, the formation of Catholic mass organizations (through the organizational strategy of the church) sowed the seeds of a Catholic political identity and created lay and low cleric activists; in a second phase, the entry of the church into the political arena and the creation of pro-church coalitions with Conservatives (through the participation strategy of the church) politicized this embryonic identity by turning Catholic associations into political organizations; finally, the electoral success of these coalitions allowed the lay and low cleric activists to engineer the formation of confessional parties despite the intentions of both the church and Conservative politicians. The Catholic political identity was fully constructed once confessional parties were formed: as Bourdieu (1987:13) points out, the construction of a mobilized or mobilizable group requires "the institutionalization of a permanent organization capable of representing it." Figure 2 illustrates the sequence of choices.

[41] Even when there was no governmental participation, the formation of confessional parties was seen as necessary by lay Catholics to avoid their absorption into existing Conservative factions. This was a point clearly made by Meda in Italy (De Rosa 1972:356).

Figure 2. The process of confessional party formation (Belgium, Netherlands, Austria, Germany, Italy)

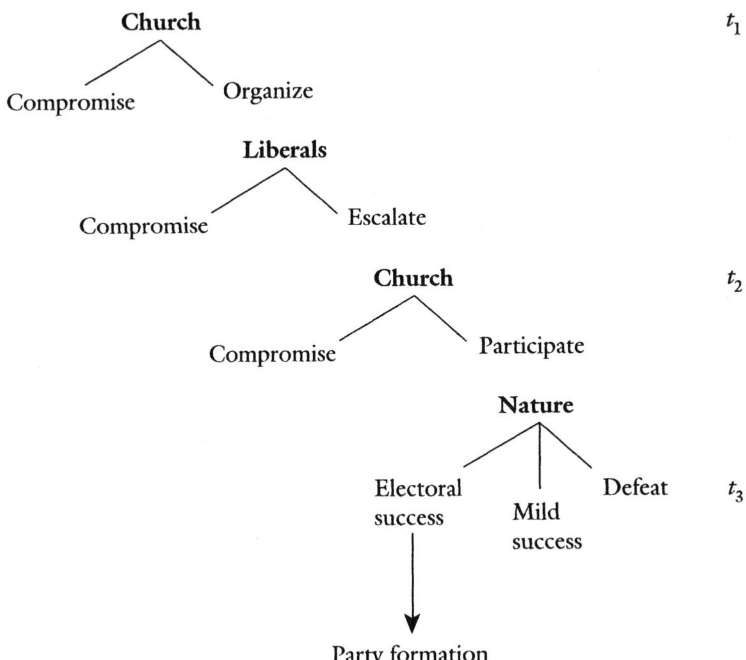

All three steps are necessary for a confessional party to emerge. The creation of an embryonic Catholic political identity through mass organization was necessary but not sufficient for the construction of a distinct Catholic political identity. While the Catholic movement, to use Traniello's expression (1982:46), "contained in its womb, perhaps from its origin on, an embryo of a party," what led to the successful birth was exogenous to the organizational strategy. No party could have emerged without the participation strategy. Mass organization alone can be contained; new outlets and alternative arenas need to be provided for it to become politicized and, eventually, autonomous. Only political participation could achieve that. Conversely, although the participation strategy developed the Catholic identity and produced collective action, it could not have led to the formation of confessional parties without prior organization. First, it was the organizational strategy that made the participation strategy electorally effective; second, even assuming that the participation strategy could produce electoral successes on its own, Conservative politicians alone would have lacked the legitimacy, credibility, and most of all the incentive to appropriate religion on a permanent basis for party building. This was made possible only through the actions of Catholic activists, the members of the mass organizations. The case of France after 1905 (and the example of Catholic Action later) is indicative in this respect: mass organization without participation could not lead to party formation. Finally, organization and participation without electoral success would have led nowhere. Religion would have proved to be a losing issue, thus destroying the efforts to build a Catholic party and inducing all relevant political actors to seek alternative strategies and issues. This is exactly what happened in France. All the potential French confessional party (the ALP) lacked was victory, declared one of its leaders, Albert de Mun, on the eve of the crucial 1906 elections (Martin 1978:194). It lost, and as a result no confessional party was formed.

The story of confessional party formation shows that once strategies have been selected and implemented, unwanted, unanticipated, and, often, inescapable consequences might follow. As Billiet and Gerard (1985:105) have pointed out about nineteenth-century Belgian Catholic politics, "The results of actions taken by various actors in this arena (episcopate, clergy, laymen engaged in social action, politicians) are never the direct prolongation of motivations and intentions of the one or the other group." When the Liberals launched their offensive against the church, nobody desired or expected the creation of confessional parties. These attacks were a necessary but not sufficient element for the formation of a confessional party. Where there was no attack, no confessional party was formed, and Ireland is a case in point.[42] But attacks against the church did not always or necessarily translate into party formation, as in the case of France. Social conflicts do not necessarily alter party systems. The emergence of a Catholic political identity was not automatic or natural and can be understood only through the actions and choices of the church and the outcomes these actions generated. To use William Sewell's words (1992:15), the Liberal offensive against the church "touch[ed] off an escalating and unpredictable chain of confrontational events that culminated in a massive and durable shift in collective identities." Rather than being a causal factor in the formation of confessional parties,

[42] Attempts to organize Catholics in England failed for the same reason. Doyle (1986:476) concludes his article on the short-lived Catholic Federation of Salford as follows: "Mass Catholic support could only be mobilized successfully when a recognisably specific threat to Catholics seemed imminent, as in 1906." When anticlericalism did not appear to be threatening, no confessional party was formed. The liberal attacks against the Spanish church in 1910–1912 are also a case in point. As Carr (1980:42) points out, "in spite of anti-clerical noises, the Church was not in danger" during this period. As a result, all attempts to form a confessional party, such as Angel Herrera's in 1911, failed. Only the anticlericalism of the Second Republic led to the formation of the Catholic Confederación Española de Derechas Autonomas (CEDA).

anticlerical attacks were a trigger that imposed constraints on the main actors and structured their options in ways that allowed room for variation in the strategies that were adopted. Both the church and the Conservative political elites had hoped that their strategies would allow them to reach their objectives safely. A decent electoral showing of the pro-church coalitions would have intimidated the Liberals into stopping or moderating their attacks. At the same time, both the church and the Conservatives thought they could roll things back after reaching their objectives and easily depoliticize Catholic organizations. Both were wrong because religious mobilization produced unexpected victories that allowed new actors to impose new political structures under their own control.

How large do institutions loom in this account? They matter a lot. Yet a quick contrast between the Dutch Catholic and Protestant parties delineates the limits of accounts that would place all their explanatory chips on institutions. The Dutch Calvinist Antirevolutionary party was formed in 1879, only one year after the introduction of anticlerical legislation. By contrast, the Dutch Catholic party was formed ten years later following the participation strategy of the church and the electoral success that followed. Calvinist and Catholic activists had similar preferences: they both wanted to form confessional parties. Churches also had similar preferences: both the Dutch Reformed and the Catholic churches wanted to avoid the formation of confessional parties. Yet the institutional weakness of the Protestant church as opposed to the strength and centralization of the Catholic one allowed the political initiatives of the Calvinist activists to flourish and result in early and relatively facile party formation. Rather than obstruct the formation of the Antirevolutionary party, conflict with the Dutch Reformed church led to its split after Calvinist fundamentalists walked out of it to form a new church. It is telling that among all cases under study only the Calvinists were able to form a party right after the anticlerical legislation and before the electoral success of the participation strategy. This is a strong indicator of the obstructing role of the Catholic church. This contrast underlines the importance of institutional structures in establishing a context that precluded some possibilities by providing varying incentives and constraints (Hattam 1992:178). Institutional structures, however, can predict only the timing of party formation, not the outcome—party formation itself. After all, Catholic parties *did* emerge. Thus the formation of confessional parties despite a hostile institutional environment indicates that institutions, though crucial, left room for choice, action, and interaction.

The emergence of confessional parties was detrimental to the interests of the three central actors at the beginning of the process. Liberals were the bigger losers. They were fatally wounded by their clash with the church, and the rise of Socialist parties would almost finish them off. Traditional

Conservative elites lost their autonomy of action, saw their policy space shrink, and were soon replaced by a new political class, the leaders of the Catholic organizations. The formation of confessional parties hurt the church in a particularly ironic and perverse way by destroying its monopoly over the representation of Catholics. In essence, the church became the victim of the success of its own strategy. True, the Liberal attack was stopped and a measure of Catholic education preserved, but nowhere did the church gain a monopoly over education—not to speak of its temporal possessions where it had lost them. Moreover, education was only one means in a wider struggle over the power and influence of the church. There is no doubt that the power of the church decreased everywhere, both in society at large and in its own constituency.[43] Furthermore, as is clear in retrospect, despite the success of confessional parties, the church eventually failed to check the progress of dechristianization. On the contrary, the church suffered a major amputation: many among its organizations moved away to join the new confessional parties. Even the Catholic organizations that were kept under church control suffered: as Pietro Scoppola (1982:18) puts it, they were emptied, losing many members to the new parties. Thus, in a paradoxical fashion, the church was simultaneously the controlling power from which Catholic laymen were being emancipated and the (unintended) agent of their emancipation.[44] Finally, priests ended up losers as well. They were instrumental in the creation of confessional parties but were eventually displaced within these parties by lay activists (see Chapter 5).

The winners were lay Catholic activists. They formed new powerful mass parties and became central (and often dominant) political actors. There was an additional winner as well. The implementation of the participation strategy and the electoral success to which it led were outcomes generated by the operation of these actors under a representative parliamentary regime. Because it shaped the arena, the political regime decisively affected the actors' choices and opportunities. In turn, the regime was shaped, although in an unintended way, by the strategic decisions of the actors. Politicizing religion reinforced the young European democratic regimes. Many confessional party leaders were initially religious integrists, enemies of democracy. The ideological project of Catholic organization was the establishment of "a clerico-

[43] It could be argued that had the church not opted for the participation strategy, it might have ended up in worse shape. This is not necessarily true. Moreover, it is generally assumed that the formation of Catholic parties strengthened the church—a dubious claim in light of the evidence.

[44] This study, then, provides an answer to the question asked by Lidtke (1986:121): "Is it possible that the hierarchy was simultaneously the agent for emancipation and the controlling power from which Catholic laymen were being emancipated? " Lidtke implies mutual exclusivity between the two options, but I show that this need not be the case.

monarchist regime or a clerico-military dictatorship, both of which spelled theocracy, the subordination of the secular power to the church and the suppression of individual freedom" (Reddick 1950:339). Yet these Catholic activists ended up consolidating representative democracy. The leaders of the new parties quickly understood that their power lay in the electorate rather than the church and that the only way to ensure their autonomy from the church was to embrace parliamentarism and play by its rules. By integrating forces opposed to parliamentarism, the process of confessional party formation consolidated the emerging democratic regimes of Europe.

CHAPTER 3

The Puzzle of Nonformation: The Case of France

—Do you want to continue being outcasts in this country?
—Shouts: No! No!
—Do you want your nuns to be expelled?
—No! No!
—Do you want your priests to be ousted tomorrow and your churches to be closed? Do you want the faith of your children to be violently pulled out from their souls?
—Increased clamors: No, no!
—Then listen well: in order to avoid all this there is . . . only one way: ***organization.*** Yes, slow, patient, organization."

—Henri Bazire, the president of the Catholic Youth organization ACJF, in a public meeting held in 1902

We must develop in men the sense of association. Why did *Catholics* count for so little in public opinion? Why were they laughed at by having laws passed against them, if not because it was known that they were not powerful, they were not united? They were the ***dispersed Catholics.***

—A speaker at the Catholic *congrès des oeuvres* in Rouen, 1922

No confessional party emerged in France during the Third Republic.[1] This absence is well known (Le Béguec and Prévotat 1992:281) and its puzzling character repeatedly underlined (Durand 1995:66; Boutry and Michel 1992:664). As the French "Christian Democrat" Francisque Gay dramatically remarked in 1935 (quoted in Durand 1995:187): "If there is a country where Christian Democracy should have established itself, put down roots, developed, and yielded profit, it was France. In all fields of action and social and democratic thought, we cleared the brush, opened paths, lay the first foundations, and the edifice was built elsewhere. . . . Why, why, why?" This

[1] The terms "emergence" and "party formation" include institutionalization, organizational consolidation, and political relevance (Bartolini 1993). Confessional (or potentially confessional) parties did appear on the French political scene during the Third Republic, but they were either stillborn (ALP) or politically irrelevant (PDP and Jeune République).

puzzle has attracted considerable scholarly attention, although the focus has overwhelmingly been on the postwar resounding failure of the MRP (Mouvement républicain populaire) rather than on the decisive period of the Third Republic, when mass politics were introduced and major party alternatives and voter alignments froze all over Europe.

Why didn't a confessional party emerge in France? Why didn't religion form the salient principle of political organization in France? The nonformation of a confessional party in France constitutes an important historical, political, and theoretical puzzle. First, it represents a crucial failure of Rokkan and Lipset's cleavage theory, which predicts confessional party formation from state-church conflict. Catholicism in France was traditionally strong and influential, and the conflict between state and church was extremely intense, tracing its roots back to the French Revolution. In fact, the state-church conflict developed into the most salient cleavage and the key ideological issue of the Third Republic. It dominated politics at all levels, from parliament to the last village, and overshadowed every other political and social question (Mesliand 1976:214; Partin 1969:vii; Hoffmann 1963:43). Second, the French case is an important test of my model of party formation, which has to account for both cases of formation and nonformation without analytic alterations.

Yet the fact that religious practice has always been an excellent predictor of French voting behavior (Boy and Mayer 1993; Derivry and Dogan 1971; McRae 1958) suggests that the absence of a confessional party might be superfluous: it is argued, for instance, that the French Right, from nineteenth-century Monarchists to contemporary Gaullists, is implicitly confessional (Lipset and Rokkan 1967:34). This claim is misleading. The absence of a confessional party in France matters. First, Arend Lijphart (1990/1981:253) has explicitly warned against confusing party ideologies and programs with the characteristics of the voters these parties represent. Mayeur (1980:9) has likewise underlined that French Monarchist parties are radically distinct from confessional parties. Second, the act of voting cannot be reduced to preexisting individual attributes; it is instead the end result of a long political process. By mediating between citizens and voting, political organizations determine to a large measure which individual attributes will become salient for politics (Przeworski and Sprague 1985). Therefore, political organizations and the political process that precedes voting matter. Third, party formation matters above and beyond the analysis of cleavages and voting because it defines the way cleavages become politicized and shape politics. Once parties representing a given cleavage have successfully emerged, "cleavages become established and organizationally institutionalized, they develop their own autonomous strength and, in turn, begin to act as an influence on social, cultural, and political life" (Bartolini and Mair 1990:218). In other words, a religious cleavage *without* a confessional party is bound to produce a significantly different political environment than a religious cleavage *with* a confessional party. For example, confessional parties (but not Conservative parties supported by religious voters) were forced to absorb Catholic workers' organizations formed earlier by the church. As a result, Catholic trade unions prospered only in countries where a Christian Democratic party emerged (Ebbinghaus 1992). Even overall union density was found to be contingent on Christian Democratic party strength (Misra and Hicks 1994). Likewise, Christian Democratic parties are linked with the growth of the welfare state (van Kersbergen 1994; Huber et al. 1993; Wilensky 1981). Finally, the *manner* in which cleavages are politicized matters a lot as Luebbert (1991:108) has shown. A focus on voting behavior at the expense of cleavage and party formation would clearly be misleading.

To restate the question: why was no confessional party formed in France during the Third Republic, given that France was torn by a state-church conflict of similar, if not greater, proportions to conflicts that led to the emergence of confessional parties in the other five countries? Lipset and Rokkan focus on the MRP but remain very vague about this puzzle, even though it is crucial to their theory. They (1967:40) refer to a "burden of historic commitments" which proved too strong and condemned the MRP to failure and mention the importance of variation in the histories of nation building on the systems of party alliances and oppositions. But what they mean by "burden of historic commitments" is never clarified, nor is the failure of a confessional party to emerge during the Third Republic addressed. Because it alludes to a vague history rather than their own theory, their argument about France is inconsistent and has a strong ad hoc quality.

There are three arguments to account for the failure of a confessional party to emerge in France. One focuses on the disorganizing effects of the regime cleavage between Monarchists and Republicans on the party formation process (Mayeur 1981; Irving 1979; Lorwin 1971). This argument is two-pronged. First, the presence of a strong and implicitly confessional Monarchist Right made the formation of an explicitly confessional party unnecessary: "It was hardly necessary for the Church to sponsor a political party of its own during this period, because most of the anti-Republican right was willing to defend the interests of Catholicism" (Bosworth 1962:239). Second, the regime cleavage divided Catholics and undermined the political entrepreneurs who attempted to organize a confessional party. According to Caroline Ford (1987:240), "Attempts to create a Catholic party on the German model failed [in France] due to political divisions among Catholics that were too great to surmount." The regime cleavage did indeed matter, I argue below, but in a different and indirect way: not as a disorganizing cleavage, but as a factor that decisively affected the risk calculations of the church in France and led it to shun mass organization.

A second argument emphasizes the decline of religiosity in France. Not enough faithful Catholics existed to provide a majority necessary for electoral victories and the formation of a successful confessional party (Durand 1995:67). This argument is empirically flawed because available data do not support the contention of a secular decline in religiosity during the period under question.[2] It is also theoretically flawed for two reasons. First, it inaccurately assumes that political relevance requires electoral majorities. In fact, nonmajoritarian parties can play a prominent political role through their coalition or blackmail potential (Sartori 1990/1976), something perfectly understood by German or Dutch Catholics. Second, it reduces parties to mere emanations of social-structural variables (Sartori 1990/1968). The failure of a confessional party to emerge has, therefore, to be accounted for politically rather than sociologically.

Finally, a third argument correctly stresses the role of political actors yet fails to draw accurate conclusions. The emphasis here is on the unwillingness of the main actors to form a confessional party. According to Boutry and Michel (1992:673), the first cause of the absence of a confessional party "is to be found in the refusal of the Catholic actors, lay and cleric, to create such a party in France." These authors point to the role of the church leadership: "The attitude of the Catholic hierarchy is explained to a great extent by the willingness to clearly disassociate the cause and the interests of the church from every political movement" (Boutry and Michel 1992:676). Although it is based on a correct observation, this account does not answer the puzzle. It is, rather, a spurious by-product of a noncomparative approach. As I show in Chapter 1, nowhere did the principal actors—church and Conservatives—desire and promote the formation of confessional parties.

Thus the puzzle remains unresolved. To unravel it, I rely on the model of party formation introduced in the first two chapters. I first outline the main argument, provide some historical background, and then examine the preferences and strategies of the church and Conservative political elites and the subsequent sequence of events.

[2] In fact, the influence of the church grew in France during the nineteenth century, particularly during the last part of the Second Empire (1864–1870). The network of parishes was reorganized and strengthened and the size of the French clergy (especially the secular one) tripled from about 70,000 to 215,000 (Cholvy and Hilaire 1985; Huard 1982; Faury 1980; Aubert 1975). Data on religious practice collected by Boulard (1982), Boulard and Hilaire (1987), and Boulard and Cholvy (1992), however, convey a mixed image. After 1875 there was an irregular decline in rates of practice. While some regions experienced decline in rates of practice, others saw rising rates, and some social groups such as sectors of the bourgeoisie were rechristianized. But the decline in religious practice can be an indicator of a new, more private, form of religiosity (Martin 1994). Indeed, Mayeur (1973:141, 103) stresses the magnitude of the French "religious awakening" and describes this trend as "Catholic restoration." Overall there is no support for the thesis of a secular, linear, and irreversible process of dechristianization in France after 1789 (Cholvy 1994; Ford 1993; Gibson 1989).

The Model of Party Formation Applied to France: An Overview of the Argument

Both the French church and the French Conservative elites had preferences that were very close to those of their counterparts in the other five countries. What made a difference, but in a dissimilar way from that usually assumed, was the regime issue. In France, contrary to the other cases, the likelihood of regime change was high. This situation affected the payoff structure of the church in the face of the anticlerical attack and foreclosed the organizational strategy by turning the conciliatory strategy in the expectation of monarchical restoration into a better choice than organization building. Following the consecutive electoral defeats of the Right, however, the surprising stabilization of the Republic, and the defeat of Boulangism (the church's last hope of an overthrow of the Republic), the church was forced to alter its strategy. Because of the church's delay in resisting the initial anticlerical measures (in the 1880s), the escalation of anticlerical attacks which made swift political action imperative, the combined cost and time of organization building, and the filling of organizational space by other forces, the participation strategy was implemented without prior mass organization. As a result, lay Catholic activists remained dispersed and disorganized, the coalitions put together by the church were defeated, and religion proved to be a losing issue in the eyes of all political actors (including political entrepreneurs). Thus no confessional party emerged in France.

Historical Background

The 1801 concordat marked the beginning of the church's postrevolutionary reorganization.[3] Initially the church was reinforced vis-à-vis the Vatican, but eventually it submitted to papal power as did all other Catholic churches during the second part of the nineteenth century (Dansette 1961). For most of the nineteenth century, domestic developments were favorable to the church. The restored monarchy fully defended the church, very much as did the Second Empire. Religious orders developed rapidly, underscoring a trend of religious revival and increase of devotion. Following the collapse of the Second Empire and the crackdown of the Commune insurrection, the 1871 elections produced a massive victory for the combined forces of the Right.

[3] The concordat, signed between Napoleon and the Vatican in 1801, formed the legal basis on which the church operated. It recognized both the confiscations of church property by the French state and the pope's right of canonical institution of the bishops, instituted the material support of the clergy by the state, and rehabilitated the church.

This victory further enhanced the position of the church, as was validated by the 1875 law on the freedom of higher education, which permitted the creation of Catholic universities. Thus by 1875 the church found itself in a very advantageous position. Public education made provision for religious and moral education, recitation of prayers before the opening of classes, and attendance at religious services. Public schools were staffed by members of the religious teaching orders. In addition, the church was free to develop its own network of secondary schools and universities.

The Preferences of the Church

The church in France sought to maximize its influence in society. As everywhere else, its action targeted the state rather than the masses. Mass organization was not an issue because the church perceived no threat. Political mobilization of lay Catholics *qua* Catholics, was not an option. Indeed, the church reacted strongly when lay Catholics and low clergy mobilized against an 1844 law project concerning education. May (1973:82) reports that "Mgr de la Tour d'Auvergne of Arras told his clergy to refrain from signing petitions because he himself looked after the interests of his diocese with the government. They could pray and keep silent. Mgr Blanquart de Bailleul echoed the same sentiment, arguing that 'laymen have no mission to concern themselves with the affairs of the church . . . they would do better to pray while the bishops made their complaints.' "

The church was suspicious of influential lay Catholics such as Louis Veuillot, the director of the Catholic newspaper *L'Univers*, and successfully obstructed any attempt at autonomous Catholic political activity. A famous case is that of the Breton priest Felicité Robert de Lamennais, who attacked the monarchy, promoted liberal views, and went so far as to ask Catholics to leave behind them exclusively religious affairs and position themselves on the "political and social level" (Molette 1968:5). He was condemned by the pope the following year and was forced to make a declaration of doctrinal submission. Likewise, Charles de Montalembert's attempt to form a Catholic political organization independent of the Monarchists during the 1840s failed (Ménager 1992:105). The absence of an immediate anticlerical threat accentuated internal divisions and helped the church to undermine this project. As Dansette (v.1 1961:236) notes, the bishops "found Montalembert's methods revolutionary and disquieting for reasons of discipline rather than politics. . . . Lay intervention advocated by Montalembert, therefore, gave rise to talk of laicism, a heresy according to which the administration of the church should be entrusted to laymen." Mgr. Félix Dupanloup (quoted in May 1973:91) warned the church leadership, in a letter he wrote in 1849: "I have only said

. . . that I have one wish above all, that is that the bishops of France unite and deliberate among themselves and decide, otherwise, religious laicism will replace parliamentary laicism and govern the church among us."

Things did not change after the launching of the anticlerical attack. In 1885, the church thwarted the most important attempt to form a confessional party initiated by Albert de Mun, a prominent Conservative politician. De Mun saw himself as the "French Windthorst" (Martin 1978:58) and announced in the fall of 1885 his plans to form a Catholic party "with the cross as its standard" (Dansette v.2 1961:66). The new party's political program was to be built around the protection of the rights of the church and the repeal of the anticlerical laws. This attempt was a threat to both Conservatives and the church and was denounced by them (Martin 1978:59; Levillain 1992:183; Gadille v.2 1967:181). Indeed, the pope in person destroyed this project before its birth (Levillain 1992:183; Dansette v.2 1961:67). The fact that de Mun was only an "isolated layman" (Levillain 1992:183), with no mass Catholic organization behind him, was decisive in the failure of his enterprise (Sedgwick 1965:16). The church was also very hostile toward the Christian Democratic congresses that were organized during the late 1890s (Mayeur 1962). The most open crackdown on independent lay Catholic activity is the case of the Sillon, an organization formed in the beginning of the 1890s that attempted to combine Catholicism with modernity and democracy. After 1906, it became increasingly politicized and well organized, claiming independence from the hierarchy, mixing political action with spiritual aims, and recruiting all over France from the ranks of both lay and clergy. The Sillon had close to twenty-five thousand members (Lapierre and Levillain 1992:73), "seemed to behave as if the lay Catholics should assume their duties independently of the ecclesiastical hierarchy" (Molette 1968:448), and was becoming "an embryo Christian Democratic political party" (Irving 1973:13). The Sillon was effectively destroyed after being condemned by the pope in 1910. Among its errors cited in the papal letter of condemnation was the "inadmissible pretension of autonomy with regard to the ecclesiastical hierarchy" (Aubert 1975:61). The pope asked its members to "offer their goodwill to their bishops without hesitation and second thoughts and submit to their supervision" (Chaline 1985:141). Indeed, the Sillon was broken down into diocesan chapters and placed under the direction of local bishops.

The Preferences of the Conservative Political Elites

The preferences of the French Conservative political elites were the same as those of their counterparts in the five other countries. Seeking reelection,

Conservatives courted the support of the church but spurned too close an embrace, while rebuffing all plans to create a confessional party.

During the first part of the Third Republic, the Right was roughly made up of three groups: the Legitimists, hard-line Monarchists followers of Count Chambord, the last heir of the French branch of the Bourbon dynasty; the Orleanists, liberal Monarchists, followers of the Count of Paris, the heir of the Orleans family; and the Bonapartists, followers of the Napoleonic legacy. Conservatives were close to the church, which they sought to defend, but their preferences often diverged: they were suspicious of "politics based on the holy scriptures" (Mayeur 1973:27). Their primary objective was the restoration of the monarchy from which a favorable situation for the church was expected to follow. As Goguel (1958:78) succinctly puts it, "Monarchists were a political, not a religious party." Even the hard-line Legitimists did not blindly follow the church. A majority among them approached the state-church question as a potentially beneficial political issue (Anderson 1974:42; Locke 1974:48). The Duke de la Rochefoucauld (quoted in Sedgwick 1965:19) made it crystal clear in 1887: "The bases of our Union are always readily apparent; the defense of the Catholic interests, the vindication of all religious and civil liberties, and the defense of material interests. But if our immediate aim is the defense of conservative principles, our ultimate aim is the Restoration." In short, the Right sought to use the state-church conflict as a political weapon in the struggle for restoration (Ravitch 1990:65; Rémond 1982:131).

Understandably, the formation of a confessional party was totally unacceptable to the Right. Such a project would compromise restoration by placing first priority on the defense of the church. Moreover, the formation of a confessional party represented a grave threat to the political position of traditional notables, who realized that Catholicism (through its newspapers and associations) competed against monarchism. As Michel Denis (1977:466–7) found in Mayenne, "monarchism [was at the end of the nineteenth century] in the process of being submerged by clericalism." This is why Monarchists went to great lengths to emphasize the primordiality of the regime issue and undermined all attempts to form a confessional party. The Monarchist newspaper *La Gazette de France* (quoted in Desaubliaux 1986:112) argued in 1889 that "in France, there is no other cause for Catholics to support and to help triumph but the legitimate monarchy, because the church will only recover its liberties under it." Marc Desaubliaux (1986:112) recounts "the fierceness used by the royalist leaders to demolish [de Mun's] Catholic party. Scorn, slander, derision, everything was good in order to crush this attempt which crossed the traditional cleavage of Catholic monarchy and atheistic republic."

The Anticlerical Attack

The 1876 elections marked the turn of the tide in France. Despite an electoral system change engineered by the Right, Republicans emerged victorious.[4] In 1877, the Republican leader Léon Gambetta introduced the famous slogan that became the symbolic referent of the central political issue in France: *Le Cléricalisme voilà l'ennemi* (Clericalism: this is the enemy). The same year, the Conservative president of the Republic Marshal MacMahon, provoked a constitutional crisis (the so-called clerical coup of 16 May 1876). He replaced the Republican cabinet with a Monarchist one and called new elections which he expected the Right to win through the use of state pressure (Pisani-Ferry 1965:23). But although the Right improved its performance, it failed to win. The by-elections of 1878 further increased the size of the Republican representation. The senatorial elections of January 1879 produced a Republican majority and led to the immediate resignation of MacMahon, who was succeeded by the Republican Jules Grévy. The presidency and the two chambers of the legislature were now under Republican control (and were to remain so until 1914). The anticlerical attack that followed the Republican victory was launched in two waves: the first between 1879 and 1888 and the second between 1899 and 1905.

The rationale of the Republicans in launching their attack against the church was similar to that of the Liberals all across Europe (see Chapter 4). In essence, anticlericalism provided the "true cement" of the otherwise divided Republicans (Mayeur 1973:106). The first anticlerical wave began with the law on religious orders (1879–1880), which drastically curtailed their power. This was followed by two decrees in 1880 which ordered the dissolution of the Jesuits and required all other religious orders to apply for state authorization. These laws were generally applied with leniency. Still, government representatives forced their way into 261 religious houses, expelling 5,643 members of religious orders, and Jesuit colleges were handed over to secular priests or laymen.[5] In the following years new laws were passed regulating many areas of civil life, from higher education to cemeteries, in ways unfavorable for the church. The most important were those affecting elementary education (June 1881 and March 1882). They provided for free, secular, and compulsory elementary education and replaced moral and religious instruction with moral and civic

[4] Who were the Republicans? Aminzade (1993:262) argues that French republicanism brought together people and ideas covering the whole ground from Liberal to Socialist and "can be understood in terms of a relatively fluid ideology and practice that combined the ability to integrate diverse, and sometimes, divergent, elements from various political traditions."

[5] Most of the religious houses were closed only temporarily. Furthermore, these laws still allowed 3,400 brothers of the Christian schools and 15,000 nuns to keep their teaching positions in public schools.

instruction. Finally, the Goblet education law of 1886 completed the secularization of elementary education by removing religious congregations from public elementary schools and replacing them with an exclusively lay personnel.

The relatively calm period from 1888 to 1899 was followed by a second anticlerical wave that was spurred by the Dreyfus affair and the continuing, if waning, presence of the church in education. Out of the 1,517 congregations operating in 1901, 774 were not authorized and would have no legal right to exist had the 1880 law not lapsed. This time, the anticlerical attack was launched by the newly powerful Radicals. Anticlericalism again became dominant within the Left because it was the only issue that held together the coalition of Progressives, Radicals, and Socialists, who were increasingly divided over social issues.

In 1899 a bill regulating congregations was introduced in parliament and a radical version of it was finally voted in 1901. The Association Law obliged all religious orders to obtain parliamentary authorization to operate legally. It was "one of the most significant legislative acts in French Republican history, and at the same time served to focus and unleash anticlerical passions that had been pent up since the founding of the Third Republic" (Partin 1969:vii-viii). The attack against the church intensified when the Radical Emile Combes became prime minister in 1902. In 1903, authorization was denied to most religious orders (many decided not to apply), and the schools they ran were subsequently closed. By October 1903 more than ten thousand schools run by religious orders had been closed down. About thirty thousand members of religious orders were dispersed, an important number of them opting to leave France. Finally, the law of 7 July 1904 forbade religious communities from providing any education. All authorized teaching congregations were to be suppressed within ten years and were forbidden to recruit members. Their property was to be confiscated and sold. In July 1904, following a complex and escalating sequence of events, France broke off its diplomatic relations with the Vatican. The crowning act of the anticlerical attack (and its conclusion), the law on the separation of church and state, was passed by the senate in December 1905. This law unilaterally abolished the concordat and deprived the church of its official status and its financial support from the state.

The Response of the Church to the First Wave

The case of France diverges from the five other cases in that the church did not respond to the first threats by implementing the organizational strategy. Nor did it fight the anticlerical legislation. In the model's notation the church selected *C* over *O*. This choice needs explanation.

Where confessional parties were formed, the foundations of Catholic mass organizations were usually laid after the Liberals sent the first signals of their intentions. Given similar actors and preferences and an anticlerical attack of comparable severity, the organizational strategy should have been implemented in France during the period 1876–1879. Yet, despite the Republican victory in the 1876 elections, the church did not create mass organizations. In fact, during the crucial 1876 elections, the archbishop of Paris refused to appeal for Catholic unity (Gadille v.1 1967:10). Some Catholic committees with pious and charitable objectives were created or revived during this period, but they were small and weak. No central umbrella organization was formed.

Even more surprising is the reaction of the church following the first anticlerical laws in 1879. Monarchist politicians called for a civil disobedience campaign and most like-minded newspapers called for a crusade of resistance similar to that of Belgian Catholics (Ozouf 1963:83; Capéran v.2 1960:192). Some bishops openly called for resistance, and lay Catholics began to set up committees of resistance all over France. The church, in an initial display of combativeness, revived a committee called Société générale d'éducation et d'enseignement created in 1868. A campaign of lectures and pamphlet publications was launched, and four hundred magistrates and civil servants resigned their positions in a public display of protest. A petition against the 1879 law gathered an impressive 1,775,000 signatures (Boulard and Cholvy 1992:25). At the same time, the church actively developed its school network. As Louis Capéran (v.2 1960:195) concludes, "An ardent bellicose movement was taking over most Catholics of France."

Yet this movement quickly waned. The church did not condemn the Ferry laws, did not impose religious sanctions on Republicans, and did not appeal for a campaign of civil disobedience. On the contrary, it refrained from further action, decided against fighting, and adopted a conciliatory attitude. Given the dearth of lay teachers, the church could have easily undermined the law by engineering a strike of congregationalist public school teachers. But it refrained from doing so. Even after the Ferry laws were passed, the church made no attempt openly and drastically to oppose them. In fact, the Ferry laws led to far less Catholic agitation than the government's action against religious congregations (Goguel 1958:53). Instructions were sent to parishes asking the faithful to obey the laws (Ozouf 1963:84). The church's position, points out Jacques Gadille (v.2 1967:246), was equivalent to "practical acceptance" of the 1881 laws. Most important, the church refused to follow the unrelenting demands of lay Catholics to set up a central Catholic committee that would coordinate local committees and generate mass organization. The church argued instead that the central committee was Rome and the local one was the bisphoric (Capéran v.2 1960:237). This decision proved fatal for mobilization and mass organization. According to Capéran (v.1 1960:257–8), "If [the church] had created, in Paris, the central committee of information and struggle that the *Univers* advocated, then a real lay movement of militant Catholic action would have been organized against the laicization of schools."

The strategy of the French church is best described as prudent.[6] "To the attacks against us let's oppose fervent prayers rather than untimely remonstrations," said the archbishop of Albi in 1881 (quoted in Faury 1980:128). The same bishop, in his pastoral letter of 1883, argued that it was pointless to rise up against the 1882 law and asked his clergy to respect it and show prudence (Faury 1980:142). Observers such as the Belgian bishops were well aware that the French episcopate did nothing to respond to the anticlerical attack (Becqué v.2 1956:365). Naturally, lay Catholics responded accordingly: "The emotion of Catholic opinion was sporadic" (Lapierre and Levillain 1992:27); "the momentum of the first days, so fertile in promises, was paralyzed" (Capéran v.2 1960:237). By the summer of 1882 the initial agitation had waned. As the Republican *Journal des Débats* pointed out in September 1882, the "crusade that started in the month of April is now exhausted. . . . It has ended like all crusades with a shining lack of success" (Capéran v.2 1960:224).

In contrast to the church, the Right attempted forcefully to turn the anticlerical attack into a political issue. For Monarchists, notes Dansette (v.2 1961:45), "it was no longer a question of safeguarding religious interests, but one of achieving political success." According to Gadille (v.2 1967:180) "This neo-legitimist opposition to the policy of conciliation was expressed then in a form that was very similar to a frontal attack against episcopal authority." But Conservatives failed to mobilize the faithful because they had no mass organization of their own, and the church reacted strongly against their appeals. In 1883, the archbishop of Paris (quoted in Gadille v.2 1967:229) reasserted the church's moderate stand, arguing that "our patience will leave to our adversaries the time to be enlightened; maybe it will inspire in them the desire to render us justice."

Accounting for the Response of the Church

This surprising attitude of the church is even more perplexing because it got nothing for its conciliatory attitude.[7] Capéran (v.2 1960:210) argues that the church opted against forming a central lay Catholic committee because of its aversion to letting lay Catholics take over the struggle. This aversion

[6] "Prudence" was an oft-used term by the episcopate. The archbishop of Paris argued in 1880 that the prudent defensive was the best tactic because it was the only possible and useful one; in 1872 Cardinal Mathieu (quoted in Gadille 1967, v.1:338, v.2:100, 256) condemned various lay initiatives as lacking prudence.

[7] A compromise between the church and Republicans was almost reached in 1880, but it eventually failed when both sides came under intense attack from their own radical wings.

was constant in all six churches, yet five of them decided to form lay mass organizations. Other authors explain the attitude of the French church by pointing to its risk calculations: the church decided against fighting after a careful calculation of the costs and benefits of resistance (Levillain 1992:179). Resistance would raise the stakes and provoke a stronger anticlerical attack so it made more sense to avoid fighting (Mayeur 1973:102, 112; Dansette v.2 1961:51). Although this explanation makes sense, it begs the question: why was the French church's appraisal of the risks of fighting so different from that of the other churches?

Most (implicit) answers to this question focus on factors exogenous to the church. It is argued, for instance, that the capability of the Republicans to harm the church and persecute its members deterred the church from resisting (Gadille v.2 1967:246). The introduction of a comparative perspective undermines this argument. Bismarck was stronger than the French Republicans, and his persecution of the church was more severe. Yet the German Catholic church opted for resistance. Furthermore, the Republican regime in France was unstable, the Right was still a credible contender for power, and elections were competitive. Another line of argument uses a modernization argument to explain internal divisions among Catholics. According to Malcolm Partin (1969:268–69): "The French church was just beginning to adjust to the exigencies of existing and functioning in modern industrial society at the turn of the century. This adjustment had not been completed when the anticlerical campaign began, and the church was forced to respond to this renewed secular attack upon its position while it was torn by internal quarrels and dissension. French Catholicism was consequently unable to counter the anticlerical attack in any really effective manner."

Levels of industrialization varied across countries in a way that does not fit any clear pattern, however, and the causal link between modernization and division is very tenuous, to say the least. Moreover, before the formal recognition of the Republic by the church in 1892, French Catholics were ideologically united in their support of the monarchy (although split among various political parties).

Institutional and organizational variables also fail to provide the answer: the role of the Vatican,[8] the nature of the state,[9] the nature of the relations

[8] The Vatican appears to have encouraged the French church to follow a conciliatory attitude out of fear that confrontation might provoke worse damage to the church (Mayeur 1973:112; Latreille et al. 1979:468; Ozouf 1963:84). Still, the position of the Vatican was ambivalent. An August 1882 letter from the pope to the archbishop of Paris appeared to encourage resistance (Capéran v.2 1960:222–23). Furthermore, the Vatican never required that the French church refrain from mass organization, and Vatican advice (as opposed to binding directives) could be sidestepped, which is what the Belgian church did when it ignored the Vatican's advice to follow a moderate and prudent course of action with regard to the 1882 law.

[9] It is argued that the creation of independent church-operated schools was more difficult in France than in Belgium because of the centralized nature of the French state (Capéran v.2

between state and church,[10] the nature of anticlerical legislation,[11] and its severity,[12] cannot account for the response of the church. Finally, internal divisions racked most Catholic churches. For instance, there were "fierce" divisions between Belgian Catholics (Remy and Voyé 1985:16; Pluymers 1984). A final argument is that French Catholicism was too weak to sustain a strategy of resistance. As Dansette (v.2 1961:51–52) tells it:

> In *L'Univers,* and legitimist organs like *La Gazette de France,* French Catholic extremists preached a similar crusade of disobedience. The general attitude, however, was not the same in France as in Belgium. In France, there were many more people who were indifferent and more who were inclined to resist clerical interference. French Catholics, on the other hand, were less enthusiastic and less well disciplined than their Belgian coreligionists. . . . Resistance would no doubt have ended in fiasco, the only result of which would have been to stimulate a strong anticlerical reaction.

Though plausible, this answer is incomplete. Why were the French Catholics "less enthusiastic and less well disciplined than their Belgian coreligionists"? Why were they, as Bessières (1924:104) puts it, dominated by a spirit of "chronic timidity" and "defeatism" that "paralyze[d] the best initiatives"? In other words, why were they not mobilizable for the defense of the church? A first answer stresses again the decline of religiosity in France: the French were indifferent about religion, and Catholics "were in a minority" (Sedgwick 1963:90; Ameye 1963:49). As Bishop Montanini argued, the faith in France was not strong enough to sustain resistance (Lapierre and Levillain 1992:63). As I argued above, however, empirical evidence does not support the claim of a secular spread of religious indifference in France during this period, and the link between religious practice and mass mobilization is

---

1960:199). The public school diploma became a requirement and the equivalence of the private school diplomas was abolished. Still, there were additional ways of fighting besides expanding private schools. For example, the church could have undermined the 1882 law by ordering the members of the congregations who staffed most public schools to strike. Conversely, if it was easier for the Belgian church initially to develop its own schools, it was also impossible to keep them going in the long run without the financial support that only the state could provide.

[10] For instance, the German church was controlled by the state as much as the French church (Spohn 1991:113; Evans 1982:256–57).

[11] The fact that the first significant measures affected only religious orders certainly helped the church decide against fighting (Lapierre and Levillain 1992:27), but this argument cannot explain the position of the church with respect to the Ferry laws.

[12] The Belgian education law was far less severe than the French one (Dansette v.2 1961:51; Capéran, v.2 1960:192) and there was less persecution against the church in Italy than in France (Binchy 1941:46). Yet both the Belgian and the Italian churches opted for resistance. On the other side, "nowhere in Europe was the struggle between church and state fought as vigorously as in the German Empire of 1871" (Lill 1981:26). Yet the German church fought back.

theoretically tenuous. In fact, various indicators suggest that the political mobilization of Catholics in Italy, Germany, and Belgium coincided with a decline of religious practice. Data from Italy indicate that the recruitment of priests declined sharply between 1881 and 1911.[13] Likewise, Richard Evans (1982:281–84) reports a significant decline of religious practice in Germany at the beginning of the twentieth century, and Aubert (1975:113), Léon de Saint-Moulin (1967), Jacques Laury (1964), and François Houtart (1953) report that during the late nineteenth century Belgium experienced a substantial decline both in the number of priests and the rates of religious practice —a decline reaching significant levels. Conversely, the revival of Catholicism in France during the second half of the nineteenth century certainly reinforced the intensity of French Catholics' faith, as witnessed by the huge pilgrimages of the 1870s (Hilaire 1977:393; Corbin v.1 1975:685–88). Furthermore, there were still more than enough Catholics available to participate in a determined and organized resistance movement. The initiation of collective action requires determined minorities rather than majorities (Olson 1971). Indeed, the problem of collective action was solved in the five other cases by the church, which used its organizational resources to generate mobilization and sustain strategies of resistance. In France, on the contrary, Catholics failed to act as a compact group and were thus electorally ineffective (Boutry and Michel 1992:676). Rather than ideological division, the problem was "lack of union and discipline" among French Catholics (Bessières 1924:104). If French Catholics remained politically divided and undisciplined it is because they were not organized by the church.

The Absence of the Organizational Strategy in France

The most striking difference between France and the five other countries is that in the former no mass Catholic movement emerged until well after the end of the state-church conflict. Indeed, the first mass Catholic organization for men was not formed until 1924. As a result, Catholics remained "condemned to act in an isolated way" (Janvier in Viance 1930:vii). The cumulative effect of the absence of organization, according to an observer (Viance 1930:15), was to push Catholics (from 1875 to 1910) into a state of "sleepy passivity that cost them dearly."

The absence of Catholic mass organization in France during the nineteenth century is a well-established historical fact (Cholvy and Hilaire 1986; Köhler

[13] The decline was both absolute (the number of priests fell from 91,205 in 1881 to 75,795 in 1911) and relative (the proportion of priests per 1,000 people fell from 2.89 to 1.87)(Brunetta 1991:436).

1981; Mayeur 1980; Bessières 1924). It is reported by both contemporary participants and observers and modern historians, national and regional alike.[14] Particularly striking is that France lacked massed organization almost everywhere, irrespective of regional variation in religiosity. Philippe Levillain (1982:50) notes that even the term "Catholic movement" is absent from the French literature on the Catholic church.

There were some attempts to form lay mass organizations, but they consistently failed because they originated from individual and isolated initiatives. The few Catholic associations formed until the mid-1890s, such as parish youth clubs, were the result of the action of isolated priests rather than the leadership of the church, which, when not openly hostile, remained totally unconcerned about them (Chaline 1981:280). No youth organization was formed until 1886 (Molette 1968:18). Albert de Mun's attempt to organize workers never took off. The Société d'éducation et de l'enseignement, never developed grass-roots appeal.[15] Although the impressive pilgrimages of the 1870s demonstrated the mobilizational potential of the church, they created among Catholics a false impression that Catholicism was in itself strong (Ozouf 1963:40–43). In reality, however, even the committees formed to organize these pilgrimages were, in the words of Gadille (v.2 1967:260), a "brilliant facade" that created an illusion of power. Prefectoral investigations reached consistently negative conclusions about their influence. It is indicative of the situation in France that the most powerful Catholic organization

[14] For instance, Gadille (v.2 1967:115–16) reports that prefectoral reports written in 1880 concluded that lay Catholic associations were too weak and represented no threat to the Republican regime. For evidence on the national level see Partin 1969:53, Rémond 1964:172, Barral 1962:260, and Bessières 1924:105–7. On the regional level see Barral 1962:262–65 for Isère, Corbin v.1 1975:689, 692 for the Limousin, Hilaire 1977:662 for the Nord and Pas-de-Calais, and Faury 1980:316 for the Tarn. Although one author (Hilaire) devotes about one thousand pages to the detailed analysis of Catholicism and the church in the Nord and Pas-de-Calais regions, he has extremely little to say about Catholic lay organizations before the 1890s.

[15] A first attempt by the priest François Picard to create (1871) Catholic committees and eventually a Catholic Union by turning charitable organizations into political ones failed. Out of sixty-seven comités catholiques formed, most had an ephemeral existence. Only about fifteen were active in 1880 and ten during the 1890s (Gadille v.1 1967:243; v.2 1967:115–16; Bessières 1924:74). The ACJF, formed in 1886, was very weak throughout the 1890s and was composed mainly of students. It started to grow after 1900, but students remained its backbone. In 1905 it claimed 60,000 members and in 1914 140,000. According to the definitive work on this organization (Molette 1968:446, 448) the ACJF started acquiring a "national standing and a regional implantation" only after 1900; it "obtained its place within the Catholic opinion" after 1907. Albert de Mun's and the Count de la Tour du Pin's Cercles d'ouvriers catholiques were a loose paternalistic network of associations targeted to workers but headed mostly by employers. They failed to attract many workers (Anderson 1974:30; Barral 1962:261; Latreille et al. 1962:443) even in Catholic regions such as Bretagne and Nord–Pas-de-Calais (Delumeau 1979:277; Hilaire 1977:645). Membership never exceeded 60,000 (Martin 1978:62), and after 1880 the circles declined and finally were absorbed in 1905 by the ACJF.

during the 1890s was a religious order, the Assumptionists.[16] Precious time was thus lost when the Republicans were still weak and divided (Vigier 1972:14–15, 19).

As a result, mass organization was missing when the second anticlerical wave was launched in 1899. The usual individual appeals for organization were then made again, but the only organizational effort was the creation of the League of French Women, "which collapsed before it advanced beyond the conceptual stage" (Partin 1969:89). As Dansette (v.2 1961:136) puts it, when the twentieth century opened, "the *Oeuvre des cercles* was moribund," and the Catholic youth ACJF and various Catholic unions "were merely ticking over. Among artisans, the attempts to form popular banks did not succeed." The fruits of the activity of lay Catholic organizers—"newspapers and groups—were all ephemeral" (Raymond-Laurent 1966:14), and "most Catholic groups were not organized for effective political pressure on the government, but only for vague 'social action' " (Bosworth 1962:28). As Poulat (1977:130) concludes, the "popular dimension" of Catholicism was missing in France, where there were "men and ideas, originality and priests-workers, but with the exception of some outbursts, Catholicism never took the form of a mass movement capable of weighing upon the destinies of the nation or of taking these destinies in its hands."

The absence of Catholic mass organization stands in stark contrast to organizational development in the anticlerical camp. By failing to mobilize and organize, the church decreased the entry costs of its competitors. The anticlerical Ligue de l'enseignement, devoted to the promotion of secular educational reforms, boasted 40,000 members in 1906 and 62,944 members in 1917, in 728 sections across the country. The Ligue developed a strong mobilizational capability on a national basis, as shown by its ability to organize two hundred anticlerical conferences in just one Sunday of 1903 (Cholvy and Hilaire 1986:102; Bessières 1924:106). This contrast becomes sharper if one looks at the tremendous Catholic organizational development in the other five countries. Whereas France's was an individually led, decentralized, weak, and incomplete effort at organization, the other countries developed

[16] The Assumptionists published the newpaper *La Croix*, which printed in excess of a hundred regional editions. In 1896 they created a network of lay Catholic committees, called Justice-égalité. These committees constituted "the only organization with enough teeth to give bite" to the Right's electoral campaign in 1898 (Larkin 1974:67). But the Assumptionists' organizational impact was limited because they were not always on good terms with the church, which often regarded them "with distrust" (Gadille v.1 1967:250). Furthermore, the mobilizational capability of a religious order was limited by its very nature because "the act of joining a religious order has always represented a radical break from the local community" (Anderson 1974:124). As a result, the mobilizing capability of religious orders was far inferior to that of the church. Religious orders were poor substitutes for a centralized mass organization under the leadership of the church.

"universal" organizations "embracing all, old and young, men and women, intellectuals and workers" (Tramontin 1981a:342). Their objective was "to coordinate and monopolize all forms of activity for the defense of the pontificate" (Gambasin 1966:307–8). They undertook from very early on to "multiply congresses on the national, regional and diocesan level" so as to increase the number of local Catholic committees (Gambasin 1969:5). Like the Italian Opera, they were "mass and robust organization[s], that coordinate and convey all the forces of Catholics toward the defense of the rights of the Apostolic See and the opposition to the liberal state" (Zerbi 1961:42).

These organizations were so effective because they combined a grass-roots character with a centralized direction and coordination from the episcopate. It is precisely mass organization that generated the "enthusiasm and discipline" that Dansette found missing among French Catholics. The stark contrast between France and the other countries, as well as its fatal consequences, were easily grasped after 1905. Peter Doyle (1986:462) reports that among English Catholics, "much was made of comparisons with the situation abroad. While Catholics in Germany and Belgium had organized themselves and were flourishing, in France this had not been done. As a result, French Catholics had failed to prevent the progress of Freemasonry and anticlericalism, and had awoken to find their position undermined, their schools closed and everything lost."

Accounting for the Absence of Mass Organization

Why wasn't the organizational strategy implemented in France? Why didn't the church proceed to form mass organizations, particularly after the first threats against it, in 1876–1880, or even following the anticlerical attacks? Why did the church fail to "sufficiently and completely understand [the laymen's] role," as the bishop of Dijon recognized belatedly in 1907 (Mayeur 1966:195)? Given the overwhelmingly negative effects of the absence of mass organization, why did the church act in such an apparently irrational way? There are two possible answers: either the church *could not* organize French Catholics, or the church could but *chose not* to organize them. I argue the latter.

The cost of the organizational strategy was no different across the six cases. In other words, the organizational strategy was not a costlier undertaking in France than it was elsewhere. Catholic laymen had proved in the past, even during the French Revolution, their ability to become activists and to fight successfully for the defense of religion by "fusing symbol and action, religion and politics" (Desan 1990:230). Grass-roots action took place. A quasi-experimental situation in the Savoie illustrates this point. Two Catholic committees were formed in the early 1870s in two similar towns in the Savoie, the first in Chambéry and the other in Chablais. The first one got no support or encouragement from the French church so it lapsed and disappeared after some initial activity. The second one, affiliated instead with the dynamic Piusverein of neighboring Switzerland, had a much more active career (Lovie 1963:537–38). There existed in pre-1870 France a vast organizational infrastructure of laymen's confraternities, charities, and even loose social organizations that could have been used as the basis of mass organization (Gibson 1989; Cholvy and Hilaire 1985; Levillain 1982; Faury 1980; Duroselle 1951). Finally, the formation in France of mass organizations by the church was not impeded by structural obstacles.

Socioeconomic factors fail to account for the absence of Catholic mass organization in France.[17] France was less industrialized than Belgium during the 1880s but more so than Italy. Nor was the level of ideological conflict higher in France than it was in Germany or Belgium, as I argued above. The claim that the French church somehow ignored the effectiveness of mass organization has also to be dismissed. In the 1880s, Belgium and Germany provided successful examples for emulation. Furthermore, the importance of organization was stressed by numerous Catholics, from Lamennais, who argued in 1829 (quoted in Poulat 1982:223) that "salvation will come and can come only from the really Catholic party, when it will organize itself," to de Mun, who called in 1885 for the creation of a Catholic party and emphasized the need for organization (Molette 1968:41). It is facile to attribute the absence of mass organization to cultural factors, as a pro-Catholic author (Viance 1930:71) did in 1930: "Let's admit it, the Frenchman, unlike, for example, the Italian lacks a naturally political spirit." But responses based on national cultures do not constitute a satisfactory answer. The absence of mass organization was not the product of a lack of associational skills inherent to the French, any more than the success of mass organization of Catholics in Germany was the product of the innate organizational skills of the Germans.[18] As a Catholic organizer pointed out (Bessières 1924:149), " 'We are Latins,' will say some and, therefore, a race inimical to organization. The Italians are also Latins. And nevertheless, in a few years, organization became a reality for them." To support his argument, Bessières (1924:149) also

[17] According to Ravitch (1990:82), "Social Catholicism in France grew only among a small Catholic élite. It was never able, as in Italy, Germany, or Belgium, to become a mass movement because a truly *popular* Catholicism was lacking in France, and the country was less urban and less industrialized than some of its neighbors."

[18] Lill (1977:74) recognizes that "the fact that Germany was the country of Catholic associationism par excellence is not explained only by the German predisposition for organization and for disciplined coordination of initiatives."

pointed to the partial and belated organizational success of the ACJF in France. In fact, French Catholics successfully organized themselves when the church coordinated and supported their initiatives after 1905.

Two more plausible arguments focus on the institutional history and culture of the French church and the endemic disorganization of French political life. According to the first argument, the concordat (through its so-called organic articles) isolated the bishops from each other and fragmented the political will of the episcopate by requiring state authorization for meetings of bishops above the diocesan level.[19] As a result, and contrary to other churches, the French bishops were unable to meet in a plenary assembly for over a century (they met only in 1905, and the Assembly of Cardinals and Archbishops was established in 1919). There is no doubt that these factors placed considerable constraints on the freedom of the church. There are, however, three limitations to this argument.

First, the reinforcement of the power of the Vatican mitigated the institutional peculiarities of the French church because "the real spokesman for the French Church was the Pope himself" (Bosworth 1962:17). Moreover, the institutional and cultural peculiarities of the French church were limited. The French church did not diverge significantly from other churches with respect to ideology, norms, organization, and state control. For instance, the Italian state, very much like the French one, "retained control over the whole machinery of ecclesiastical life through a complex network of laws" (Einaudi and Goguel 1952:3); and, though the reactionary ideology of the French church and its alliance with the Right has often been emphasized (Ravitch 1990:167; Whyte 1981), it was no different from the posture of the other churches: ultramontanism affected all of them more or less equally.

Second, the extent to which the concordat isolated the French bishops from each other has been exaggerated. Recent research (Dougherty 1994) has decisively challenged this perception by underlining the ability of the bishops to use alternative new means of communication, such as Catholic newspapers, to coordinate their action and act as collective body. In addition, bishops often managed to meet informally (Capéran v.2 1960:200).

Third, this argument could explain the lack of positive action by the church (its inability to form mass organizations), but it cannot explain its negative action (the fact that the church sabotaged and destroyed all organizational efforts). Yet the failure of the attempts made by priests and lay Catholics to

[19] Theoretical support for such arguments is found in Levine (1992), who emphasizes the importance of episcopal norms, hierarchical control, and control over resources, in short, the ideological mind-set and resource base of the local episcopacy, on the development of autonomous lay Catholic movements in contemporary Latin America.

establish a centralized mass Catholic organization was to a large extent caused by the opposition of the church.[20]

The second argument points to the endemic disorganization of French political life, its loose structure of associations, and the absence of centralized mass parties during the Third Republic. This disorganization can be attributed to the organization of French society, institutional constraints, the continuing prevalence of the countryside, and a mode of industrialization based on crafts production—in other words, French exceptionalism[21] (Hoffmann 1963). Indeed, disorganization and division were not the exclusive property of Catholics. Throughout the 1860s and 1870s the Republican party remained decentralized, nonbureaucratic, and localized (Aminzade 1993). As the Republican leader Jules Simon wrote in 1868 (quoted in Aminzade 1993:16), "There are so many parties in France, and so many divisions within parties, that there is no longer a single word in our political language that is perfectly clear." Clearly, structural and institutional factors, such as the revolutionary Le Chapelier law, which restricted combination and thus stifled associational life, constrained the organizational options of all political actors, including the Catholic church. Despite these constraints, there was still room for choice.

First, although the sociostructural point about modernization might hold for economic interests or class, it hardly accounts for the lack of religious mobilization, which is supposedly found in economically less developed environments. Stanley Hoffmann (1963:37) recognizes that the Catholic church was extremely effective in organizing a Catholic agricultural youth movement after 1905.

Second, although the Le Chapelier law had deleterious effects on associational life, it failed to wipe it out. As Tarrow (1994:63) points out: "It is true that the Revolution ended feudalism, destroyed the guilds and passed the Le Chapelier law suppressing association. But corporatism remained in spirit, and often in practice, the language of labor in the regimes that followed. Workers and peasants, masons and notaries retained a strong spirit of association that emerged in their collective action and during every regime crisis."

Indeed, there is evidence of important associational lay Catholic activity

[20] The *cercles* faced, initially at least, the indifference and even hostility of the church (Molette 1968:14; Dansette v.1 1961:342; Chapman 1962:329). The activity and expansion of the ACJF were often obstructed by bishops, who viewed it as a threat to other church-sponsored services (Chaline 1981:123–24; 285–86; Molette 1968:25–26). Molette (1968:479) emphasizes that it is not the bishops' political preferences that explain this hostility, but rather the danger of loss of control represented by the development of the ACJF.

[21] Stanley Hoffmann (1963:11) has argued that French society is characterized by "atomism," a "peculiar associational life," and "individualism." He imputes those characteristics to the "slowness of industrialization and the isolation of agriculture," which led to the "defense of the various interests" being "undertaken through the traditional structures of the notables."

during the nineteenth century (Gibson 1989:58–59). Conversely, there were many institutional impediments to mass organization and centralized political action in countries where strong Catholic movements did develop and grow. In Prussia, for instance, the Law of Association forbade until 1899 the formation of centralized political parties, making German parties "relatively disjointed organizations" even after the law's repeal (Ritter 1990:27).

Third, as Charles Tilly (1986) has shown, though the French tended to act on a local basis and through the medium of local authorities and patrons up to the middle of the nineteenth century, in the second half of the century collective action was no longer local and patronized but national and autonomous. This is confirmed by the work of Maurice Agulhon (1970), who recounts the gradual development of mass politics in the south of France during the second half of the nineteenth century, and Melvin Edelstein (1993), who reports that the high rates of electoral participation during the Third Republic indicate a "nationalization of politics." In other words, not only was the lack of a centralized Catholic mass movement not predicated on some general structural conditions prevailing in France, it was even at odds with the prevailing trends of collective and political action.

Fourth, the focus on general disorganization is not sufficient to explain the attitude of the church. If there was one organization capable of organizing in a disorganized environment, it was the church. Although in the five other cases the church did not invent or introduce political clubs, it was the first to initiate large-scale mass organization, thereby raising the stakes of the electoral game and forcing the other political actors to emulate it. This was the case because the church, with its centralized leadership and national implantation, had a formidable competitive advantage in organization. In addition, early entry in the mobilization market yielded higher returns. Yet, instead of engaging in organization building, the church actively sabotaged promising organizational efforts.

Fifth, numerous studies (particularly of local politics) have shown that first the Republicans and later the Radicals had a head start in mass politics by creating a relatively better organization than the Right or the church, even in regions considered traditionally Catholic.[22] True, Republicans failed to become a mass centralized party, but as Raymond Huard (1982) has shown

[22] Rivet (1979:440) refers to the "lag" of the Right compared to the Left in organization in the Haute-Loire. Armengaud (1961:452–53) describes how Republicans set up local associations and permanent electoral committees in the Est-Aquitain region starting as early as 1870. Likewise, Republicans began organizing in the Bas-Languedoc at the end of the Second Empire, and the years after 1876 saw "an associational expansion without precedent" and a "spectacular progression of republican circles" (Huard 1982:331–32). Moreover, electoral analyses show a correlation between votes for Republican candidates and the presence of Republican organization (Huard 1982:226).

in his study of the Bas-Languedoc, they successfully reached urban and rural masses by creating hundreds of local organizations. In his analysis of the 1871 elections, Jacques Gouault (1954:110–11) contrasts the Monarchist committees, "composed of a small number" of notables, with the Republican ones, "true preparatory electoral assemblies which often assembled several hundreds of people representing the different *cantons* and diverse professional activities of the *département*." In his study of the Haute-Loire, Rivet (1979:421–59) shows that the Right and the church were far behind the Republicans in organization, and Mayeur (1968:109) reports a similar lag in the traditionally Catholic district of Hazebrouck in the north.[23] Besides Republican committees, ancillary organizations such as the Ligue de l'enseignement grew and became increasingly politicized after 1873, acting as "a major arm of the emerging Radical party" (Auspitz 1982:145). When it came to the press, the major instrument of propaganda, the Right lagged behind the Republicans both quantitatively and qualitatively and the gap was widening (Irvine 1989b:64). Overall, the overwhelming Republican political domination of the late nineteenth and early twentieth centuries is an indicator of the Republicans' superior organization.

When Republican efforts stagnated, the Radicals took over. Gérard Baal (1977:261) has shown that a tremendous growth of local committees and other Radical organizations took place, particularly after the official creation of the Radical party in 1901.[24] Furthermore, the extremely successful "Republican discipline" became, after 1881, a substitute for centralized organization: Republican voters united in the second round to support the most successful Republican candidate. This mitigated the lack of centralization and the effects of factionalization and established a de facto unity in the Republican camp when that mattered most[25] (Huard 1982:343–44). This situation was not ignored in Monarchist circles, where it was "the subject of endless discus-

[23] Rivet (1979:433) reports that all the "associations with a well-defined political orientation" belonged to the Left. Republicans began substantial efforts to create a national and centralized organization in the 1830s (Aminzade 1993:29–31). These efforts eventually failed because of state repression but left important traces behind them.

[24] When the Radical party created a national organization, around 1,000 local and regional committees, Masonic lodges, newspapers, and other organizations applied for membership (Kayser 1962:301). Baal (1977:263) found 2,334 Republican and Radical committees and political organizations during the period 1899–1905. For all the shortcomings, there was a "true flourishing" of committees on the Left (Baal 1977:265). The Right was no match for that. It is true that the Radical party remained largely decentralized, with the local and regional organizations of the party successfully preserving their autonomy from the executive committee. At the same time, however, the local committees of the Radical party became increasingly structured and permanent, and the coordination between local associations and central offices improved markedly after 1901 (Berstein v.1 1980:33–34).

[25] As a result of their coordination, Republicans usually did better during the second round than Monarchists.

sions in the 1880s, and the unfavorable comparison with republican organization was a constant theme" (Irvine 1989b:62). According to a Monarchist agent (quoted in Irvine 1989a:37), Monarchists were losing ground because "there was no conservative electoral organization that could match and resist this formidable organization constituted by the coalition of the government and all the factions of the republican party; they are legions, when we have all the trouble in the world to reform the small group of our friends; they have ramifications in every *commune*, when we can just count on the fidelity of our correspondents; they command, they demand, they menace or they promise, when we are reduced to invoke the principles and to appeal to the dedication."

To summarize, even though the French church faced some additional constraints compared to Catholic churches of other countries, the absence of mass Catholic organizations was mostly a result of factors not independent of its will. Past successful electoral mobilization (Jones 1985:7), the phenomenal mobilizational and organizational ability displayed by the church during the mass pilgrimages of the 1870s (Blackbourn 1994:38–39), and the post-1905 organizational effort all indicate that the potential was there. The French church could have created mass organizations but chose not to do so.

If the absence of Catholic mass organization is the key to the absence of a confessional party, and if this absence was the church's choice, then the puzzle is to explain this apparently self-defeating choice. The answer requires a focus on the risk calculations of the church. As I argued in the first chapter, the creation of Catholic mass organizations was perceived as a risky venture by the church everywhere and was undertaken only as an extreme defensive measure. The model of party formation laid out in the first chapter posits that the church selects the organizational strategy O only when mass organization is perceived as being significantly better at preserving church influence than the conciliatory strategy C ($i_O > i_C$). The French church decided against implementing the organizational strategy because the influence it would obtain from it was not expected significantly to exceed the influence generated by the conciliatory strategy (see Figure 3). In other words, the cost of the organizational strategy was not justified by its expected benefits. But why was this the case in France?

The answer is that in France, the issue of the regime decisively altered the opportunity costs of the church. This was the case because of two cleavage overlaps: the main cleavage in the party system was a regime cleavage, which, in turn, overlapped with the state-church cleavage. First, the distinction between Right and Left was built around the issue of the regime: republic versus monarchy. As a result, the French state under the Third Republic became highly partisan, indistinguishable from the Republicans: as Goguel (1958:48) puts it, "The ideology, the program, the temperament of the Left

Figure 3. Costs and benefits of the church's strategies in France (t_1)

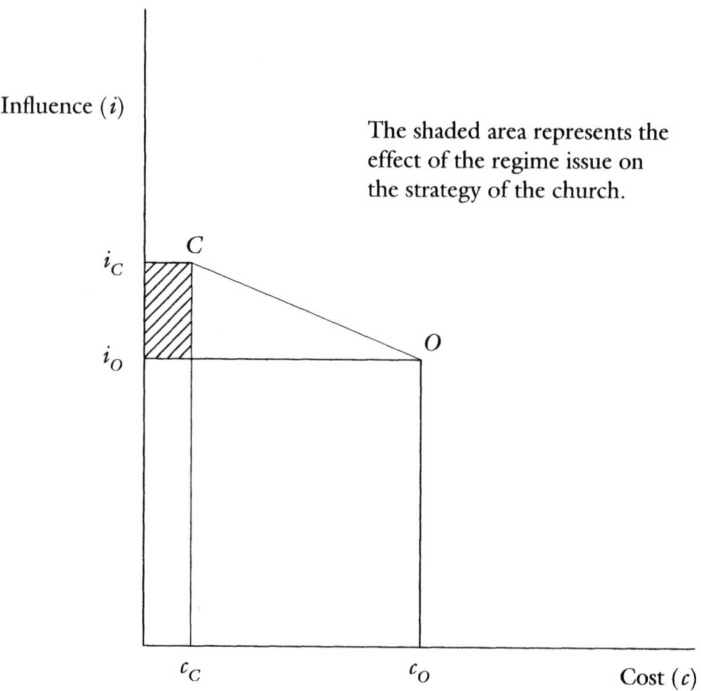

Strategies C : Compromise (conciliatory) strategy
O : Organizational strategy

Costs c_C : cost of C
c_O : cost of O

Influence i_C : influence generated by C
i_O : influence generated by O

became bound up with the institutions and the state itself." Second, the Republican regime made anticlericalism its central concern: "Create the *école laïque* is also to create the Republic," argued the Republicans (Mayeur 1973:113). As the Republican leader Louis Barthou argued in 1910 (quoted in Goguel 1958:53), "The great and just laws that made the *école laïque,* suppressed congregationalist education, and separated the church and the state are the criteria with which republicans recognize each other." Thus republicanism and anticlericalism quickly became indissolubly linked. To quote the French historian Maurice Agulhon (1981:182), "The Republic was at the same time a new sovereign power set up against real monarchs; virtually a new cult opposed to established religion, and a popular force against the dominant powers in society." As a result, it became obvious to all that an eventual Conservative political domination would lead to the restoration of the monarchy and would make anticlericalism impossible by simultaneously restoring "the legitimate pretender and the social order of the Syllabus" (Latreille et al. 1962:440).[26]

Third, contrary to the other countries, the prospects for state clericalism, through the replacement of the republic (the anticlerical regime) by the monarchy (the pro-clerical regime), were high. When the church faced the first threats against its influence in 1876 and the first wave of the anticlerical attack in 1879, the viability of the Republican regime was universally questioned. To begin with, the Republic was born by default after the French defeat in its war with Germany and the collapse of the Second Empire. For the Conservative politicians who had assembled at Bordeaux to provide France with a new form of government, the Republic was a temporary solution chosen as "the least disagreeable among several unwelcome choices" (Partin 1969:3). In fact, Monarchists saw the Republic only as a regime of transition leading to a restored monarchy (Goguel 1958:41–42). Nobody imagined that this constitution would last (Chevalier and Conac 1991:255). Moreover, the Republic suffered from its history: it was a regime associated at best with the instability of the Second Republic and at worst with the Jacobinist terror of the First Republic. Finally, the Republic was viewed as a regime theoretically incompatible with large countries, fit only for microstates[27] (Dupeux 1991:119–20). As Irvine (1989b:21) puts it, "When France became a republic in 1870 there was good reason to believe that the new regime would last no longer than the two previous republics." As a result, and "for a long time," as Pierre Birnbaum (1993:9) points out, "the Republic appeared fragile, uncertain, almost foreign to the national identity, having ensured no legitimacy." The belief that the Republic was doomed (and the restoration of the monarchy most likely) persisted throughout the 1880s.[28]

[26] The association of Catholicism with the Right first became naturalized during the French Revolution (Gibson 1989:53). For Catholics, the restoration of the monarchy came to be equated to the arrival of a "new Constantine" who would free them from persecution (Mayeur 1968:34). The monarchy, it was thought, would protect the church from the danger of anticlerical legislation, even in a parliamentary regime with universal suffrage. As Irvine (1989a:35) points out: "In his celebrated manifesto of 1887, the Count of Paris formally embraced universal manhood suffrage but simultaneously rejected the principle of responsible government. Even his acceptance of universal suffrage was disingenuous since his private drafts of the constitution of a restored monarchy plainly showed that he intended to disenfranchise large numbers of Frenchmen."

[27] The only republics in Europe at that time were Switzerland, Andorra, and San Marino.

[28] The first attempt to restore the monarchy failed in 1871 after the legitimist candidate to the throne, Count Chambord, issued a manifesto that was judged too extreme. A second

This belief was reinforced by two additional factors: the Third Republic's chronic political instability[29] and the history of regime duration in France, which displayed regularly short cycles. Every post-1789 regime had a duration of fifteen to eighteen years.[30] When, in the late 1880s, restoration began to fade as a credible option, Boulangism (the vigorous antirepublican populist movement led by General Georges Boulanger) prolonged for a short time the Monarchist hopes.[31]

Sharing the belief that "the Third Republic was not destined to a longer life than its two predecessors" (Partin 1969:21), the church played the restoration card. As Aubert (1975:83) notes, "During the first years of the Third Republic, the majority of the Catholic notables, bishops on top, compromised themselves in clumsy tentatives of monarchical restoration." The first anticlerical wave reinforced this belief by contributing to the creation of a climate of "catastrophism" and "millenarianism," which led "the Catholic opinion [to] expect, with a confidence which for some functioned as political

---

attempt failed in 1873 because of Chambord's insistence on the issue of the flag (he pressed for the old Monarchist white flag). Still, the prospect of a restoration remained "possible and even probable" (Goguel 1958:41). The Monarchist majority in the parliament extended the presidential term of MacMahon to seven years expecting a solution following the death of Chambord, while the failed constitutional coup of 16 May 1877 was an attempt by the Right to block the ascension of Republicans (Bertocci 1978). Hopes persisted even after the electoral successes of the Republicans in the late 1870s: an electoral victory by the Right would lead to restoration. Chambord's death in 1883 reignited the hopes for a monarchical restoration by uniting the various monarchical factions around the Orleanist pretender, the Count of Paris (Irvine 1989a:33). As Joly (1983:311) points out, even though monarchism retreated during the last two decades of the nineteenth century, it still represented a real danger for the Republic.

[29] As late as 1891 the Republic was still seen as unstable. Partin (1969:3) notes that "after some twenty-odd years of existence [the Republic] had offered little evidence that it was destined for a long or honorable life." Likewise, Irvine (1989b:71) reports that "by the late 1880s, the situation of French royalism was desperate but not beyond hope. Royalism remained the largest, most coherent, and most powerful alternative to the republican regime. . . . The sins of the regime had weakened the republican loyalty of a critical segment of the voters, and under the right circumstances an antirepublican majority was conceivable." Financial scandals in the early 1890s (the Wilson and Panama scandals), as well as ministerial instability, indicated that the Republic could still be expected to fall one way or another.

[30] The Consulat and Empire lasted for fifteen years, and so did the Restoration. The July monarchy had a duration of eighteen years, the same as the Second Empire that followed. At the time of the Boulanger affair the Republic had lasted for seventeen years (Rémond 1982:122).

[31] After the Count of Paris left France in 1886, "the monarchical cause had been dealt a fateful blow" (Osgood 1960:42). But the Boulanger movement provided, from 1886 to 1889, a renewed concrete possibility of the overthrow of the Republic. Right and church alike saw in Boulanger and his vigorous mass populist movement the instrument needed to topple the Republicans (Lapierre and Levillain 1992:35; Irvine 1989a:46). They funded and supported Boulanger because, as de Mun (quoted in Irvine 1989b:162) pointed out, "the monarchist party existed only among the elite, with no roots among the masses." Initially electorally successful, Boulanger failed to lead a coup against the Republic when the opportunity opened up in January 1889, bitterly deceiving his Monarchist supporters and thwarting their hopes.

sense, the double miracle that would simultaneously restore the pope and the king" (Rémond 1982:133). Only after the Boulanger disaster in 1891 did the hope of restoration vanish. In sum, restoration had looked certain until 1876, an extremely good bet until January 1879, and a serious possibility until roughly 1891. This is why the church bet on restoration until 1891, rather than implement the organizational strategy. To use Jean-Pie Lapierre and Philippe Levillain's (1992:33) felicitous phrase, during this period, "dynastic legitimacy" prevailed for the French church over "the exercise of the suffrage."

To summarize, the church's opportunity costs were affected by the probability of an overthrow of the Republic. Since the Republic was equated with anticlericalism and its fall was perceived as very likely, it made more sense for the church to wait on the side for the collapse of the Republic than to engage in a costly and risky active resistance and organization building. This point was clearly made by the abbé Lemire, who publicly accused the church in 1888 of "accepting without grumbling the blows to its freedom . . . in the hope that the regime [*pouvoir*] will change" (quoted in Mayeur 1968:56).

It is important to show how the situation in France was, in this respect, different from that prevailing in the other five countries. In the latter, the regimes associated with anticlerical attacks were rock-solid. No hope existed for their overthrow and the advent of an openly pro-clerical regime. As in France, Catholics in Italy and Germany resented and rejected the prevailing regimes, but military defeat had left them with no hope that they would be overthrown.[32] In Belgium, the Netherlands (where Catholics were a minority), and Austria, Catholics did not question their regimes, but their emperor and kings showed no willingness to block the Liberal anticlerical attacks nor did they consider overthrowing the Liberals. On the contrary, they proved willing to collaborate with them (see Chapter 4). As a result, the church could expect no salvation through monarchy. Thus in both instances (and contrary to France) there was a lack of alternative institutional options, which made the costs of the organizational strategy acceptable for the five churches, whereas the availability of such an option in France made the organizational strategy there unacceptably costly.

The Effects of the Absence of Organization

The absence of Catholic mass organization in France accounts cumulatively for the failure of a confessional party to emerge there. First, it impeded the emergence and neutralized the action of actors central in the process of

[32] In Italy, Catholic forces were militarily defeated in 1862 and 1870; the military defeat of Austria by Prussia in 1866 amounted to a defeat of German Catholicism. The subsequent unification of Germany turned Catholics into a minority.

confessional party formation. Second, it made the church politically ineffective. And third, it contributed to the successive electoral defeats of the Right.

The absence of the organizational strategy in France undermined the emergence and limited the influence of the two actors necessary for the formation of a confessional party: the militant lower clergy and the lay Catholic activists. Without mass organization, no distinct Catholic political identity and no collective action based on this identity could emerge because the potential agents of this identity remained restrained and dispersed.

The lower clergy in France were as potentially militant as those elsewhere in Europe. Gadille (v.2 1967:223) notes their "aggressive ardor," and Dansette (v.2 1961:19) confirms that the "pugnacious outlook, exceptional in the episcopate, became the rule with the lower clergy." In fact, the lower clergy proved very effective at electoral mobilization after 1848 (Jones 1985:5; Faury 1980:25; Dansette v.2 1961:21), while between 1850 and 1880 the social influence of rural priests reached its apex (Hilaire 1977:306). As elsewhere, the electoral activity of priests was usually discouraged by the episcopate (Dansette v.1 1961:271), and a cleavage formed between the hierarchy and the rural priests (Faury 1980:293). Sometimes bishops went so far as the bishop of Quimper, who in 1902 accused the politically active abbé Hippolyte Gayraud of encouraging "clerical insubordination and class conflict in the region" (Ford 1987:121).

Priests quickly realized what a handicap the lack of mass organization was and took organizational initiatives in numerous regions—but without any coordination. They even attempted to create a Catholic party.[33] The initiatives taken by members of the lower clergy were doomed to failure because, at best, they lacked church support and coordination and, at worst, they had to face the open hostility of the church (Raymond-Laurent 1966:19–20;

[33] In 1882 the *chanoine* Lémann formed in Reims the Alliance catholique; in Isère, the abbé France created in 1897 an organization called Action électorale catholique, intended to be electorally oriented and mass based, using "recruiting sergeants" to attract "humble people with faith" (Barral 1962:331). The abbé France argued that, once organized, "the Catholics would rapidly progress and would soon impose themselves, as they did in Germany and Belgium" (Barral 1962:332). The role of priests would have been central because as the same abbé pointed out, "without action from the priest, how could this action remain Catholic?" (Barral 1962:331). Another priest, the abbé Lemire, was central in these efforts. In 1893, he was elected to the parliament, "in the teeth of his Archbishop's disapproval," an act that became "a symbol of the revolt of the lower clergy against the ecclesiastical hierarchy and the great Catholic notables" (McManners 1972:95). Lemire led a group of priests (known as the *abbés démocrates*) who organized clerical congresses in 1896 and 1900. He also participated in an attempt to form a Christian Democratic party in the late 1890s, an attempt that ended in "complete failure" (Raymond-Laurent 1966:19). Lemire had to face the open hostility of his bishop, who attempted without success to prevent, and then undermine, his candidacy for the parliament. Lemire was suspended from his priestly functions in 1914. Numerous other priests were also silenced by the church (Arnal 1985:54–59).

Rémond 1964:viii). The absence of mass organization made church repression of independent lower clergy action easier and more effective; it also made the priests vulnerable to persecution from the hostile Republican administration, in contrast to Germany, where mass organization helped shield priests against the persecution of the Kulturkampf.

The mass of lay Catholics was initially as passive as in the other five countries. Contrary to these countries, however, French lay Catholics remained passive. Lay Catholic activists, a product of mass organization, did not emerge in France until very late. A survey of the "clerical" world around the 1880s by Jean Faury (1980:285–301) yields only three actors: the clergy, the clerical notables of mainly legitimist aristocratic extraction, and the *hommes d'oeuvres,* lay Catholic notables running the charities of the church. These *hommes d'oeuvres* were disinclined to political action and the vigorous promotion of their faith (Hilaire 1977:723). Recognizable primarily for their piety and devotion, they were a far cry from politically active Catholic militants (Faury 1980:299).

Yet French Catholics were famous around Europe for their intellectual qualities (Gramsci 1995:105) and took a great number of organizational initiatives. Montalembert's and de Mun's efforts (in the 1840s and 1880s respectively) failed because of the church's reaction. In a letter sent to the pope in 1883, the bishop of Nancy denounced "the radical Catholics who attack the authority of the clergy, the bishops and the pope, who want to put the laymen in the position of the hierarchy, and who, consequently, attack the basis of the church's constitution" (quoted in Gadille v.2 1967:246). As a result, the church gradually reinforced its control over the laymen and systematically cracked down on every attempt at autonomous political action. As Gadille (v.2 1967:263) notes, the episcopate "gradually took over the government of church matters, in a more coordinated way from diocese to diocese, imposing on itself and on its auxiliaries, clerics and lay, an increasingly tight 'discipline.' " The absence of mass organization greatly facilitated this trend.

Although the church's decision not to form a mass organization made control over its members very effective, it badly hurt its mobilizational capability. Without mass organization, Catholics remained both undermobilized and divided—hence politically ineffective. In short, they never constituted a force to be reckoned with in politics.

As Mayeur (1973:102) puts it, "With the exception of some *départements,* the Catholic right did not succeed in mobilizing the masses against the *laicité* policy." The result was a "mass of Catholic people relatively passive, even indifferent, with the exception of some regions" (Le Béguec and Prévotat 1992:232). As a result, Catholic support for Monarchist candidates declined with every new defeat (Irvine 1989b:55). As the papal nuncio (quoted in

Bosworth 1962:27) concluded in one of his letters, "political action by Catholics is zero." When the church mobilized in 1861 to protect the temporal power of the pope, Catholics followed timidly (Dansette v.1 1961:289). Fifty years later, in 1906, when the archbishop of Paris was forced to leave his episcopal palace, the abbé Frémont (quoted in Lapierre and Levillain 1992:63) noted that "about 5,000 people escorted the cardinal and sang *cantiques*, a quite mediocre number for Paris. . . . The indifference of the population is general." Lapierre and Levillain (1992:63) confirm that "the general indifference of the Catholic masses surprised the episcopate and the most fanatic adversaries of the separation. Of course, the [church's] intellectual elite attacked without interruption the Freemasons' anticlericalism, but the mass of the faithful did not react at all." Besides passivity and undermobilization, the lack of mass organization had an additional pernicious effect. Political division of Catholics persisted and grew: Catholics never formed a unified political bloc (Le Béguec and Prévotat 1992:281; Boutry and Michel 1992:676). This situation eventually led numerous lay Catholics to seek alternative means of political action and allies away from Catholicism (Barral 1962:332).

This disunion, which amounted to the political neutralization of Catholics, is singled out as a major reason behind the lack of political effectiveness of the church and its political allies (Bosworth 1962:25–26). As de Mun (quoted in Martin 1970:677) summed up in 1903, "We are persuaded that the multiplicity of parties, [and] the dispersion of resources and of efforts which is its consequence, is one of the principal causes of the weakness of the conservatives." Still, the political division of Catholics was far from insurmountable. Although it was generated by factors exogenous to the church (such as the regime issue), it persisted and grew because of the church's choices. Only the encapsulation of French Catholics by a mass organization could have induced the discipline and unity necessary for effective political action. Indeed, it was the vigorous intervention of the church through its organizational strategy that prevented the translation of the ideological disunity of Belgian Catholics into political division and organizational incapacity (Soete 1986:48–49). Without organization and unity, church interventions in the electoral field were, as Gadille concludes (v.2 1967:269), "doomed to fail."

The French Right kept losing elections. As Dansette (v.2 1961:436) notes, "The conservative parties to which [Catholics] entrusted the religious destinies of the country suffered eleven electoral defeats in a space of twenty-eight years during the period between 1876 and 1914." Losing elections was not only bad in itself; it also demonstrated to Republicans that anticlericalism was paying off and provided an added and significant incentive for stepping up the attacks against the church. Moreover, this string of electoral failures acted as a self-fulfilling prophecy and reinforced the spirit of fatalism that pervaded the church. The French bishops sank into an attitude of resignation. The bishop of Avignon argued in 1883 (quoted in Gadille v.2 1967:246) that "the triumphs of religion are not necessarily essential . . . since God himself lets us be subjected to the influence of the events"; he went on to use the three centuries of Catacombs as the most fitting metaphor for his times.

Why did the Right suffer such crushing defeats? The answer hinges to a large extent on the electoral behavior of the peasants. France was a predominantly rural country, and peasants constituted the main pool of potential supporters of pro-Catholic parties. Why, then, did the majority of the peasantry support the Republicans? This is one of the central debates of French history and the object of considerable controversy.[34] Surprisingly, the focus of this debate has been more on how the Republic won the peasants than how the Right, and especially the church, lost them.

Once more, dechristianization has been cited for the inability of the French Right to win elections under the Third Republic. Besides being empirically flawed, this argument assumes a direct translation of individual religious beliefs into political behavior, in other words, of the Catholic religious identity into a Catholic political identity. Although religious practice and support for the Right often correlated, they did not necessarily coincide. A review of relevant studies concludes that "the relationship between religion and politics cannot be so easily reduced to equating religious fervor with the political domination of the Right and religious indifference with the preponderance of the Left" (Ford 1987:231–32).

The problem was not dearth of religiosity but rather the failure of religiosity to translate into political support for the Right. The preservation (even growth) of religious practice in the 1880s coincided with a gradual shift of the electorate toward Republicanism. Electoral data indicate that in numerous regions (with varying levels of religious practice) practicing Catholics voted for Republicans rather than right-wing candidates (Faury 1980:489; Hilaire 1977; Loubère 1974:136). For example, in the Ille-et-Vilaine, districts where religious practice reached 90 percent voted for Republican candidates at the same rate (Lagrée 1980:412). The village priest of St. André in the Tarn noted in 1901 that although 90 percent of the village men went to church for Easter and all came to church on Sunday, three-fourths of them voted for the Radicals (Faury 1980:231). Numerous prefects reported that "the population was at once devoted to religious practice and [politically] anticlerical as well" (McManners 1972:11).

The church realized what was happening. The archbishop of Rennes com-

[34] This literature has focused on the economic integration of peasants, as well as the role of the Republic in providing benefits to agriculture. The major initial disagreement concerns the timing of the peasant conversion to Republicanism with some authors pointing to the Second Republic and others to the Third (see Weber 1991; Judt 1979; Corbin 1975; Agulhon 1970; Wright 1964; Vigier 1963). Weber (1976:493) argues that the French peasants became fully politicized only in the "two-score years on either side of 1900."

plained in 1881 that in an area of his diocese, "the people rise *en masse* in demonstrations competing for the honour of manifesting . . . their religious convictions, but if tomorrow they are called to the ballot box they will vote for candidates hostile to religion" (McManners 1972:11). Eleven years later nothing had changed. A French bishop complained to Cardinal Mariano Rampolla that though his rural diocese was "one of those where the Catholic consciousness has been best conserved," on election Sunday people went from the church, "where they assisted piously in the mass," to the electoral booth, "where they gave their vote to the candidates who are the least favorable to religion" (quoted in Vismara Chiappa 1982:228). The crucial question, then, is asked by Faury (1980:489–90): "Why did large fractions of the rural or urban population attached to Catholicism prefer to follow the Republicans in politics —who often were Freemasons or freethinkers—rather than the traditional [political] structures? . . . Why didn't the clergy succeed in rallying all Catholics to its positions? Why was [the clergy] powerless in checking the mounting flood of anticlericalism on the political level, while it managed to limit the diffusion in depth of [anticlericalism's] ideology and practice?"

In the words of Mgr. Isoard (quoted in Vismara Chiappa 1982:232), why wasn't the average French Catholic behaving politically as a *"homo religiosus"*? Institutional factors fail to provide an answer to this question: electoral rules were very similar in France and Germany. Yet suffrage rules and parliamentary sovereignty varied considerably within the group of countries in which successful mass Catholic organizations emerged.[35] The material benefits that the Republic provided to peasants were undeniably a major factor (Weber 1991:188), but only well into the 1880s. A more plausible answer focuses on the monarchy as an issue. Important segments of the rural electorate supported the Republicans for fear that a return of the monarchy would bring back feudal rights and the abhorred feudal tax *dîme*. This answer is not sufficient, however. The Right, after all, had fought and won elections under universal suffrage before the 1880s. The crucial problem for the Right was clearly one of organization rather than issues: "Mass politics—in the form of political democracy—presented an insoluble problem for French royalists" (Irvine 1989a:33). According to Irvine (1989a:35–36):

> Political platforms do not win elections and even a successful outward transformation would not have solved the monarchist dilemma. [Royalists] needed above all an effective political organization. This became dramatically apparent only in the 1880s. Political organization is the weapon of the weak and royalists had initially seen no need for it. Until the 1870s royalists

[35] For instance, Germany and Austria had limited parliamentary sovereignty, while the Netherlands, Belgium, and Italy were full-fledged parliamentary democracies.

Table 4. Electoral results and abstention rates in France

Year	Republican seats	Conservative seats	Abstention rate (%)
1876	393	140	26
1877	323	208	19.4
1881	372	88	31.4
1885	383	201	22.4
1889	366	210	23.4
1893	317	93	28.8
1898	254	86	23.9
1902	321	266	20.8
1906	420	190	20.1

Sources: Bon 1978; Lancelot 1968; Charnay 1964; Bomier-Landowski 1951.

and their allies had dominated both the higher and lower administration of French society and it had been republicans who had required an efficient political organization to struggle against the entrenched power of traditional élites. By the mid 1880s the tables had been turned.

The crucial 1881 elections, which followed the first wave of anticlerical legislation, provide an example of the way the Right lost elections. Conservatives fought these elections "in a profound state of division and discouragement" (Goguel 1958:58). They were so badly organized that they failed to field candidates in 252 out of 541 districts (Levillain 1992:180). The results were dismal: "The Right suffered a crushing defeat" (Goguel 1958:55). From 208 deputies in 1877 the Right fell to just 88. Despite pressure from the Right, the church resisted turning anticlericalism into a political issue and supported the Right only in an unsystematic way (Gadille v.2 1967:191–92).

In the few instances when the Right managed to form a unified block, it came close to victory. Despite inadequate church support (Barral 1962:401, 411), the Union des droites almost won the 1885 elections, obtaining 40 percent of the votes. The Right needed only a mere extra 5 percent of the vote to win a parliamentary majority. As Irvine (1989a:33) puts it, "Control of the regime was but a few hundred thousand votes and few score seats away." That the Right came so close to winning in 1885 indicates that its defeats were not structurally predetermined. Irvine (1989a:45–46) points out that "as late as 1885, royalists and their allies held the allegiance of a substantial minority of French voters. It was reasonable to hope that a revitalized image and a modern party structure might convert that minority into a majority, especially in the light of the persistent crises and scandals of the republican regime." A systematic look at electoral turnout is enlightening (see Table 4).

As shown in Table 4, the size of electoral abstention and the performance of the Right vary inversely. The incidence of high abstention rates in traditionally Catholic regions and among Catholic voters is also supported by historical studies[36] (Jones 1988:287; Bon 1978:43; Mayeur 1973:102, 209; McManners 1972:39). This trend is striking because Catholic abstention is unusual both longitudinally and cross sectionally. The findings of electoral research in France show that Catholic turnout rates are generally higher than those of the population at large (Berger 1987:116; Rémond 1965:69–70), whereas the findings of electoral research in Germany indicate a very high rate of turnout among Catholics from 1887 to 1912 (usually higher than 75 percent, and in two elections even higher than 85 percent; in fact, voter turnout in Catholic constituencies initially exceeded that of Protestant ones by about 50 percent)(Ritter 1990:32; Suval 1985:69).

The absence of Conservative party organization was not unique to France. Such organization was absent across all five cases and it also translated into electoral defeats for the Right. Unique to France, however, was the absence of Catholic mass organizations that would have allowed the Right to tap huge reserves of voters. Studies of local politics such as Rivet's work on the Haute-Loire (1979) and Georges Dupeux's work on the Loir-et-Cher (1962) show clearly how harmful was the absence of organization for the Right. As Dupeux (1962:467) puts it, "the Right renounced organization." Mass organization would have been instrumental in mobilizing voters who abstained, minimizing division and enforcing discipline—particularly during the second round of elections—and attracting new voters. Indeed, the electoral system in use, with its small districts and two rounds, penalized the less organized side. For instance, Conservatives once lost nearly sixty seats by margins of fewer than one thousand votes (Irvine 1989a:46). Finally, the emergence of Catholic activists attuned to mass politics would have made a tremendous difference. The example of abbé Lemire is revealing. In 1893, forming an organization from scratch, he ran an electoral campaign of a new kind: whereas traditional Conservative candidates held a few private meetings with local notables, he held as many as six public meetings daily. As a result of this mobilization, electoral participation peaked and he won the seat (Mayeur 1968:12).

When some degree of organization existed (the ALP in 1902), the Right

[36] The department of Ardèche provides a striking illustration of these trends. In 1877, the Right won 41 percent of the votes and the abstention rate was just 17 percent. It was defeated in 1881, getting just 19 percent of the votes with the abstention rate rising to 34 percent but came back in 1885, obtaining 40 percent of the votes while the abstention rate receded to 22 percent. This pattern was repeated in 1888 (24 percent for the Right, 38 percent abstaining) and 1889 (37 percent for the Right, 23 percent abstaining). In 1902 and 1906, voting patterns reflected the mobilization of the Right: 39 percent and 36 percent of the votes with a 24 percent and 23 percent abstention rate, respectively (Siegfried 1949:84, 92).

both mobilized most Catholic voters and expanded its influence beyond its traditional clientele. Likewise, in Belgium, electoral districts that previously had supported Liberals and Conservatives in a balanced fashion became safe Catholic constituencies after the church implemented its participation strategy (Stengers, in Lamberts and Lory 1986:190). A quick focus on Lower Britanny (and particularly the department of Finistère) is revealing as to the political effects of mass organization. Priests and lay Catholics used the strong regional identity as a resource independently to build a local Catholic movement. The development of mass Catholic organization generated popular mobilization against the 1902 laws, which in turn broadened the basis of the Catholic movement and allowed it to survive in the face of church reaction (Ford 1987:159, 163–64). Organization minimized division among Catholics and achieved a dramatic shift in the political orientation of the peasantry to Catholic republicanism (Ford 1987:87). As a result, Catholic activists were able to turn their movement into a local Catholic party, the Féderation des républicains démocrates du Finistère (FRDF), which was instrumental in the formation in 1924 of the Parti démocrate populaire (PDP), a small but "mass-based party with a highly developed and effective political organization" (Ford 1987:228). These events in Lower Brittany suggest that political developments in France could have paralleled those of the five other countries had the organizational strategy been implemented.

Conservatives were aware of the handicaps of failing to organize and "in the 1880s were obsessed by the problem of organization and talked about it incessantly" (Irvine 1989a:37). Yet they could not and did not organize. The local committees that were set up to run electoral campaigns were composed of aristocratic notables hostile to mass organization: "A 'democratic' political organization held little appeal for a socially exclusive caste—the more so if the reluctant increase in royalist political effectiveness meant a corresponding loss of influence for local notables" (Irvine 1989a:39). Conservative candidates often avoided public meetings, holding private meetings instead (Rivet 1979:518). At the same time, they were increasingly unable to meet the skyrocketing costs that modern electoral campaigns entailed (Locke 1974:224–25). As a result, "royalist distrust for the masses hampered their political efforts at every level" (Irvine 1989a:41). The cost of the absence of organization was also recognized by some circles in the Vatican—although after it was too late. As the papal secretary of state Cardinal Mariano Rampolla (quoted in Sedgwick 1965:90) privately argued in 1896: "Obstacles have made it difficult to realize the benevolent designs of the Sovereign Pontiff with regard to France, chief among which is the lack of organization and unity among well-intentioned citizens which renders them incapable of exercising a salutary influence upon the government and upon the Chambers. Such lack of coordination does nothing but help the enemies of the Church."

The absence of the organizational strategy of the church was, therefore, crucial. Without mass organization, which only the church could build, the Right could not overcome its division and lack of coordination to win elections. Furthermore, by contributing to successive electoral defeats, the absence of mass organization demoralized militant priests and laymen and convinced them, along with everyone else, of the futility of undertaking the formation of a confessional party.

The Strategy of Participation: The Implementation of the Ralliement

"It would be very good to reestablish the monarchy, of course if we could!" argued the Monarchist Pierre Veuillot in 1890 (quoted in Barbier v.2 1923:272). "But since we cannot!" he added; "Soon we shall have been working on this for twenty years, and still the republic continues. In fact, we must admit that it draws new strength from each assault against it." Indeed, there was little doubt after 1891 that the Republic was there to stay. The consecutive electoral defeats of the Right and the stabilization of the Republic demanded a radical reassessment of the situation. After the Boulanger debacle in 1889, the church realized that restoration was unlikely. As Ozouf (1963:170) points out, for both Conservatives and Catholics the failure of Boulangism sounded "the death knell of monarchy."[37] Relying on the Monarchists now became a handicap for the church. De Mun, who had supported Boulanger, in 1889 reached the conclusion that "in order to save Catholicism, it is necessary to separate it from the throne" (Desaubliaux 1986:105).

Thus, like the five other churches, the French church had to face a new reality, with no alternative institutional choices in the face of anticlerical attacks. Contrary to the other churches, however, institutional defeat and resignation came for the French church years after the initial launching of the anticlerical attack. This delay had important consequences.

To begin with, the church abandoned the monarchy in a period of relative religious peace, when the first anticlerical wave had ended and the Republicans appeared disinclined to continue their anticlerical attack. Moreover, the cost of organization had gone up since the late 1870s. Postponing mass organization had increased its cost. The creation of mass organizations is slow and arduous; it was now even more costly because the market for mass mobilization was cornered. As parties and other political actors began building local organizations, options for individual citizens expanded—while

[37] There is a general consensus among historians that the failure of Boulangism was the crucial event in the church's realization that restoration was unlikely (Martin 1978:86; Aubert 1975:84; Soltau 1965:35; Poulet v.3 1944:336).

simultaneously shrinking for the church.[38] The organizational space was filled, and the church was just one among many competitors—and running behind. Yves-Marie Hilaire has confirmed that the rise of political militantism and political participation through mass organizations covered an increasing number of citizens: at the beginning of the twentieth century, a French citizen had a wide range of political choices, being able to choose between, among others, Nationalist, Socialist, Radical, and Progressive organizations (Hilaire 1977:698). Yet for all their great number and their superiority with regard to the church, these organizations were overall relatively weak and French political life was still decentralized. These factors, together with the relative religious peace of the time, led the church to skip mass organization. Indeed, Pope Leo XIII "clearly perceived" that Catholic organization and a Catholic party would produce a rise in anticlericalism by provoking "appeals for an anti-catholic defense which would target the existence even of Catholicism in France" (Lapierre and Levillain 1992:35). Rejecting monarchy and reneging on its alliance with the Monarchists, however, had the merit of not provoking the Republicans while allowing the formation by the church of a wide coalition that would include moderate factions of Republicans. Thus for the church participation was preferable to organization *(P > O)*. As a result, the church went directly from compromise to participation. Coherent and comprehensive mass organization was a step skipped in France.

The church implemented the participation strategy through the so-called Ralliement. The 1892 papal encyclical *Au milieu des sollicitudes* officially recognized the Republic. Alexander Sedgwick (1965:vii) correctly points out that the Ralliement was more than a way to settle the regime issue: "In most histories of the Third Republic the Ralliement is described as an attempt by the Vatican to persuade French Catholics to accept the Republic. However, it was much more than that. The Ralliement represented an effort on the part of the French Royalists, Bonapartists, and Opportunists to change their political habits by joining together to form a conservative party within the constitutional framework of the Republic."

This strategy consisted of setting up a wide coalition of moderate Conservative forces, fully backed by the church. Indeed, the pope "rejected political

[38] In a comparable way, Luebbert (1991:9) explains the weakness of working-class movements in a number of countries where political entrepreneurs failed to organize the working class in coherent and encompassing trade unions early. After 1919 it was too late; the organizational space was already filled. Likewise, Valenzuela (1979) shows how the filling of organizational space during crucial phases of labor development froze organizational alternatives within the labor sector in Latin America. Finally, Harvey (1995) argues that the failure of women's organizations to organize women politically right after suffrage was won in the United States allowed established parties to fill the organizational space and destroyed the possibility of the political organization of women on the basis of gender.

action on a strictly Catholic basis" (Sedgwick 1965:52) and called on Catholics to unite "with non-Catholics who, without being antireligious in principle, strove against the church because they thought it hostile to the Republic" (Dansette v.2 1961:88). It also appeared to make sense electorally because all Monarchists were Catholic, but the opposite was not true. Monarchist voters were thus seen as a captive market, while there were plenty of moderate voters to be won by moving away from monarchy.

The central objective of this coalition was to protect the church from new attacks and if possible to reverse the anticlerical legislation. De Mun (quoted in Levillain 1992:201) made this point clear when he argued in 1892 that "by placing ourselves on the constitutional field, we are Catholics and nothing more. We demand the revision of the school and the military laws, the abrogation of the divorce law, the reintegration of the Sisters in the hospitals." Likewise, the pope argued in an 1892 letter to French cardinals that "only through Catholic and conservative unity could the church be saved" (Sedgwick 1965:53). In Goguel's (1958:77) felicitous phrase, "The moment was well chosen for attempting a political operation through which, by 'accepting the Constitution,' the Catholics would obtain the means of 'changing the legislation.' " As the bishop of Grenoble (quoted in Barral 1962:412) declared in 1891, "I enter in the Republic, but in order to fight in every way against the republicans on the electoral level and throw them out." Cardinal Rampolla (quoted in Sedgwick 1965:40) described in 1890 the essence of the participation strategy: "Consequently, when the interests of religion demand it, and there is no just reason to oppose it, it is right that the faithful *participate* in public affairs in order that through their zeal and their authority, existing institutions and laws will be modeled on the rules of justice, and that the spirit and salutary effect of religion will influence the general welfare of the state" (emphasis added).

Reactions to the Ralliement were mixed. Many bishops initially reacted, and the Legitimist Right opposed the project. But the Ralliement prevailed quickly. The reluctant bishops followed the official line, as did many Conservative politicians. The consecutive defeats of the Monarchist Right proved the most powerful argument. A former local Legitimist (quoted in Dupeux 1966:590) asked his colleagues bitterly in 1902: "During long years you have been the only Catholic leaders in the Loir-et-Cher and where are your victories? What did you do with this department which was neither radical nor socialist, and where honest people were perfectly united, following you, something that would certainly lead to triumph?"

Not surprisingly, the Ralliement's immediate effect was the destruction of the Monarchists as a significant political force. But Monarchist parties were not replaced by a new and solid political organization because there was no mass Catholic organization to fill the gap. As Dansette (v.2 1961:101) notes,

"It is easy enough to speed the death of a dying party, but much more difficult to create a new one." At the same time, the church failed to achieve its electoral objectives. Church-supported "Republican Catholic" candidates were consistently unsuccessful between 1889 and 1902 (Barral 1962:413). The result was further demoralization and depoliticization of French Catholics (Hilaire 1977:702). Because of successive electoral defeats and the concomitant escalation of anticlerical attacks, the church was forced to experiment and France became a laboratory for various versions of the participation strategy (see Table 2).

The first version of the participation strategy began as a pact between moderate factions of the Right and the Left around a parliamentary group called Droite Constitutionnelle, formed in March 1890 by the Conservative deputy Jacques Piou. This group recognized the Republic and promoted a program emphasizing the defense of the church (Sedgwick 1965:34). It intended to provide parliamentary support to moderate Republican candidates (the so-called Opportunists) in exchange for favorable legislation in religious matters. It aimed, furthermore, to emerge as a key actor in the 1893 elections by endorsing Opportunist candidates in exchange for commitments to revise anticlerical legislation. These somewhat narrow objectives did not preclude wider party-formation ambitions.[39]

Electoral objectives were initially limited and the group (now renamed Droite républicaine) fielded only ninety-four candidates for the August-September 1893 elections, widely considered as a test of the Ralliement (Levillain 1992:201). Still, these elections proved a disaster for the ralliés, who secured only 35 seats (winning about 5 percent of the vote). All three leaders of the group (Piou, de Mun, and Lamy) were defeated, while overall the Right lost 122 seats compared to the previous election. The electoral strategy had failed. On the one hand, an important segment of the Conservative electorate, particularly those close to the rural Royalist nobility, abstained (the abstention rate was the second highest since 1876 and was particularly high in traditionally Catholic regions). On the other hand, precisely because the *ralliés* were seen as a small group of parliamentarians with limited appeal (as opposed to leaders of a mass organization), they were not taken seriously by the moderate Republicans, who did not reciprocate with support in the second round. As Sedwgick (1965:70) puts it, "Although the *Ralliés* were anxious to cooperate with the Opportunists the latter were not interested." The electoral returns confirmed their expectations and, as a consequence, moderate Republicans did not commit themselves to revise the anticlerical

[39] The ultimate objective of the faction, according to one of its members, was the formation of "a great party . . . consisting of members of the clergy, moderate Republicans, Conservatives of good faith and sincere patriots" (Sedgwick 1965:47).

reforms. Thus the first attempt to translate the Ralliement into a new non-anticlerical majority through a pact with moderate Republicans failed.

This failure is usually imputed to division within the Conservative camp (Partin 1969:52), but this division was made possible by the absence of mass organization. Strong organizational structures could have fostered unity among Catholics, enforced discipline upon them, and turned the Catholic vote into an attractive bargaining chip—as was the case with the Gentiloni pact in Italy.

The second version of the participation strategy, implemented from 1894 to 1898, mixed parliamentary with electoral objectives and introduced the element of mobilization. The Vatican shifted the focus of its strategy because it realized that the pact with moderate Republicans in the absence of electoral leverage could only lead to defeats. According to Sedgwick (1965:74), "The focus shifted from the Conservatives to the Catholics. The significant aspect of this phase was the effort made by Catholics both in France and in Rome to coordinate Catholic political activity in view of the 1898 elections." In this vein, the pope (quoted in Sedgwick 1965:85) reiterated his concern about the division among French Catholics in instructions that appeared in the Catholic newspaper *L'Univers* in June 1897: "Catholics must work closely, putting aside political differences. They must employ all honest and legal means to improve the hostile legislation."

To implement this new version of the participation strategy, the pope hand-picked Etienne Lamy, a moderate Catholic politician. Lamy was summoned to Rome in January 1896 and asked "to promote unity and organization in Catholic ranks in order to give them a sense of direction, in conformity with the principles laid down by the Holy See" (Sedgwick 1965:90). This required the centralization and coordination of all Catholic activity and the federation of existing Catholic organizations. In April 1897 representatives of various Catholic groups met at Lamy's residence and agreed to form the Fédération électorale.[40] They also sketched the broad lines of their strategy: "At this meeting it was unanimously agreed to create a solid alliance between groups. . . . It was also recognized unanimously that the purpose of the *Fédération* was to prepare a common program and a common list of candidates for the elections of 1898" (Sedgwick 1965:101). At the same time, an attempt was made to reach an agreement with moderate Republicans. Cardinal Rampolla was quoted as saying, "We ask only one thing and that is that the Opportunists do not refer to the laic laws as

[40] The Fédération consisted of seven organizations: the Union Nationale an organization created by the abbé Garnier, the Catholic Republicans (known as the Politique nouvelle group, headed by Lamy), the Christian Democrats (the *abbés démocrates* Lemire, Gayraud, Naudet), the Justice-Egalité committees connected with the Assumptionists and their newspaper *La Croix*, the Comité des congrès nationaux catholiques, the ACJF, and the Association catholique du commerce et de l'industrie.

intangible" (Sedgwick 1965:111). In the summer of 1897, the pope announced his support for Lamy's effort and called on the French bishops to realize that "it is necessary that everyone strive to put an end to those unfortunate divisions, which afflict Us so profoundly, by uniting all decent men" (quoted in Sedgwick 1965:107). The official announcement of the formation of the Fédération électorale was made in December 1897 in a national Catholic congress held in Paris and presided over by Lamy.[41]

As Dansette (v.2 1961:164) concludes, however, "Lamy's efforts proved vain." The absence of a centralized network of Catholic organizations under the control of the church made effective mobilization impossible. The leaders of the Fédération failed to convey their directives to the Catholic voters in the provinces (Martin 1978:126). The leadership of the ACJF, for instance, was unable to direct and control its local groups (Molette 1968:231–32). Antagonistic Catholic organizations as well as local Catholic groups "were particularly jealous of their prerogatives and tended to resent the kind of interference which would become inevitable if a central committee with any kind of authority came into being" (Sedgwick 1965:93). The only organization worth its name was the order of the Assumptionists (Larkin 1974:68), and they demanded that "they and not Lamy should determine Catholic policy toward the elections" (Sedgwick 1965:112). In spite of their adherence to the Fédération's propositions, "they did not abide by them" and made their own endorsements of candidates (Sedgwick 1965:110). As Sedgwick (1965:114) puts it, "The tensions and the divisions within the *Fédération électorale* made the outcome of the elections a foregone conclusion." Fédération candidates won about thirty-two seats. The outcome was an obvious failure.

Lamy had rightly understood that "in order to bring all Catholic elements into line with his conciliatory policy, he would have to subject them to central control" (Sedgwick 1965:117). Right after the elections, he attempted to turn the Fédération into a permanent and centralized structure under the label Fédération catholique et constitutionnelle. This proved to be impossible because the participating organizations reacted to Lamy's demands and recalled their delegates in June 1898. Thus the Fédération, this "dismal attempt" at participation (Gadille 1974:196), was officially dissolved in 1899. One more time, the absence of an encompassing and disciplined mass Catholic organization made itself felt.

[41] The ACJF issued a resolution declaring that its action would now be placed "in all domains, including the electoral one"(Molette 1968:231). Its president (quoted in Molette 1968:232) declared in 1897 that "[our] action should place us in contact with the people, since we live in a democracy; it should be exercised on the electoral field, since it is only there that the next victories will be won; it should be inspired by the Catholic interests only, since we have no other objective than God's triumph to whom are attached the greatness and prosperity of France."

The relative religious peace ended with the Dreyfus affair in 1898. The elections of the same year turned the Radicals into the dominant force of the Left. In 1901, they launched a new anticlerical attack. The church reacted by initiating the third version of the participation strategy.

Catholics responded to the new anticlerical legislation almost with apathy. No demonstrations took place in favor of the congregations (July 1901-March 1902), and there were few demonstrations in 1902 after hundreds of private schools were closed (Partin 1969:68; Barral 1962:417). The 1903 parliamentary debate on the government's refusal to authorize most congregations produced less public outcry than anticipated (Partin 1969:172). The ACJF complained about the "apathy of too many of its coreligionists" (Molette 1968:325). A book on Catholics published by a priest in 1903 had the telling title *Le découragement des catholiques.* Catholics remained demobilized.

The third version of the participation strategy, which began in 1901, aimed to reverse this trend and mobilize Catholics. The objective was now to form a wide and, this time, electorally effective pro-church coalition. A new parliamentary faction, the Action libérale (AL), was formed in 1901 by a small group of ralliés led by Piou and de Mun. Contrary to the Droite constitutionnelle (a loose parliamentary faction with no credible ambition beyond brokering parliamentary deals) and the Fédération électorale (an umbrella organization with no authority over its component parts), the Action libérale was designed as a longer-term effort intent on evolving into a permanent party—although not a confessional one. In the speeches he gave in 1901 Piou (quoted in Martin 1970:666) "warned that only if Catholics trooped to the polls in rigid formation, uniting behind the Action Libérale in a 'severe discipline [and] a precise program,' could these [anticlerical] assaults be repelled." As a result, the following years saw a "return to confrontational elections" (Siegfried 1949:87).

Leo XIII called Catholics to unite behind the two AL leaders (Martin 1970:666), and the French church backed the effort (Ameye 1963:44). The 1902 elections were, again, seen as critical: "Either we will obtain at least a reasonable majority in the next elections or everything will be lost," warned the auxiliary bishop of Cambrai in 1901 (quoted in Ameye 1963:44). But though the Right was in 1902 "better organized and coordinated than ever before, [so] too was the Left"[42] (McManners 1972:129).

The 1902 elections were fought around the state-church issue and the Right lost once more, albeit by a very small margin. The Right obtained

[42] Out of roughly 600 constituencies only in 108 did candidates from the three groups of the Right face each other in the first round—the three groups being the Action libérale, the Progressives, and the Independents. In the second round candidates of the Right never faced each other (Martin 1970:667). On the other hand, Republicans, Radicals, and Socialists also formed, in 1901, a common committee to prepare for the elections.

altogether 49 percent of the votes and came only two hundred thousand votes (out of about 11 million cast) behind the Left in the first round. The AL increased its parliamentary representation from fifty-eight to seventy-eight, but fell short of its goal of one hundred deputies (Martin 1970:669). Yet the outcome was interpreted by all political actors as an electoral defeat for the AL. As Benjamin Martin (1970:669) notes, "The result of the voting had a profound effect upon the bitterly disappointed opposition groups. The closeness of the popular ballot and its proof that their ideas found many adherents in the nation hardly compensated for the government's continued ascendancy in the Chamber." The AL leaders were fully aware that it was the absence of mass organization that undermined them. The mobilization of Catholics was again seen as "incomplete" (Le Béguec and Prévotat 1992:216). The official party journal asserted in April 1902 that "despite the efforts of the Action libérale, it is by the absence of organization that the opposition has sinned" (quoted in Martin 1970:669). The closeness of the vote, however, gave the AL a second chance. Right after the elections, Piou and de Mun announced the formation of the Action libérale populaire. The word "popular" in the label stood for the intention to create a mass party "whose network would descend to the most humble village and whose membership on the local level would be extensive" (Martin 1970:669). In other words, the ALP intended to do what the church failed to: organize Catholics.

The ALP was a *potential* confessional party.[43] Although it claimed to be aconfessional and made no appeals to Catholic principles in its program, it emphasized the defense of religious liberties.[44] The ALP's focus on the religious issue was manifest. Many priests as well as members of church organizations (such as the ACJF) helped and often even joined the ALP (Lapierre and Levillain 1992:76). Piou pointed out that the new party "cherished aspirations of becoming primarily a Catholic party, deriving cohesion from its central purpose of combating the government's anticlerical measures" (Partin 1969:117). The party's local activities underscored its confessional concerns. As soon as a local branch of the party was formed in the Mayenne, it organized a protest campaign against the closure of religious schools (Denis 1977:490).

It became clear to all that to establish itself credibly as *the* Catholic party of France, the ALP needed an electoral success: all the party needs is victory,

[43] The ALP is described as a Catholic party (Goguel 1958:126) or "almost but not quite a confessional party" (Anderson 1974:172). I treat the ALP as a potential confessional party because, had it survived, it probably would have evolved into a confessional party.

[44] Boutry and Michel (1992:674) argue that the claim of aconfessionality made by the ALP (and its successor parties) "is evidently explained by the political context particular to France, that is, by the political and legislative reality of anticlericalism." This is yet another instance of a noncomparative flawed insight.

declared de Mun in the 1905 party congress (Martin 1978:194). The anticlerical attack, which intensified during the Combes ministry in 1902, offered the party a splendid opportunity to mobilize Catholics. The party "hoped most to convert" the "apathetic Catholics and conservatives" (Martin 1970:672). To that end, the ALP organized mass demonstrations in Paris and the provinces and appealed for mass organization. In a rally held in Nantes in 1902, Piou (quoted in Martin 1970:673) asserted that "it is not sufficient merely to unite; we must have organization; not for an ephemeral demonstration, not for an election on its eve, but for a long, patient, and persevering struggle. From particles of dust, organization can create granite." The ALP made serious progress toward organization. At the same time, the party managed to build a wide anti-Left coalition bringing together moderate Republican and Monarchist politicians.[45] The 1905 Separation Law and the 1906 inventory of the church's goods raised the political tension even more, and the ALP tried to capitalize on these events. Expectations ran high, and the Catholic newspaper *La Croix,* somewhat imprudently, announced that the elections would be "a grandiose referendum" (Mayeur 1966:159).

Contrary to these expectations, the ALP suffered a severe defeat.[46] The 1906 elections "represented the triumph of radicalism" (Dansette v.2 1961:240). They were "a bitter disappointment" for the church (Larkin 1974:158) and constituted a "decisive defeat" for the ALP (Anderson 1974:180). In the words of Martin (1978:200), the ALP coalition "suffered a serious reverse" and the ALP itself "sustained a major setback." The defeat was magnified because the organizational activity of the ALP during the preceding years had made the party and, by association, its victory in the forthcoming elections, "truly credible" (Martin 1978:188). The consequences of the defeat were a very shaken morale and the beginning of the party's end.

Why did the ALP lose the 1906 elections? The Radicals had realized that the ALP was a real threat. Louis Bonnet, the secretary of the Radical party, warned in 1904: "The battle will be warmer in 1906 than in 1902. . . . We have never before fought an organization so strong, so extensive, so well-endowed" (Martin 1970:679). Combes even introduced an updated version of Gambetta's old slogan: *"l'Action Libérale Populaire, voilà l'ennemi"* (quoted in Martin 1970:678). As a result, Radicals were particularly well

[45] Paul Beauregard, the leader of the Progressives, and Denys Cochin, a well-known Monarchist, appeared together with Piou on the stage of the 1905 party congress (Martin 1970:683). The party claimed 160,000 members and 700 local committees in 1904 and 200,000 members and 1,200 local committees in 1905. Two successful congresses were organized in 1904 and 1905. Studies of local politics confirm that the party began to build a local organization (Rivet 1979:525; Denis 1977:490–91).

[46] The coalition headed by the ALP obtained 41 percent of the vote and 190 deputies, about 60 fewer than in 1902. The ALP lost 14 seats.

prepared in those elections. The main reason, however, was again the absence of Catholic mass organization, a point emphasized by Bosworth (1962:24): "More important [in accounting for the failure of the ALP] was the absence of groups such as Catholic Action. . . . At the turn of the century the *ad hoc* Catholic groups existing with the ALP were not able to perform this function."[47] Although the attempts of the ALP leadership to create a mass organization looked impressive on paper, this organization was soft, and frail, as indicated by its collapse after the electoral defeat (Martin 1970:686–88). Moreover, while the church supported the ALP and recognized that "the mission of the clergy is to introduce Catholics into politics en masse" (bishop of Périgueux in 1904, quoted in Weber 1991:170), its mobilizational capacity was limited because of the absence of its own mass organization. This is why Piou (quoted in Martin 1978:187) complained in 1905 that notwithstanding the organizational effort of the ALP, too many Catholics "groaned, looked sad, and remained silent, playing the soldiers who will not fight . . . the congregation of folded arms and weeping willows."

Parties operate under very tight time constraints and are subject to high expectations, especially when they are new. The ALP was a political party under probation. It was thus under tremendous pressure to prove its political viability (and that of religion as a winning issue) in the 1906 elections. It was unrealistic to expect that this party would build a powerful mass organization within just four years while in competition with parties that already had a head start in organization. Only centralized and institutionalized organizations like the church had the resources and time to undertake the painstakingly "slow, arduous, and tedious strategy" of "comprehensive, coherent organization" that could deliver the level of mobilization necessary to win elections (Luebbert 1991:9). In addition, such organizations did not have to face an immediate and decisive electoral test. This is why almost all mass parties have been "externally" formed (Duverger 1954).

The cumulative consequences of the two consecutive ALP defeats are obvious. Without electoral success, the ALP proved stillborn. As Martin (1970:687) concludes, "The election of 1906 destroyed the vast hopes of the

[47] There are two accounts of the ALP's defeat. Moody (1953:161) goes back to dechristianization and claims that "France was not a Catholic country in 1905. . . . The Church in France no longer enjoyed the loyalty of the masses." Besides the problems of the dechristianization argument, analyzed above, the ALP's electoral performance in 1902 and 1905 was good enough, even in the absence of strong mass organization, to disqualify this argument. Martin (1970:685) claims that the ALP lost because of Clemenceau's decisions "to halt enforcement of the Separation law and to charge the ALP with revolutionary conspiracy." He adds (1970:686), however, that "even without Clemenceau's machinations, there had been only slight chance of an opposition triumph." The reason was that "the average French voter in 1906 sought stability, and found the ALP, especially with its new burden of royalists, unlikely to provide it" (Martin 1970:686).

ALP." After 1906 the ALP ceased to be a credible threat to the Radicals and gradually vanished into political insignificance. Local organizations built with great effort began disbanding and political mobilization dwindled (Loubère 1974:151). It has been calculated that between 1906 and 1910 the Catholic Right lost one-third of its electorate (Jacques, cited by Bosworth 1962:27). Political entrepreneurs attempted to recast the Right by replacing religion with new issues, particularly nationalism.[48]

Beyond the ALP, the 1902 and 1906 defeats spelled the death of any prospect for a confessional party in France. Coming after a string of defeats, the 1906 setback unequivocally proved that religion was a losing issue for the Right. For example, the outcome of the 1906 elections was seen in the town of Tourcoing as confirming that "a candidacy with confessional character is not rewarding" (Ameye 1963:56). McManners (1972:173) outlines the prevailing feeling: "It had been demonstrated again that the mass of nominal Catholics could not be transformed into Catholic voters." The lesson that the church could only lose by getting into politics was internalized and constructed as experience: years later, Dansette (v.1 1961:236) would report that "experience has taught Catholics that the expedient of a 'confessional party' is particularly dangerous in a country as liable as France to resent any ecclesiastical interference in politics."

What if the ALP had won? Local politics allow for reasonable extrapolation. The ALP leadership in Mayenne, made of a new breed of politicians strongly disliked by the traditional Monarchist notables, built the nucleus of a strong local party with formal procedures for fielding candidates and carefully planned electoral campaigns. After the ALP candidates won all five seats of the department in the 1906 elections, they went on to form what was called a "Catholic parliamentary group." This move was not followed by grass-roots demobilization. On the contrary, the local party organization was strengthened to fight in the forthcoming regional elections (Denis 1977:493). The developments in Mayenne strikingly mirror political developments in countries where confessional parties were formed. They suggest that had the ALP won, it could have evolved into a confessional mass party similar to the other European confessional parties.

[48] Nationalist organizations began to emerge after 1887 (Rémond 1982:150). The supporters of the best-known such organization, the Action française, put it clearly: "Action libérale works hard . . . toward a new and resounding defeat. . . . Better be divided and defended than united and regularly crushed" (Denis 1977:509). Gramsci implicitly argued that Catholicism and nationalism were competing for the same segment of the political market. According to Fulton (1987:213), "Gramsci sees the power of nationalism posing a double threat for Catholicism in that it adopts a similar strategy to Catholicism, by high-jacking from contemporary religion the use of fanaticism as a preserver of unity, while at the same time developing its own culture from the same popular base of common-sense or material values."

The Aftermath: Late and Incomplete Organization without Participation

The Separation Law of 1905 and the ensuing defeat of the ALP in 1906 concluded this phase of state-church conflict. Anticlericalism subsided, and the religious question ceased to be the dominant political issue (Berger 1987:116; Mayeur 1966:10, 187).

The Separation Law forced the church to reorganize and to tighten its control over priests and laymen (Hilaire 1977:767; Mayeur 1966:194). The prevailing feeling of isolation and defeat altered the incentives of the church and led to a gradual, belated, and incomplete implementation of mass organization. Ironically, the situation facing the French church in 1905 was similar to that faced by the churches in the five other countries *before* the anticlerical attack: defeat was complete and unquestionable. The organizational strategy now made sense and the church accepted, as Rivet (1979:337) tells it, that it had "somewhat neglected to reach the [people's] hearts and consciousness through the medium of associations." The incentives and energy of Catholics for political action dissipated, however, and the majority among them, with a feeling of bitterness, opted for private piety over politics (Bosworth 1962:31). The church never again "envisaged relying on a political organization" (Boutry and Michel 1992:675).

Organization quickly became a buzzword unremittingly repeated by the Catholic press, which also called for the creation of "organizations of religious defense and reconquest" (Hilaire 1977:763; Cholvy and Hilaire 1986:150–58). Annual Catholic congresses were organized on a regular basis, and the church began to build a centralized network of parochial committees and diocesan Catholic unions explicitly placed outside electoral politics and subjected to tight episcopal control (Dansette v.2 1961:254). Control over existing organizations was decisively reinforced, a more clerical structure introduced, and the church did not shy from cracking down on organizations that attempted to remain autonomous. For instance, the church reasserted its control over the up to then semi-independent lay committees charged to run Catholic schools and repressed the union of confessional schoolteachers. As André Lanfrey (1991:383) puts it, the objective of the church was to "reduce the lay Catholic forces (such as associations and unions) which had ensured Catholic school continuity in a way that didn't suit the taste of many bishops."

The growth of Catholic mass organizations between 1905 and 1914 was impressive and is confirmed by regional studies (Cholvy 1982:246; Chaline 1981:280–81; Rivet 1979:338–40; Hilaire 1977:726–70). Its novelty struck observers across the political spectrum (Hilaire 1977:779). Still, mass organization in France never reached the level achieved by German Catholics (Cholvy and Hilaire 1986:154). The church faced the consequences of a late start, the presence of increased competition, and a record of electoral defeats that had demoralized Catholics. As Eugen Weber (1991:170–71) puts it, the church's decision to begin mass organization after 1904 "came very late in the process of peasant politicization." Moreover, contrary to the other cases, the French church's long and unsuccessful electoral experience precluded a future participation strategy and made organization a terminal strategy. Eventually, the advent of World War I proved a crucial blow to this fledging organization: the church did not have the time to form a national federation, while its diocesan unions were still few (there were only twenty-one in 1914) and lacked "the solid national organization that might have saved them from downfall" (Bessières 1924:40). Clearly, timing matters a lot.

After the end of the war, a renewed organizational effort took place, now spurred by a change in the political context: the specter of a new anticlerical attack following the victory of the Left (the Cartel des gauches) in the 1924 elections. At last, the church "understood that the time had come to create a national Union of French Catholics" (Viance 1930:24). A retired general, Edouard de Castelneau, was asked to lead the Féderation nationale catholique, the first French mass Catholic organization for men. The growth of the FNC was impressive both in size and rapidity.[49] The role of the church was crucial. For example, the Union des hommes of the diocese of Rennes was very successful precisely because the local bishop required that every parish organize a group of members (Delumeau 1979:281–82). The FNC began to enter electoral politics and claimed in 1928 that it helped elect 277 deputies who agreed to promote its main demands (Viance 1930:120). Impressed by this initial success, some FNC activists called for its transformation into a Catholic party. But this time the Left quickly retreated and the threat to the church dissipated. As a result, the church forced Castelneau "to abandon the political field" (Boutry and Michel 1992:676). The FNC was renamed Action catholique générale des hommes and was effectively neutralized. In 1931, Catholic Action was reorganized in a way that once again reinforced hierar-

[49] The bishop of Versailles argued in 1924 that "a new organization is absolutely necessary to assure the collaboration of the laity with the clergy, all while safeguarding the immutable rules of holy hierarchy, that is the subordination of the faithful to the direction of their spiritual leaders" (quoted in Bessières 1924:11). Castelnau (quoted in Viance 1930:27) called Catholics to "unite tightly and organize methodically." The FNC was closely supervised by the episcopate and explicitly excluded politics from its action; it was made up of 82 diocesan committees, organized 14,814 conferences in 5,073 parishes in one year, and had over two million members in 1925 (Arnal 1985:95–96, 118–19; Cholvy and Hilaire 1986:288; Viance 1930). The impressive development of regional affiliated organizations is confirmed by regional studies (Rivet 1979:445; Delumeau 1979:281–82; Denis 1977:540–41; Barral 1962:265, 336).

chical control and eliminated any political leaning (Hilaire 1982:64). In the 1930s the focus of the church shifted to evangelization through specialized organizations (Barral 1962:267).

Two independent attempts at confessional party formation failed unequivocally.[50] The absence of mass organization seems also to have contributed to the failure of the postwar Mouvement républicain populaire as well. This party, formed in 1944 with ambitions similar to those of the Christian Democratic parties of Germany and Italy, was essentially a regional party (Irving 1973:14) and disappeared in 1967—but remained politically significant only until 1951, when it lost half its voters in a single election. The causes of the MRP's failure cannot be addressed in the context of this study (see Warner 1995), but it appears that the lack of links between the party and existing mass Catholic organizations was a significant factor (Mayeur 1980:173; Irving 1979:19; Coutrot 1965).

Although a large number of Catholics were pushed into private piety by the church's exit from the political process after 1906, many others became available for recruitment by the primarily Nationalist (but also Monarchist and Catholic) Action française (AF), which advocated open resistance to the Republic. According to Oscar Arnal (1985:64), "Within an eight-year period, from 1906 to 1914, the Action Française came to exercise a profound influence over French Catholics." The AF recruited particularly among the most active lay Catholic militants, those who under different circumstances might have supported a Catholic party (Arnal 1985:64–65; Rivet 1979:528; Hilaire 1977:766). Abbé Paul Naudet (quoted in Latreille et al. 1962:495) bitterly complained in 1900 of "the disaggregation of [our] groups in the face of nationalism. This is so," he added, "because nationalism is something alive." By 1908 numerous ALP cadres were drifting away to Action française (Martin 1978:217, 221), while it is estimated that priests made up about 10 percent of AF recruits during the 1906–1914 period (Arnal 1985:64). Things evolved differently in the few instances where religious mobilization led early on to the development of Catholic mass organization, as, for instance, in Lower

[50] The Parti démocrate populaire was formed in 1924 by left-leaning Catholics. It was a regional party that remained isolated from the church and its organizations and never became a significant political force. According to Lönne (1987:5), the PDP "achieved only a modest significance and was not even able to attract to itself all Christian Democrats, let alone a substantial proportion of Catholic deputies." Both the PDP (thirteen deputies in 1924 and twenty deputies in 1928), and the Jeune République, another attempt to form a Catholic party by former members of the Sillon (three deputies in 1932, one in 1935, and four in 1936)(Callot 1978:44), are discounted as irrelevant based on Sartori's (1990/1976:319–22) criteria of political relevance: they were very weak in parliamentary representation; they lacked coalition potential (they were not needed for any feasible coalition majority); and they lacked blackmail potential (they did not alter the direction of competition).

Figure 4. The process of failure of confessional party formation (France)

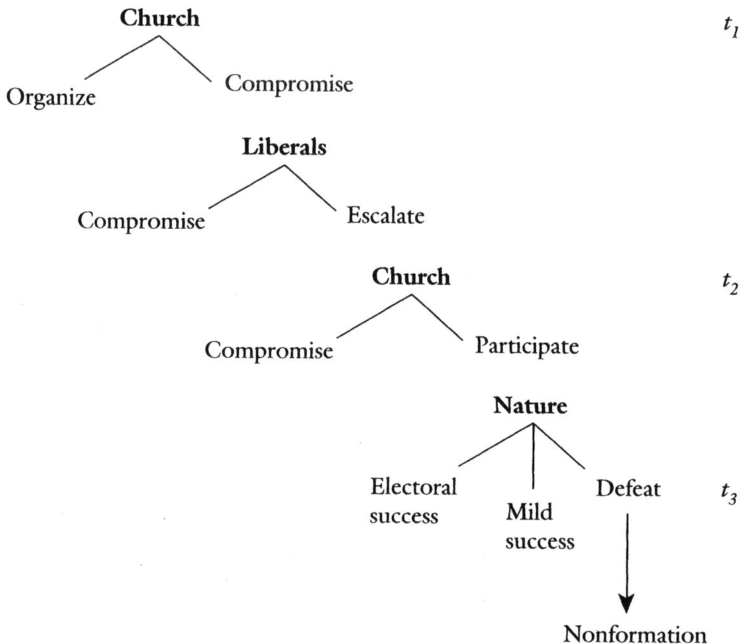

Brittany. There, as Ford (1987:16) points out, "religious conflict served as a catalyst for the political integration of an area."

The most immediate answer to the puzzle of the failure of a confessional party to emerge in France lies in the repeated electoral failures of the Right and the various coalitions that fought for the defense of the church. This "uninterrupted series of failures" (Dansette v.2 1961:23) was interpreted as proving that religion was a losing issue for the Right. My model of party formation predicts that without electoral success no confessional party would be formed. Figure 4 summarizes the process that led to the failure of confessional party formation in France.

The cause of the successive Conservative defeats and, hence, the answer to the puzzle of the failure of a confessional party to emerge in France is that the church implemented a participation strategy without previously implementing an organizational strategy. As Malcolm Anderson (1974:172) puts it, "no 'federator' emerged to harness the passions unleashed by the anticlerical attack." To put it more precisely, no *successful* federator emerged. Although many attempts at federation (coalitions in the context of the participation strategy) were made, they were doomed to failure without prior implementation of the organization strategy. The absence of organization operated in three ways: it impeded the emergence of Catholic political activists; it reproduced passivity and undermobilization among Catholics and made church action politically ineffective; and it contributed to the Right's successive electoral defeats and turned religion into a losing electoral issue.

The church decided against forming Catholic mass organizations because of the opportunity costs it faced. Having to choose between compromising and resisting, the church chose the former. Both choices were costly and risky. But contrary to the decision made by churches in the five other cases, it was rational for the French church to avoid the cost of fighting because of the presence of an alternative: the high likelihood that the anticlerical Republic would be overthrown and replaced by a pro-Catholic monarchy. This probability structure turned resistance and organization building into an unacceptably costly and risky course of action. When, the Boulanger coup failed in 1889 and the church realized that there was no hope of restoration, the remaining alternative in the face of the ever escalating anticlerical attacks was the participation strategy. After having relentlessly denounced the Republic, the church, under pressure from the Vatican, officially recognized the Republican regime in 1892 and entered the political process by implementing a variety of electoral strategies. But in the absence of prior strong and coherent mass organization, the participation strategy did not deliver electoral victories. Catholics remained undermobilized and divided.

The formation in 1902 of the Action liberale populaire was too little too late: it was too little because there was not enough time to develop a mass party from scratch, anticlerical political forces already had a head start on mass politics and cornered the market for organization, and the ALP had limited resources of its own; and it was too late because the church squandered its competitive advantage in organization building by bypassing its chance to organize the masses before everyone else. The failure of a confessional party to emerge in France is a perfect illustration of path dependency: the path of historical development matters; once certain choices are made, they constrain future possibilities (Aldrich 1995:5; Krasner 1988:67).

After 1905 a generalized feeling of missed opportunity prevailed. As a priest lamented in 1910 (quoted in Capéran, v.2 1960:258), "Even today, after more than thirty years, after so many deceptions and ruins, many regret that a decisive struggle following this method [the creation of a central lay Catholic organization] was not implemented. . . . The field was excellent; after that, we did not find a similar opportunity again, and the church was incessantly enfeebled." This feeling of missed opportunity was probably best captured by the papal secretary of state, Cardinal Rafael Merry del Val (quoted in Larkin 1974:124), when he exclaimed during a private discussion in 1906:

"Ah, if only the policy of resistance had begun twenty years ago! What a splendid situation the Church in France would have had today!"

The failure of a confessional party to emerge in France had profound political implications. According to Anderson (1974:172), "The major structural and organizational problem that the Right faced at the beginning of the 20th century, and one which it failed to solve, was the integration of the Catholic electorate into the political system in a manner which convinced the majority of its members that they were effectively represented." Likewise, Gilles Le Béguec and Jacques Prévotat (1992:285) point out that the failure of the ALP "deprived the Catholic masses of a true instrument of integration within the republican democracy and made more difficult their entry into political modernity." This failure greatly facilitated the rise of nationalism and antiliberalism among Catholics. And the Nationalist, as opposed to a hypothetical confessional Right, fought openly against parliamentarism (Rémond 1982:155). Indeed, it is generally accepted that the Vichy regime was not just the result of German occupation (Birnbaum 1993; 1991; Paxton 1982). To be properly understood, Vichy has to be placed in the context of the long-term consequences of the failure of political Catholicism in France.

CHAPTER 4

The Formation of Confessional Parties in Historical Context

This chapter contains five case studies. Using "causal" (Sewell 1992:27–29) or "analytic" (Aminzade 1993:27) narratives, I describe confessional party formation through the analytical lens of the model laid out in the first two chapters. The focus is on both the fundamental similarity of all cases and the peculiarities of each one. I begin by placing the anticlerical attack in its historical context, turn to the efforts made by the church to obstruct the development of political Catholicism, and then proceed with the case studies.

Catholics and Liberals

Political identities are not static. They are fluid, continually and dynamically shaped by competing social and political forces. Originally, Catholicism did not appear poised to enter the political arena in a party form or likely to dominate the Conservative space. During the first part of the nineteenth century, the Catholic church lost much of its political weight.

Ideology can be a bad predictor of political action. The ideological opposition between Catholicism and Liberalism cannot alone explain the formation of a distinct Catholic political identity. For all its ideological hostility toward Liberalism, the action of the church did not always translate into blind identification with Conservative factions or monarchical regimes. A disjunction between religion and political regime subsisted even in the most difficult moments of the church's history. For instance, numerous French Catholics were initially not hostile to the French Revolution and later remained indifferent on the issue of the regime. The split between revolution and the church was not necessarily preordained (Gibson 1989:54).

The relationship between church and state was often congenial, even when the state was not controlled by pro-church forces. For instance, the Prussian state, while championing Prussian Protestantism against Austrian Catholicism, did not repress Catholics. On the contrary, it guaranteed the rights of its Catholic citizens on a level equal to that of Belgium (Aubert 1952:137). As a result, the church strove to preserve cordial relations with the government (Windell 1954:65). Moreover, where they coexisted, Catholics and Protestants were not automatically or naturally pitted against each other. As Helmut Smith (1991:24) points out, "Despite a long and troublesome history, religious conflict was not a natural fact of social and political life in Imperial Germany." Before the Liberal attack against the church, a growing number of practicing Catholics were members, even leaders, of Liberal parties. Even after the anticlerical attack, numerous Liberal voters and leaders remained practicing Catholics. Conversely, the experience of Catholics under Conservative regimes was not always a positive one because Conservatives, even when protecting the church, tended to impose a great deal of control over it (Whyte 1981:34). Conservatives sometimes even supported anticlerical attacks. In Germany, the Kulturkampf was supported by Protestant Conservatives even though it was launched by the National-Liberals with the approval of the Progressives (Spohn 1991:115). Finally, given its traditional respect for established political authority, the church tended to be respectful of all governments, including Liberal ones, and numerous instances of church-Liberal collaboration took place during the first half of the nineteenth century. They followed a remarkably similar pattern in every country under study, with the exception of Italy.

In Belgium, Conservative and Liberal notables governed the country together from its independence in 1830 up to 1847. The unionist compromise between Conservatives and Liberals originated in the alliance forged against the Protestant Dutch king William I that led to the revolt of 1830 and the creation of Belgium. Following the constitution of the new country, the state provided the church with material support and refrained from interfering in its internal affairs, in exchange for the establishment of liberal freedoms "that were anathema in other Catholic lands" (Lorwin 1960:150)—but where, nonetheless, similar pacts also took place. Belgian Catholics supported the constitution despite the explicit papal condemnation of modern Liberalism in the encyclical *Mirari vos* (1832). Conservatives were more sensitive than Liberals about the protection of the church and its rights, but their differences were modest. Indeed, unionism made religion an irrelevant cleavage and politics were structured around local issues. For the majority of Catholics, the issue of church-state relations found a satisfying solution with the constitution, and the church saw no reason for political mobilization (Beaufays 1973:57). As the Belgian historian Charles Terlinden (v.2 1929:39) notes, "If we use the term *Catholic* in a religious sense . . . the immense majority of the congress was composed of catholics, since most liberals were at that time believers and practicing [Catholics]." Pascale Delfosse and André-Paul

Frognier (1988:63) found it impossible to classify deputies based on their voting on major issues (including education) between 1845 and 1855. In fact, until as late as 1870, the majority of Liberals were "still Catholics" (Claeys van Haegendoren 1967:415). During the 1850s, conservative Catholics took some "very cautious steps" in developing a Conservative rather than a Catholic party (Kossmann 1978:246). In 1864, the party's program was still explicitly nonreligious (Simon 1958:80). Furthermore, as Simon (1958:100) reports, among lay Catholics there was "an absence of will for organizing a party." As E. H. Kossmann (1978:166) sums up: "Political opinion divided between progressives and conservatives for under the cover of Unionism, left-wing Catholics and liberals were free to join against right-wing Catholics and liberals. . . . At any event, in this period political life in Belgium adopted the classic pattern of two parties not embarrassed by religious factors and disagreeing on purely political matters: just as in France and England, it was not so much liberals and Catholics but progressives and moderates who found themselves confronting each other."

It was only the rising anticlericalism of the 1860s and 1870s that made religion a political cleavage. Through the mediating action of political actors, this development forced faithful Catholics among the Liberals to decide which of their now conflicting identities would have to prevail: the Liberal senator Prince de la Ligne, for example, followed his religious identity when, in 1879, he voted against the anticlerical Van Humbeck law—and immediately after resigned (Pirenne 1932:235). Likewise, Edouard Ducpétiaux, who was connected with the Liberals until 1858, became the organizer of the Catholic congresses (Leblicq 1978:219).

Since Catholicism in the Netherlands was a minority religion, it had more political saliency. Furthermore, the Catholic minority was excluded from the political, economic, and cultural life of the country and remained deprived of its civic rights until the end of the eighteenth century. But this saliency, a vestige of the religious wars, was declining and religion repeatedly failed to generate Catholic political action on a group basis (De Kwaasteniet 1990:15). Dutch Catholics developed instead a long tradition of cooperation with Liberals. The first time the Catholics of the North Brabant and Limburg asserted themselves politically was at the time of the French Revolution, when they supported the revolutionary legislation of the Patriot party (Van Kessel 1976). After the Restoration, politically active Catholics "tended for several decades to hold liberal views" (Evans 1984:94). Pro-Catholic politicians found in the alliance with Liberals the means to gain rights for the church and to counter Calvinist power. They supported the Liberals from the 1850s to 1864, and in exchange, Liberals pushed for the emancipation of Catholics and restored (in 1853) the Catholic hierarchy despite a virulent Protestant reaction (Bakvis 1981:25). Most Protestants supported Conservative factions rather than seek a confessional political organization (Daalder 1960:201).

In Austria, politics were dominated by the issue of centralization, and Catholics were split along these lines. Most Conservatives were proponents of the federal structure and often looked for allies outside the Catholic church (Bled 1988:91). After the reestablishment of constitutional politics in 1867 and until the end of the 1870s, a faction of Catholic Conservative politicians allied with moderate Liberals under the auspices of the emperor and the discreet support of the church. This alliance was built around the defense of the centralized Habsburg empire and against the federative concept supported by ethnic nationalists and the major part of the Catholic nobility. In general, the church maintained a close relationship with the Conservatives without, however, supporting them in an organized fashion. In fact, the church tried to preserve its good relationship with the Liberals even after they passed anticlerical laws. For instance, the archbishop of Vienna Rauscher voted on most questions as a member of the liberal Constitution party in the upper house (Zeps 1979:80).

Following the 1848 revolution in the German states, Liberals and pro-church politicians allied against the princes (Mann 1968:135). In the 1848 Frankfurt national Assembly, the Catholic delegates were divided among various political factions but supported the Liberals in their attempt to introduce liberal freedoms as a guarantee against Protestant domination. As John Whyte (1981:35) points out, "The possibility of Catholics building themselves up into a cohesive structure must have seemed more remote than ever. They were too much dispersed along the political spectrum for the minimum necessary unity to be achieved." Recent quantitative research (Best, cited in Anderson 1986:83) discounts confession as a variable that accounts for political divisions within the Frankfurt Assembly. Studies of voting behavior in 1848 in the Rhineland reveal considerable Catholic support for the demands of the democrats, both from ordinary Catholics and clericals, priests and members of the various Pius Associations (Anderson 1986:83). Sperber (1980:179) reports that "in 1858 the fronts were still blurred. In the electoral district Wiedenbrük-Halle-Bielefeld the Liberals and clericals worked together. Similar instances of Liberal-clerical cooperation could be found in the lower Rhine and in the Bergisches Land." Until the late 1860s confessional issues were politically irrelevant, a trend encouraged by the Progressives, who claimed that they "will not drag religion into politics" (Sperber 1980:187). In fact, during the 1860s, Catholic voters joined and voted massively for the Liberals and the Progressives (Anderson 1991:688; Evans 1981:18; Windell 1954:58). A Catholic newspaper (quoted in Sperber 1980:223) commented after the 1861 elections: "It is unfortunately true that . . . at the election many Catholics, as a consequence of religious indifference, have left the field free for Jews and Freemasons." Anderson (1986:87) concludes that "there was before 1866 no necessary relationship between Catholic confession and conservative politics. Quite the contrary." In fact, there was no connection between religion and politics. The attempt to introduce political Catholicism into Prussian politics proved a total failure. When used, religion proved ineffective as a mobilizing issue. In the 1861 elections, "appeals from the pulpit and in the Catholic press to defend endangered religion and turn back the rising tide of atheism and freemasonry were even more ignored" (Sperber 1980:189). The formation of a Prussian Catholic parliamentary faction ended in total failure: the Zentrumsfraktion declined gradually until it disbanded after the disastrous results of the 1866 elections. In short, until the formation of the Zentrum Catholics showed no tendency to act as a bloc (Windell 1954:155–57).

In Italy, many Catholics, including priests, participated in the Risorgimento movement up to 1848, but most left when they realized that the Piedmontese leadership was becoming increasingly anticlerical and willing to dispossess the pope from its territorial authority (Vaussard 1956:219; Hall 1975:307). In contrast, the moderate Liberals *(moderati)* were no ideological enemies of the church; most were even practicing Catholics (Suardo 1962:49). Even in France, where the French Revolution associated Catholicism and monarchy, religion did not immediately lead to a clear-cut political cleavage. As Lapierre and Levillain (1992:17) report, "There existed conservative republicans who were Catholics." In fact, the Republican leadership included many faithful Catholics. Until the late 1870s, this was true at the local level as well, where Republican leaders were often "deists" or even "convinced Catholics" (Hilaire 1977:371; Loubère 1974:136). Conversely, important members of the Orleanist faction were not practicing Catholics (Dansette v.1 1961:327). In fact, during the 1840s (although before 1848), an important number of Catholic notables and members of the clergy were moving toward Liberalism (Hilaire 1977:212). Finally, Catholic extremists were not necessarily associated with Conservatives. The ultramontane movement that developed in France after 1850 was, initially at least, mostly apolitical (Lapierre and Levillain 1992:16).

The evidence from all six countries suggests that the politicization of Catholicism was neither inevitable nor inevitably conservative in nature. Without the Liberal attack against the church and the political choices that followed there is every reason to think that religion would not have served as the basis for the formation of a distinct political identity and new political parties. Catholic political factions that represented Catholic minorities in Protestant states probably would have vanished following the example of the Prussian Zentrumsfraktion.

The Attack against the Church

In the second part of the nineteenth century, Catholic Europe became "the scene of unbridgeable conflict between those who were determined to limit or abolish the ancient church's rights and influence and those who saw damnation, temporal as well as eternal, in a divorcement of church and state" (Jenks 1965:122). The attempt by Liberal state-centralizing elites to curtail the influence of the church and to increase the authority of the state put in motion a process that, under conditions specified in the first two chapters, turned Catholicism into a political identity.

Liberals attacked the church driven by several motives. A narrow political rationale aimed at the creation of a cleavage which Liberals thought would benefit them, both by mobilizing masses on their behalf and by neutralizing their internal divisions. A wider institutional rationale aimed at state building, modernization, centralization, and national unification and entailed the suppression of social and political forces that could contest state sovereignty. Both rationales were underpinned by the ideology of the Enlightenment, which sought to destroy religious obscurantism. Radical Liberals, often Masons, were convinced that the church represented a real danger for both the nation-state and modern liberties. They argued that the church intended to impose a regime of rule by priests—*pfaffenherrschaft* in the words of German and Austrian Liberals, or *gouvernement des prêtres* and *ministère des curés,* in those of the French ones. Confronting the church became akin to fighting for progress against medieval obscurantism; for parliamentarism against absolutism; and for national independence against the supranational domination of the Vatican and its local representatives, in the words of a Belgian Liberal, "the political militia of the Roman church" (quoted in Guyot de Mishaegen 1946:75). Liberals were further enraged by the growth of ultramontanism, whose central tenet was that "Christ must also reign upon earth" (Gibson 1991:115). As the Larousse *Grand dictionnaire universel du XIX siècle* asserted, the *Syllabus* was "revolting for human consciousness and reason . . . from now on, an unbridgeable gap exists between the Vatican *(la papauté)* and the modern world" (quoted in Gibson 1991:115).

The Liberal attacks against the church were also partly motivated by constraints that were the result of the rise of a new and dynamic radical wing within Liberal parties which provoked an internal crisis. These radicals turned the party's position on education and state-church relations into the central piece of their challenge to traditional Liberal leaders. In Belgium, for instance, the Liberal leader Frère-Orban repeatedly pointed out (quoted in Pirenne 1932:231) that "liberalism would commit suicide by descending into the religious field."[1] Until the 1870s the moderates managed to resist radical

[1] Likewise, in France, the Republican premier, Waldeck-Rousseau, had no intention in 1899 of pushing the anticlerical attack as far as separation, but this outcome was reached because of internal party pressure: "In a very real sense, the Prime Minister was captive to the will of his parliamentary supporters on this vital issue, and events were to demonstrate that Waldeck was not always free to choose the direction and the pace that the anticlerical movement would take" (Partin 1969:263).

pressure, but they eventually lost the battle because they depended on radicals for the operation of the party machine and the successful contestation of elections. Moreover, the rise of the Socialist Left turned anticlericalism into the only issue that could make bourgeois Liberalism attractive to the masses. As a result, anticlericalism became the cement that held Liberal parties together, their "only common denominator" (Witte 1973:377; Partin 1969:263; De Meeus 1962:324). Indeed, "Frère-Orban was able to maintain agreement between the [factions] and carry on with the government, only by initiating a political struggle against the church. This was inevitable because of the internal cleavage within the party" (De Meeus 1962:324). As Pirenne (1932:233) reports, Frère-Orban "was the prisoner of the radicals."

The church had been able, through its direct access to power, to thwart the first feeble Liberal attempts at educational reform which got under way after the revolutions of 1848. In Belgium a first attempt of educational reform made in 1850 failed because of the direct intervention of the church. In the Netherlands similar attempts were made from 1857 to 1864 with no results. In Germany, where the church was very close to some princes and monarchs, and in Italy (with the exception of the Piedmont), the church was generally not threatened at all. In Austria, not only did the concordat of 1855 between the empire and the Vatican reassert the privileges of the church, it even provided for additional ones, provoking intense reaction: the Austrian concordat is aptly called "the church's great negative gift to Austrian Liberalism" (Boyer 1981:20). The end of the 1850s, however, saw the rise of new aggressive Liberal governments which passed effective anticlerical legislation around the 1870s. In Belgium, the Netherlands, Austria, and France this attempt primarily took the form of the institution of state (or near-state) monopoly over education. In Italy and Germany educational reform, though significant, was only part of a far wider attack against the church that took the form of the destruction of the temporal sovereignty of the pope (in Italy) and the close regulation of the internal life of the church (in Germany).

The conflict developed in a spiral fashion rather than as the result of carefully planned moves intended to turn religion into the dominant political issue. Anticlerical legislation provoked the reaction of the church, which, by fulfilling the Liberals' worst image of it, led to Liberal escalation. Windell (1954:183–84) describes this process in Bavaria:

> Perhaps the feature of the [1869] campaign which aroused the greatest liberal indignation was the direct intervention of the Catholic clergy on behalf of the Patriots. Clergymen often refused to grant absolution to Catholics who persisted in reading liberal newspapers, and many of them campaigned actively for Patriot candidates. In such a situation, religion itself could hardly escape becoming an issue. As the campaign progressed, anticlericalism, and even anti-Catholicism, became more and more the focus of

the liberal attack. Ever more frequently was heard the demand that the people of Bavaria and of Europe be freed of the domination of an obscurantist clergy.

The Catholic Church and the Rise of Mass Organizations

Constraints affected the action of the church as well. They explain why the church tolerated the gradual independence and growth of Catholic organizations and the formation of confessional parties, even though it was opposed to these developments. The two strategies implemented by the church (organization and participation) were certainly based on trade-offs, as the church sacrificed some degree of control to protect its influence. Although the church failed to foresee the emergence of confessional parties, it did everything in its power to prevent this prospect from becoming reality.

Initially, the church took a variety of preemptive measures to strengthen its control over both its personnel and its members. When these measures proved insufficient, the church openly and directly cracked down on any attempt toward independence, autonomy, or uncontrolled politicization of the Catholic organizations. To quell the move of Catholic organizations toward political autonomy, the church followed two broad methods. First, it destroyed the organizations that openly promoted independent political action and imposed religious sanctions on their leaders. This was the strategy of repression. Later, when outright repression became extremely costly, the church attempted to block the emergence of independent Catholic organizations and confessional parties: this was the strategy of obstruction. Finally, once confessional parties emerged, the church was forced to recognize their existence. But this recognition was followed by an energetic attempt to reclaim its members from the new parties. This I call the strategy of recuperation. In addition, when political circumstances were favorable, the church went ahead and crushed these parties altogether.

The eagerness and initial ability of the church to repress any attempt at independent Catholic political action are indicated by consistent evidence across all cases. The church dissolved Catholic organizations that demanded independence and autonomous politicization.

The attempt of the Belgian journalist Bartels and his newspaper *Le Journal de Flandres* to create a Catholic party during the late 1830s failed "under the concerted action of the nuncio Mgr. Fornari, the king, and the Jesuits" (Guyot de Mishaegen 1946:59). The Union catholique, the first attempt to create a mass Catholic organization in Belgium with sections in every parish, was dissolved in 1871 after its members refused to accept a bishop as leader and restrict their activity in the field of charitable and religious work (Preneel 1982:121). The attempt by Dommer van Poldersveldt in 1848 in the Netherlands to create a Catholic party also failed because of church reaction (Bakvis 1981:60), as did later the interconfessional trade union Unitas, which was sabotaged and destroyed by the church against the wishes of the priests who promoted it (Bakvis 1981:31). The Katholikenverein, the first Austrian Catholic political association, was renamed, placed under the direct authority of the archbishop of Vienna, and turned into a philanthropic organization (Bled 1988:101). Likewise, two politicized clerical reform movements, the Austrian Clerustag and the Czech Jednota, were repressed by the episcopate in 1902 and 1907, respectively (Boyer 1981:165). In Prussia, the Zentrumsfraktion, the first Catholic political group, failed in part because it was used by the church in a deal to turn Prussia into the protector of papal Rome after the defeat of Austria (Hansen, cited in Windell 1954:59). In Italy, an attempt by lay Catholics and Conservatives to create a pro-Catholic party, the Partito nazionale conservatore, was condemned by the Catholic Congress of Modena in 1879 and thwarted (De Rosa 1972:135). The main Italian Catholic organization, the Opera dei congressi, was dissolved in 1904, when it came under the control of "christian democrat" activists who advocated participation in elections and planned to turn the organization into an independent Catholic party (Webster 1960:15). A similar fate awaited the Lega democratica nazionale of the priest Romolo Murri, which emerged as a result of the opposition of Catholic activists to the strategy of supporting Conservative candidates and demanded full autonomy from the hierarchy on questions unrelated to religion and morals (Giovannini 1981b:305). The Lega was neutralized in 1906 through the publication of the encyclical *Pieni l'animo,* which forbade priests to join it (Gherardi 1967:45; Menozzi 1983:66). The church did not hesitate to impose heavy religious sanctions, including excommunication, on activists who took independent initiatives: Murri was suspended *a divinis* in 1907, and excommunicated in 1909[2] (Menozzi 1983:66).

It is important to emphasize that the repression of independent Catholic political activity had organizational rather than ideological causes. For instance, the church did not crack down on the Italian Lega because of its position on the Roman question, since the French Sillon, which did not meddle with this issue, met with the same fate. Rather, the church repressed the Lega for three reasons: first, because it was seen as a rival of the official church-sponsored organization Unione popolare; second, because it claimed

[2] The church effectively undermined the formation of confessional parties and successfully repressed Catholic political activity in a number of other countries as well (such as Poland and Slovakia) where attempts had been made to form and develop Catholic parties (Durand 1995:85; Osa 1992:75).

autonomy and independence from ecclesiastical authority; and third, because it opted for political action (Agócs 1988:98). Likewise, the Vatican did not condemn the Action française for ideological reasons, as is often assumed, because the official Catholic organization, FNC, advocated similar ideas. This condemnation was "more the reassertion of the Church's own authority over the Catholic laity than a repudiation of political or social conservatism" (Ravitch 1990:121).

Thus repression was successfully implemented and the threat of destruction became a credible deterrent that prevented many Catholic organizations from rebelling. In addition, Catholic organizations, especially in their early stages, could not possibly survive without church approval. Most Catholics, particularly in rural areas, were closely connected to the church and would have never followed an excommunicated political leader or an organization explicitly disavowed by the church. Yet repression gradually became the exception rather than the rule and was implemented only under exceptional circumstances. First, the cost of repression became increasingly high: since Catholic organizations attracted more support, more Catholics would have been alienated by their church-sponsored destruction. As Jemolo (1960:60–61) puts it, most of these organizations in Italy "ended up by gaining the allegiance of the ecclesiastical hierarchy, by making it feel that its opposition would have alienated numerous good Catholics." Second, the emerging assertiveness of Catholic organizations coincided with the worst wave of anticlerical attacks. The church could ill afford to open a second (internal) front and squander its resources (Horner 1987:30). Third, following their politicization through the participation strategy, Catholic organizations were able to claim a new and exclusive source of legitimation: voters. This the church could not ignore. Altogether, these factors made the cost of repression forbidding. All the church could do was impede the transformation of Catholic organizations into political parties.

Simon (1958:23) points out that the Belgian bishops saw the organization of a political party as an obstacle to their leadership. Likewise, Serge Noiret (1994:88) reports that the church "was loath to promote a partisan political organization," and Jean-Luc Soete (1983:196) points out that one of the main causes of the delayed formation of a Catholic movement and a confessional party in Belgium was "the resistance of the bishops—who feared that religious influence might pass to the hands of laymen." As Wladimir Plavsic (1968:242) concludes, "It [wa]s not the church that . . . created and organized the Catholic party." Cardinal Engelbert Sterckx repeatedly in 1834, 1837, and 1841 asked priests "not to deal with politics from the pulpit [and] to abstain from everything that could . . . offend in any matter" (Guyot de Mishaegen 1946:60). During the 1850s, Sterckx refused to encourage and fund the creation of a Catholic newspaper (Cordewiener 1970:43). Conservative politicians, such as Adolphe Dechamps in 1875, pointed out in private that the church was resisting the expansion of the Catholic movement into the field of politics (Guyot de Mishaegen 1946:157). The same Dechamps (quoted in Kossmann 1978:246) claimed in 1865 that "the Catholics had done all they could to prevent the emergence of a Roman Catholic party." In 1867, the church decided to end lay-organized Catholic congresses in order "to take back the direction of the struggle" (Preneel 1982:121).

In the Netherlands, attempts to form a first Catholic electoral committee in 1848 failed because of the intervention of the church (Bakvis 1981:60). Hans Daalder (1955:6) points out that in the late 1880s, "the episcopacy, if not openly against attempts at founding a special Catholic party, was hardly in favour of the idea." Supported by the church, "a number of Catholic politicians felt that their needs were best served by supporting the Conservative party" (Bakvis 1981:62). In 1883, the priest Herman Shaepman provoked "perplexity and indignation" among church leaders when he issued a political program intended to lead to the formation of a Catholic party (Beaufays 1973:374). Wilhelmus Van Eekeren (1956:30) remarks that "his remained the lonely voice in the desert." The pro-Catholic press either ignored his appeal or attacked him openly: "In all kinds of writings Shaepman's fellow-Catholics opposed the idea of his party. History was called upon to prove that victory in the struggle for principles did not lay in a political formation" (Van Eekeren 1956:37). Shaepman's religious orthodoxy was questioned by influential church leaders (Beaufays 1973:374) who accused him of endangering the position of Catholics in the country by arousing with his actions "the ire of the non-Catholic majority" (Bakvis 1981:23). As a result, the bishops forbade him to speak in public and tried to undermine his project (Van Eekeren 1956:39). The church continued this tactic even after the formation of the Catholic party. In 1904, "the bishops ordered that an association of reform-minded priests and lay Catholics be disbanded on the grounds that priests and laymen could not consort with each other in a common society" (Bakvis 1981:23). The same year the church blocked the creation of a centralized party by inducing local associations not to join. According to Bakvis (1981:63), "At this point [1904] the Bishops were still ambivalent about Catholic participation and thus made no effort to ensure a cohesive Catholic party." Thus the General League of Roman Catholic Electoral Associations, as the Catholic party was known, remained until as late as 1926 a loose coalition of local Catholic electoral associations.

According to Boyer (1981:123), "Modern political clericalism in Austria was effected in large part against the Austrian bishops." Although the Austrian episcopate was the "most compliant and weakest sector of Catholic resistance" to anticlerical legislation (Boyer 1981:32), it did not show weakness in its attacks against Catholic activists. Jean-Paul Bled (1988:119) reports that the archbishop of Vienna "was observing the efforts that Catholics made to organize themselves politically with a distrust difficult to hide." During the late 1860s, newspapers close to the church attacked the Catholic activists "for using the problems of the church to serve political interests" (Bled 1988:121) and "using the issue of the church only as a lever for political participation" (France 1975:198). In 1873, the archbishop openly accused Catholic activists of using religion for political purposes (Bled 1988:122). Catholic organizations were often deprived of both material and moral support and were able to survive and grow only through the help of the lower clergy. Bishops were infuriated by the political activity of the lower clergy during the late 1880s. This activity was crucial in transforming the Viennese Christian Social movement into a political party. In 1894, after a decade of vacillation, the cardinals of Vienna and Prague issued a direct condemnation of the Christian Social movement and sent an official delegation to Rome to obtain a papal condemnation of the Christian Socials. But by then it was too late. The attempt to curb the Christian Socials by postponing the Catholic congress of 1894 failed, and the Christian Socials organized their own Catholic congress against the wish of the bishops. The church leadership realized that the creation of a competing national Catholic political association under its control was unfeasible given the Christian Socials' popularity (Boyer 1981:343). As Boyer (1981:348) concludes, "The bishops could grumble and complain, but now they had to come to terms with the Christian Socials."

The Catholic church in the German states obstructed the formation of a lay Catholic political movement for a long time. During the 1850s several Prussian bishops openly opposed the formation of a Catholic party and raised various obstacles to lay political activity (Whyte 1981:31). In 1857, the church attempted to eliminate the governmental position of the director of church affairs in Berlin, which was occupied by a Catholic layman. The director, Matthias Aulike, complained and expressed frustration about the role of the hierarchy (Yonke 1990:187). The Prussian archbishop Paulus Melchers officially prohibited clerical participation in the crucial electoral campaigns of 1867 (Windell 1954:280). In a letter he addressed later to the Vatican, Melchers (quoted in Mayeur 1966:162) pointed out that "there exists among the Catholics of Prussia a small faction of men, excellent Christians, full of faith and devotion toward the church who, however, are not endowed of a similarly remarkable prudence."

Württemberg church leaders reacted to the formation of a confessional party during the 1870s because, as Blackbourn (1975:846) remarks, they "preferred the discreet lobbying of ministers on specific concessions to the Church, not the instigation of a mass party which cut across the lines of their own authority." In 1877, Bishop Karl Joseph von Hefele told the local Catholic leader Probst that he was unwilling to see a Zentrum group in the lower house because he felt it to be "inopportune" (Blackbourn 1975:846). Likewise, in Alsace-Lorraine "efforts to create a Catholic party" were stymied "by an upper clergy which was troubled by the idea of direct clerical involvement in politics" (Gaines 1993:209). In Bavaria during the late 1860s, the hierarchy "was reluctant to approve any [Catholic] program which set the masses politically in motion" (Windell 1954:179). Southern (1977:xi) reports that "the attitude of most of the higher clergy, especially the bishops, towards Catholic agitation was cool or hostile." The most open enemy of Catholic organizations was the archbishop of Passau, who "opposed on principle every form of lay organization within the church, whenever it threatened to escape the guiding hand and leadership of the hierarchy" (Southern 1977:199). He "set out to curb their influence and to maintain a wall between their activity and his diocesan clergy" (Southern 1977:230). In 1867, he forced the local youth organization to abandon the use of the word "Catholic" in its title and ordered clergymen under his jurisdiction to cease participation in its activities (Windell 1954:179–80). In newspaper articles, published in the summer of 1872 and widely believed to have been written by him, he submitted the Bauernvereine, peasant Catholic organizations, to a very tough critique: "Filled with hate and aversion for the laws [and] for authority, disrespectful towards the clergy, hostile to officialdom and the educated classes, mistrustful of its former leaders, the peasant estate is on the lookout; it trusts no one any more" (quoted in Southern 1977:97). Yet "to a large extent, the policy and attitude of the Bishop of Passau was a failure, for it was in the Passau diocese that a large number of young and mostly lower ranking members of the clergy, especially among the *Cooperaten,* founded or were among the leaders in numerous political associations, some of which took on a populist coloration" (Southern 1977:230–31). Repression was directed particularly against priests. Under the leadership of such a priest, Dominic Gröbl, the Catholic Volksverein of the village of Beilngries in Franconia attracted close to one thousand members within just eight months from its creation in December 1871. In July 1872, Gröbl's activities were condemned by the church and he was forced by his bishop to declare publicly that he was quitting the organization and ceasing his activity (Southern 1977:291–95).

The Kulturkampf weakened the German Catholic church so much that rather than obstructing the formation of the Zentrum, it became instead totally dependent on it. By 1876 every bishop in Prussia was either in prison or in exile and by 1880 about 1,100 out of 4,600 parishes were without pastors (Ross 1976:16). The removal, exile, or isolation of the bishops allowed both the lower clergy and the lay Catholics to gain extraordinary leverage within the church (Anderson 1986:109). Lay Catholics were even allowed to run parishes (Yonke 1990:234). But when the anticlerical attack subsided, the church vigorously reasserted its authority (Anderson 1981:475). For instance, between 1900 and 1914 the church used various means (episcopal directives, threats of suppression, and papal pronouncements) to suppress the interconfessional Christian trade unions (Ross 1976:99).

Until 1919, the Vatican refused to recognize the new Italian state and formally prohibited the political participation of Catholics and, by implication, the creation of a confessional political party. The *non expedit* was first promulgated in 1868, although the formula *né eletti né elettori* (neither elected nor electors) was unofficially guiding the action of the faithful from 1861 (Gherardi 1967:39). This prohibition was formally reinforced in 1874 and 1886, but the *non expedit* established a common political practice for all Catholics, unintentionally creating the basis for the emergence of a Catholic political identity. The formula *preparazione nell'astensione* (preparation through abstention), launched in the 1880s and 1890s, was a means used by Catholic activists to turn electoral abstentionism into organizational preparation for future political struggles (Ambrosoli 1958:13–14). Gradually, it became increasingly difficult for the church to control lay Catholics. When, as a result of the 1904 partial relaxation of the *non expedit,* a few Catholics were elected to the parliament, the pope forbade them to form a Catholic parliamentary faction (Howard 1957:75); when, in 1916, the Catholic leader Filippo Meda decided to participate in the Boselli cabinet, the Vatican declared that he represented only himself and his friends, not the Catholics (De Rosa 1972:378).

The Vatican strongly resisted the transformation of the Catholic lay organizations into a political party. The story of these organizations is one of unremitting conflict over their control between the church (supported by conservative lay Catholics) and Catholic activists demanding political participation and organizational autonomy. The attitude of the pope on the national level and of most bishops in their dioceses toward Catholic organizations was at best one of "formal approval, but distrustful and discouraging detachment" (Belardinelli 1979:61). The Vatican decisively blocked a first attempt by some Catholics to form a party during the years 1882–1888 (Webster 1960:7). The congress of the Opera dei congressi in 1901 resulted in structural modifications that gave the Opera "an even more ecclesiastical character." The Opera ended up depending on the College of Cardinals "as if it was a fraternity or an association of priests and not of laymen" (De Rosa 1972:208–9). In 1904, the Opera was dissolved. Richard Webster (1960:15) points out that "the Vatican had escaped the danger of an Italian Catholic party, which under Murri would have cut loose from any hierarchical control and might have dragged the church into dangerous adventures. Murri's party would have been Catholic without being papal, and its leader would have been a political primate imperiling the unity of command within the church." In 1905 Meda's project of a Catholic party modeled after the German Zentrum failed when it became clear that "the intentions of Pius X moved in a different direction from what Meda and his friends dreamed" (Vecchio 1987:29).

Azione cattolica, the organization that replaced the Opera, was placed under direct control of the bishops. In a papal circular sent to the bishops in 1904, it was pointed out that "Azione Cattolica would be in the future under the direct control of the bishops. Diocesan congresses would be held only under episcopal control, and national congresses could not be held without the authorization of the pope. The pope would also have the exclusive right of appointing the head of Azione Cattolica" (Howard 1957:74). The church effectively thwarted all attempts by lay Catholics to take control of their organizations. Attempts to wrest control of the Unione popolare, the main Catholic organization, failed in the 1906 and 1910 congresses. In 1910, the supporters of the Vatican won by prematurely closing the congress and declaring its fidelity to the pope (Howard 1957:86). After the 1913 Gentiloni pact, the official Vatican paper *L'Osservatore Romano* argued that the need for a formal political party of Italian Catholics was shown to be unfounded (Cunsolo 1993:44). Although Catholic activists managed at last to form the Partito popolare italiano in 1919, the role of the church in its formation was at best irrelevant (De Rosa in Magleri 1969:xii), at worst openly hostile: the PPI "was not only expendable to the Vatican, but more positively it had to be dismantled" (Molony 1977:13). At the same time, the church reasserted its control over the lower clergy by reducing its quasi-union, the FACI, into a charitable organization of the clergy (Erba 1990; Carillo 1992).

Thus historical evidence suggests more than just a sporadic and incidental church reaction to the emergence of independent Catholic political organizations. Indeed, the pattern of repression and obstruction is consistent across cases. Yet obstruction failed and confessional parties emerged. The church could not afford to turn its back on the newly formed confessional parties. Repressing them would have been incredibly costly given their newfound popular legitimacy, acquired through impressive electoral victories won with a pledge to defend religion. The difficulty of repressing the parties is illustrated by the case of the abbé Lemire in France. Although his bishop suspended him from his priestly function in 1914, he was reelected. As Mayeur (1968:517–18) describes it, "a district, considered among the most catholic in France, elected in the first round a suspended priest."

The church tolerated these parties for four reasons. First, it was easier to try to control them from within by playing factions against each other. Second, toleration was a form of damage control. After all, if Catholics *had* to be organized politically, better it be by pro-Catholic parties. Third, these parties were, up to a certain point, a political guarantee against future anticlerical attacks. Confessional party leaders used this argument to win church support.

For example, the German Carl Bachem pointed out that should "electoral losses enfeeble the Centrum, the Roman church's interests in Germany would be in jeopardy" (quoted in Ross 1976:116). Fourth, the rise of socialism was a factor of utmost importance in the calculations of the church, although only after confessional parties were formed. In addition, the Socialist threat provided an incentive for the church to help preserve the unity of Catholic movements and parties once these movements were an established and inescapable reality (Mabille 1985:114; Belardinelli 1979:154).

These four reasons were also a way for the church to rationalize an inescapable reality. As Molony (1977:6) remarks, "The Vatican acquiesced to the formation of the PPI because . . . it could not prevent it." Once these parties became a reality, the church could do nothing but try to live with them and make the best of a bad situation. Still, it never gave them unconditional support. In some cases, the church withdrew from active politics and left the parties "to fend largely for themselves" (Houska 1985:28). "Once major church political goals had been achieved, such as the public support of religious schools, and some of the dangers of both overinvolvement in politics and overdevelopment of organizations had been exposed, church leaders were far less willing to continue close support of a particular political party and the goals of its elite" (Houska 1985:131). In some cases, however, the church took advantage of a favorable political context to destroy autonomous Catholic organizations and even the confessional parties themselves.

The formation of confessional parties had negative consequences for the church. Because they grew independent from the church (see Chapter 5), these parties reduced the range of the church's political action and diminished its bargaining capacity. The church now had to share Catholics with the new parties and compete for the right to represent them. The recognition by the church of this new reality was therefore coupled with an active strategy of redressing the balance of authority and control which had been shaken by the creation of confessional parties and winning back the Catholics who came under these parties' fold. The strategy of recuperation was not new for the church. The medieval Catholic church often responded to internal movements of protest with a tactic that "consisted in the elimination or co-optation of the leaders of a movement, and the integration, after that, of what was left of it into the official organizational structure of the Church through creation of religious orders" (Vaillancourt 1980:30). Gramsci (1995:37) has nicely described the strategy of recuperation: "It is to be noted that all innovations within the Church, when they do not stem from an initiative on the part of the centre, contain within themselves something heretical and end up by explicitly taking on this character until the centre reacts decisively, throwing the innovatory forces into disarray, reabsorbing the waverers and excluding the refractory elements."

Recuperation was implemented with particular intensity after the ascendance of Pius XI to the throne of St. Peter in 1922. As the British minister to the Vatican reported to the Foreign Office in 1927 (quoted in Rhodes 1973:15), "Pius XI wishes to withdraw the Church as far as possible from politics, so that Catholics may unite on a religious and moral basis." According to Arnal (1985:115), "Influential autonomous Catholic groups were looked upon with disfavor by the pontiff, and whenever he could, he engineered their replacement by organizations under the direction of the hierarchy." To weaken the confessional parties, the church actively discouraged priests from engaging in political action. To win back those church members who were now primarily active in politics, the church resorted to the development of Catholic Action. The 1922 papal encyclical *Urbi Arcano Dei* for the first time recognized that lay Catholics had a role to play within the church. Catholic Action was defined as "the participation of the Catholic laity in the apostolate of the hierarchy, for the defense of religious and moral principles, for the development of healthy and beneficial social action, under the leadership of the ecclesiastical hierarchy, outside of and above all political parties, in order to bring about a restoration of Catholic life in family and society" (quoted in Osa 1992:66). Catholic Action was thus given an exclusively religious and apostolical role; it was explicitly nonpolitical and "was to eschew politics entirely" (Rhodes 1973:15); and it was placed under very stringent control: as Bosworth (1962:74–5) reports, "All Catholic Action groups are organized in diocese federations, whose officers receive a mandate from the bishop. This allows the organizations to share in the apostolic work of the diocese. It also means that the bishop has a control over the 'tendencies' within Catholic Action. The bishop can withdraw his mandate and suspend the operation of any Catholic Action group within his diocese." Laura Gellott (1987:74–75) contrasts the features of Catholic Action in Austria to those of previous church organizations.

> First, religious apostolic concerns dominated the activities of the organizations, to the exclusion of political interests. . . . Secondly, Catholic Action emphasized an *official* church form of organization, in contrast to the previous *Verein* situation, which existed apart from the hierarchical structure of bishops, pastors, and parishes. Third, Catholic action was above all a lay movement, albeit one directed from above, through the clerical-episcopal structure. In it, the laity were called not to independent action, but to cooperation with church interests as defined by the hierarchy. There was no pretense at democratic organization and decision-making in Catholic action, as had existed in fact in the *Vereine*. Finally, Catholic action returned the focus of Catholic involvement to what bishops considered to be its proper environment—the parish and not partisan politics.

Besides the development of Catholic Action, the church sought to guarantee its rights through the signing of concordats with national governments, in exchange for which it willingly participated in the destruction of confessional parties. Concordats upgraded the status of the church by treating it as a sovereign power quasi-equal to the state, guaranteed substantial church privileges, and, in some cases, provided for state sanctions of religious offenses. For instance, the Italian concordat banned from certain public offices apostate priests and people under religious censure. Concordats were particularly effective for purposes of recuperation when signed with authoritarian governments, as in Austria, Germany, and Italy, but recuperation took place everywhere. Following the Catholic victory in the 1884 Belgian elections, the church forced one of the most important Catholic organizations, the Union nationale pour le redressement des griefs, to exit the political arena and dedicate its energies to social relief. In implementing this strategy, the church allied itself with the Conservative political elites and moderate Catholics who disliked the radical Catholics of the Union. Furthermore, the church separated social from religious activity and forced priests out of the former (Billiet and Gerard 1985:90). In 1919, the church set up a new organization, the Association catholique de la jeunesse belge, which excluded all nonreligious activity and was tightly controlled by it: every local group was under the direct supervision of a priest (Preneel 1982:130). The formation, in 1928, of the Jeugdverbond voor Katholieke Aktie provoked a confrontation between the church and the Catholic student organization, which refused to renounce its autonomy (Preneel 1982:131). During the same period the church tried hard to depoliticize a number of organizations—particularly working-class ones (Remy et al. 1985:401). Likewise, Gellott (1987:65) reports that most Austrian bishops "felt also that the [Christian Social] party and the organizations affiliated with it had become, by virtue of association, too much part of the parliamentary system. In so doing, they had become too independent from the church and had moved away from the task of advancing Catholic principles. A new structure of Catholic organization was needed, one which placed authority squarely in the hands of the bishops, and one which would work on behalf of confessional interests."

After 1901, the Austrian episcopate developed a comprehensive strategy to regain control of "its often unruly subordinates" (Boyer 1995:303). In 1905, the church attempted to win its members back by launching the Katholische Union von Österreich, which had "only limited success" (Gellott 1987:72). After the collapse of the empire, the church increased its hostility toward the party: the archbishop of Vienna was "unsure of the merits of close identification with the Christian Social party," and the church questioned "the value of relying on a political party to represent [its] interests (Zeps 1979:297, 312). When the Austrian concordat was signed in 1933, the church ordered all eighteen clerics holding parliamentary mandates to relinquish them. The rise of the Dolfuss dictatorship allowed the Austrian church to destroy the Vereine, the organizations that formed the backbone of the Christian Social party. In 1934, the forty-five thousand-member-strong Katholische Volksverein of Upper Austria was barred from participation in the Christian Social party and was transformed, against considerable resistance, into a diocesan organization of Catholic Action. Strict cultural and religious objectives were imposed, and the organization was placed under the tight control of the bishops (Gellott 1987:86–89). Most other organizations quickly followed, and by May 1934 the bulk of Christian Social organizations had been dissolved by the church (Gellott 1988:578). In a display of hypocrisy, the bishops praised the members of those organizations as "*Freicorps* for the church, fighting for its rights and freedoms . . . as Catholic politicians and parliamentarians." They simultaneously pointed out that the need for such action had passed and that Catholic Action was now "the sole proper forum for lay activity within the church" (Gellott 1987:92–93).

The church followed a similar course of action in Germany. In 1872, Windthorst blocked the formation of a competing Association of German Catholics spearheaded by the church. Anderson (1981:180) underlines "Windthorst's determination to preserve the Zentrum's monopoly on political Catholicism and the tactical freedom it guaranteed." At the end of the 1880s, the church pressed again for the creation of a new mass anti-Protestant organization with purely confessional objectives named after the pope, the Leoverein (Iserloh 1977:59). This attempt eventually failed because Windthorst, in a masterful political move, managed to create instead a phenomenally successful party organization, the Volksverein. Its spectacular growth dismayed the bishops, who viewed the issue as a "question of power for the Catholic episcopal authority in Germany" (Ross 1976:59). Noting its huge growth, a supporter of the church argued "that the time had come to ascertain the *Volksverein's* position within the ecclesiastical framework and the authority to which it must subordinate itself. Lest the *Volksverein* be misused, [he] concluded, it must be closely supervised by the episcopate" (quoted in Ross 1976:59). Where possible, the hierarchy managed to keep the Volksverein out, as was the case in Silesia (Mendershausen 1973:57).

After World War I, the church was more successful in asserting its control over Catholic organizations (Hürten 1986). During the 1920s and 1930s, the rise of Hitler provided the church with the opportunity to concur in the Zentrum's destruction (Casanova 1994:33). The church sent out public signs of its indifference about the party, and when Hitler offered the church concessions over religious education in return for the pope's withdrawal of support from the Zentrum, the Vatican accepted (Rhodes 1973:174). The British minister to the Vatican reported in 1933 that "the Vatican really viewed with indifference the dissolution of the Centre party" (quoted in Rhodes 1977:175). He added that "in conversations I have had with Cardinal Pacelli and Mgr Pizzardo, who both played an important part in the German concordat, neither gave me the feeling of the slightest regret at the eclipse of the Centre, and its consequent loss of influence in German politics" (quoted in Rhodes 1977:176). As soon as the concordat was signed, the Zentrum was banned.

The formation of the PPI provoked a similar reaction from the Italian church. Once the PPI was formed in 1919, the Vatican called all Catholics to join the official Unione popolare, which "was centralized, reliant upon ecclesiastical authority and directed fundamentally at the spiritual rather than at the civic or political" (Molony 1977:14). As Molony (1977:55) points out, "In the first few months of existence the seeds were sown for a conflict of loyalties between Catholic Action and the PPI." Count Dalla Torre, the head of the Unione popolare and a man of the Vatican, "saw the inevitable signs of a mass exodus from his own organization to the PPI" (Molony 1977:51). Dalla Torre (quoted in Molony 1977:52) declared that Catholic Action "never will admit that a catholic political party can arise in its place." Just after the formation of the party, Pope Benedict XV (quoted in Molony 1977:81–82) complained about the move of Catholics from official church organizations to the new party, a move he refused to accept and which, he thought, would be ephemeral: "We do not want anyone to forget that the Popular Union is the principal agent of Catholic Action. If other activities have been able to arise, even recently, in different fields, they are nothing but little streams springing from the regal river. The little streams of the Tiber and the Po can fade away while the Tiber and Po will always continue their majestic course through the cities and villages."

The church moved swiftly to assert its prominence over the PPI. The official Vatican newspaper *L'Osservatore Romano* consistently overlooked the activity of the party and often attacked it, denying that it was a Catholic party at all (Molony 1977:82). Moreover, many bishops showed little respect for the PPI and were openly hostile toward it (Vecchio 1979:72). The advent of fascism provided the church with the opportunity to spearhead the dissolution of the PPI (Casanova 1994:33). In 1923, Pius XI asked Sturzo to resign from parliament and disband the party. Sturzo obliged and went into exile. The church quickly ordered all priests to resign from the PPI, which was formally suppressed in 1926. In exchange, the church won, through the 1929 Lateran agreements, the recognition of its sovereignty by the Italian state, the granting of special privileges including the right to keep the Catholic Action organizations alive, the teaching of religion in schools, and considerable financial assistance (Vaillancourt 1980:186–88; Wolff 1979:2–3).

Obviously, recuperation strategies were successful, leading to the destruction of independent Catholic organizations where authoritarian regimes gave the church concordats and took away from the church the burden of directly eliminating confessional parties—in Italy, Austria, and Germany. Authoritarian regimes lowered the costs of destruction, partly by liquidating competing parties as well. It is telling that the arguments used by these regimes to justify the destruction of confessional parties were derived directly from the church's ideological arsenal. As the Milanese newspaper *L'Italia* (quoted in Vecchio 1987:15) argued in 1926: "Now, the thought of the Holy Father is clear: it is to subtract the defense of the sacred religious right from the baneful influence of the political struggles and the factions. The persecuted unite in the religious, not in the political domain, because in the latter case they should build a party, which even if it is good in itself, it is not immune to the shortcomings and errors of politics."[3]

I now turn to the five case studies.

Belgium

Liberals began their attempts to reduce the church's power in 1850 with the Rogier law, which sought to curtail the high level of clerical influence on education (Aubert 1968; Laury 1979:51–53). This attempt, coming on the heels of the creation of the Liberal party in 1846, destroyed the Unionist compromise and polarized the political class. In 1857, 1859, and 1860 a series of mild anticlerical legislative actions were implemented. The Liberals became increasingly anticlerical in the 1860s. Their program condemned religion as an "obstacle to progress," and Catholicism was proclaimed "an aberration to be destroyed at any price" (Verkade 1965:30).

The church began to carry out an organizational strategy as a response to these first threats. The gradual implementation of this strategy was spearheaded by the realization that the old way of direct intervention did not work anymore. Moreover, Conservatives appeared too weak successfully to face the Liberals and too fearful of adopting the defense of the church as their main issue. They were divided and trailed the Liberals in organization (De Trannoy 1905). As a result, the church leader, Cardinal Sterckx, asked laymen to help in the defense of the church (Mayeur 1980:76). There was, however, no thought of political organization. Sterckx's appeal (contained in his *Lettres sur la Constitution*), lacked any reference to the possibility of forming a Catholic party. Laymen, uninvolved in parliamentary politics, responded by organizing three Catholic congresses in Malines, in 1863, 1864,

[3] Likewise, the Vatican explained the demise of the Zentrum in the following semiofficial statement (quoted in Vaillancourt 1980:189): "The determination of Chancellor Hitler's government to eliminate the Catholic party coincides with the Vatican's desire to disinterest itself from political parties and confine the activities of Catholics to the Catholic Action organization outside any political party."

and 1867 (Guyot de Mishaegen 1946:124). These congresses, particularly the first, encountered the "rather reserved tolerance of the episcopate" (Aubert 1982:213). The motivation of both organizers and participants was not to create a political party, but rather to coordinate their action in view of the education laws (Mayeur 1980:76). Political action was explicitly rejected (Delfosse and Frognier 1988:73). As a result, these congresses, "although successful in a missionary and educational sense, did not succeed in formulating any direct political aims" (Verkade 1965:29). Nevertheless, the Malines congresses were extremely important because for the first time, they brought lay Catholics together for the defense of the church. They thus unintentionally sowed the seeds of the future Catholic political identity (Aubert 1952:171). The inaugural speaker at the 1863 congress put it very clearly: "Not daring to admit we are Catholics is a weakness hardly worthy of our cause" (quoted in Guyot de Mishaegen 1946:130). This speaker was not referring to religious affiliation, which no one would fear to acknowledge in a nation of Catholics, but to a new political identity.

The Malines congresses spawned two projects, both explicitly rejecting any interference with politics (Guyot de Mishaegen 1946:134). The first was a national organization for the defense of Catholic interests, the Union catholique de Belgique, which never formed probably because of the reluctance of the church to encourage the creation of a centralized national organization in a period when the danger of anticlerical legislation was not acute. The second project was a loose federation of local semireligious lay associations. This project succeeded, and in 1868 the Fédération des cercles catholiques was born. This lay organization controlled by the church was not intended for parliamentary action (Simon 1958:107). Some *cercles* were formed from 1853 as traditional religious associations, but the creation of the Fédération increased their number from thirty-one in 1869 to seventy in 1877 (Guyot de Mishaegen 1946:138, 144). In the meantime, the Conservative Right had followed the example of the Liberals in forming an organizational structure. The Comité central conservateur was formed in 1852 and the Association constitutionnelle conservatrice, a loose federation of local committees of notables, in 1858. Association and Fédération were two distinct organizations with different objectives, membership, and identity. The Association was a political organization composed of traditional politicians who upheld conservatism. It often appealed to Catholics for support, as to a different, subordinated body (Guyot de Mishaegen 1946:145). In contrast, the Fédération was a semireligious organization, controlled by the church and composed of lay Catholics with no parliamentary or political activity. The Fédération supported (in a nonsystematic way) the Conservatives when they defended the church and criticized them when they failed to do so (Guyot de Mishaegen 1946:139, 144). No alliance existed between the two organizations. Jules Malou, the parliamentary leader of the Right, was "a stranger to the Fédération" (Guyot de Mishaegen 1946:156). The organizational effort made by the Fédération was superior to that of the Association. The Conservative defeat in the 1878 elections is attributed to internal division and lack of organization (Becqué v.2 1956:322). In sum, though the Catholic organizational network remained weak, its foundations were laid out in the period 1864–1878.

The Conservative victory in the 1870 elections led to a decline of Catholic organizational efforts. Because there was no formal link between Catholic lay organizations and Conservative parliamentarians, the latter tended to neglect the interests of the church, displayed a marked reluctance to deal with confessional issues, and were often criticized by lay Catholic activists (Beaufays 1973:59). In the 1878 elections, Conservatives were defeated and the Liberals formed a new cabinet, promptly initiating a major attack against the church. The Van Humbeck law, passed on 10 July 1879, stipulated that the state would take over primary education, reduce (but not exclude) religious instruction from the curriculum of public primary schools, and abolish the church inspection of schools. This law was followed by a break of diplomatic relations with the Vatican in 1880 and supplemented by a law on secondary education passed in 1881. A final law, passed in 1883, made attendance in primary schools compulsory.

A contemporary observer (Carton de Wiart 1948:7–8) reports that the school laws generated among Catholics the feeling that "this time the whole spiritual heritage of our country, including what is sacred and essential for the believers, was the object of a premeditated aggression." The church quickly realized that most options were unavailable. On the one hand, Liberals ignored a collective letter of the bishops appealing for the repeal of the law and two official denunciations of the law by the church. On the other hand, the king did not block the Van Humbeck law but sanctioned it, notwithstanding expectations and rumors that he would not (Lubelski-Bernard 1983:388). Thus it became clear that only the further development of mass organization and participation in the political process could reverse the anticlerical legislation, and the church consequently decided to fight a "total war" (Becqué v.2 1956:365). This decision was taken without consultation with the Conservatives, who felt they had no other choice but to follow, even when dissenting on tactics (Terlinden v.2 1929:146; Laury 1979:714).

Catholics mobilized as soon as the law was passed in 1879. The resistance to the law was "systematic, intransigent, and often passionate" (Lubelski-Bernard 1983:383). To begin with, the church asked Catholic teachers to resign from public schools, forbade Catholics to send their children to public schools, and introduced heavy religious sanctions (such as the refusal of sacraments) for the parents who disregarded its directives. The archbishop Mgr. Dechamps ordered all dioceses to create committees composed of clerics and laymen to take over the running of a new network of primary confessional schools. These committees became "powerful organizations where the political and the religious became entangled" (Simon 1961:14). An organization called the Denier des écoles catholiques was created for fund-raising. The Catholic school network was very successful; in just two years it absorbed the majority of children.[4] The cost of running the new school network was extremely high, however. Legislative action for the repeal of the anticlerical laws was needed, and this required political participation.

The network of Catholic associations created under the organizational strategy was vastly expanded and reinforced under the direction of the church.[5] Committees of resistance and Catholic school committees, which included the philanthropic organizations of the church, sprang up everywhere. According to Laury (1979:711), "The expansion of the 'Catholic movement' " was "stunning" and it "took over Belgium within months." The right-wing press launched violent attacks against the law. Public meetings were organized all over the country, and a petition against the law collected 317,000 signatures. The Jeune garde catholique, a militant youth organization, was formed in 1879, and a Central Catholic Committee (Comité central catholique) was set up in Brussels to coordinate the struggle against the Liberals. Overall, as de Moreau (1929:521) reports, "innumerable" Catholic associations participated in the well-coordinated struggle. The term "Catholic movement" was by then widely used (Preneel 1982:123). Belgium had never witnessed a political opposition "so rapid, so general, so enthusiastic, so organized" (de Moreau 1929:520).

Supported by the expanding Catholic organizations, Conservatives began a campaign "for the defense of religious education" (Guyot de Mishaegen 1946:163–64). The main organization of lay Catholics, the Fédération, was transformed into a political organization. In 1879, in an act of great organizational and symbolic importance, it merged with the Conservative organization, the Association constitutionnelle conservatrice.[6] The new organization, the Fédération des cercles catholiques et des associations constitutionnelles conservatrices, an amalgam of local Conservative electoral committees and Catholic lay associations, received the full support of the church. As a result, it quickly grew to 104 local branches by 1883, constituting a "powerful structure" (Soete 1983:199). The publication, in 1884, of the Catholic newspaper

[4] Catholic schools attracted, in 1880, 455,179 children compared to 90,125 in 1878, or 60.73 percent of all students, while enrollment in the official schools went down to 294,356 students from an initial 597,614. By the end of 1884, 2,253 teachers had resigned from the public schools to join the new school network (Capéran, v.1 1960:199; Guyot de Mishaegen 1946:171, 169).

[5] These associations were not strictly speaking mass organizations. Relative to the very narrow electorate, however, they were huge organizations and constituted powerful political machines. The Catholic movement became a truly mass movement during the 1890s (Billiet and Gerard 1985).

[6] The statutes of the Fédération were altered in February 1884 to provide for the participation of parliamentarians in the executive council of the organization. "From now on," Soete (1983:201) asserts, "a narrow and official link exists between the Fédération and the right."

Patriote, at last made the pro-Catholic press equal in strength to the Liberal one (Delfosse 1979:470). In February 1884, four months before the elections, a new organization was created by lay Catholic activists called Union nationale pour le redressement des griefs. It grew rapidly to reach a membership of over six thousand within a few months (Soete 1984:213). This openly political organization was created without consultation with the parliamentary Right or the church (Soete 1986:61). Its purpose was to lead the electoral battle against the Liberals. "The Union is a war machine against liberalism," declared its leaders; "its objective is to be the general and direct instrument of the Catholic democracy; it wants to be the support of the Right in the country" (Guyot de Mishaegen 1946:176, 179). At the same time, the movement aimed to "absolutely prevent the return to power of an autonomous Right, which would not take into account, as it did in the past, the demands of the Catholic world" (Preneel 1982:124). This movement became known as *programmisme* because it was based on the idea of imposing a binding mandate on the Right.[7]

In June 1884, the Conservatives, with the help of the church and their political organizations, which collaborated closely during the electoral campaign, defeated the Liberals. The elections were dominated by the issue of religion (Falter 1986:191). Simon (1955:107) reports that "the [electoral] campaign was animated, enthusiastic, marked by religious mysticism, solidly helped by the local *comités scolaires.*" The victory of the pro-Catholic coalition was surprisingly big. Seventy Conservatives (plus sixteen Nationaux-Indépendants, allies of Brussels) were elected, up from fifty-nine in the previous elections, while the Liberals elected fifty-two deputies, down from seventy-nine. As a newspaper put it: "Ce n'est pas une défaite, c'est un écrasement" (this is not a defeat, it is a debacle)(Terlinden v.2 1929:152). This victory turned religion into a permanent institutional feature of the political landscape. Establishing its electoral potential, religion helped recast the Right from Conservative to Catholic. The president of the Fédération, Auguste Beernaert, appealed before the 1884 elections directly to Catholics, while people cheered in the streets shouting *"Vivent les Catholiques!"* (Guyot de Mishaegen 1946:184). This success is considered by most Belgian scholars to mark the emergence of the Catholic party in Belgium. As Beaufays (1973:60) puts it, "from Conservative before 1884, the party becomes Catholic."[8]

[7] As a result of this activity, the period 1878–1884 was dominated by an intense conflict between organized ultramontane Catholics and the parliamentary Right, with the church as an uneasy arbiter (Billiet and Gerard 1985:87).

[8] Lode Wils (1986) argues against this view. What happened in 1884, he points out, was not the formation of a confessional party but the subordination of the party to the will of its (confessional) electorate. The point remains that, one way or another, the post-1884 Catholic party was very different from the pre-1884 Conservative party. After 1884 there was no doubt about its confessional identity.

Following these elections, the Catholic coalition "organized itself into a party very quickly in order to consolidate its gains" (Delfosse and Frognier 1988:74). One of its first measures was to abolish the Ministry of Public Instruction (created by the Liberals in 1878) and repeal the Van Humbeck law. The Jacobs law, passed in September 1884, was more clerical in its content than the status quo ante, the law of 1842. It included the obligation of the state to subsidize Catholic schools and the right of the communes to introduce the teaching of religion into state school curricula. Still, it left the church unsatisfied because it recognized a dual system of education instead of establishing a church monopoly.

The Conservative leader Malou once more became the prime minister of Belgium. But he was now a mere relic of the old conservative times. His government included politicians such as Charles Woeste and Victor Jacobs, who were committed Catholics in control of the Catholic organizations (Pirenne 1932:298). They were "the most authentic representatives of the dominant religious tendency within the new party" (Simon 1958:84). After a short tenure, Malou resigned and was replaced by Beernaert, the president of the Fédération. Beernaert was politically moderate but had projected himself as a Catholic leader. During his tenure he was increasingly forced to rely on the confessional right of the party (Simon 1958:302). In the meantime, Charles Woeste consolidated the party organization through a series of reforms. The Union nationale was turned by the church into a social organization, while the Fédération became officially the political organization of the Parti catholique, as it was now called. The party remained in power until 1914. When universal, but plural, male suffrage was introduced in 1893, the Catholic party triumphed, electing 104 deputies, as opposed to 34 for the Socialists and 14 for the Liberals. Although it had not been its intention to create a Catholic party, the church had to accept the fait accompli. As Beaufays (1973:61) points out, "The church did not create the Catholic party but episcopal action supported it once the party was formed."

The Netherlands

A first mild law providing for nondenominational, yet still Christian, primary education passed by the Liberals in 1857 led to a first break with their Catholic allies in 1860 and spurred the first Catholic and Calvinist organizations. The 1870s saw a new attempt by the Liberals to reform the educational system. The reaction of the Liberals to the pope's loss of his territories in 1870 and the decision of their government in 1871 to recall the Dutch legation from the Vatican ended the Liberal-Catholic collaboration.

In 1868 the Catholic bishops issued a collective pastoral letter condemning the neutral orientation of public education, calling for the establishment of Catholic schools, and asking the faithful to unite. This letter marked the beginning of the church's organizational strategy. The first Catholic associations, mostly unstructured and ephemeral, were formed in 1868 (Brachin and Rogier 1974:373). A more structured organization, the Roman Catholic Electoral Association of North Brabant (R. K. Kiesvereeniging Noord-Brabant) was formed in 1870 with vague objectives. On the Protestant side, a radical mass Calvinist movement emerged in the beginning of the 1870s. A Protestant cleric, Abraham Kuyper, created in 1872 a militant daily newspaper *(De Standaard)* and a league against the school reform (evolved from the Society for Christian National Education formed in 1861), which was "consciously modeled on the British Anti-Corn Law League" (Daalder 1960:201). The league grew nationally with the quick creation of more than a hundred local branches (de Kwaasteniet 1990:15). In the meantime, despite its break with the Liberals, the Catholic church continued to consider them a less dangerous foe than Protestants. The chasm between Catholics and Calvinists remained large—a remnant of the religious wars.

The 1877 elections were won by the Liberals. The first anticlerical educational law was passed in 1878 by the Liberal government of Joannes Kappeyne van de Coppello. The education act introduced by the Liberals included important improvements in education, compulsory for all schools, but unequivocally forbade any financial assistance to nonpublic schools. In other words, "while considerably raising minimum educational and hygienic standards, [the law] did nothing to assist denominational schools to attain them" (Verkade 1965:41). New anticlerical laws followed in 1879 and 1883.

The 1878 law proved a "great boost for the clericals" (Beaufays 1973:373). It led to the implementation of the participation strategy through a pact between Catholics and Calvinists, both of whom reacted forcefully against this law. The Calvinists organized a massive petition movement against the school law which obtained 305,689 signatures at a time when the electorate was only a little over a third of this figure, and a similar petition by Catholics gathered 164,000 signatures. Abraham Kuyper drafted a party program that appeared in the *Standaard* in 1878. The Antirevolutionary party (ARP) was formed in 1878 and held its first national convention the following year.[9] The party adopted Kuyper's program, the Declaration of Principles, proclaimed resistance against the world of 1789, and pioneered modern mass-party orga-

[9] Antirevolutionary voters clubs were created during the 1860s by the Calvinist Guillaume Groen van Prinsterer, but they were marginal, isolated, did not form a national organization, and had little political significance. According to Vanden Berg (1960:96), "Although the Antirevolutionary party had already existed for many years under Groen's personal leadership, 1878 is correctly considered the birth year of the *organized* Antirevolutionary party" (emphasis added).

nization techniques. Popular response was extremely encouraging: as Kuyper (quoted in Vanden Berg 1960:52) declared, "Among our men the conviction is visibly gaining ground that the strength of our movement lies in the appeal to the consciences of our people." Instead of forming a Catholic party, the church focused its attention on the creation of a network of Catholic primary schools. From 1868 to 1887 the number of these schools swelled from 46 to 266. But the costs mounted as well and the realization came that participation in the political process was necessary.

The educational reform law, which the Calvinist leader Kuyper labeled *decretum horribile* (Verkade 1965:41), provoked so strong a sense of danger among the Christians that it contributed to the elimination of the Catholic-Protestant divide by burying the enduring legacy of the wars of religion. This legacy was still so sharp that Abraham Kuyper had been proclaiming that the chasm which separated the reformed church from Rome—and, by implication, from local Catholics—could never be closed (Brachin and Rogier 1974:107). In 1872 Kuyper had published a brochure on the tercentenary of the Saint Bartholomew massacre which was notable for its "sheer power of graphic, dramatic, startling recital of deeds of blood and horror and inhumanity" (Vanden Berg 1960:166). Likewise, a prominent Catholic politician (quoted in Van Eekeren 1956:26) had argued that "we Catholics (even if we might have the same wishes in education) can never make common ground with the Anti-Revolutionary Party."

Anticlerical legislation drove the Catholics "into the arms of the Calvinists" (Verkade 1965:42), leading to a previously unthinkable alliance. This alliance, implying organizational distinctiveness among Calvinists and Catholics (Vanden Berg 1960:167), was implemented in 1887 when it was adopted by the national convention of the ARP. It was dubbed Unio Mystica by Kuyper but "monstrous alliance" by the Liberals (Vlekke 1945:319), and it included Catholics, Calvinists, and assorted Conservatives. Its objective was to reverse the anticlerical reforms. In 1888, ten years after the formation of the Antirevolutionary party, Catholics created the Popular Catholic Union (RK Volkbond), a federation of Catholic organizations. The purpose of this federation was to participate in the forthcoming elections as a partner in the antiliberal coalition. The Catholic organizations were thus transformed into a political organization electorally promoting the defense of the church.

Aided by the electoral reform of 1887, which increased the number of eligible voters from 100,000 to 350,000, the Calvinist-Catholic coalition defeated the Liberal Union in the 1888 elections. Calvinists and Catholics coordinated their action by supporting a single candidate in each district. The Conservatives, until then the main opposition to the Liberals, were swept away by the force of the new religious cleavage and vanished as an autonomous force after 1888. A section of the Conservative party fused with a wing of the Liberals, while another wing joined the Calvinists (von der Dunk 1978:746). The elections produced a House composed of twenty-eight Antirevolutionaries, twenty-six Catholics, forty-four Liberals, one Conservative, and one Socialist. In 1889 the new government promptly replaced the 1878 law with the clerical Mackay law, which provided for state financial support for the denominational schools (Edmundson 1922:423).

The Catholic party was formed in 1888, ten years after the formation of the Antirevolutionary party. It was less radical and independent than the ARP because of its relationship with a centralized institution, the Catholic church.[10] The Catholic party was formed through the independent initiatives, often condemned by the church, of a priest, Herman Shaepman. In 1883, Shaepman drafted an outline for political action modeled after the German Zentrum's program. Because of church opposition, his activity failed to produce a Catholic party immediately (Beaufays 1973:374; Bakvis 1981:23). The Algemeenen Bond, a weak national organization he created, did not survive. It was the electoral success of the Catholic-Calvinist coalition and its participation in the government that led to the transformation of the RK Volkbond into a political party under Shaepman's leadership. The party was very slow to centralize because of church opposition and regional divisions between northern and southern Catholics. In 1896 the Catholic members of the Second Chamber decided to unite under a common party program. Local organizations accepted the Catholic program in 1897, but a central organization was not formed until 1904. According to Bakvis (1981:63), "At this point the church was still ambivalent about Catholic participation in politics and thus made no effort to ensure a cohesive Catholic party." Still, the effects of centralization were impressive. Whereas in 1897 candidates from confessional parties were competing in sixty-five constituencies, in 1905 such competition took place in only five constituencies. This event, according to Jan Verhoef (1974:215), "marks the final stage of the process of institutionalization of the religious parties at the national level." The Catholic party was enormously successful and became, in 1901, the strongest party in the country. A fully centralized party, the Roman Catholic State party (Roomsch-Katholieke Staatspartij—RKSP), emerged in 1926.

[10] For instance, after he resisted the extension of the franchise proposed by the Liberals and supported by the majority of the ARP, the leader of a minority faction within the ARP, Lohman, was accused as one of the "plutocrats and title holders in the ARP" (Verkade 1965:46). As a result, Lohman's faction broke away from the ARP and established the Christian Historical Union (Christelijk Historische Unie—CHU) which was more aristocratic, more loosely organized, and less radical than the ARP.

Austria

The Austrian case is original in the following way.[11] The organizational strategy was initiated by the church after the anticlerical attack but was subsequently left to lapse. Nevertheless, mass organization was subsequently developed by Catholic activists against the open resistance of the church. Likewise, the participation strategy was implemented autonomously from the church by those same activists. This was possible because of the peculiar significance of Viennese politics within the empire and the use by Catholic activists of the international position of the Austrian Empire to appeal directly to the Vatican and overcome the reaction of their national church.

The neoabsolutist period (1849–1859) was marked by the renovation of the altar-throne alliance, which culminated in the 1855 concordat. The concordat granted the church broad concessions in areas ranging from matrimonial law to education. This period came to an end with the Austrian military defeat in Königgrätz in 1866. The ensuing political democratization brought to power a new generation of Liberals, determined to reduce the church's power, which they viewed as the main cause of their country's backwardness. They won the 1867 elections and formed the Constitution party in the Austrian Reicshrat. Their particular target was the concordat, which they considered a shameful text.[12]

The Liberal government (known as Bürgerministerium because it was controlled by the champions of the German bourgeoisie) sought to abrogate the concordat unilaterally and simultaneously to advance the cause of educational reform. In July 1867, Liberals introduced a motion in the Austrian parliament which included the restoration of the matrimonial law to the jurisdiction of the civil courts, the emancipation of the public schools from the influence of the church, and the regulation of interconfessional relations to assure non-Catholics equal treatment (France 1975:1). Although this motion was

[11] Austria refers here to the Austrian (or Cisleithanian) half of the Austro-Hungarian empire, which after 1866 was divided in two parts (the other half was the Transleithanian or Magyar part).

[12] For the Liberals, there were two particularly unacceptable stipulations of the concordat (France 1975:2): article ten, which provided that since "all cases of Church law, particularly those concerning the faith and sacraments . . . belong under the jurisdiction of ecclesiastical authority, matrimonial affairs are to be decided by ecclesiastical judges according to the holy canonical law"; and article five, which required that the "entire instruction of Catholic young people, in all public as well as private schools, will be made suitable to the teachings of the Catholic religion. The bishops will exercise the power of their own pastoral offices over the education of the young and carefully guard against anything that might be contrary to the Catholic faith and to moral purity." Both rights were exercised before 1855 by civil authorities. The Liberal newspaper *Die Presse* (quoted in France 1975:124) referred in 1868 to the concordat as an "instrument of torture, [a] glowing iron thumb screw."

initially blocked by the ministry of Count Ferdinand Beust, the first laws were passed in the Lower Chamber in October 1867 followed by passage of a new constitution. The concordat was repudiated in 1868 and abrogated in 1870. A bill introducing civil marriage passed in March 1868, followed by a law regulating interconfessional relations in May 1868. Liberals voted two education bills, the school supervision law in May 1868 and the imperial school law or Reichsvolksschulgesetz, in May 1869. Known as the May laws, they "signaled the end of the singularly privileged position of the Catholic church in Austrian society" (Bowman 1989:250). These laws took away from the church its extensive supervision and administrative rights and replaced them with state control over the schools. In the new supervisory councils the church had only a minority position. Under the new system, priests were responsible only for religious instruction. These reforms allowed confessional schools to operate freely but barred them from receiving state subsidies. According to C. A. Macartney (1968:574), "It was their confessional legislation which the Liberals pressed most strongly of all."

Because the emperor Franz Josef relied on the Liberals for the regeneration of the empire, he was compelled to yield to their program (France 1975:iii). This came as a shock to the church, which depended exclusively on the state for its protection. As Pope Pius IX (quoted in France 1975:141) put it, "the Emperor has sold himself to the liberal party." Indeed, Carl Schorske (1967:361) confirms that the emperor "had since 1860 evidently become a prisoner of the Liberals." Thus, "as political exigencies forced Francis Joseph to abandon his defense of the concordat, it became increasingly clear to clerical Conservatives that in a constitutional, parliamentary state they themselves had to assume the defense of the church's interests" (France 1975:iii).

The anticlerical legislation provoked vehement reactions. The Austrian bishops met in Vienna in September 1867 to discuss means of combating what was dubbed "the War against the church." They issued a public address calling for imperial intervention (France 1975:16, 18). After the emperor took the side of the parliament against the church, the bishops condemned the laws in pastoral letters (Wandruszka 1977:153). "Austrian citizens who were devout vowed to reverse the decisions of 1868, particularly the new School Law" (Jenks 1965:123). The Liberal attack "awoke in the Catholic circles a spirit of combativeness which made *croyant* Catholicism a more living force in Austria than it had been, perhaps, since the days of Maria Theresa" (Macartney 1968:621). According to the Austrian historian Max Hussarek (cited in Zeps 1979:84), it was a demonstration in support of the imprisoned Bishop Franz Rudigier, which took place in Linz in 1869, that marks the birth of popular political Catholicism in Austria. Between 1867 and 1869 numerous Catholic associations were formed with the specific purpose of fighting the Liberal laws. France (1975:59) notes that "by November 1867 . . . a mass political movement in its embryonic" form had appeared. Catholic lay associations, such as the Katholische Volksverein in Linz with a membership of fifteen thousand in 1870, the Katholisch-Konservative Volksverein in Styria with four thousand members in 1869, and the Katholisch-Patriotische Volksverein, were created on a local (mostly rural) basis, were led by the clergy and remained outside politics. At the same time, Carl von Vogelsang's newspaper *Das Vaterland* developed in 1867–1868 the main themes of the ideological critique of Liberalism.

Yet, after this initial reaction, the church returned to a moderate and conciliatory course emphasizing direct negotiations. According to Schorske (1967:361), the hierarchy "offered little resistance to the dismantling of the church's traditional authority"; it "clung to the imperial system as the rock on which the ship was wrecked, worked through the *Honoratioren* and the court, and tried to keep out of trouble. . . . It bowed to the inevitable and bore its sufferings as a patient victim, without self-examination and without doubt." This tactic led to fragmentary concessions from the Liberals and a moderate application of the laws. Despite his ratification of the May laws, Franz Joseph remained a guarantee for the church. France (1975:141) reports that he "gave his approval to the laws, again 'with heavy heart,' and restrained his ministry from seeking 'the right to obtain further, more far-reaching measures in religious and ecclesiastical affairs. . . . 'I will never again offer my hands toward [causing] a break with the Church,' he vowed." No longer feeling in immediate danger, the church was able to slow the development of Catholic organizations and obstruct the efforts of Catholic activists to assert their independence and to participate in politics.

The defeat of the Liberals in the 1879 elections contributed decisively to the moderation of the church. This defeat was provoked by the question of nationalities rather than church intervention. The Liberals lost their parliamentary majority and their cabinet fell, to be replaced by one led by a pragmatic Conservative, Eduard Taaffe. The new cabinet was based on an alliance of Conservatives, Slavs, and various independents. The advent of the Taaffe government marked the end of the Austrian Kulturkampf through an even more moderate application of the anticlerical laws (Wandruszka 1977:162). Taaffe, however did not run a clerical cabinet. The Right was divided along ethnic lines and its pro-Catholic component (the Hohenwart Club) was weak and divided as well "by provincialism and nationalism" (Zeps 1979:133). The Upper House, in contrast, remained for some time under Liberal control and effectively blocked all attempts to repeal the May laws (Macartney 1968:621). Moreover, Conservatives failed to obtain control of the Ministry of Education: Taaffe selected a person reputed to be neutral on the question of confessional schools (Zeps 1979:118). Finally, despite pressure from the Conservatives, Taaffe refused to repeal the school laws: "He fended off the clerical attack on the school system as long as he commanded some rapport with the Liberals" (Jenks 1965:124). Thus Catholics were unable to reverse the anticlerical legislation as they did in Belgium and the Netherlands. An amendment to the 1869 law with some concessions to the church was passed in May 1883, but Catholics were far from satisfied (Papanek 1962:29). Conservatives made a last effort to achieve abrogation of the 1869 law in 1888. The Conservative parliamentary leader, Alois Lichtenstein, proclaimed a "second crusade" to secure the "proper principles" in the Austrian school system, but his attempt failed, and the legal reforms of 1867–1869 remained in effect until 1934.

The conciliatory position of the church provoked a conflict between Catholic activists and the church, which, in 1873–1875, almost spilled into the public arena (Bled 1988:124). Not until 1877 were Catholic lay activists able to overcome the reluctance of the church and organize the first Catholic Congress of Austria, held in Vienna. It is revealing that the final obstacles to this congress were removed only with the death of the archbishop of Vienna, Cardinal Rauscher. The congress was attended by 2,300 delegates, including 684 churchmen, and proved a success. Following the familiar pattern, this congress had a high symbolic value but no political impact besides the condemnation of the school laws and the affirmation of its Catholic identity. According to Michael Zeps (1979:113), this congress revealed "the embryonic state of Catholic organization in political matters on the imperial level."

The church underestimated the frustration felt by lay Catholics and priests: "There was ferment in the ranks of the Catholics over a new direction for political Catholicism" (Zeps 1979:141). Disillusioned by what they viewed as lack of progress, Catholic activists used the existing organizational infrastructure to build a new Catholic movement: according to France (1975:4), "A dynamic clerical Conservative movement, culminating in the formation of the Christian Social Party, grew inexorably out of the struggle over the May confessional legislation." This movement vastly differed from the traditional Right, which was led by "federalist Bohemian noblemen and provincial Conservatives from the Alpine lands," and whose "parliamentary clubs were *Honoratiorenparteien,* small groups of notables" alarmed by "modernity and all its works and pomps" (Schorske 1967:361).

Organization building was arduous. On the surface, the period 1874–1887 was a stagnant one for Catholics. The failure of the legislative attempt to repeal the May laws in 1888 marked the low point of Catholic political influence. But Catholic activists, both lay and priests, were busy laying the foundations of the Catholic movement. The failure to reverse the school laws and the growth of the strongly anticlerical Social Democrats, committed to secular public education, facilitated their work. The Katholische Schulverein, an organization that coordinated the action against the school law, was created in 1886. This organization, with 20,610 members and 151 parish chapters in 1891, became "the most important lay Catholic voice in the politics of education before World War I" (Zeps 1979:127–28). In 1887, Viennese priests formed the Christian Social Association, which advocated the creation of confessional schools as a precondition for effective social reform (Boyer 1981:114). These clerics were supported by Catholic lay leaders who sought to form an alliance with other antiliberal groups to fight the Liberals and eventually create a Catholic party (Boyer 1981:160). As early as 1868 the newspaper *Das Vaterland* had called for the creation of an "antiliberal confederation" that would include Catholics, Federalists, the nationalities of the empire—particularly the Czech aristocracy—and those who "suffered from the financial and material consequences of the recently adopted system" (France 1975:149–53). Various programs along these lines were formulated, but no such coalition was formed before 1887, when it contested by-elections in Vienna. The electoral results were impressive, helped by the 1882 electoral reform, which significantly increased the number of eligible voters. For the first time since 1870, a non-Liberal was elected to the Reichsrat from an urban constituency in Lower Austria. The success of this strategy led to its repetition during the same year and, again, to its success, to the astonishment of Catholics and Conservatives (the "German Nationals") alike, "who had been trying for years (with no success) to break down Liberal power in provincial Lower Austria" (Boyer 1981:218). As a result, the All-Austrian Catholic Congress of 1887 displayed a "new mood" for action and called for organization and combat (Schorske 1967:361–62).

The surprising electoral successes of 1887 led Catholic activists and Conservative leaders to proclaim the creation of a Catholic-Conservative coalition called United Christians. This coalition brought together democrats of the Viennese suburbs, small petty-bourgeois shopkeepers, conservative Catholics, and German nationalists united by anti-Semitism and a common opposition to Liberalism and capitalism (Wandruszka 1977:165). In February 1888 the Christian Social associations organized a United Christians meeting from which they excluded their Pan-German allies, thus establishing their control over the coalition (Geehr 1990:74). A clever political entrepreneur, Karl Lueger, the leader of the Vienna "Democrats", climbed on the bandwagon of this alliance, and "from the multiform group of the 'United Christians' . . . formed his christian-social party"[13] (Wandruszka 1977:166). Although the United Christians had a brief existence, no central leadership, and no

[13] According to Boyer (1981:419), "The decision of Lueger and the other secular politicians in the movement to adopt a quasi-religious facade for their party was an act of the highest prudence. Not only did the priests and Vogelsang [the leading Catholic journalist] provide important cadre-level resources and valuable political propaganda, but the association of a vague Christian motif with the movement helped to tone down its state-political radicalism."

program, they were the medium through which the politicized low clergy and lay Catholics successfully developed their initiatives toward the creation of a confessional party. According to Schorske (1967:363), the Christian Social party grew out of the United Christians, and Klemens von Klemperer (1972:23) underscores the importance of this coalition by referring to the Christian Socials as "originally called United Christians." Likewise, Boyer (1981:220) points out that "only the precedent of the alliance of 1887 made the later Christian Social experiment . . . possible." The participation strategy was, therefore, implemented autonomously by Catholic activists through the United Christians coalition.

In September 1888, the newspaper *Das Vaterland,* which evolved into the "chief mouthpiece" of the coalition, proclaimed Lueger the leader of the United Christians and suggested the adoption of the label Christian Social (Geehr 1990:75–76). Lueger consolidated his position by appearing as a speaker at the 1889 Catholic congress. The 1889 municipal elections in Vienna marked a significant increase in the strength of the anti-Liberal coalition (Geehr 1990:79). With the implementation of the participation strategy, the Catholic associations (Vereine) became politicized and were transformed into the political machine of the Christian Socials (Boyer 1981:162). "The small parish associations devoted to a variety of pietistic purposes now became centers of agitation," while the large city-wide Catholic associations were used to "establish lines of communication with thousand of potential voters, as well as to recruit future party activists" (Boyer 1981:120–21). The role of priests was crucial: between 1887 and 1890 hundreds of priests worked for Lueger and his coalition in Vienna. The school question remained a central issue for the Christian Socials: "On one point neither Lueger nor his party ever compromised . . . education and schools must remain Catholic and clerical" (Papanek 1962:33).

That the transformation of the Catholic organizations into political ones and their participation in the electoral process was implemented outside the church made this movement particularly vulnerable to attacks from the hierarchy. The church openly tried to repress the movement, leading to constant conflicts. A pastoral letter published before the 1891 elections was openly hostile to the party. In 1894, the bishops of Vienna and Prague publicly condemned the Christian Social movement, something no other church did in the cases under study. The hierarchy unsuccessfully attempted to postpone the Austrian Catholic Congress scheduled for April 1889. In a symbolic gesture, Lueger attended the congress and went so far as to accuse the church establishment of collusion with the Liberals (Boyer 1981:338). In 1893, with contributions from priests and lay Catholics, Christian Socials created the *Reichspost,* the only major Catholic newspaper to be independent from the hierarchy. Naturally, it became the hierarchy's central target (Boyer 1981:339).

Because of this intra-Catholic crisis, the church postponed the fourth Catholic congress scheduled for 1894. The Christian Socials, however, decided to organize their own Catholic congress in Lower Austria and were even able, using their connections to the papal nuncio, to secure indirect papal approval against the will of the hierarchy. The church reacted, and Cardinal Anton Gruscha did not attend the congress. More important, a delegation of bishops headed by Cardinal Franz Schönborn was sent to Rome to obtain an official condemnation of the Christian Socials from the Vatican. But the Schönborn mission failed in its task. It succeeded only in getting the Vatican to ask Austrian clerics to reaffirm their loyalty to the bishops; however, it was unable to secure any written statement expressing the displeasure of the Vatican with the activity of the clerics or condemning Christian Social activities (Boyer 1981:348).

The Austrian hierarchy failed to destroy the Christian Social movement because Catholic activists were able to mobilize two resources: the international position of Austria and urban politics. First, using the pope's need to secure protection from Austria, they were able to defy the Austrian hierarchy and get indirect legitimation from the Vatican. The Vatican expected that the Austrian emperor, poised by the rise of Social Christian influence, would play an active international role in its favor. Still, it is important to emphasize that the Vatican acted as a facilitator of party formation rather than as its cause. Second, they enjoyed the advantages of urban politics and quickly acquired so much mass support among the Catholics of Vienna as to made repression very costly. The unusually heavy weight placed on Viennese politics, was thus crucial.

The Christian Social party was formed as a mainly Viennese, loose protoparty in 1890. In November 1889 Lueger announced publicly that he was leading the new party, in February 1890 he formalized his new allegiance in the parliament and in 1891, he outlined the party program in a Reichsrat speech. The Landtag campaign in the fall of 1890 was the party's operational starting point. It received a big boost when, in 1890, the parliamentary leader of the traditional Catholic-Conservatives, Alois Liechtenstein, "grew weary of his lack of tactical success" (Jenks 1965:13) and left his faction to join the Christians Socials, thereby giving them respectability. By 1891 the party had fourteen deputies and its first real program drafted by the clergyman Martin Schindler. No permanent central party bureaucracy was formed until 1897, but by 1895 the party was "adopting some of the 'attributes' of a 'mass' party" (Boyer 1981:368). In 1895, Karl Lueger was elected mayor of Vienna, although his election was blocked until 1897 three times by the emperor, backed by the Liberals and the episcopate. This victory provided the necessary impetus for national expansion. The party staged its first peasant congress in 1896. In the first comprehensive campaign for the Lower Austrian Landtag forty-six Christian Socials and nationalists were elected as compared to twenty-eight Liberals, and the Christian Social party became the leading party in the Landtag. In the 1902 Landtag elections Christian Socials obtained a two-thirds majority, and in the 1908 Landtag elections they achieved control of nearly three fourths of the seats. In the Reichsrat elections of the next year the party won thirty seats; in the 1907 elections, the first to be held under universal male suffrage, the Christian Social party won sixty-eight seats. During the same year the party absorbed the traditional Katholische Konservative Volkspartei, a party of notables created in 1895. The fusion between the Viennese Christian Socials and the rural Conservatives, a complex process that took ten years to complete, turned the Christian Social party into the largest party in Ceislithanian Austria, surpassing even the Social Democrats.

The Austrian case shows that under exceptional circumstances, the participation strategy could be implemented by Catholic activists alone and a confessional party could emerge despite a particularly hostile church. This peculiarity carried a heavy price. The Austrian Christian Social party was more vulnerable to the action of opportunistic urban political entrepreneurs and became, as a result, more radical and populist than its counterparts in other countries.

Germany

As in the Netherlands, most Catholics in the German states lived in a religiously mixed environment that was conducive to the development of a religious cleavage, especially until 1815, when congruence between state and confession was the rule (Smith 1991:21). The presence of substantial religious minorities sustained traces of this cleavage past the end of confessional states.[14] For instance, with the annexation of the Rhineland region, Prussia, a state officially identified with the Lutheran church, acquired a large Catholic minority (on the top of its Silesian one). For all its strength, this religious identity did not become politicized. Attempts to create Catholic parties based exclusively on the Catholic-Protestant cleavage failed before 1870, as the fate of the Prussian Zentrumsfraktion indicates.

This parliamentary faction first appeared in 1851 as the Katholische Fraktion and was renamed Fraction des Zentrums in 1858. This was the only political

[14] According to Smith (1991:23), "Despite increasing social interdependence, Protestants and Catholics continued to be divided over issues of culture, whether written, symbolic, or sacred. This division was most severe in areas where the Catholics suffered and Protestants benefited from the impact of modernization." Yonke (1990:81) reports that "in confessionally homogeneous cities, the Catholic burgher tended to feel secure in his cultural Catholicism. . . . Cities with a Protestant/Prussian community transplanted to a native Catholic population experienced heightened confessional tensions. Members of the Catholic Bürgertum used religious affiliation in these settings to underscore religious identity."

group to claim a confessional identification in pre-1866 Germany. It was concerned mostly with educational issues and demanded parity for both confessions (Anderson 1981:106–8). In fact, its concerns were connected with the demands of the Prussian Catholic minority rather than with the defense of the church; in other words, it addressed traditional anti-Catholicism rather than anticlericalism. In addition, this group was extremely loose. The voting pattern of its members in the parliament diverged significantly across issues (Goyau v.3 1909:242). In spite of the faction's confessional outlook, its members were, as Joseph Rovan (1956:38) remarks, totally different from the future Catholic deputies. They were more responsive to regionalist appeals than to religious ones, reflecting an "incomplete" assimilation of Rhineland into Prussia (Goyau v.3 1909:289, 245). Finally, the Zentrumsfraktion never became representative of all Catholics or attained the degree of Catholic mobilization later achieved by the Zentrum (Whyte 1981:38). In the Rhineland, Westphalia, and Hohenzollern between 1862 and 1866, Catholics voted for Liberal candidates more often than for clerical ones by a ratio of approximately three to one (Anderson 1986:84–85). The Zentrumsfraktion gradually declined and completely disappeared after its disastrous showing in the 1866 elections. Its main leader, August Reichensperger, retired from politics.

The first anticlerical attacks were launched during the 1860s in the states of Baden and Bavaria.[15] Relations between the Prussian state and the Catholic church deteriorated in the same period. As early as 1853, Bismarck (quoted in Goyau v.3 1909:263–64) denounced the power of the church and emphasized that "the invading spirit that dominates the Catholic camp will force us, in the long run, to fight a battle." These signals, together with the promotion of anticlerical legislation in some states, distressed the church, which became increasingly active in supporting candidates favorable to its interests (Windell 1954:29).

The main threat to the Catholic church came when Austria was defeated in its 1866 war against Prussia, which opened the way to a unified Germany under Protestant Prussian rule (the *kleindeutsche* option), turning Catholics into a minority. As Sperber (1980:243) points out,"The war of 1866 brought home the message of endangered religion in a direct and visible fashion." It was Ludwig Windthorst's belief that "the great struggle began with the Battle of Königgrätz in 1866" (Southern 1977:48). The Austrians were partly responsible for generating this attitude because they had been promoting a confessional interpretation of their conflict with Prussia, calling on Prussian

[15] Attacks against the Catholic church took place earlier as well, but they were neither systematic nor were they inspired by a comprehensive secularizing ideological project. In 1837, for example, the archbishop of Cologne was jailed by the authorities, an event that provoked riots.

Catholics to refuse military service (Anderson 1981:98). In addition, the Protestant press made vehement anti-Catholic statements during the war, further alienating Catholics (Ross 1976:11). "The world is collapsing!" exclaimed the papal secretary of state upon learning of the defeat of Austria (Anderson 1981:98). As a result, Catholics shifted to an anti-government position while Liberals became pro-government. The defeat of a motion in 1867 that would have incorporated into the organic laws of the new German confederation the paragraphs from the Prussian constitution of 1850, which protected freedom of religion and guaranteed the independence of the churches and their administration, further increased Catholic anxiety.

A first network of lay Catholic associations was created after 1848 and expanded during the 1850s and 1860s (Heinen 1993). Although an attempt was made to politicize these organizations in the wake of the liberalization of 1848, the ensuing political reaction led them to profess political neutrality and to focus on ecclesiastical objectives (Lill 1977:85). These associations remained weak and nonpolitical, and had little immediate effect on the politics of the late 1860s.[16] As Sperber (1980:84) points out, before the late 1860s "there were essentially no sociopolitical organizations in German Catholicism. Notions of charity and moral improvement remained the dominant conceptions for the clergy and Catholic notables. . . . The predominant form of association remained the religious brotherhood whose sociopolitical workings were limited to the possible existence of a mutual benefit fund." It was only after the war of 1866 that new organizations appeared, "which, while

[16] As a result of the wars following the French Revolution, the organization of the Catholic church in Germany was disrupted and groups of lay Catholics were able to mobilize popular support in defense of the church; this led to the early formation of Catholic organizations (Sperber 1987:980; Hürten 1986). The most important early network of Catholic associations, the Piusverein, was created in the wake of the 1848 revolutions together with the first pro-Catholic newspapers (Wettengel 1989). The emergence of these organizations before 1866 is related to a great extent to the minority status of Catholics in the German lands. Most associations either disappeared or turned their attention to regional issues and charitable work both because of legal restrictions on political activity that followed 1848 and developments within the hierarchy, which "was in a process of a far-reaching consolidation of power, which Pius IX painstakingly cultivated" (Yonke 1990:99, 186). In any case, the political activity of these associations in 1848–1849 had not been very successful because of organizational weakness and lack of clarity on the issues, leading many Catholics to vote in a nonconfessional fashion (Yonke 1990:113). Annual Catholic congresses were organized as well. The first Katholikentag took place in October 1848. As Goyau (v.3 1909:103) remarks, through these congresses "the aspirations of the lay element to become a part of the church were simultaneously satisfied and limited." These congresses proved an outlet for the "civic apprenticeship of Catholics" (Goyau v.3 1909:92). They provided political inspiration for foreigners as well. The Belgians Ducpétiaux and Dumortier were impressed by the fifteenth general assembly of Catholic associations in Augsburg (Guyot de Mishaegen 1946:128), and the Venetian Paganuzzi was inspired by these same German congresses in pushing for the organization of the first Italian Catholic congress (De Rosa 1972:57).

obviously related in form to the earlier types, were openly political in character" (Windell 1954:34).

The organizational strategy was implemented through the formation of new Catholic associations after 1867. In the following three years a dense network of Catholic associations sprang up. Sperber (1980:251) found it "striking how many [northern Rhineland and Westphalia organizations] were founded or reorganized between 1867 and 1871." Similarly, Eric Yonke (1990:244) reports that in Düsseldorf Catholics began to mobilize through their associations after 1866. Finally, Southern (1977:67, 236) shows that a first wave of organizational activity in Bavaria took place in 1868–1870, followed by a second, larger, one in the winter of 1871–1872. In Bavaria alone, about 170 associations with a political character were created or revived during this period (Southern 1977:330). The church played a central role in the creation of these associations. Southern (1977:236) reports that the Swabian Vereine, created in 1871–1872, had statutes that were identically or nearly identically worded, suggesting, besides a concerted effort by Catholic activists, the existence of church coordination. The church tried hard to keep these organizations under its control, but this attempt met with limited success (Southern 1977:315).

The electoral strategy of the church during this period vacillated between neutrality and nonparticipation on the one hand, and timid, indirect, and unsystematic support of friendly candidates, on the other. For instance, the church remained neutral in the August 1867 elections, both in Prussia and in the parts of Germany where no anticlerical legislation was enacted (Windell 1954:59). "Priests were not allowed to stand for office, nor to preach on the election, nor to engage in any other form of political agitation" (Sperber 1980:248). In addition, the church issued no pastoral letters of political advice between 1867 and 1870 (Sperber 1980:271). During the time of the organizational strategy (1866–1870) the church leadership was also worried about lay Catholics, who began to enter the political arena in a way that indicated signs of autonomy and independence (Sperber 1980:270).

In two states, Baden and Bavaria, the church moved from the organization to the participation strategy before the unification of Germany. These states were precisely the ones where the first anti-Liberal parties with a Catholic orientation emerged. These parties, especially in Bavaria, were primarily regionalist and anti-Prussian. Given Prussia's Protestantism, Catholicism tended to fit well with regionalism. These parties participated in the 1868 elections for the Zollparlament.[17] Eventually, most failed to survive because

[17] The Zollparlament was the all-German chamber for the representation of the state members of the customs union (the Zollverein). For the first time these elections were held under universal male suffrage, which was imposed on the German states by Bismarck with the expectation that Liberals would win and transform the session of the Zollparlament into a showcase for German unity.

the surprisingly quick and successful German unification destroyed their fundamental purpose. But because they are instances where the party formation dynamic put forth in the previous chapter applies, they deserve a quick look.

In Baden the anticlerical attack was launched in the mid-1860s. When in 1864 the Liberals introduced a moderate law on education, the church reacted immediately by calling for a boycott of the forthcoming elections, which turned out to be successful: only 27 percent of Catholics participated in these elections (Goyau v.3 1909:102–3). A petition demanding the revocation of the law gathered thirty-seven thousand signatures. The government of Julius Jolly reacted by forbidding the activity of the militant Catholic youth associations. In 1868, a new law on education was introduced and an attempt was made to pass a law on civil marriage as well. At the same time, the Liberal prime minister attempted to interfere in the process of nominating the archbishop. After an attempt at direct negotiations and the boycott of elections failed to produce political change, the church supported a coalition of Conservatives and Catholics, which under the label Opposition obtained about 50 percent of the votes in the 1868 elections. Out of this coalition grew a Catholic party, the Katholische Volkspartei, but it did not have time to consolidate its position because it lacked a strong organizational base. When relations between church and state eased somewhat and German unity was achieved, the party lost an important part of its appeal and was able to win only two out of fourteen available seats in the 1871 national elections. Religion lost its saliency as a local political issue in Baden and an important number of party members, including the leader of the party's parliamentary group, left it to join the National Liberals (Mayeur 1981:60).

Confessional conflict erupted in Bavaria in the late 1860s, after the Liberals attempted to bring Bavaria into the new Prussian-led German state and to set up a Liberal anticlerical regime there. The proposal to reform the educational system in 1867 "was the most hotly debated issue" in Bavaria (Windell 1954:176). The state was to have the primary responsibility for the organization and supervision of the schools, with the exception of purely religious schools. The inspection boards of schools would include a majority of laymen and a minority of clergy. "The measure provoked a tremendous amount of agitation among members of the hierarchy and among Catholic laymen, who felt that their children would thereby be turned over to the mercies of the godless state" (Windell 1954:176). Such was the reaction provoked by this issue that the 1868 Zollparlament elections were won by the Bayerische Patriotenpartei, an anti-Prussian regionalist party that recast itself as a Catholic party to take advantage of the religious issue. This surprising victory was achieved by the combined activity of the lower clergy and the Catholic organizations that sprung up after 1868. In Munich alone, there were thirty different Catholic organizations (Southern 1977:191). As Southern (1977:158) notes, "Of the many grievances that concerned Bavarian Catholics it was perhaps the defense of the Catholic church and belief which occupied them the most in terms of time, energy, and effort." These Catholic associations became the political machines of the Patriotenpartei, which won the November 1869 Landtag elections and obtained a majority in the lower house. As a consequence of the Catholic victory, the Liberal premier Prince Hohenlohe was overthrown in 1870, although the government remained in the hands of the Liberals because of the king's support and their domination of the upper house. The Prussian sympathizers, troubled by this result, predicted in 1869 that in three years Bavaria would be "in the hand of the priests" (Windell 1954:190). German unification, however, ruined the regionalist appeal of the Patriots. In the 1871 Reichstag elections, their share of votes fell and they won only nineteen of the forty-eight Bavarian seats. The anticlerical attack intensified in 1871, and the law "against the abuse of the pulpit" was introduced; in 1872 a law expelling the Jesuits was passed, and an attempt in 1873 to impose "simultaneous" (mixed) schools was finally abandoned after ten years of efforts. This new anticlerical wave led to a renewed organizational attempt: in January and February 1872 alone, twenty-two Catholic Vereine were created in the Bavarian province of Swabia, and twenty thousand new members joined Catholic organizations all over Bavaria during the winter of 1872 (Southern 1977:69–70). Still, the Patriotenpartei never became a confessional party and remained primarily regionalist in character. As Goyau (v.3 1909:191) notes, "The preoccupation of numerous Catholics was, then, more national than religious; between a Bavarian Liberal and a Prussian Catholic, didn't they, sometimes, prefer the first?"

In Württemberg relations between the church and the state were calm, and pro-Catholic politicians remained dispersed among numerous parties (Windell 1954:161). Catholic voters tended to back an anti-Prussian Conservative-democrat alliance. In Hesse, although the church was attacked, direct negotiations between church and state proved effective and no Catholic party was formed. This is a rare instance of successful negotiations between church and state.

The decision of Prussian Catholics to participate in the 1870 Landtag elections under the Zentrum banner was provoked by the rise of anticlericalism in the context of a Protestant-dominated Germany—the "Protestant empire," as both Liberals and (Protestant) Conservatives insisted on calling it. As Ronald Ross (1976:13) points out, "anti-Catholicism was rampant," fueled in particular by the Vatican council's decision on papal infallibility. This was exemplified in a dramatic way by the Moabit affair, the attack in 1869 on a Catholic monastery by a crowd of young artisans. This *klostersturm* coincided with the beginning of anticlerical parliamentary activity. In 1868, demands were made in the parliament for the introduction of nonconfessional schools, and the Liberals launched a campaign for secular public education. In December 1868, the Prussian government resurrected a long-forgotten cabinet order to suppress one of West Prussia's three Franciscan monasteries. By 1870 the situation of the Catholic church in Prussia seemed to be deteriorating quickly. Anderson (1981:134–35) summarizes:

> Why did the Catholics move to re-create their own party now? The swelling tide of the liberal, nationalist euphoria that accompanied the founding of the empire was creating a political climate hostile to all minorities: regional, linguistic, and confessional. The Protestantverein, which numbered many influential Liberals among its ranks, explicitly aimed at completing the territorial unification of Germany with its cultural unification under a national church. In such an atmosphere, many Catholics felt their traditional interests to be threatened. All of their platforms, for example, alluded to the need to defend the religious orders, and understandably so.

As a result, lay Catholic pressure for political participation grew stronger. In the 1869 Catholic congress, the Baden Catholic leader Jacob Lindau called for the creation of an all-German Catholic party (Goyau v.4 1909:117). During the third annual conference of the lay Catholic organizations (Katholikenvereine) of Rhineland and Westphalia, the archbishop of Cologne Melchers expressed the hope that the assembly would clarify for the public the attitude of loyal Catholics on crucial political issues "so that the bases of the country's constitution, so important and beneficial, will remain in force, unimpaired" (Windell 1954:280). In June 1870, in view of the forthcoming Prussian Landtag elections, Melchers withdrew the prohibition he had imposed in 1867 on clerical participation in political campaigns because of "the special importance of this election" (Windell 1954:280). Then the church moved a step further. Three weeks before the elections (and on the same day that Catholic candidates precommitted themselves to support the Soest program) the archbishop issued a pastoral letter calling for the election of devout Catholics. Only such men, he pointed out, would be certain to fight to preserve both the constitutional freedom of the church and "its rightful influence on the school, on marriage, and on the family" (Windell 1954:280). The church threw its organizational might into the electoral campaign. Melchers's letter made it a duty of parish priests to give political instruction to the faithful and to use their influence in all possible ways to ensure a favorable outcome in the election (Windell 1954:280). The bishops of Trier, Münster, and Ulm issued similar pastorals. As the Liberal *Pfalzer Kurier* pointed out, the priests were campaigning so actively that the landscape appeared "completely black" (Windell 1954:126). Within three years, the church had made a volte-face, shifting from prohibition to requiring clerical participation in elections.

The participation strategy in Germany was implemented by a coalition built around a political program. The Soest program, as it became known, was adopted just before the 1870 elections. The original draft of the Soest program began with the declaration that the Liberal campaign for a secular state school system meant that "religion is in danger" (Sperber 1980:269–70). The final draft, though more moderate, referred to the increasing attacks on the church and emphasized opposition to secular public education and civil marriage; its objective was the defense of the freedom of the church. As Sperber (1980:270) notes, "In comparison with the religious issues—which . . . were the real vote-getters among the mass electorate—the political and social planks of the program were noticeably less precise." The Soest program was the result of a tripartite alliance between church, Conservative politicians, and Catholic organizations. It was drafted by the brothers August and Peter Reichensperger and Hermann von Mallinckrodt, leaders of the old Prussian Zentrumsfraktion, and Karl von Savigny, who had helped found the Prussian Free Conservative party and had won many Catholic deputies to it. The program was endorsed by numerous organizations, including the largest local groups of what would develop in 1871 into the Westphalian Peasant League, as well as a number of *Landräte* (state functionaries ranking below provincial governors) and other Catholic Conservative state officials (Sperber 1980:269–70). To complete the picture, Catholic associations throughout Rhineland and Westphalia agitated and drew up political programs for a Catholic party (Anderson 1981:134). Likewise, in the South, Catholic organizations were transformed into political machines, which, besides campaigning during elections, acted as local Zentrum or Patriotenpartei (in Bavaria) branches[18] (Southern 1977:237). In fact, leaders of important Catholic organizations competed in the elections and most were elected. Although no party was formed or planned at that time, the pro-church candidates agreed to support the Soest program after the elections in exchange for electoral support from the church and the Catholic organizations.

The Prussian elections of November 1870 "marked the triumphant return of an organized political Catholicism" (Sperber 1980:271). Electoral success was, of course, concentrated in the Catholic regions of western Prussia.

[18] Southern (1977:237) reports that the Augsburg Casino "served as a forum for reports on the activities of the Center party in the Reichstag" and that the Eichstätt Casino in Franconia "seems to have functioned as a local branch of the loosely organized Patriotic Party whenever elections occurred on either the Bavarian or *Reich* level" (1977:290). This Casino, as was probably the case with most, retained its religious character for a while, organizing ceremonies and small demonstrations of honor for the bishop and other members of the hierarchy (Southern 1977:290). Similarly, the Bamberg Casino in Franconia, founded in late 1871, was active in elections at every level and "was even said to have become a kind of central committee for the clerical party in all of Upper Franconia [during the period before the local elections in November 1875]" (Southern 1977:296).

Pro-Catholic candidates captured every seat in the predominantly Catholic constituencies of northern Rhineland. In Düsseldorf, the Progressives, who had represented the district for the previous eight years, were crushed (Sperber 1980: 271–74). All over Prussia roughly one-hundred pro-Catholic candidates were elected. This victory was achieved because of the combined activity of priests and Catholic organizations (Sperber 1980:274).

Less than half of the elected pro-Catholic candidates (forty-eight, including nineteen priests) were Soest signatories. They decided after long discussions to establish a new Catholic faction in the parliament. This faction aimed to defend exclusively, as its program made clear, "the freedom and independence of the church and its institutions" (Brose 1985:44). The discussions about the form the new party would take began during the special session of the North German Reichstag in December 1870. The decision was finally made to minimize the confessional character of the party and name the new organization Zentrumspartei Deutschlands (Verfassungspartei).[19] The first electoral appeal to voters, issued in January 1871, in view of the spring national elections to the Reichstag, avoided references to Catholicism and mentioned only the struggle for religious freedom and "the rights of religious organizations against all potential attacks of hostile parties" (Windell 1954:286). August Reichensperger (quoted in Mayeur 1980:61) declared in 1871 that the "essential objective of the group [is] to push back any attack against religious freedom and the Christian character of the schools." The founders of the party hoped that by emphasizing the Christian rather than the Catholic character of the party they would be able to attract Conservative Protestants. This attempt failed. Catholics, especially in Rhineland, disliked the prospect of having Protestants join the party and, in any case, Protestants did not join it because the party could not convincingly promote a non-Catholic image (Windell 1954:284). The Protestant church, moreover, contrary to the situation prevailing in the Netherlands, was not threatened by the state and, therefore, remained strongly anti-Catholic (Hatfield 1981b).

In the first elections of the German Empire (which took place under universal, direct, and equal manhood suffrage on March 3, 1871) the designation "Zentrum" was used only in Prussia. Pro-church candidates did extremely well. Fifty-seven Catholics willing to cooperate in the establishment of a confessional party were elected. They obtained 18.5 percent of the votes and formed the second largest party after the National Liberals, who won 120 seats. One-third of the Catholic deputies came from the Rhineland region. The party was formally organized in March 1871 after the Reichstag con-

[19] Verfassungspartei: Constitutional party, a reference to the demand that the guarantees toward the church included in the Prussian constitution be kept in the new German constitution.

vened.[20] A few days later it published its official program, which listed three objectives: the preservation of the federal character of the empire; the protection of civil and religious freedom for all citizens; and the freedom of the members of the party to retain their own opinions within the party (Windell 1954:289). The party began its life with a parliamentary defeat. It failed to include the Prussian guarantees of religious freedom in the new Reich constitution. Windthorst (quoted in Windell 1954:290) declared that "in the new Germany the legal rights of Catholic citizens will be crushed."

The originality of the German case lies in the fact that the confessional party was formed *before* the main attack against the church. As Sperber (1980:392) states, "It must be asserted that the *Kulturkampf* did not lie at the origin of the political allegiance of the Catholic masses. All these developments were complete by 1871—before the *Kulturkampf.*" But the party was still weak, and the mobilization of Catholics had only been partial: the Zentrum had obtained the votes of only 57 percent of German Catholics (Anderson 1981:182). More than half of the Catholic deputies were not members of the party, and the party remained essentially Prussian, unable to attract Catholics from other regions. In southern Germany only the Katholische Volkspartei of Baden gave definite signs of willingness to cooperate in the formation of a national Catholic party. The Bavarians, in contrast, were not interested (Windell 1954:287). To top it all, the party had a loose, "virtually nonexistent" organization (Evans 1981:34). As Anderson (1981:194) remarks, "In 1871, the survival of the infant Zentrum was by no means certain."

The party was able to survive and grow strong because of the launching in 1872 of a state attack against the Catholic church, which evolved into "the major religio-political conflict in nineteenth century Germany" (Ross 1976:15). Sperber (1980:320) describes the Kulturkampf as follows: "The ministry, with the enthusiastic support of the Liberal parliamentary majority, attempted to re-assert the predominant influence of the state over the church in a wide variety of arenas, ranging from the control of the educational system to the legal validity of marriage, to the education, appointment and discipline of the Catholic clergy." The Kulturkampf's causes lay at the intersection of Bismarck's plan to unite his government with the Liberals, and the ideologically driven Liberal plans to destroy the power of the church (Sperber

[20] The party was unitary on the Reichstag level but remained a coalition of loosely united state parties until the 1890s. In Württemberg there was no local Catholic party until 1894. The Bavarian and Hessian Catholic parties took the name "Zentrum" in 1887, and Baden followed in 1888. But local identities remained strong, and the party's strength was concentrated in the Rhineland region of Prussia, where most German Catholics lived. The party remained quite decentralized until the formation of a national coordinating committee for imperial Germany in 1914.

1980:320). The Kulturkampf served as an excuse for the Liberals to jettison their principles and instead support the policies of Bismarck. It also prevented the split of the party, which would have proved ruinous for Bismarck's project. As Anderson (1981:192) points out, "The Kulturkampf was the cement that held the National Liberals together."

The Kulturkampf was launched when Bismarck abolished the Catholic section of the Prussian ***kulturministerium*** in July 1871. A series of laws and decrees were enacted from 1871 to 1874 with the objective to "restore the rights of the state in relation to the church" (Evans 1981:54). These laws and decrees censored church sermons by severely punishing priests who would misuse the pulpit for political purposes (*Kanzelparagraph,* 1871); they censored the publication of church documents; they attempted to establish state control over education and defined school inspectors as state representatives, abolishing the automatic right of priests to be school inspectors (1872); they forbade Jesuits and their corollary organizations to operate within the German Empire (1872); they attempted to establish state control over the appointment of clergy by regulating the internal organization of the church (laws of May 1873); they dissolved all but one religious order (*Klostergesetz,* 1875); and they made, in most cases, the instruction of religion the task of lay teachers (decree of 18 February 1876).

The church's reaction was prompt and strong. The German bishops' conference condemned the May laws in 1873, and in 1875 Pius IX followed up by issuing an encyclical condemning them and declaring them null and void. Bishops refused to apply the May laws, and Catholic students refused to take the state's "culture exam." The state responded by repressing the church. A large number of members of the clergy, both priests and bishops who refused to obey, were removed from their offices, imprisoned, or forced to leave the country, especially in 1874.[21] Catholics reacted by participating in gigantic demonstrations and other acts of resistance characterized as "events of unparalleled size and intensity" (Sperber 1980:347). The Mainzer Verein, created in 1872 with the statutory goal to defend the freedom and the rights of the Catholic church and bring Christian principles to bear on all aspects of public life, was the first mass organization to be created in Germany (Sperber 1980:324). A consequence of the Kulturkampf was the weakening of the church, now composed of "exiled and harassed bishops" and "punished and harried priests" (Anderson 1981:238). This led to the temporary assumption of church control by lay Catholics. The hierarchy was forced to allow the

[21] By 1879, nine of the twelve Prussian bisphorics stood vacant, as were 955 parishes. In the four Prussian Catholic theological faculties the number of students declined from 999 in 1870 to 515 in 1878 (Hatfield 1981a:473). As late as 1883, and only in Prussia, 207 of 703 parishes remained vacant and fifty other pastoral positions continued unfilled, while the bishops were forced to meet in secret (Anderson 1981:309–10).

laity a greater role within the church, especially on the local level: "Parishes without pastors were essentially placed in the hands of the parishioners. The laity maintained church properties and the archbishop approved the election of parish councils. . . . The *Kulturkampf* failed to dismantle clerical authority in Catholic Germany, but it forced the clergy to depend more heavily upon the laity in the public realm" (Yonke 1990:234). Agócs (1988:168) describes the organizational consequences of the German Catholic church's institutional weakness: "The formidable success of the Germans in organizing the Catholic masses was due to a very large extent to the fact that laymen, whom the circumstances of the *Kulturkampf* thrust to the fore of Catholic Action, remained active and relatively independent from direct and everyday control by the church hierarchy, at least as far as their political activities were concerned." This weakness also accounts for the church's relative lack of reaction to the rise of autonomous Catholic political action and the formation of the Zentrum during the years of the Kulturkampf.

The Kulturkampf peaked between 1874 and 1878. By 1878 it had become clear that persecution had failed. Between 1879 and 1882 many of the administrative measures of the Kulturkampf were repealed and educational reform plans relegated to the archives (Sperber 1980:377). After 1882, diplomatic relations with the Vatican were reestablished and the Kulturkampf laws canceled. Bismarck, however, was extremely skillful in preventing the formation of an alliance between the Zentrum and the "deeply Protestant" (Anderson 1981:151) Free Conservative party. Invoking the "Roman menace," "he drowned Conservative fears that the struggle against Catholicism was beginning to undermine respect from religion in general by a rousing attack on the Pope as an enemy of the Gospel and a danger to salvation" (Anderson 1981:177). As a result, Protestants did not mobilize politically as Christians (as they did in the Netherlands). Accordingly, a large anti-Liberal interconfessional coalition was made impossible.

The nature of the anticlerical attack accounts for the exceptional organizational strength of the party. The Kulturkampf considerably strengthened the party, which obtained its highest electoral scores during this period. Four out of five voting Catholics voted for it, and it was able to secure about 100 of the 397 Reichstag seats until 1914.[22] The Zentrum became the church's only hope: "Catholic Germany's sole leverage now lay in the strength and durabil-

[22] In 1871, the Zentrum got 724,000 votes (18.6 percent of all votes and 63 Reichstag seats). In 1874, during the height of the Kulturkampf, the party doubled its votes to 1,446,000 (27.8 percent and 91 seats). In the 1874 elections the party augmented its share of votes from Catholics to 83 percent, up from 57 percent in 1871. The party was the second strongest in both the Prussian house (following the 1873 Landtag elections) and the Reichstag. After the end of the Kulturkampf the party's electoral support began to erode, especially in the South, where it got 19.4 percent in the 1907 elections and 16.4 percent in the 1912 elections (Mayeur 1980:66; Sperber 1980:340; Anderson 1981:182).

ity of their separate political machine" (Anderson 1981:196). As a result, "from 1870 onwards the bishops' attitude towards the Center party was one of unreserved support" (Sperber 1980:270). Windthorst exploited this situation to force the Vatican to recognize the party's independence (Fogarty 1957:175). The party began to build its own political basis, particularly through the parallel activity of the Mainzer Verein, which encouraged the formation of local Catholic political clubs and "created a mass base for a political organization dominated by the Catholic elites" (Sperber 1980:327). The Catholic press, which until 1871 had been insignificant, grew rapidly to respond to the anti-Catholic attacks; most Catholic newspapers became part of the Augustinusverein, which, in 1918, included 950 members with a total of 2,624,900 subscribers (Mendershausen 1973:31–33). The most important organizational achievement of the party (and the best guarantee of its independence from the church), however, was the creation, in 1890, of the Volksverein für das Katholische Deutschland, "an essential appendage of the Zentrum providing the party with the kind of secular, mass organizational support it needed to move into the post-Bismarckian era" (Anderson 1981:393). Several of its leaders were Zentrum deputies, and the principal speeches at its yearly congresses were always delivered by party leaders (Agócs 1975:44). The membership of the Volksverein—which in a highly symbolic move named Windthorst as its honorary president—grew at an amazing pace, rising from 108,000 members in 1891 to 805,000 in 1914—13.6 percent of the total male Catholic population (Iserloh 1977:60; Mendershausen 1973:36). In Catholic areas there were Volksverein local leaders ("trustees") "on every street, every block, one for each hundred or two hundred Catholic inhabitants," and in 1909, it released 20,705,006 pieces of propaganda literature (Agócs 1975:35–37). At the same time, a vigorous effort was made to develop ancillary organizations. One could find the Catholic Merchants' Association, the Catholic Officials' Association, the Rhenish Artisans' league, and, particularly, the Catholic Workers Association, founded in 1904, with 400,000 members in 1913 and the Association of German Christian Peasant Associations, formed in 1900, with more than 450,000 members in 1918. By 1912 there were more than 3,000 Catholic workers clubs with almost 500,000 members (Evans 1982:279). A contemporary observer noted that in the town of Bochum, Catholics formed so many separate clubs that almost every profession and trade "divided itself up along confessional lines" (quoted in Crew 1979:129).

Italy

The first anticlerical laws were passed in the kingdom of Piedmont, which became an "experimental site" for the reduction of church privileges (Passerin d'Entrèves 1981:2). The 1848 Boncompagni law decreased church influence in education and provoked a strong reaction from the church (Pazzaglia 1981:72–73). In 1850 the Siccardi laws abolished the jurisdiction of ecclesiastical courts in civil and criminal cases affecting the clergy and forbade ecclesiastical corporations from acquiring property without the consent of the government. A law promulgated in 1855 suppressed most religious organizations and stipulated that no new order could be established without the consent of the government. The 1859 Casati law strengthened the autonomy and the laicization of the state. According to Jemolo (1960:13), "Naturally, the adoption of such laws . . . prompted many Catholics, who in 1846–1848 had supported the unification movement to oppose it."

The kingdom of Italy was proclaimed in 1861. The pope lost all his territories with the exception of Rome, which fell in 1870. In 1865, anticlerical legislation was passed that provided for civil marriage and led to the suppression of religious bodies. Many of the most ancient monasteries and convents were taken over by the state, and numerous ecclesiastical organizations were suppressed (Jemolo 1960:30). During the 1870s anticlericalism was on the rise (De Rosa 1972:126). A series of laws were passed seriously curtailing the influence of the church and diminishing or suppressing the role of religion in schools[23] (Pazzaglia 1981:74). According to Vincenzo Sinistrero (1967:158), "With the framing of these laws, the supplanting of the church by the State in the schools became definitive." In the 1890s many Catholic charitable institutions were taken over by the government. But the worst blow to the church was the destruction of the papal state. Although the anticlerical measures enacted in Italy were milder than those adopted in Germany, they "constituted a more revolutionary break with the past, a more dramatic attack upon the position of the Church than those carried out by Bismarck in a land where Catholics had long been a minority" (Reinerman 1993:762). The Vatican reacted by refusing to recognize the new state and forbidding Catholics from participating in Italian political life.

The first steps toward organization were taken in 1868, when the pro-Catholic newspaper *Unità Cattolica* called for the organization of Italian Catholics into Catholic associations (France 1975:177). A number of small local organizations, approved by the pope or local bishops, were created

[23] In 1870, the minister of education issued a circular stating that religious instruction in elementary schools would be provided only upon request. The chairs of theology in the state universities were abolished in 1872, the "religious houses" in Rome in 1873, and the exemption of priests from military service in 1875. In 1877 the Coppino law extended the Casati law to all Italy. The same year, two new laws were passed, one that eliminated from schools the position of spiritual director, and a second that replaced compulsory religious instruction in elementary schools with civic instruction. In 1888, a law making religious instruction in schools available only upon parental request was passed.

independently during the late 1860s.[24] But only after the fall of Rome underlined the impossibility of reversing the unification process through foreign policy did the church undertake a serious organizational effort.

In 1874, lay Catholics, with papal approval, convened a Catholic congress in Venice. The congress called for the formation of local associations in every parish and one central organization, the Opera dei congressi, to be placed under the direction of a permanent committee.[25] The congress of Florence, which took place the following year, passed a program of action which led to growth "superior to any expectation" (Gambasin 1969:133). The church promptly placed the Opera under its direct authority and used it as a mere "auxiliary of the Holy See" (Webster 1960:4). According to De Rosa (1972:47), the objective of the organization was to "defend the pope and obey his orders." The organizational strategy was officially sanctioned by the church in 1882 with the papal encyclical *Etsi nos,* which called Catholics to form lay organizations throughout the country. Catholic newspapers were created and cooperatives and rural banks were developed in agrarian areas. By 1892, Catholic organizations formed a giant network that "commanded respect" from the enemies of the church[26] (De Rosa 1972:159). Still, the church had no intention of turning this organization into a political party. The Opera was seen as a one-issue movement, the "only defense against the

[24] A short-lived organization, the Associazione cattolica italiana per la difesa della libertà della Chiesa in Italia—with a membership requirement of "the most complete submission to the pope" (De Rosa 1972:48)—was created in Bologna in 1866. The Associazione della gioventù cattolica was formed in 1868, and smaller local associations, such as the Promotrice in Florence, the Società per gli interessi cattolici in Rome, and the Società veneziana per gli interessi cattolici in Venice, were created in the same period.

[25] The organization was renamed, in 1881, Opera dei Congressi e dei comitati cattolici in Italia to reflect the importance of local committees. The Superior Council of the Societies of the Catholic Youth, presided over by Count Giovanni Acquaderni, was instrumental in setting up the new organization. The Opera defined itself as ***intransigent,*** since it accepted the ***Syllabus*** and the pontifical directives; ***lay,*** since it was founded and presided by laymen; ***papal*** since it concentrated all Catholic efforts and organization in the service of the pope; and ***hierarchical,*** since its organization replicated the hierarchical constitution of the church (Gambasin 1966:308).

[26] Just in the three first years of the Opera (1874–77) 3 regional, 16 diocesan, and 533 parochial committees were formed (Tramontin 1981a:338). In the congress of 1897, the president of the Opera, Paganuzzi, presented an "impressive result" (Tramontin 1981a:341): 17 regional, 188 diocesan, 3,982 parochial committees, 708 youth sections, 17 university circles, 588 rural organizations, 688 workers' societies, 116 circles of the Gioventù cattolica, 24 newspapers, and 155 periodicals. The Opera grew mostly in northern Italy, particularly in the Veneto and in Lombardia. It remained weak in central Italy (including Rome) and the south (Gambasin 1969:122–23). During the 1890s, however, the Catholic movement grew even in those regions. The leaders of the Opera emphasized organizational growth to an extreme degree. Organizational statistics composed a major part of both the congresses' published minutes and the official newsletter of the movement *Il mondo cattolico.* Gambasin (1969:97) refers to the "organizational obsession" of the Catholic movement.

agnosticism of the middle classes and the aggressive irreligiousness of the mass movements, whether democratic or Socialist: a Catholic mass movement aimed first at safeguarding Catholic interests, many of which were often no longer protected by the State, and ultimately at Catholic 'reconquest' of national life" (Webster 1960:4). Despite the *non expedit*, the organizational strategy of the church included some measure of sporadic and uncoordinated (albeit growing after the late 1890s) participation by Catholics in local elections.

The Catholic movement was divided into two main tendencies, although there were often cross-cutting divisions depending on the issue. The issue of autonomous Catholic action pitted "demochristians" against conservative intransigents (even though not all supporters of political autonomy shared the social concerns of demochristians). Demochristians, such as the priest Romolo Murri and his followers, pushed for "the principle of autonomous responsibility of Catholics in the political and social field," independent Catholic organizations, and, eventually, the creation of a Catholic party (Giovannini 1981:305; De Rosa 1972:183). Conservative intransigents envisaged Catholic organization only as a papal auxiliary, an organization operating outside the political system as part of the struggle against the Liberal state. They supported the church in advocating economic and social but not political organization. The members of this faction were fittingly labeled by their opponents "bishops in tall hats" (Webster 1960:6). Theirs, argued the demochristians, was not obedience but subjection (De Rosa 1972:183). The intransigent faction began to lose control of the Catholic movement after 1898 and in 1904 the church dissolved the Opera and replaced it with a new federation of five unions *(unione)*, each tightly controlled by the Vatican.[27] The prospect of an independent Catholic political organization vanished.

While tightening control over the Catholic organizations, the church gradually introduced elements of political participation. The reason for this change of orientation was the "rebirth of a more polemical and more aggressive anticlericalism" (Scoppola 1977:110), connected with the rise of the So-

[27] The 1905 organizational reshuffle created the Unione popolare formed as a general organization of Italian Catholics on the model of the German Volksverein. Membership was individual and reached 70,000 in 1907 and 110,000 in 1919 (Tramontin 1981d:394); the Unione elettorale, which was to coordinate the action of Catholics with regard to local elections; and the Unione economico-sociale, which included all social and economic associations: in 1905 there were 835 rural credit associations, 774 mutual aid workers' societies, 69 banks, 21 peoples' secretariats, and 107 cooperative institutions (Tramontin 1981b:390). These three organizations were joined by two others, the Società della Gioventù italiana (created in 1868), and the Unione fra le donne cattoliche italiane (created in 1908). The five organizations constituted the Azione cattolica. They were independent of each other and each had its own local committees in every diocese (Howard 1957:76–77, 94). From 1915 on, the Azione cattolica was governed by a central council but remained under the direct control of the pope.

cialist movement. A parliamentary debate in 1908 about full laicization of education and a more rigorous application of the 1877 Coppino law alarmed the church even more (Scoppola 1977:110). From 1904 on, some pro-Catholics were independently elected to the parliament. The first organized instance of political participation took place in Bergamo in 1904, prompted by a general strike during which violence was committed against churches and clerics (De Rosa 1972:284). The Catholic voters of this region, chosen because it was particularly "docile" to the pope (Belardinelli 1979:154), were expected to deliver their votes for the conservative Liberal candidates (the *moderati*) with nothing in exchange.

This still timid shift was made official with the 1905 papal encyclical *Il fermo proposito,* which, though maintaining in principle the *non expedit,* modified it and specified that Catholics should vote when the bishops decided that such action was necessary to block the election of a "subversive" candidate (Howard 1957:75). This encyclical asked Catholics for the first time to prepare themselves for the prospect of participation in political life. But as Mario Belardinelli (1979:159) points out, this was a prospect of nonautonomous party intervention. The Unione elettorale was formed in 1905 to coordinate this effort. The 1909 elections brought twenty-one independent Catholic deputies to the parliament, up from ten—still a very limited opening. The great majority of Catholics abstained from voting, and the church was undecided about its participation in the political process. Moreover, these pro-Catholic deputies were formally forbidden by the church to form a political party and were asked instead to ally with the conservative wing of the Liberals (Howard 1957:79).

The church implemented the participation strategy in 1913 following the introduction of universal manhood suffrage under which Catholic abstention would have produced a Socialist victory. The Gentiloni pact, named after the head of the Unione elettorale, was based on an explicit, but secret, contract: the church would support conservative Liberal candidates who would promise (in a signed written statement) to promote mild pro-church policies and refrain from supporting anticlerical legislation[28] (Jemolo 1960:135). Catholics

[28] The alliance between Catholics and conservative Liberals became known as *clerico-moderatismo.* Both Gentiloni and Giolitti denied that an explicit pact was formally signed on the national level (Coppa 1967:227). But the Unione elettorale declared openly that it would support on a local basis individual Liberal candidates who would agree on the seven following points (the *eptalogo*): (1) defend liberty of conscience and association as established in the constitution and therefore oppose any bill inspired by hatred of the religious congregations or which tended to disturb the religious tranquility of the nation; (2) support the principle that with the increase and development of the public school system, no attempt be made to discredit the work of private institutions, whose work was to be considered an important factor in the elevation and diffusion of national culture; (3) remove any uncertainty about the legal right of parents to have their children provided with religious instruction in the public

delivered their votes to these candidates in 330 constituencies; 228 of them were elected with Catholic support (Webster 1960:38).

This way, the church entered the electoral process without undertaking the risk of putting together an electoral coalition. The obvious advantage of this move was, as Webster (1960:14–15) points out, that "the Catholic vote, enlarged by universal male suffrage, became a pawn, moved by the Vatican through an intermediary, in the Italian political game. It had no normal means of self-expression; the Catholic masses began voting as a minor under papal guardianship." A drawback, however, was that the church had no way to enforce the pact inside the parliament. Numerous Liberals initially denied the existence of such a pact, while the combined pressure of Liberal newspapers and the radical anticlerical wing of the Liberal party, who publicized the pact, made its implementation impossible (Jemolo 1960:135). If the Gentiloni pact proved generally to be a sweet deal for the Liberals and, to a certain extent, the church, it was a bitter pill for the Catholic activists, who simultaneously realized the extent of their electoral leverage and their total impotence: the pact was for them nothing but a "prostitution" of their vote.

The advent of World War I temporarily froze political developments: this explains the lag between the implementation of the participation strategy (1913) and the formation of the confessional party (1919). The rise of socialism after 1913, often expressed in violent anticlerical actions, created a sense of heightened danger within the church. During the "red week" of June 1914, churches and priests were attacked and Catholics acutely sensed their weakness. The Unione elettorale called the Catholics (addressing them as Catholic voters) to defend themselves (Webster 1960:43). Accordingly, the municipal elections of 1914 saw the repetition of local pacts between moderate Liberals and Catholics.

During the war, debates about political participation multiplied within the Catholic organizations. According to a conservative Catholic (Dalla Torre, quoted in De Rosa 1969:4), during the war "it became difficult to keep political discussions and votes away from the *Azione cattolica*." The priest Luigi Sturzo, who had, in the meantime, become the secretary of the central council of Azione cattolica, got restless: "His discourses during the war were not about Catholic but political action; they were oriented toward the

---

schools; (4) resist any attempt to weaken family unity and hence absolutely oppose divorce; (5) recognize the equality of economic and social organizations before the law, irrespective of the social or religious principles that inspired such organizations; (6) advocate gradual but continuous reform in fiscal matters in the sense of an increased application of the principle of social justice; and (7) uphold a policy tending to conserve and reinvigorate the economic and moral forces of the country, increasing Italian influence in the developing international civilization (Coppa 1967:226).

direction of fully preparing the consciousness of Catholics for public life" (De Rosa 1969:4). Local Catholic committees, Gambasin (1969:158) reports, gradually lost their ecclesiastical character and were being transformed into a "party or syndicate." The growth of expectations about direct political participation had gone so far that the Catholic weekly *Settimana Sociale* asserted in 1916 that membership in the Unione popolare was the Catholic equivalent of party membership in the Socialist camp (De Rosa 1972:372). This led to a serious crisis within the organization.

In 1916, the thirty-four independent Catholic deputies supported the moderate Boselli cabinet, and the Catholic lay leader Filippo Meda entered the government. After the end of the war, pressure to form a Catholic party intensified. In July 1918, a Catholic committee was created to study postwar political problems. The pressure was such that the church silently approved —by not condemning—the formation of the party. In January 1919, the Partito popolare launched an appeal to the nation in which it emphasized its aconfessional character. The church removed the last barriers from the political participation of Catholics and declared that the new party did not represent it (Webster 1960:52). The party took part in the November 1919 elections and won 20.5 percent of the votes, making "a forceful entry into the public arena" (Molony 1977:67). This electoral success firmly established the new party.[29]

Why did the church allow the formation of a Catholic party? Couldn't it just implement a new Gentiloni pact against the socialists? According to the autobiography of Count Dalla Torre (quoted in Howard 1957:108–9): "*Azione Cattolica* had turned, at the end of the war, toward an increasingly more intense political activity, and the Vatican hierarchy reached the conclusion that they had either to put an end to the political activity of the Catholics, or to make it entirely different from the activity of the *Azione Cattolica*." The first option was too costly. The fear of socialism helped the church accept the formation of a Catholic party. Molony (1977:66) concludes that the available public evidence "clearly indicates that the PPI was in no sense a creature of the Vatican and that any judgment of it made by the authoritative Vatican sources was largely negative."

[29] The party was joined by 100,000 members and was pledged support by twenty daily papers and sixty-two weekly ones. By 1919 the party claimed 20 provincial committees and 850 local sections, and by 1920 it had grown to 3,137 sections and 251,740 members, a sign of fast development (Malgeri 1981:355).

CHAPTER 5

After the Formation: The Confessional Dilemma and the Construction of a Catholic Political Identity

Christian Democracy is not the Church.

—Luigi Sturzo

How did the party formation process affect the nature of confessional parties and, by extension, the politics of the societies within which they operate? I argue that the Christian Democratic phenomenon cannot be properly understood without examining the confessional party formation process. Hence the focus of this chapter is on the construction of a Catholic *political* identity, which emerged as a result of the process of party formation and transcended and superseded the preexisting religious identity from which it sprang.[1] In turn, confessional parties shaped and molded this new political identity to suit their interests and overcome the constraints they faced. This produced political and societal effects unanticipated at the time of party formation. In essence, confessional parties detached the Catholic political identity from the church and eventually even from religion. Thus I provide an account of the secularization of confessional parties which views the loss of their religious character as a process endogenous to these parties that took place *during* and *right after* their formation. This account goes against a prevailing assumption according to which the secularization of confessional parties was an exogenous process imposed upon them by a rapidly seculariz-

[1] The leader of the Dutch Calvinists, Abraham Kuyper (quoted in Barnouw 1940b:190), pointed to the distinct implications of these two identities when he declared to his followers that "as faithful Calvinists you ought to oppose Rome in all dogmatic and religious matters, but to reckon on their support if you find them willing to fight for your Christian school and for the Christian foundation of the state."

ing societal environment that took place after World War II.[2] (Hanley 1994:4; Fleet 1993:136; Mény 1993:69–70; Boswell 1993:60; Leonardi and Wertman 1989; Houska 1985; Wolinetz 1979:119; Kirchheimer 1966:177–200). A theoretical implication of this account is the emphasis on the active (as opposed to the reactive) nature of political parties.

I approach the issue of the construction of the Catholic political identity by first focusing on conservatism and Catholicism as competing forces for the same political space. I then examine the central political dilemma faced by confessional parties (what I call the confessional dilemma): how to escape from the constraints of their confessional origins while maintaining a distinctive identity. I show how confessional parties resolved this dilemma and suggest what the consequences of the solution were for politics and society at large.

The Catholic Movement and the Conservative Political Space

The launching of the anticlerical attack by the Liberals goes a long way toward explaining the association between conservatism and Catholicism, even though it cannot account for the filling of the Conservative political space by confessional parties. It is true that following the French Revolution, the Catholic church became closely identified with Conservative, even reactionary, political forces. The Dutch Calvinists, the only non-Catholic confessional party, expressed this point with unequaled lucidity when they decided to call their party Antirevolutionary.

A practicing Catholic was likely to be a Conservative or a Monarchist and joined or voted for these parties—but this was not always the case. Numerous Catholics were Liberals or, more often, remained outside politics. As Anderson (1986:87) remarks about Germany, "There was before 1866 no necessary relationship between Catholic confession and Conservative politics. Quite the contrary." Religion was not politically salient and fostered many different forms of political action. As I argued in the first chapter, it made more sense for pro-church politicians to join nonconfessional parties than to form a confessional party. For example, following the 1867 elections in the

[2] I use the term "secularization" to refer to the declining strength of the relationship between individuals and churches. In this sense, the "privatization of religion" (Fox 1982) falls under secularization. I, therefore, agree with van Kersbergen's (1994:43) view of secularization as representing "the condensation or transference of religious morality into secular ethics. Secularization may be looked upon as comprising a transformation of religious contents into worldly substance." For a discussion of the various meanings of the term see Kselman (1988:328–30). For a general discussion of theories of secularization see Martin (1978), Lechner (1991), and Bruce (1992).

Prussian Rhineland, ten elected representatives who had been supported by the church joined the Free Conservatives, one the National Liberals, four the old Prussian Left, and six remained unaffiliated. A similar dispersion took place after the 1870 elections (Windell 1954:61, 282). The attack against the church affected this trend and led numerous Catholics to join Conservative parties. Political formations in which practicing Catholics became active initially used Conservative labels.[3] Although the initial reaction of Catholics was to identify with Conservatives, the emergence of the Catholic movement led to the gradual establishment of a distinct political identity, which was reflected in the subsequent coexistence of Conservative and Catholic labels.[4] Still, exclusively confessional labels were usually avoided at this stage.

Because the attack against the church came from the Left, political Catholicism was pushed to the Right. Its eventual success implied a competition with conservatism and ultimately required the elimination of the initial Conservative identification. This does not mean that Catholics ceased to be Conservatives; it suggests, however, that they became instead primarily Catholics. In this vein, Montalembert, who attempted to create a French Catholic party during the 1840s, asserted (quoted in Dansette, v.1 1961:235) that Catholics "did not just happen to be Catholics but were Catholics before anything else" and that one is not Catholic *après tout* but *avant tout* (Denis 1992:61). The strategy of the church following the anticlerical attack eventually led to the elimination of the distinct Conservative political identity. This identity shift was not originally planned by the church but was rather the unanticipated result of decisions imposed by the political necessity of the moment; yet it had far-reaching consequences, a fact underlying the importance of decisions taken in response to pressing circumstances. The elimination of conservatism as the primary political option for Catholics took place in two steps parallel to the two strategies implemented by the church.

The first step was undertaken in the context of the organizational strategy, when the objective of the church was to isolate and control Catholics. Accordingly, the church stressed distinctiveness and dissimilarity between the Catholic and Conservative identities. When Catholics attempted to associate with Conservative parties in ways that escaped church control, Catholicism was promoted as a distinct ideology and identity, superseding all political

[3] Some examples: Association constitutionnelle conservatrice in Belgium; Grossdeutsche Konservative Partei in Hesse; Partito conservatore nazionale (the abortive attempt of some Italian Catholics to organize a party in the 1880s).

[4] For example, Fédération des cercles catholiques et des associations constitutionelles et conservatrices in Belgium; Katholisch-Konservative Volksverein in Styria; Katholisch-Konservative Partei in Bavaria. Patriotism—usually meaning regionalism—was also used as a label: the Bavarians created the Bayerische Patriotenpartei, while the label used later in Low Austria was Katholisch-Patriotische Volksverein.

identities. In their first congress in 1874, Italian Catholics (quoted in Tramontin 1981a:337) declared: "The congress is Catholic . . . and nothing else than Catholic. . . . Catholicism is not liberal, is not tyrannical, is not of any other quality. Whatever quality might be added is a very grave error . . . Catholicism is the doctrine that the Highest Pontiff, bishop of Rome, vicar of Jesus Christ, infallible doctor of faith and moral, teaches either alone from his own chair or jointly with the bishops, the successors of the apostles. Every dissimilar doctrine [about what is Catholicism] is schism and heresy."

Likewise, the members of a Milanese Catholic youth association (quoted in Vecchio 1987:82) defined themselves as "neither monarchists, nor republicans, neither traditionalists, nor pro-Austrians, neither pro-Bourbon, nor pro-Savoia, but clericals only." These declarations, made in the context of an overall rejection of politics, contributed to the gradual rise of a distinct Catholic political identity. Next, the point was made that Catholicism was separate and dissimilar from conservatism. Ruggero Bonghi, an Italian lay Catholic, argued in 1879 against the attempt of some Catholics to form a party in association with Conservatives: "This exchange between Catholics and Conservatives is a great error and is very suspect. The Catholic feeling is not necessarily conservative, and the conservative feeling is not necessarily Catholic"[5] (quoted in De Rosa 1972:136).

The second step was undertaken in the context of the participation strategy, when the church used its organizations to support coalitions run by Conservatives. Now stress was put on the complementarity rather than the dissimilarity between the two identities. The president of a Belgian *cercle* emphasized the affinity between Catholicism and conservatism when he declared to "unanimous applause" in the 1875 congress of the Fédération (quoted in Guyot de Mishaegen 1946:143): "Some people think it is unfortunate for the Conservative party to have the name Catholic appended to it. For me, this is one of its principal glories. A Catholic can only be conservative and we are proud of being Catholics." To avoid the assimilation of its members by Conservatives, however, the church stressed the superiority of Catholicism vis-à-vis conservatism. The situation was thus reversed. Whereas Catholicism used to be an attribute of conservatism, now conservatism became one of many possible attributes of Catholicism. Lay Catholic activists, like Meda in Italy, were actively promoting Catholicism as superseding the Conservative identity fostered by the parliamentary Right. The essence of

[5] Conservatives were called, in the 1879 congress of Modena, *amici dubbi* (untrusted friends)(De Rosa 1972:135). Later, the leaders of the new confessional parties would follow through and emphasize the dissimilarity of the confessional and the Conservative identity. The Dutch Calvinist leader Kuyper (quoted in Vanden Berg 1960:187) declared in 1894: "Our battle is . . . against conservatism, not conservatism of a specific brand but against conservatism of every description."

the Ralliement in France was that Monarchists were necessarily Catholics while Catholics could (and after some point should) also be Republican. Still, even when the church mobilized Catholics in support of Conservatives, it never stopped to emphasize the distinctiveness of the former vis-à-vis the latter so as to keep them under its control. In 1914 in Italy, for instance, after having used Catholic organizations to elect Nationalist candidates, the church exhorted its members through its official paper *L'Osservatore Romano* to "distinguish between a temporary resemblance of intentions [and] an identity of ideas, a fortuitous conjunction [and] the thorough amalgamation of the two [Nationalists and Catholics]" (quoted in Cunsolo 1993:51).

Once the participation strategy demonstrated the electoral potential of religion and confessional parties were formed, political Catholicism was established; it dominated the "bourgeois" political space and replaced conservatism (which disappeared as a distinct political option in Belgium, and the Netherlands). In Austria, conservatism became gradually identified with German nationalism. In Germany, Conservative parties survived the advent of the Zentrum as an essentially Protestant parties. In both Italy and Germany Conservatives were able to survive the advent of confessional parties when the activation of the nationalist issue preceded the emergence of confessional parties, a possibility only where movements of national unification arose. Still, nationalism eventually proved only a temporary barrier to the domination of political Catholicism. Nationalism led to the rise of authoritarian movements and regimes, which eventually discredited conservatism. Thus the end of World War II sealed the Christian Democratic domination of the nonsocialist space in both Italy and Germany.

Confessional Party Leaders: Old and New Political Class

Understanding the evolution of confessional parties requires a focus on the twin evolution of their leadership. It is possible to distinguish between two political classes, broadly defined to include attributes such as social and political origin, ideology, and political education. Traditional Conservative leaders tended to be aristocratic or upper-bourgeois in origin, conservative in politics, moderate in ideology, and connected with the old parliamentary Right. They represented the era of the politics of notables. Confessional party leaders tended to be bourgeois and petty-bourgeois in social origin, were concerned about the social question, and were more radical in their ideology. They emerged from a long apprenticeship in Catholic mass organizations and were radically different from traditional notables whom they sought to replace (Boyer 1995:47; Yonke 1990:131; Mendershausen 1973:29; Maier

1969:37). They represented the era of mass politics[6] (Poulat 1982:224). Anderson (1981:369) reports that "their political power was grounded neither in rank nor wealth, but in the press, the clergy, and the growing machinery of local party organizations: upstarts all, as far as political authority in Germany was concerned." They are described as "a group of ragtag outcasts" (Boyer 1995:451), "Catholic underdogs" (Anderson 1986:109), or simply as "outsiders" (Guyot de Mishaegen 1946:180).

That this new political class came from the ranks of the Catholic organizations usually indicated the presence of religious devotion, although not always.[7] The background of two of the leaders of the Katholische Volkspartei in Baden suggests divergent motivations. Jacob Lindau was a fervent lay Catholic, who "discovered" his Catholic political identity during the Aachen Catholic congress; Ferdinand Bissing used Catholicism as a tool to combat the Prussian domination of Germany (Windell 1954:20). Karl Lueger, the leader of the Austrian Christian-Socials, was the quintessential political entrepreneur, "a man who was hardly a fervent communicant" (Zeps 1979:133). Finally, there were Catholic leaders who initially came to confessional politics from movements of regional protest: Joseph Edmund Jörg in Bavaria, Victor Jacobs in Belgium, and Alcide de Gasperi in Austrian-controlled Trento are three such examples. While the boundaries between the two political classes were well-defined, a few politicians managed to make the transition from old to new political class. The leader of the German Zentrum, Ludwig Windthorst, is probably the best example. During the Zentrum's first ten years, Windthorst's outlook was traditional, hardly surprising because his political background was in traditional Hanoverian politics. Yet he managed to transform his political style and actions during the beginning of the 1880s. According to Anderson (1981:268), "No other political figure in imperial Germany made the transition from notable to mass politics more swiftly and more easily than he." Conversely, the Italian Filippo Meda emerged from

[6] Southern (1977:40–41) describes the main cleavage within the Bavarian Catholic movement as follows: "From its inception the movement was thus divided into two roughly defined groups: a group based on some members of the Catholic nobility, most of the bishops, and some sections of the Catholic middle class, which tended to be conservative and comparatively sympathetic to the *Reich;* and a group based on the peasantry and the small town lower and lower middle classes as well as guild strata, lower clergy, and workers, which tended toward broadly populist and in some cases democratic goals. . . . There also existed a division between moderates and extremists, with the extremists normally coming out of the populist wing of the movement."

[7] Religion seems to have been used instrumentally by some confessional leaders. To use Kitschelt's (1989) typology, second-generation leaders were mostly "ideologues" (i.e., organic intellectuals) and "lobbyists" (members of ancillary organizations). This mix is the outcome of a political situation characterized by sharply polarized cleavages.

Catholic mass organizations, argued for political participation, and supported the autonomy of Catholics from the church but had a hard time making the transition to the modern politics of mass party, parliamentary discipline, and extraparliamentary structures (Vecchio 1988:36).

When Conservative politicians decided to turn the defense of the church into a central political issue, they thought they would be able to avoid a permanent association with the church and religion. Yet the defense of religion proved surprisingly successful from an electoral point of view. At last, popular mobilization was being used for the benefit of the Right. As a contemporary Belgian observed, the Conservative party "found, in a crusade conforming to its true ideals, a marvelous means of rejuvenation and rallying" (Carton de Wiart 1948:12). But electoral success came at a heavy price for Conservative politicians. To begin with, the temporary pro-Catholic coalitions of the participation strategy quickly developed into more permanent political structures, first on the parliamentary level, where electoral gains had to be consolidated (Delfosse and Frognier 1988:74), and later on the mass level. The transformation of the old Conservative factions into new mass parties and their concomitant literal "conversion" to religion was, according to a Belgian historian (Guyot de Mishaegen 1946:121), "not the work of the parliamentarians . . . but of a handful of men who were not [up to then] actively participating in politics," of "outsiders" (Guyot de Mishaegen 1946:180). Catholic activists had engineered the stunning Catholic electoral victories and expected fully to taste the fruits of their victory. Their clash with the old political class was as inevitable as was its outcome.

It is no exaggeration to say that Catholic activists felt almost contempt for the parliamentary Right. As Simon (1958:110) puts it, "the lack of esteem that the Right inspired was too strong" among the leaders of Catholic organizations. This attitude had both organizational and ideological causes. Conservatives were perceived as lacking "program, energy, and true unity" (Soete 1986:46). They were also seen as opportunists: a French priest (quoted in Mayeur 1968:135) expressed the feeling of acute resentment about Conservative politicians experienced among Catholic activists when he wrote that "our Catholics let themselves be led by men without principles or convictions." Consequently, Catholic activists claimed that Conservative politicians were not the true representatives of the Catholic people. Moreover, Catholic activists had strong political and policy preferences (especially on the issues of religion and the social question) that clashed with those of the Conservatives. Bavarian Catholic activists were intensely dissatisfied with the parliamentary group of the Patriotenpartei: "They wanted the ideological lines in the movement drawn more sharply, not blurred. . . . [They] sought 'action' and a 'real change', and felt this would occur only when the compromisers were out of the movement, and particularly out of the *Landtag* fraction" (Southern

1977:147–48). The Belgian Catholic leader Charles Woeste (1927:132) made plain what he thought of the Conservative leader Malou and his government: "How much satisfaction did Mr. Malou give to the Catholics from 1871 to 1878? We must recognize it: very little." Catholic activists sought to "restrain the freedom of the right vis-à-vis the 'real country' " (Soete 1986:57). Following the Belgian Conservatives' defeat in the 1878 elections, the Catholic activist Arthur Verhaegen (quoted in Soete 1984:202) argued in a newspaper: "Let's courageously liquidate the old Conservative party, and let's constitute in our dear Belgium a political party that will be Catholic before everything else. . . . Let's constitute now in the Chambers, not a purely Conservative and constitutional right anymore, but a Catholic right, composed of frank and vigorous champions of the Church." Even the few and weak French Catholic organizations developed openly antagonistic relations with Conservative political elites (Rivet 1979; Denis 1977).

Conservative parliamentarians thus had good reason to see Catholic organizations as a threat. The Belgian Conservative politician Dechamps (quoted in Guyot de Mishaegen 1946:157) went so far as to say that "there are two Catholic parties: the old parliamentary Conservative party, and the party, that in exaggerating some true principles, and applying them in a false way, would destroy the political traditions of the first [party]." Dechamps added that "fortunately, the cardinal and the bishops are resisting this impulse of the press [to back the second party]." In the Netherlands, where the Catholic press, controlled by "bourgeois reactionaries," had attacked Shaepman for his efforts to form a Catholic party (Van Eekeren 1956:37), a wide gulf remained between the parliamentary party and the members of Catholic organizations (Bakvis 1981:60).

Conservatives tried to block Catholic organizations from infiltrating the party. The relations between Conservatives and Catholic organizations became antagonistic and often erupted into open conflict. This was usually a three-way contest fought by Conservative political elites, the church, and Catholic activists. Opportunistic alliances were often struck among those actors, depending on the prevailing balance of power. Mass politics was the way of the future, however, and the attempt by Conservative elites to preserve their control over the emerging confessional parties was a lost battle. Catholic activists were eventually able to take over the new parties and establish themselves as their indisputable leaders. For instance, after the electoral victory of the Belgian Catholic coalition in 1884, the local notables of aristocratic extraction who dominated the Right were gradually replaced by what Delfosse and Frognier (1988:77) call "institutional notables," the petty-bourgeois leaders of Catholic organizations. Using their organizational might, Catholic activists were able to gain control of the candidate selection process and gradually strengthen the power of the party executive by imposing voting discipline on the parliamentarians. As the German Free Conservative Count Fred von Franckenberg, a Catholic (quoted in Anderson 1986:92), quipped: "So far, gentlemen, I thought that only Social Democrats issued binding mandates to their voters."

Nowhere was the struggle between Conservative elites and Catholic activists more apparent than in Austria. This was the case because, unlike elsewhere, Conservative Catholics and Catholic activists belonged to competing parties for more than twenty-five years. While the Christian-Social party was formed and grew in Vienna, aristocratic elites dominated the Conservative party in the Austrian provinces. As a result, the competition between the two groups was not concealed by a common organizational frame as in the other four cases. The antagonism between the two factions broke out into the open, particularly during the Catholic congresses of 1892 and 1896. According to Zeps (1979:149), "The school issue, which had previously united the Catholics, became an occasion for division in the drive of the Christian Socials to discredit the Catholic-Conservatives and win support for themselves. . . . By criticizing the Conservatives on a confessional issue they could prove their loyalty to the church at the same time they were attacking the opportunism of the Conservatives."

The Christian Socials were able to emerge victorious from this competition. After the 1897 elections, Conservatives were still dominant, having elected forty-three representatives compared to thirty for the Christian Socials. The introduction of universal male suffrage in 1907, however, proved a test Conservatives could not pass. The Christian Socials overtook them by electing sixty-eight deputies, while the Conservatives fell to twenty-eight. The eventual outcome of this conflict was the absorption of the Conservatives by the Christian Social party in 1907. Conservatives lost because they had discredited themselves by not being able to reverse the anticlerical legislation despite their participation in the government coalition and appeared, as a result, unprincipled and willing to compromise with the Liberals. Also, Conservatives shunned organization and tended to rely on the bishops and the church instead of creating their own political machine. According to Ross (1976:124), this was why the conservative pro-church wing of the German Zentrum lost the internal struggle over the control of the party: "By relying on the acquisition of episcopal support and the backing of the church, they doomed their cause to failure. That support was of limited value in the political quarrels dividing the Centrum because the church's influence waned in the face of the party's secularization and the laicization of its leadership. Neglect of the party apparatus cost the confessional wing a determining role within the Centrum."

Of course, the process of elite replacement was never totally linear and clear-cut. Segments of the old elites managed to survive, while confessional party leaders were later overtaken by the emerging leaders of the party's working-class organizations. As Jaak Billiet and Emmanuel Gerard (1985) have pointed out about Belgium, the formation of the Catholic party did not end the tensions between the parliamentary party and mass organizations. Political institutions acted as intervening variables, facilitating or hindering this process. For example, the restricted franchise of pre-1919 Belgium helped protect the power of the parliamentarians within the party, while the introduction of universal suffrage greatly increased the leverage of mass organizations and their leaders. As a result, mass Catholic organizations managed to impose a new form of organization after 1918 *(standen)*, and in 1936 they even "evicted" from the party thirty-three parliamentarians of the party's "old-guard" (Billiet and Gerard 1985:101).

This process of political elite replacement was certainly democratic in nature given the class differential of the two groups. As Anderson (1986:109) points out about Germany, "A neglected consequence of the Kulturkampf seems to have been a democratization of the Catholic Germany's own elite structure. The old notables, at least in part, were pulled down." Denis (1977:494) reaches a similar conclusion about a region of France where Catholic organizations were able to develop: "The democratic and popular spirit . . . won over the oligarchic and aristocratic one." By pushing for universal manhood suffrage, Catholic activists also had a democratic impact on politics in general.

The irony of this story is that although the Catholic activists who took over the confessional parties were, as a rule, more fervent and sincere Catholics than the Conservative parliamentarians, they were the ones who, once at the helm of the new parties, would push them away from the church. Aemilian Schöpfer, a Tyrolean priest and member of the Katholische Volkspartei was inspired by the radicalism of his fellow Viennese clerics. He seceded from his party and formed a Christian Social association in Innsbruck beginning the "Bruderkampf" that tore Tyrolean Catholicism apart. He "was a priest whose cultural beliefs were as orthodox and integralist as those of the conservatives with whom he battled. He shared with the Viennese party, however, an unwillingness to be manipulated by the arch-conservative episcopate and a frenetic confidence in the virtues of electoral democracy in a province with a solidly Catholic *and* predominantly rural voting base" (Boyer 1995:94–95). The Italian Giuseppe Sacchetti, who was "the most extremist and unilateral journalist"of the Italian Catholic movement, "the quintessence of aggressive intransigentism," also demanded "the greatest possible distance from the sacristy" for lay Catholics (Suardo 1962:35;66). The German Felix Porsch, a man who rose through Zentrum ranks to become a leading "party boss," a "stodgy, unsympathetic representative of the integralist wing of prewar political Catholicism is transformed after 1918 into a committed defender of the very democratic polity he had struggled against so long" (Anderson 1992:316). Explaining how this transformation took place is akin to understanding why confessional parties did not turn into religious fundamentalist parties nor did they seriously attempt to "rechristianize" society, as the initial objective of Catholic organizations dictated.

The Constraints of Religion

The leaders of the new confessional parties quickly realized that the identification of their parties with religion, which they had themselves engineered, was a double-edged sword. For all its proven advantages, religion also entailed very serious dangers. These dangers became clear once confessional parties were formed. To begin with, the confessional nature of these parties circumscribed their electoral appeal. Confessional parties were easily and convincingly branded as clerical organizations, instruments of the church and of the supranational interests of Rome, hence treated as outcasts. For example, Bismarck denounced in 1872 the idea of a confessional party as dangerous and divisive (Evans 1981:56). These parties were often placed in an unfavorable electoral situation with a restricted ability to appeal to nonpracticing, nonreligious, and non-Catholic voters.[8] Furthermore, their confessional character restricted their ability to strike alliances with nonconfessional parties. This was a particularly acute problem where Catholics were a minority, confessional parties had not been able to secure electoral majorities early on, and there was a majority electoral system. In western Prussia, for instance, "pluralities were often so narrow that the margin of success depended on attracting a broader electorate or on accommodation with other political parties and groups" (Ross 1976:45). Przeworski (1985:26) has pointed out that "the search for allies is inherent to electoralism," and this point was made clearly in 1896 by the French pro-Catholic politician Etienne Lamy (quoted in Sedgwick 1965:91): "In France at the present time the majority are not true Catholics. Thus Catholics cannot be expected to help themselves unless they are allied with those elements in the ranks of unbelievers which are honest. These elements have a good reason not to associate themselves with Catholics in an effort to restore the Church to its privileged position because by doing this they would be acting contrary to the egalitarian and liberal principles of the Republic. Catholics must appeal to the ideals on which modern society is based in order to vindicate their belief."

[8] Most confessional parties were largely unsuccessful in attracting non-Catholic or nonreligious voters. In Germany, electoral research indicates that the Zentrum received very few non-Catholic votes. "In the elections from 1874 to 1887, the party won, on average, two-thirds of all the votes in constituencies with clear Catholic majorities, whereas it acquired fewer than 2% of the votes in districts with clear Protestant majorities" (Ritter 1990:35).

Besides purely electoralist concerns, the association of confessional parties with religion was the source of two additional constraints. First, the mobilizational capability of confessional parties and their ability to appeal to Catholic voters were hurt once the danger facing the church declined. Anderson (1981:262) underlines the "inevitable loss of interest among parish priests and Catholic devotional groups in the technical legislative matters that increasingly occupied the time and efforts of parliament." Blackbourn reports that "by the 1890's to be a Catholic was still a necessary but by no means a sufficient condition for voting Centre" (1978:165). By 1912, the Zentrum's share of Catholic votes cast at Reichstag elections had fallen from 83 percent (in 1874) to 54.6 percent (Schauff cited by Blackbourn 1978:165). Second, participation in democratic politics implied rejection of the antiliberal and antidemocratic doctrines of the church: "How would the Belgian people," asked a Belgian author and politician (Mélot 1935:8), "support a party whose program implied the adoption of an authoritarian regime? To demand the votes of the electorate while proposing to limit their power would be attempting the impossible." Lamy (quoted in Sedgwick 1965:90–91) succinctly expressed this dilemma in 1896: "Catholics must choose between two policies: either to present to the public a picture of the ideal Christian State and demand for the Church all the privileges necessary to fulfill its divine mission, setting the principles of the Church against the ideals of civil society; or to attack this society on its own grounds and demand . . . the cessation of religious persecution in the name of its most cherished principles—liberty, equality, and fraternity."

The realization that electoral majorities were hard to achieve, especially after the anticlerical attacks ended, and that politics was necessarily a game of compromise certainly impelled confessional parties to reassess their identity and strategy. The French priest and parliamentarian Lemire (quoted in Mayeur 1968:182) made this point crystal clear to his fellow Catholics: "You had imagined politics to be perfect . . . you had imagined a worldly society similar to the Catholic Church"; but, he added, politics "is a reality that we must grasp in the time we are, in the place we live." The leader of the Austrian Christian Socials, Albert Gessmann, was more blunt. In a special session of the parliamentary group held before the 1911 elections, he insisted (quoted in Boyer 1995:268) that "in politics the only thing that counted was success."

In fact, both electoralist and ideological concerns hinged on a second-order consideration: the connection between confessional parties and religion ultimately undermined the parties' political position. These parties were the products of religious mobilization, having being formed through a religious appeal. Yet religion was not controlled by them, but by another power, the church. The inescapable implication of there parties' connection to the church was the limitation of their electoral appeal, independence, and autonomy. To confront this problem, confessional party leaders stressed as much as they could their independence from the church and indeed claimed that their parties were "aconfessional". As Vecchio (1979b:54) notes, the delicate relationship of these parties with the church did not deter them from seeking autonomy and their own identity. In spite of church pressure and internal dissent, they deemphasized religion, declericalized party organization, and displayed a surprising spirit of political moderation. They did so not just because of electoralist concerns (to attract nonpracticing and non-Catholic voters and strike alliances with non-Catholic political forces) but also to break their dependence on the church. Their drive toward aconfessionality was as unrelenting as it was fraught with seemingly insurmountable obstacles and apparently insoluble dilemmas.

The Limits of Aconfessionality

The attempt of confessional parties to deemphasize religion and move away from the church was limited by two related factors: their nature and their organizational dependence on the church. Both factors allowed for church intervention in party decision making; they were particularly pronounced when confessional parties were young and had not yet consolidated their hold on their voters.

The political coalitions that evolved into confessional parties had as their central goal the defense of the church. The leaders of the new parties, having learned their politics in the context of Catholic organizations, were initially imbued with the urge to defend the church, and they did so even at a high political cost. Indeed, the connection of the confessional parties with the church was these parties' "reason of being" (Howard 1957:79). "How could the Catholic party be fully and entirely independent of the church since it has as its mission to defend it?" asks Mélot (1935:44).

The confessional nature of these parties carried a high cost. On the one hand these parties proclaimed loudly to be political parties, not religious interest groups. On the other hand, they retained a highly religious coloration and placed a high priority on confessional issues. Issues related to religion and the church enjoyed political priority for a long time, and it was on such issues that legislative discipline was primarily enforced. One of the very first actions of the parliamentary group of the Italian Popular party was a pledge to work for the freedom of religious teaching in the school system (Molony 1977:53). According to Blackbourn (1980:126), "It is a telling sign that the Centre was able to compromise with the government and the other parties over measures of local government and fiscal reform, and that it was the two central issues where the position of the church was at stake—the constitution and education—where it dug in its heels." Indeed, while the

Zentrum avoided any mention of Catholicism in its program and downplayed its confessional character in the hope of attracting non-Catholic voters, its first parliamentary combat as a party concerned the Roman question. The party introduced in the Prussian Landtag an address to the throne protesting the abolition of the papal state and requesting government action to secure the rights of the pope. As Anderson (1981:148) puts it, most Zentrum leaders "would have been glad enough to keep [the Roman question] out but they were trapped by their own recent history." Although this proposition was defeated, it demonstrated that the Zentrum was indeed, and contrary to its assertions, a confessional party. The confessional nature of the party was forcefully underlined by the party statutes which stipulated that only practicing Roman Catholics could be nominated as candidates of the party. Likewise, though Dutch Calvinists and Catholics remained allies for decades, overcoming important policy differences, their coalition broke down in 1925 when the Catholics demanded appropriations for the continuance in office of a Netherlands envoy to the Vatican. The Calvinists rejected this demand, and their defection "caused a break in the Christian Union that was slow in healing" (Barnouw 1940a:250). While Austria was torn in 1922 by an acute economic crisis, the Christian Social leader Ignaz Seipel set as his condition for accepting the post of chancellor that the under secretary of education be a Christian Social. The Social-Democrat newspaper *Arbeiter-Zeitung* (quoted in Zeps 1979:306) reacted to the confessional priorities of the Christian Socials as follows: "At this terrible moment, what is the greater concern of the man who is supposed to become chancellor tomorrow? It is not only the greatest concern, it is a precondition for taking over the government. Reported exactly, it is that the education ministry be occupied by a Christian Social member of the parliament! At this moment, this future head of the government thinks only of clericalizing the school."

The ideological commitment of confessional party leaders to church-related issues explains only part of their persistence in emphasizing confessional matters. Catholic leaders were not just ideologues. They were also politicians interested in political success and religion was essential to it since it was what attracted voters to confessional parties in the first place. As the Zentrum deputy Franz Bitter (quoted in Ross 1976:67) asserted in 1910: "Catholic voters come to our party on account of their ideology." This had profound consequences.

Confessional parties represented a multitude of often conflicting social interests and related ideological viewpoints. *Because* religion was their primary appeal, confessional parties became heterogeneous interclass parties—in sharp contrast to their early competitors, which were relatively homogeneous parties. As Thomas Nipperdey (1992:188) points out, membership in a confession is for confessional party voters "an absolute priority over membership to a social group or strictly political considerations." As Henri Haag (1953:281) remarks, "The Belgian Catholics constitute a characteristic group in the nation. The link that unites them is not material interests; in fact, there are broad differences among Catholic aristocrats, bourgeoisie and proletarians. Their distinguishing mark is their acceptance of the leadership of the Roman Catholic church." In fact, social and political heterogeneity was the distinguishing mark of these parties: the "cohabitation of clashing social movements within the Christian blocks" (Lorwin 1971:148) in Belgium and the Netherlands is well documented. The Belgian Catholic party was an interclass party composed of aristocrats, bourgeois, farmers, and workers (Soete 1983:202). In Italy, the members of the PPI ranged "from old conservatives to young radicals, from large capitalists to small farmers, from directors of the Bank of Rome to small shareholders in credit societies" (Molony 1977:56). It is indicative of this heterogeneity that the leader of the trade union wing of the party, Guido Miglioli, suggested that the party be named "Party of the Christian Proletariat" (Molony 1977:62). As Romolo Murri (quoted in Molony 1977:56) complained, the PPI was "not a homogeneous and strong party but a gathering of men held together only by electoral interests." The Austrian Christian Social leader Albert Gessmann (quoted in Boyer 1995:103) pointed out at the 1907 party congress that Christian Socials were "a true trans-class party encompassing peasants, the urban bourgeoisie, and the workers." According to von Klemperer (1972:232), the party under the umbrella of the Catholic faith "included many interests and opinions: liberals as well as integralists, monarchists as well as republicans, conservatives as well as social reformers, friends and foes of a coalition with the Left and also of the Anschluss, centralists as well as federalists, anti-Semites as well as Jews." The leader of the Bavarian Patriot party, Joseph Edmund Jörg, explicitly recognized that his party was a mobilization platform of various groups to such a degree "that any attempt to construct a detailed political program would be injurious and perhaps fatal to the Party" (Southern 1977:39–40). Bismarck (quoted in Zeender 1976:3) made a similar point when he claimed that "there are not two souls in the Center but seven ideological tendencies which portray all the colors of the political rainbow from the most extreme right to the radical left." As one of the leaders of the Zentrum, Peter Reichensperger (quoted in Anderson 1981:141), complained, the party was composed of "damned heterogeneous elements." Klaus Epstein (1971:44) reports that the Zentrum "was compelled to develop social policies that could win the endorsement of Silesian landlords, Ruhr trade unionists, Rhenish industrialists, Swabian artisans, and Bavarian peasants alike. Considerable tension between a Right and a Left wing was inevitable, and this was accentuated by regional differences." The party itself recognized the diversity of its members' interests and forsook party discipline on most issues—with the exception of questions pertaining to religion and the church, where voting discipline was to be maintained (Ross 1976:43). Thus confessional parties were catch-all parties from their very inception, and it is right to assert, as van Kersbergen (1994:39) does, that "in contrast to Kircheimer, one could argue that catch-allism in the case of Christian Democracy is not so much an effect of the transformation of Western European party systems and of the growing intensity of electoral competition, but rather the manifestation of the very nature of these parties. Christian Democracy was a catch-all party *avant la lettre.*"

This heterogeneity, eventually reflected in a peculiar organizational structure based on autonomous class-based or "social" organizations, such as the *standen* in Belgium, was the outcome of the religious character of the mobilization from which confessional parties emerged and gave religion the political weight it commanded. Religion was the cement that held these parties together. As Zeps (1979:213) points out, "the confessional issue was a rallying point which cut across provincial lines to unite all Christian Socials"; and as Southern (1977:328) remarks, "the Catholic faith was indispensable as a cohesive element in a socially and politically disparate movement." So, when a leader of the Zentrum in Hesse (quoted in Zucker 1984:26) complained that "material interests" were taking precedence over "those of principle," his concern was not of an ideological nature: material interests, he argued, "were threatening party harmony." It was, therefore, impossible to suppress religion altogether and erase the confessional character of these parties because of political and strategic rather than ideological considerations. In short, the catch-allism of confessional parties was not the result of ideological choice but of the constraints imposed by the particular process of formation of these parties, which is to say the result of their history.

Confessional parties could not afford to disregard the resources of the church in the face of mounting electoral challenges during their early years. Organization building takes time, and emerging Socialist parties represented a more formidable threat than Liberal ones. As a result, confessional parties initially had to rely on an electoral strategy that "resorted intensely to defense-of-the-church slogans" to mobilize their constituency (Blackbourn 1980:108). Sometimes they even had to appeal directly to the church for support. For instance, the Belgian Catholic party was forced to request church support during the crucial 1912 elections (Stengers 1981:63), and the Zentrum had to resort to the organizational help of the clergy during the challenging 1907 elections. "Just once allow the clergy to remain neutral in an electoral campaign and the Centrum will be shattered," argued the Zentrum deputy Franz Bitter in 1910 (Ross 1976:67). A Zentrum cadre in Baden (quoted in Anderson 1988:367) pointed out that "for the ordinary Catholic citizen in the countryside, the priest was and remained the representative of the Center party. Inquiries and assignments from the district and central party leadership, leaflets and election newsletters to be distributed, requests for funding these and other campaign activities, all went to him." In other words, "every contemporary, Protestant and Catholic, knew: no clergy, no Center" (Anderson 1988:367). This dependence was reinforced by the clerical presence in party organization. The first congress of the PPI, for instance, was marked by the presence of a large contingent of priests (Molony 1977:63). Furthermore, numerous priests were elected on the tickets of confessional parties and some of these parties had even priests as their leaders. Finally, dependence on the church was also reinforced by an initial laziness that led to organizational inertia. Anderson (1981:260–61) reports that in Germany, "the Zentrum did not at first require a dense network of regional organizations because it could rely on the clergy and make use of numerous parish and diocesan associations originally set up for devotional and charitable ends. . . . The ready availability of so many Catholic clubs enabled the Zentrum to tap [the Catholic] constituency inexpensively and effectively." Likewise, the PPI initially relied on the pro-church press instead of creating its own party press. Jemolo (1960:173–74) describes the initial dynamic between the Italian Catholic party and the church. The PPI, he notes,

> during elections necessarily attached peculiar importance to the support of the bishops, to the warmth with which parish priests commended its programme to their flocks, and which at such times would have a second electoral office (in reality the most important) in every presbytery. The Popular Party was a non-confessional party; but a difference of opinion between the provincial leaders of such a party and the local bishop was not to be thought of; such a difference if it arose, would have to be composed —if necessary by the leaders in question. The Popular Party was a party independent of ecclesiastical authorities inasmuch as the latter in effect dissociated themselves of many of its initiatives and aims; but neither it nor any avowedly Catholic party would find it possible, either now or later, to oppose the [Vatican's] Secretariat of State whenever it issued a directive on any question. . . . An organization of Catholics which sought to defy the Pope had been for a century at least a contradiction in terms, a practical impossibility.

The dependence of confessional parties on the church was resented by party leaders. A contemporary pro-church Belgian observer (quoted in Simon 1955:153) illustrated this situation by denouncing the behavior of the first Catholic deputies: "They are powerless in the elections without the help of the clergy. [But], as soon as they are elected they move away from it, sometimes they bitterly criticize it, and they present themselves as independent from clerical influences, as they say." The main negative consequence of this dependence was that the church retained an important leverage over the parties. The obvious danger was, as Molony (1977:66) points out, that "what was so gratuitously and enthusiastically given could equally as readily be withdrawn." Indeed, party leaders realized that church support could not be taken for granted (Zeender 1976:5). Above all, church support was not gratis; it came at a stiff price: church intervention in party decision making. The Italian Catholic Murri argued in 1920 that a completely independent Catholic party was a contradiction in terms and that the religious identity and origin of confessional parties in itself justified church intervention (Howard 1957:140). Murri imagined the following dialogue between church and party. The pope could say to a Catholic party: "You declare that you want to bring back religion to the state and to society; at the same time it is from me that you accept religion and it is to me that you profess obedience in the matter of religion; either, therefore, it is my religion that you accept from me and want to apply on the state and the society and then you must receive directions from me; or it is another religion, and I have the right to repudiate and unmask it" (quoted in Howard 1957:141). Likewise, the bishop of Trier Michael Felix Korum (quoted in Ross 1976:61) asked himself: "What's the Centrum for us?" He answered: the Centrists "are our defenders in Berlin." Because this was their mission, he added, "they should devote themselves to the church's interests and serve with complete trustworthiness."

Confessional parties were thus subject to intense church intervention. Initially, the church regulated this intervention on the basis of a division of the policy space into two spheres of action: secular, where the party was free to act, and religious, where the church could intervene. As Mélot (1935:45) points out, the issues of no interest for the church were considered "free issues," a "vast field where the Catholic party is perfectly autonomous." Windthorst (quoted in Anderson 1981:350) made this point in 1887: "The Holy Father expressed a very important principle, that is, the principle that in questions of a secular nature the Zentrum fraction can, just as any Catholic, judge and vote with complete freedom and according to its conviction, and that the Holy Father does not mix in these secular things." But this mutual indifference about political priorities gradually evaporated. On the one hand, party leaders progressively grasped the political cost of delivering unremitting support to the church. On the other hand, the perception that the secular and the religious spheres of action were clearly delimited and that in the secular one the confessional party was completely free and independent proved to be an illusion. Church leaders soon discovered logrolling: through the parties' mediation, policy issues could be used as bargaining chips for winning concessions on matters of church interest. As a result, the church often intervened in the secular field to extract concessions from governments in the religious field. The realization that the religious and secular spheres were intertwined was expressed by the pope himself in a note sent to the Zentrum about Bismarck's military bill (known as the Second Jacobini Note). According to Anderson (1981:343), "By insisting on the connection between religious and political spheres, the Pope had sharply undercut his own avowal of the Zentrum's complete freedom, 'considered as a political party'. Mosler expressed the real sentiments of [Windthorst] when he complained that while the Pope 'concedes that the matter is in itself purely political', he insists that the bill has '*rapports d'ordre moral et religieux*. . . . Now I ask you, couldn't you say precisely the same thing about other questions of equally secular and political nature: for example, of the tobacco and whisky monopoly'?"

In other words, as Jemolo (1960:174) concisely points out, "the power to fix the limits between that which was purely political and that which concerned morality and religion in such way as to legitimate the intervention of the ecclesiastical authorities would always remain with the last-named." A famous example of church intervention is the Vatican's pressure on the Zentrum to vote for Bismarck's military budget in exchange for concessions in Germany's religious policy and diplomatic relations with Rome. According to De Rosa (1972:137), "The pope did not hesitate, in 1887, to require the sacrifice and submission of Windthorst, the leader of the German Center, to the domestic policy of Bismarck, which was the condition set by the German chancellor for a reconciliation with the Holy See." Another instance of open church intervention in the party's decision making was the obstruction of the alliance between Catholics and Socialists in Italy during the 1920s which opened the road to fascism (Einaudi and Goguel 1952:17). In such situations the church was prompt to remind the party of its confessional character. Indeed, the Italian pro-church press depicted a Catholic-Socialist coalition as nothing less than a break of the contract between church and party: this move was "neither decent, nor opportune, nor *lawful*" (Einaudi and Goguel 1952:19; emphasis added). To quote a Belgian author, "*L'Eglise est toujours présente et pesante*" (the church is always present and always matters)(Beaufays 1973:60).

Generally, only rarely did the conflict between church and parties break openly into the public realm. Even in cases of intense confrontation, the conflict remained relatively muted. Windthorst skillfully covered the Vatican's intervention and his own anger at it, while the Italian church let it be understood in 1923 that it did not support the Popular party rather than condemn it publicly (Webster 1960:95). In general, confessional parties avoided publicly defying the Vatican. Party leaders had to make sure that church tolerance for confessional parties did not turn into open disapproval. What is certain is that church pressure was much resented by party leaders and members: "No

Center deputy . . . wanted any bishop or pope to tell him how to vote in the Reichstag." (Anderson 1988:368). In sum, despite the benefits it provided, the religious origin and nature of confessional parties limited the parties' electoral appeal, allowed for church intervention, and carried high political costs.

The Politics of Adaptation: The Confessional Dilemma

There was no easy way out of this state of affairs. To begin with, confessional party leaders were unwilling to maximize votes at the expense of their principles and ideology—not least because forgoing these principles and moving away from religion would prove counterproductive and could even provoke the disintegration of their parties through the combined effect of the loss of legitimacy conferred by the association with the church and the loss of the parties unifying bond. With the religious connection proving to be such a constraint, confessional party leaders had to act in an imaginative and decisive manner if they wanted both to overcome the disadvantages of their association with religion and the church and to preserve its advantages. How could they deemphasize religion without destroying the confessional character of the parties which guaranteed unity and electoral support? On the surface, this confessional dilemma was one, as Durand (1995:21) puts it, of "deciding between fidelity to an identity and the definition of a strategy." In fact, the situation was more complex because identity and strategy were not distinct from each other. On the one hand, the parties' identity constrained their choice of electoral strategies and, on the other hand, the strategy selected would shape their identity in dramatic ways. Ross (1976:xiv) describes this situation as a self-defeating dilemma:

> On the one hand, [the Zentrum] could seek to deemphasize its confessional identity and purport to be a purely political party. This would exorcise traditional Protestant fears regarding the party's ties with Rome and facilitate the working of a Centrist legislation through the national and state parliaments. On the other hand, it could adopt an intransigent pose, immuring itself as it were in a beleaguered citadel, and seek to infuse strength into its ranks by raising the cry of religious persecution. In short, the Centrum had to decide if it was a political party or a religious interest group; it had to choose between secularism and sectarianism. Both options were self-defeating. Without its sectarian penumbra, the party jeopardized its internal unity. If, however, the Centrum comported itself as a religious organization, it relegated itself to political isolation.

Yet contrary to Ross, this confessional dilemma was not self-defeating. Declericalization could be achieved without jeopardizing the parties' support and existence. In fact, confessional parties could *both* achieve declericalization and retain a confessional identity. The key was redefining their confessional identity and reinterpreting the role of religion in politics and society.

Initially, the Conservative politicians who had allied with the church tried to resolve this dilemma by insulating the parliamentary party from Catholic organizations. This proved impossible to achieve, and the leaders of Catholic organizations took over the new parties. These new leaders found a way out of the confessional dilemma; it was simple but had long-lasting effects. They retained their parties' confessional identity, thus preserving unity, keeping the confidence and support of their religious constituency, and maintaining the church's tolerant stance toward them. At the same time, they transformed their parties into independent and secular organizations with secular priorities, relaxed their dependence on the church, averted church intervention, and became major players in the politics of their countries, unconstrained by the church. Confessional parties managed, as Anderson (1988:374) points out, "to function both as an interest group and a political party, asserting and protecting the particular interests of Catholics, yet accepting responsibility for the well-being of the whole: to be *both* Catholic *and* universal." Party leaders became capable of "freely exploiting the resources and authority of the church as the apparatus for [their] lay party, yet keeping the essential decision-making of this party in [their] own hands" (Anderson 1988:369). How was this possible?

The declericalization of confessional parties took place on two levels: organization building and identity. On the first level, a successful effort was made to free the parties from their dependence on the church through organization building. On the second level, confessional parties successfully repudiated clericalism by reinterpreting the meaning of religion for politics and society.[9]

Confessional parties broke their organizational dependence on the church by building a lay mass organization of their own with membership allegiance and loyalty directed exclusively toward the party. Although the original Cath-

[9] A party is clerical when it acts as the political arm of the church, largely relying on clerical personnel and seeking to impose a religious identity on civil society. A party is confessional when it has a Catholic identity, is supported by Catholic voters, the clergy, and the church, and is concerned about confessional issues. For a discussion about confessionalism that points to the same elements, albeit not distinguishing confessionalism from clericalism, see Anderson who points out (1988:367) that "if, however, clericalism meant the determination of party policy by the hierarchy, then the Center was no clerical party. . . . On the other hand, if clericalism meant the inclusion of religious demands on a political agenda, then the Center was certainly a clerical party."

olic organizations initially proved to be excellent party machines, they could not sustain the party in the long run. Parties seek full control over their organizational resources, something incompatible with the reliance on traditional Catholic associations that were organized on a parish and diocesan basis, were often supervised by priests, and constituted easy recuperation targets for the church. Catholic organizations were the building blocks in the construction of the new party organizations. The creation, in 1890, of the Volksverein für das katholische Deutschland provides the most impressive example of confessional party organization building. Like all confessional parties, the Zentrum was forced, during its early years, to "rel[y] upon the church apparatus and laymen's organizations under clerical sponsorship for its very existence" (Ross 1976:58). The Volksverein was formed mainly by priests and initially supported by the church (the original intention was to call it *Leoverein*) because of its pronounced anti-Protestant profile. But this organization was quickly hijacked by the party. According to Ross (1976:58), "The *Volksverein* was and remained an appendage of the Centrum given its tasks of strengthening and tightening party organization. It assumed the task of campaign agitation and political education within the party, and maintained and cultivated the ties between the Centrist electorate, especially the workers and the urban middle-classes, and the party." By 1908 the Volksverein exerted direct influence over five newspapers and in the course of a single year distributed around thirty million leaflets. By 1914, it reached a membership of eight hundred thousand (Ross 1976:59). At the same time, a host of other organizations were created as well. According to Blackbourn (1980:111), the "proliferation of auxiliary organizations . . . constituted a victory for Gröber's [a Zentrum leader] conception of political organization over the clerical conservative conception."[10]

The lower clergy were instrumental in the creation of the new organizational structure but were eventually removed from it and replaced by laymen. The presence of priests in party organizations was strongly criticized. According to Ross (1976:63), "The cleric was being challenged within the Centrum party by the emergence of the laity as an interest group with concerns separate and distinct from the Roman church itself." An Italian contemporary commentator (Fanelli cited in Molony 1977:64) argued that it was a great weakness of Sturzo that "he had not rejected the hordes of inopportune priestly colleagues whose presence branded the party as clerical . . . and who then deserted Sturzo in his hour of need." The development of the

[10] Likewise, the Belgian Catholic party strengthened its organization during the late 1880s and was thus able to pressure the church into reducing its political interventions (Stengers 1981:62). In Italy, PPI activists urged the creation of a party press "rigidly obedient to the prescriptions of the central direction" (F. L. Ferrari, quoted in Vecchio 1988:14).

Volksverein into the party's main mass organization marked the beginning of the decline of clerical participation in German politics: as Ross (1976:64) points out, "After the creation of a separate party organization the clergy did not long remain a preponderant factor in the Centrum." Indeed, the party bureaucracy and the parliamentary group were gradually purged of priests in a process that was completed by 1914.[11]

As expected, the process of organizational declericalization provoked sharp criticism. Count Hans Georg von Oppersdorff denounced it in 1913, arguing (quoted in Ross 1976:65) that "in this systematic de-clericalization of the party organization" was to be found "the simple explanation for the decreasing intercession of the Centrum for the religio-political demands of the Catholic people. . . . With the exclusion of the 'clerical' element the old Catholic Centrum has disappeared and in its place has stepped a new interconfessional, democratic, nationalistic party that possesses naturally little zeal and understanding for specific Catholic claims." Priests protested against their gradual exclusion from the party, and in 1911, at a meeting held in Ratibor, they signed a petition stating that "as the born leaders of the Catholic people," they wanted "a powerful and truly Catholic Centrum" (Ross 1976:65). But they failed to stop this process. The replacement of clerical personnel by lay cadres reinforced the independence of confessional parties and had long-lasting effects on their political development.

Besides building their own organization, confessional party leaders sought to construct a distinct political identity. Because they could not and did not want to shed the confessional character of their parties, they altered its connotation and recast its meaning. The construction of this political identity was achieved through a radical reinterpretation of Catholicism that challenged the church's monopoly in defining the relationship between religion and politics. In a process of symbolic appropriation, confessional party leaders reinterpreted Catholicism as an increasingly general and abstract moral concept, controlled and mediated by them rather than the church. "Concepts such as 'Christian,' 'moral,' 'religious inspiration,' 'values of christian civilization,' even 'humanism' replaced Catholic doctrine and the interests of the church as the foundation of the parties' ideology and program" (Billiet and Gerard 1985:100). As Lorwin (1971:168–69) observes, these concepts were "as vague as the doctrine of the Catholic church was detailed and specific." Catholicism was thus drained of its religious content even while being legitimated as a political identity. The French Catholic thinker Jacques Maritain

[11] Within the Zentrum's Reichstag group the number of clerics declined from eighteen (20 percent) in 1903 to eleven (10.9 percent) in 1912. A similar process took place among candidates for the Reichstag. While in 1903 clerics made up 15.3 percent of the party's candidates, by 1912 they made up only 8.5 percent (Ross 1976:64).

understood this development and grasped its consequences: he identified the "so-called Christian parties" as the reason behind the total destruction of any hope for truly Christian policies (Durand 1995:125).

The redefinition of Catholicism by confessional parties allowed them to solve the problem of the tension between religious faith and political practice at the expense of the former. Political Catholicism was gradually yet decisively detached from both the Catholic church and religion. Confessional parties could now claim to be simultaneously Catholic and secular. As a result, they contributed to making religion less relevant for politics. To use Formigoni's (1988:28) felicitous term, they "desacralized" politics. The political priorities of confessional parties shifted. The original objectives behind the formation of Catholic organizations, rechristianization and the building of a Christian society, were swiftly recognized to be chimeras and were discarded. As Zeps (1979:478) remarks, "In the process, the Catholics realized more than ever that the Christian Social party could not be used as a tool to rechristianize Austria." The church's concerns and interests became secondary for the parties. Anderson (1981:401) reports that "what Windthorst was never capable of doing, was to identify Catholic interests too narrowly with the concerns of the Church's visible institutional apparat, implicitly denying its universal claim." Ernst Lieber, Windthorst's successor at the helm of the Zentrum, declared in 1898 (quoted in Vecchio 1979a:52) that "the Zentrum is not a religious, confessional, ecclesiastical party, but a political [one]." In sum, confessional parties were gradually transformed from "Catholic parties" into secular "Christian Peoples' parties" (Gerard and van den Wijngaert 1982). These parties, according to Gregory Baum and John Coleman (1987:xix), "while firmly Catholic, were not interested in protecting the institutional privileges of the Church. They wanted the church to be the source of spiritual values that could become the foundation of a democratic society." Thus, in a paradoxical way, the politicization of religion contributed to the secularization of politics.[12]

Luigi Sturzo, the leader of the PPI, is considered by many (such as the Italian priest and theologian Gianni Baget Bozzo, quoted in Vecchio 1979b:65–66), to have "effectively revised the 'Catholic party' model then existing, taking away its still decidedly ecclesiastical character and placing it in the context of civil society." Baget Bozzo (ibid.) adds that "the non-confessional formula expresses, through the party, the original distinction

[12] For Vecchio (1987:7) this move was a transition from the "Catholic party" to the "party of Christian inspiration" or "Christian Democracy." He argues (1987:7) that Catholic parties were directly tied to the hierarchy, to the confessional idea, to the defense of immediate and ineluctable catholic "interests," and to the attack against the Liberal state; while parties "of Christian inspiration" are necessarily aconfessional and lay organizations because they express a "national" interest and promote their own opinion on every important political issue.

between the Church and political society: in defining itself as non-confessional the Christian party shows that it belongs to the latter." Indeed, Sturzo made a sharp distinction between the political and the religious fields by arguing, as early as 1899 (quoted in Molony 1977:24), that "in the platform of Christian Democracy . . . there can be no place for a direct plank on the condition to which the revolution had brought the Holy See, just as there could be no place for a statute of the League against blasphemy." In 1905, Sturzo (quoted in De Rosa 1972:275) clearly delineated what the central choice for Catholic activists would be: "The political, administrative, civil and social camp chosen by Italian Catholics: will it be open, organically national and lay, or diocesan and dependent on the bishops?" Sturzo's choice was clear: "We search in religion the vivifying spirit of all individual and collective life; but we cannot transform ourselves from a political party into a religious order, we don't have the right to speak in the name of the Church, we cannot be an emanation of ecclesiastical organizations and depend from them, and we cannot validate our own political action with the power of the Church" (quoted in Gherardi 1967:52–53). This point was epitomized in Sturzo's dictum: *"La democrazia cristiana . . . non é la Chiesa"* (Christian democracy is not the church)(quoted in De Rosa 1972:250).

Even though theoretically elaborated by Sturzo, the same choice was made by hundreds of Catholic activists in Italy and elsewhere. When, for example, the lay activist Agostino Cameroni asked, in 1907, the Florentine Catholics to elect him to the parliament, he pointed out (quoted in Formigoni 1988:106) that the Catholics did not intend to become "a true Catholic parliamentary party with official, Vatican, character" because this would, among others, "be a gravely dangerous misunderstanding, a reciprocal diminution of the freedom of the Church and of the Catholic parliamentarians." In short, political Catholicism could not be a program of the church, and a confessional party could not be the political arm of the church: "Catholics are not the permanent army of religious authority," declared Sturzo (quoted in De Rosa 1972:278).

It is important to emphasize that the symbolic appropriation and redefinition of Catholicism by confessional parties was inherently linked to their formation process. Ultimately, this outcome was the unintended consequence of the church's strategies of organization and participation. The "Christian people" as Poulat (1982:224) points out, changed: after having remained "on their knees" *within* the church, they had to stand up and defend religion *outside* the church. But once outside, they did not come back. Well before the emergence of a confessional party in Austria, the Catholic activist Ferdinand Brandis (quoted in Bled 1988:123) asserted: "We are seeing the moment that lay Catholics would have to determine their political strategy away from the bishops." As Zeps (1979:310) notes about Austria, "In a way, the Christian Socials were practicing a grass roots separation of church and state by refusing to become the secular representatives of the hierarchy when church interests conflicted with the needs of the country." Once formed, confessional parties encouraged these tendencies further and shaped the new Catholic political identity in a way that served their interests and legitimized them. The redefinition of Catholicism by confessional parties had tremendous consequences. To many Catholics, Catholicism became as much a religion represented by the church as a secular ideology represented by a political party. The claim of being a Catholic in politics denoted no official or practicing connection to Catholicism or the church. As van Kersbergen (1994:45) remarks, people today can be "Christian Democrats even if they do not believe in God." Therefore, it became possible to be simultaneously Catholic and secular, to claim, in other words, two mutually exclusive identities.[13] The most striking recognition of this contradiction is perhaps to be found in the Belgian Catholic party's (Parti social chrétien–Christelijke Volkspartij, PSC-CVP) famous 1945 "Christmas Program." This program (quoted in Pasture 1996:266) designated the party as Christian "because it claims the human values which form the basis of our western civilization" and went on to add that these values have become "the common heritage of believers and unbelievers alike."

This process amounted to an emancipation of Catholics from the authority of church. The Italian Mario Missiroli (quoted in Molony 1977:48) reflected this development when he asserted in 1919 that the creation of the Partito popolare was a step by which Catholics "liberated themselves permanently from Vatican subjugation."[14] Loyalty to Catholicism often shifted from attendance at religious services and participation in church-related events to participation in the political and social activities of the Catholic organizations. In the early stages of party formation, sacral functions were hijacked into political activities, while church services and other religious activities lost their original spiritual content and were transformed into pure political events: "When the defense of the religion became a, or more appropriately, the political issue, then participation in a religious event became a political statement" (Sperber 1980:341). Thus the rise in attendance at mass services (as noted, for example, in 1901 by the Austrian bishops) did not indicate an increase in peoples' religiosity but rather their increasing politicization. Catholic services became politicized, and "the line between cultic worship and political mobilization was frequently difficult to draw" (Boyer 1981:119). In

[13] In a more extreme and less widely applicable formulation, "it was equally possible, as Reinhold Knoll has rightly observed about Lueger himself, to be both pious *and* anticlerical" (Boyer 1995:168).

[14] In a more circumspect way, Sturzo "defended autonomy for the layman as a way of 'gaining personality' " (Agócs 1988:169).

Germany traditional religious events such as the Kevelaer pilgrimage were transformed into party events, shows of support of the participants for the Zentrum (Sperber 1980:343). The annual Catholic congresses "had become by the mid-1880's an opportunity to see, hear, and fete Windthorst rather than an occasion for the meeting of the leaders and members of Catholic associations" (Zeender 1976:17). In fact, these congresses were gradually transformed into congresses of the Zentrum. Analyzing data on participation in religious events and elections from the region of Trier, Smith (1991:32) found that a large group of Catholics identified with their confession and the Zentrum "but were no longer bound to the church." The intellectual interests of lay Catholics shifted as well. A content analysis of the *Revue Générale*, the main Belgian Catholic periodical (Piepers 1968), found that the coverage of religious issues decreased after 1880. Among the religious issues still covered, religious history themes prevailed at the expense of religious doctrine and actuality. Thus the Zentrum critic Edmund Schopen was not too far from reality when he argued, in 1910, that the downgrading of the party's religious identity and its declericalization "led inevitably to religious indifference and loss of faith" (quoted in Ross 1976:67). The Austrian Dominican theologian Albert Maria Weiss was equally right when he argued, in 1925, about the Christian Social party (quoted in Boyer 1995:167) that "the Christian and the Catholic might be two different religions, or even stand in direct contradiction to each other." He added that this produced "a Christianity existing without the Church, without the sacraments, without liturgical services, a kind of deism with Christian names."

The redefinition of Catholicism by confessional parties provoked justifiable reactions. According to Anderson (1988:352), "Not surprisingly, some Catholics took a dim view of any retreat from Catholic, and toward merely 'Christian,' organizations." Numerous priests denounced the absence of a genuine "Christian soul" in the PPI (Father Gemelli, cited in Vecchio 1979b:54), while prominent bishops openly displayed their hostility toward the party (Vecchio 1979b:72). Cardinal Pietro Gaspari, papal secretary of state in the 1920s, considered the PPI an "irreligious" party (Webster 1960:53). Accusing party leaders of deism, even heresy, became increasingly common (Blackbourn 1978:163). Confessional party leaders such as Julius Bachem in Germany were repeatedly attacked for setting "aside the Catholic basis of the most important organization of German Catholicism in order to substitute a 'so-called nondenominational Christian basis' as the party's guiding philosophy" (Ross 1976:57). Confessional parties were able to thwart these attacks, however, and thrive under democratic regimes because party leaders never repudiated Catholicism, built their own organizational resources, and relied on the fear that the church felt for emerging Socialist and, later, Communist parties.

All confessional parties implemented processes of declericalization with varying degrees of intensity. Declericalization was not a linear process, and at times the church was able to reinforce its authority vis-à-vis the confessional parties and push for a more pronounced Catholic party outlook (Boyer 1995). In the long run, however, declericalization was achieved in all cases.

In Belgium, the Catholic party leaders ceaselessly emphasized that their party appealed to "all people of goodwill, that it is not a confessional party, but a true party of constitutional freedom" (Guyot de Mishaegen 1946:194). Even though the party repealed the Liberal education law, it did not overturn most of the Liberal legislation as the church expected it to do (Urwin 1970:324). According to Aubert (1968:31), the leaders of the Catholic party "had the wisdom . . . not to abuse their victory, despite the desires of a part of the clergy and of the ultramontanes." For instance, the inclusion of religious instruction in the official curriculum of public schools, which was abolished by the Liberals in 1879, was not reintroduced in 1884 and the matter was left to the discretion of the communal authorities. As a result, the bishops felt "immense disappointment" and, although they asked for changes, they failed to get them (Stengers 1981:69). Overall, the Catholics were extremely careful and restrained when revising the Liberal legislative edifice. De Moreau (1929:562) points out that the party was able to remain in power until 1914 mainly because of its moderation. Even Liberal authors (such as Stengers 1981:69) recognize that "we should not imagine [the Catholic party] as being under the command of the episcopate." During the 1930s, declericalization was pursued with renewed vigor (Billiet and Gerard 1985:100). The party developed its own organizational resources, and its links to the church declined markedly (Pasture 1996:267). Likewise, in the Netherlands, the Catholic leader Herman Shaepman declared early on that the Catholic party should not be an instrument of the church (Brachin and Rogier 1974:111). He retained his independence vis-à-vis the hierarchy (Durand 1995:75) and argued (quoted in van Eekeren 1956:32) that "what the Catholics just want to make impossible in the future is that they count in the political field only as supporters of the Roman Catholic faith." These were not merely cheap tactics but reflected a genuine attempt to differentiate church and party in the ways outlined above.

In Austria, the leaders of the Christian Social party made clear, through both discourse and action, that their party was independent from the church. As Zeps (1979:214) puts it, "The concerns of the Christian Socials in politics and economics went beyond those of the bishops. The bishops formed a special interest group in the party, powerful, to be sure, since the party needed the endorsement of the church, but independent nonetheless." Party leaders, Boyer (1995:199) points out, were not willing "to take orders from the Vatican." The party ignored (at least up to 1910) the wishes or needs of the bishops "unless those needs also served the party's own tactical interests." In turn, the episcopate "remained suspicious of Lueger down to [his] death" (Boyer 1995:167). Furthermore, the party saw itself as the servant and executor of the "Christian people" rather than the church (Boyer 1995:164). It shaped a Christian, as opposed to Catholic, identity and "did not emphasize 'Catholicism' as an independent political variable deserving decisive and exclusive prominence on its own" (Boyer 1995:167). Indeed, a British embassy officer noted that the party clearly distinguished "between the appellation 'Christian' and 'Catholic' " (Boyer 1995:105). All in all, the party "wore its religion lightly" (Boyer 1995:164).

The Christian Socials played down confessional issues in 1922, even though they were "numerically in a better position than any earlier Catholic party to press demands for confessional schools" (Zeps 1979:310). To ally with the secular Pan-Germans the following year, they ignored pressure from the church and suppressed the school issue. As a result, the gap between the church and the party widened and tension escalated. Their relations, "always strained to some degree, had deteriorated over the schools question, which plagued religious and political circles in Austria for much of the decade of the 1920's . . . What the controversy did accomplish was to bring into the open the long-festering differences between the church and the party" (Gellott 1987:68–69). The church, according to Gellott (1987:69), perceived the party as "untrustworthy in representing confessional interests such as education." According to Zeps (1979:309–10):

> The Christian Socials had always taken a broader approach to politics than that dictated by the interests of the church. They represented the lower middle class and farmers who, as [archbishop] Piffl noted, might be lukewarm or irreligious. Confessional goals had never been foremost, a fact that Cardinal Schönborn stressed when he tried to have the Holy See condemn the party. Rather, the Christian Socials formulated a more general response to the times that protected the place of religion while it stepped back from confessionalism to stand on Christian principles rather than on the immediate wishes of the bishops.

The leader of the party, the priest Ignaz Seipel, made clear in 1924 that "since the party was thoroughly based on a world view, it had always kept an interest in the school question. The goal of the party was received from the church, but thereafter it was up to the party to decide the possibilities presented by the political situation and the methods of proceeding" (quoted in Zeps 1979:343). In doing so, Seipel laid himself open to fierce attacks from the church (von Klemperer 1972:15). Moreover, Christian Socials "faced loss of church support or erosive independent action by the bishops" (Zeps

1979:314). By the end of 1926 there was a split in the party between the followers of the church and those of the party leadership. The struggle probably would have been won by the party leadership, but the advent of the Dolfuss dictatorship altered the situation and doomed the Christian-Socials. When Seipel resigned as head of government in May 1929, "he was hurt perhaps more than anything else by defections from the church which seemed traceable to his involvement in politics" (Zeps 1979:526).

According to Blackbourn (1980:20), "The Catholic-ness of the Centre party was not contingent but central to the party's nature. This is not to say, however, that the Centre party was a clerical party which acted as the political arm of the Catholic church." When the party was formed in 1871, it adopted a neutral label. Rejected labels included Conservative People's party and Christian Conservative People's party (Evans 1981:33). Blackbourn (1980:27) reports that a conscious effort was made to avoid the use of terms such as "Catholic" or "Christian:" "[T]he name of the party was deliberately chosen to reflect the fact that it was not a clerical party." In its first declaration, the party avoided any mention of Catholicism and downplayed confessionalism. The trend away from too close an identification with the Catholic church was temporarily interrupted by the advent of the Kulturkampf. As the Silesian Zentrum leader Felix Porsch wrote to the bishops, however, after the end of the Kulturkampf the Zentrum men would not blindly follow the church (Blackbourn 1980:28). Similarly, the Württemberg leader Adolf Gröber "was unwilling to see the cause of the Württemberg Catholics remain the preserve of the hierarchy" (Blackbourn 1980:94). Gradually, the balance of power between party and church was altered in favor of the former. As Anderson (1986:113) points out: "By 1887 the social and political authority of the German hierarchy was no longer what it had been in the days before the Kulturkampf unleashed its emancipatory force. A bishop's overt role in politics was perhaps greater. But his freedom of decision was now hedged about by the proliferation of other centers of Catholic authority, legitimized by their role in this struggle: the lower clergy, insofar as they were politically prominent; the press; the Center Fraktion and its local affiliates; and later, the *Volksverein*."

Instead of the church imposing its will on the party, the party tended to prevail. For example, the party even had a say in the appointment of bishops. Anderson (1986:110) reports that "Windthorst, a lawyer and a layman, was not only dictating to Prussia's bishops the correct 'line' on mixed marriages and other episcopal policies but he also had a major say in episcopal appointments." Usually conflicts between church and party were hushed, but sometimes they escalated. For instance, in Bavaria in 1872, such a conflict between the main Catholic organizations and the bishop of Passau erupted into the open. In general, there was "one basic tension" between the German episcopate, which sought "centralized and monopolized control," and the laity, which "did not want to be the instrument merely for a one-way communication" between society and church (Dietrich 1992:468).

Blackbourn (1980:20) locates the "marked de-clericalization" of the Zentrum "at the level of both policies and personnel, measures and men" in the 1890s. He reports (1980:31) that "the [party's] emphasis was not so much on the position of Catholic worship and the Catholic church within a recently unified and still loosely federal Reich, but on the economic, social and political equality of Catholic citizens within the consolidated German state." It is indicative of this shift that the Vatican's attempt to impose its will on the Zentrum on the issue of Bismarck's military budget, described above, failed miserably. The party refused to follow the church. Even though a wing of the party went so far as to threaten a split, the party let it be known that "it is absolutely impossible for [it] to accept directives in matters of non-ecclesiastical legislation" (Fogarty 1957:313). Of the party's ninety deputies, only seven followed the church's directives and voted for Bismarck's bill. The Vatican was thus forced to retreat. The church swiftly reacted to the party's promotion of its own political and legislative priorities. In 1898, Bishop Georg Kopp complained that the party ignored the church's interests on the issue of the repeal of the Jesuit law and was trying instead to ameliorate its political position in the Reichstag (Ross 1976:61), while the bishop of Breslau refused to permit freedom of action for the Volksverein in his diocese: "Political agitation and organization were to remain in his hands, subordinate to the hierarchy's interests" (Ross 1976:62). The party leadership, however, remained unified in its promotion of autonomy from Rome and the church: "German Catholics who enjoyed the ear of the Curia were far removed from power in the party" (Blackbourn 1975:823).

Declericalization proceeded in a more decisive fashion after 1906, when the prominent Zentrum politician Julius Bachem published his famous newspaper article *"Wir müssen aus dem Turm heraus!"* (We Must Come Out of the Tower!). As Ross (1976:38) puts it, "Julius Bachem, with the concurrence of many Centrists, concluded that the moment had come to discard the sectarian label, attract non-Catholic voters, and make the party more attractive as a political ally." Anderson (1988:353) describes the essence of this article: "In the Tower article, as it became known, Bachem argued that the popular logo depicting the Center Party as an impregnable fortress, although once an important symbol for resistance to oppression, was now—along with the mentality it symbolized—an obstacle to the party's mission. Catholics would never overcome the prejudices against them if they remained behind barricades. It was time for them to 'come out of the tower,' and indeed to take the initiative in demonstrating to outsiders that the Center was in fact a political, not a denominational, party."

The publication of this article led to one of the gravest party crises, known as the *Zentrumsstreit* (Zentrum conflict).[15] The bishop of Cologne—Bachem's city and the center of his movement—called Bachem a "misfortune for the Catholic cause" (quoted in Ross 1976:46). Additionally, "Churchmen in Rome, who were not much inclined to accept political advice from lay Centrist leaders in Germany, had only contempt for Bachem's line of thought" (Ross 1976:55). The Prussian envoy in Rome reported that the Vatican viewed "the entire Cologne faction" and its "Bachenism" as an abomination (Ross 1976:55). The church attempted, but failed, to suppress this trend. The bishop of Cologne tried to suppress Bachem's newspaper and set up a rival one but was restricted by the party's organizational might. Intraparty strife also occurred. Under the slogan "a truly Catholic Center," the pro-church "Berlin faction" attempted to revive the Catholicness of the party and to reassert the influence of the church over the party and especially over auxiliary organizations like the Volksverein (Hendon 1976:603). It criticized the "Cologne faction" for sacrificing ecclesiastical interests to serve the party's interests (Ross 1976:67). For the Berlin faction, the party's official agenda was "to free the public life of Catholic Germany from the influence of the episcopate and orthodoxy. . . . The 'Berliners' expressed alarm about the 'de-Catholicization' of the party's platform, the secularization of its organization, and the laicization of its leadership" (Ross 1976:56). They denounced to the Vatican some of the Cologne faction's leaders as fit candidates for excommunication (Epstein 1971:67). In 1911, this faction formed a movement within the party, named Catholic Action, which declared that in all its actions the party must work in close conjunction with the church hierarchy (Ross 1976:65).

Because of its strong organization, the party was able to silence internal dissenters: "Twice—in November 1909 and October 1910—the bulk of the party united behind statements reaffirming the definition of the *Zentrum* as a political and not a confessional party" (Ross 1976:36). Following these events, the party asserted its secular identity in an even more aggressive way. In 1914, Theodor Wacker, a priest and a Zentrum Landtag deputy from Baden, delivered an address titled "The Zentrum and Church Authority," in which he condemned the efforts by the Berlin faction to stress the sectarian nature of the party, which, he claimed, only increased the party's political difficulties and fed the accusations of the National Liberals and the Social Democrats about the "priest-ridden" Zentrum. Wacker strongly asserted that the hierarchy had no voice in party affairs. His speech so upset the

[15] Anderson (1988) has convincingly argued that this conflict was more complex than it appears on the surface, ultimately pitting against each other two opposite views, one that wanted the Catholics to become part of the *Kaiserreich* society versus another that wanted Catholics to maintain their particularism.

Vatican that its published version was placed on the index of forbidden books, an action intended as a "blow aimed at the Centrum" (Ross 1976:62). The same year, the party made a new declaration affirming, for the third time, its nonsectarian character, and the party's central committee asked every Reichstag and Landtag deputy to sign it. "In the face of the coercive machinery of the party organization, the dissidents either capitulated or were expelled" (Ross 1976:126). At the same time the debate over interconfessionalism in the trade union movement ended in a way that severely weakened whatever was left of the hierarchy's leverage on party affairs (Mendershausen 1973:18). Zentrum members stood by the party rather than the church, and as Blackbourn (1980:30) concludes, the party leaders "never allowed the bishops, or Rome to dictate the politics of the party." Likewise, Catholic associations successfully resisted the attempts of the episcopate to bring them under its control, at least up to 1914 (Hürten 1986). In fact, the party's organizational might made it impossible for the church to initiate a recuperation strategy: in Germany the church was not able to create Catholic Action organizations (Gramsci 1995:108).

A similar process took place in Italy, where the Partito popolare, following the decision of Sturzo and his followers, was formed as an explicitly independent and aconfessional party. The label Partito popolare italiano was chosen over Partito popolare cristiano (Howard 1957:106). In March 1919, Sturzo (quoted in Einaudi and Goguel 1952:12–13) remarked that "the Popular Party is born as a non-Catholic Party, an aconfessional Party, a strongly democratic Party inspired by Christian idealism but which does not take religion as an element of political differentiation." Sturzo added that "our Party is a Party of national integration. It cannot and will not take religion as its flag." The pro-PPI review *La Politica Nazionale* (in Vecchio 1988:111–12) explained, in 1922, the meaning of aconfessionality: "That we were and are neither a party of faithful to a given historical faith, as such, nor a political instrument in the hands of ecclesiastical power for the achievement of ecclesiastical objectives: that the PP does not depend hierarchically on the church, nor does it officially engage the church, nor pursues ends that the church judges as its own and reaches by its own means." The party's objective from early on was to attract non-Catholic voters: "Sturzo hoped that many voters outside the Catholic action organizations and even outside the Catholic fold itself would rally to his program" (Webster 1960:53).

Again, declericalization provoked intense reactions. The party had to face "the open enmity of the Church" (Einaudi and Goguel 1952:23). The first congress of the party (Bologna, 1919) was the scene of a vehement debate: "The non-confessional character of the party, its desire to free itself from the authority of the Church, the 'liberal poison' that was to creep into it, its failure to assume the Catholic label as its distinctive emblem, the lack of an explicit reference in its programme to the absolute freedom, sovereignty, and independence of the Pope—all these deficiencies were castigated" in a 1919 pamphlet written by two priests, Agostino Gemelli and Francesco Olgiati, with the telling title "The Program of the Italian Popular Party. How It Is Not and How It Should Have Been" (Molony 1977:56). Sturzo prevailed, however, and the congress stressed that the PPI was "a perfectly political organization," not "a second face of the Catholic Action" (Proceedings of the congress, quoted by Malgeri 1981:355). Still, this victory turned to be short-lived. The advent of fascism allowed the church to participate in the liquidation of the party.

It is logical to infer that a French Catholic party would have followed a similar path. Both the small interwar PDP and the short-lived postwar MRP stressed aconfessionality as part of their identity. Similar concerns had emerged earlier, during the late 1890s, in the context of the attempts to form a Christian Democratic party. The abbé Garnier, one of the leaders of this effort, used the term "non-confessional Catholics," and a newspaper of the movement proposed cooperation of all Christians in "a non-confessional Christian party" (McManners 1972:97).

Confessional parties moved away from the church as the institution on which they depended and defined their identity in a way that both deemphasized and reinterpreted religion. These parties did not achieve aconfessionalism and were not transformed into traditional Conservative parties. A total and radical break between the church and confessional parties made no sense in the context of democratic politics. In turn, the church avoided repudiating these parties because the ensuing rupture would have produced a conflict of unpredictable dimensions in the Catholic world, alienating a great number of its members, while simultaneously leaving it unprotected from the emerging Socialist parties. Confessional parties never discarded religion because it defined their identity and guaranteed their unity. Parties and church were locked into a permanent yet loose relationship, usually skewed in favor of the party. This uneasy relationship was maintained after World War II.[16] The tension between the two sides decreased significantly, but then their relationship also decreased in significance.[17]

[16] In a sense this relationship was an equilibrium like the initial one between church and Conservative factions, but its consequences were different: the church was worse off because it lost its monopoly over the definition of Catholicism and the representation of Catholics.

[17] Recent sociological research in Belgium (Billiet and Dobbelaere 1985; Remy et al. 1985; also Post 1989) recorded a variety of disconcerting phenomena about the relation between religion, church, confessional party, and confessional ancillary organizations. Confessional parties are electorally successful, and ancillary organizations (unions, cooperatives, and the like) grow even though religious practice declines. At the same time, most active members of

Though they did not discard religion, confessional parties constructed their political identity in a way that redefined Catholicism. They symbolically appropriated Catholicism, subtracting most of its religious content and disconnecting it from the church. They became declericalized: nonclerical, secular organizations, organizationally and ideologically autonomous from the church. This development was the culmination of a process that began with the response of the church to the Liberal anticlerical attack. Declericalization was launched by the parties to solve the critical problem of their dependence on religion and the church. This was, therefore, a process endogenous to confessional parties, initiated right after their formation. Hence it is inaccurate to see, as the political science literature does, the secularization of confessional parties as both a post-World War II phenomenon and a reaction imposed on these parties exogenously by a secularizing societal environment.[18] Przeworski and Sprague (1986:44) observed a similar phenomenon among students of Social Democracy: "There is a peculiar tendency among contemporary observers to see the strategy of appealing to a heterogeneous class base as a relatively recent effect of the deradicalization of Socialist movements. . . . This view is simply inaccurate."

The declericalization of confessional parties had important consequences that were not anticipated at the time of their formation. Confessional parties reduced the political salience of religion and eroded their members' links to the church. In that sense, they affected their societal environment in a way that contributed to general secularization. Paradoxically, organizations formed to bring religion back into politics and society took it out.

---

these ancillary organizations (and a number of their middle-level officers as well) have ceased voting for the confessional party. In turn, though the Catholic "pillar" remains externally intact, it has been undergoing a dramatic internal transformation that points to a renewed process of declericalization: cutback of clerical personnel, further reduction of its ties to both the church and the confessional party (with an increase of the party's influence at the expense of the church), and a shift of ideological references from Catholicism to Christianity or simply humanism.

[18] The observation that after World War II "larger denominational . . . parties have faced a different problem: decreasing religiosity and changing class and occupational structures dictate a wider appeal if only to stay in the same place. As such, Christian Democratic parties must find ways to attract those who are not regular church attenders" (Wolinetz 1979:119) applies to a far earlier time.

CONCLUSION

Toward a Theory of Christian Democracy

The founders of Christian Democracy were not democrats.

—Joseph Hours

This book aims to be a starting point for a theory of Christian Democracy. It also proposes an analytical approach to party formation and evolution and provides a sustained focus on the politics of identity formation. Its wider ambition is to contribute to a truly comparative, analytically grounded, and historically sensitive political science.

The first theoretical contribution of this book is the delineation of the conditions of applicability of Lipset and Rokkan's cleavage theory through the introduction of some of its micro-foundations. A second contribution is the application of a theory of party formation (with a particular focus on confessional parties but, possibly, a more general and lateral applicability) based on rational choice assumptions with a particular focus on how parties construct political identities and shape their political and societal environments.[1] Both points share a common underlying theme: even though actors are rational, political developments can be, and are frequently, unintended and unanticipated.

Confessional parties were not the historically predetermined and automatic reflection of preexisting identities and conflicts, nor were they the emanation of structural, economic, or political modernization. They were, instead, a contingent outcome of the struggle among various organizations facing a multitude of challenges under tight constraints. Neither the Catholic church nor the various conservative factions desired or planned this outcome. Confessional parties emerged despite the preferences and intentions of both

[1] Contrary to Aldrich's recent book (1995), the focus here is on the formation of mass parties which mobilize one particular issue dimension and are formed through the action of organizations external to the parliament.

actors as a by-product of the church's response to Liberal anticlerical attacks. This response produced new collective entities, mass Catholic organizations, and new individual political actors, Catholic activists. The spectacular and surprising electoral successes of the temporary coalitions of church and Conservative parties turned these new actors into significant political players, permanently and structurally associated with both the religious cleavage and the nonsocialist political space. These parties radically transformed the existing categories of social and political action. Through its quick normalization, the association of religion and politics under the particular form of confessional parties established itself in the minds of collective actors and citizens alike as the obvious state of political affairs and the obvious category of political thought and action.

The formation of confessional parties was not only an unintended outcome; it was also an unfavorable one for both actors involved in the process —conservative political elites and the church. On the one hand, conservative elites were displaced by a new political class that emerged from Catholic mass organizations. On the other hand, confessional parties, far from being a dependable instrument of the church, became antagonistic to it, first, by competing with the church for the right to represent the same constituency and by undermining its hierarchical structure, and second, by redefining Catholicism in a way that eliminated most of its religious content. As a result, confessional parties shaped their political and societal environment in a way that disrupted the links between individuals and the church.

The formation of confessional parties had important consequences for politics. Looking today at the benign Christian Democratic parties, one can easily forget the aliberal and often intolerant nature of the Catholic movement from which they emerged. Catholic mobilization occurred as a counterrevolutionary reaction against Liberalism. In fact, the whole Catholic movement was built around the intransigent opposition to the Liberal state as expressed by the church in the *Syllabus*. This political project was, in many ways, fundamentalist and openly theocratic[2] (Papini 1993; Loth 1991; Lamberts 1984; Gambasin 1969; Zerbi 1961). Even social Catholicism and Christian Democracy were rooted in this intransigent Catholicism[3] (Ritter

[2] Gambasin (1969:122) equates the Opera with the phenomenon of intransigence. According to Vecchio (1979a:22), Catholic intransigentism was "fiercely papal, radically opposed to all tendencies of contemporary society, [and] connected to an unmerciful struggle against liberal ideology in the name of the eternal values of Christianity." Mayeur (1981:159) confirms that "we know it today better, intransigent Catholicism played a determinant role in the genesis of the Catholic movement." Gambasin (1969:3–4) puts it nicely: the Catholic movements of Europe "waved the papal program as an essential condition for the civil and religious restoration."

[3] Social Catholicism and the Christian Democratic movement, with their concern for workers' welfare and its critique of laissez-faire capitalism, developed out of Catholic intran-

1990:39; Jadoule 1990:49). Intransigent Catholics, who rejected the notion that any spheres of life lay beyond the reach of religious regulation, were instrumental in creating and running the Catholic movement (Berger 1987:126; Aubert 1982:207–8; Mayeur 1972; Gambasin 1969:26). They constituted the vast majority of the Catholic camp (Vecchio 1979a:21) because their ideas were representative of those of most Catholics (Suardo 1962:39). In turn, the Catholic movement reinforced the intransigence of the organized Catholic masses. The priest Bartolomeo Sandri, one of the founders of the Italian Opera, remarked that the purpose of the Opera was to unite all Catholics against the so-called liberal Catholics who preached moderation and a settlement with the Liberal state.[4] Those Catholics, added Sandri, were the worst enemies of the church because they "were infected by ideological equivocation and religious-political compromise" (Gambasin 1969:74–75). The abbé Bernard Goudeau (quoted in Sedgwick 1965:97) sketched this philosophy in a discourse he gave at the 1896 congress of French Christian Democrats: "We must have the courage to admit that intolerance is necessary and legitimate. In the social as well as in the philosophical order of things any organism which has the right to live has the right to be intolerant. The Church wants to live. The Church is a mother and there is nothing in the world more legitimately intolerant than a mother. The right to think and to publish one's thoughts without being subject to any rule whatsoever is not in itself a right which the state should support. Free thought is more often than not the cause of much evil."

Naturally, such an ideology lends itself easily to theorizing about the antithetical relationship of religion (particularly Catholicism) and democracy.

---

sigentism and ultramontanism. Social Catholics opposed liberal Catholics, who supported economic liberalism. The term "Christian Democracy" denoted the impossibility of the existence of a purely secular democracy (Vecchio 1979a:21, 28). As the Italian Catholic activist Vico Necchi (quoted in Vecchio 1987:85) argued, "The democracy of tomorrow will be Christian or will not be." Vecchio (1979a:29) concludes that "[the] Christian democracy of the end of the century is not a fruit of liberal Catholicism . . . but it was grafted on the trunk of intransigentism and Leonian teaching." Similarly, Poulat (1977:117) points out that "social Catholicism is a historical development of intransigentism," and Mayeur (1972:490) stresses the persistence of this connection over time. Soete (1984) and De Maeyer (1984) have shown how the Christian Democratic movement in Belgium grew out of the ultramontane movement.

[4] Liberal Catholics were hostile to mass organization as a method of political action and to ultramontanism as an ideology. Their "creed was political moderation, parliamentarism, liberal constitutionalism, and a basic (though increasingly disillusioned) conviction of the compatibility of modern society and Catholicism in a liberal, Christian state. Their tactics reflected the liberal tradition. They were suspicious of democratic and popular opinion—public enthusiasm always struck them as demagogic, vulgar, potentially violent, and undisciplined. Counterrevolution was essentially a 'radical' appeal to political passions, prejudices, and hatreds, the kind of mass sentiment they found frightening and associated with the Left" (Grubb 1977:368).

Indeed, it has been repeatedly argued that the "injection of religion into political controversies tends to hamper working out the pragmatic accommodations needed by a functioning democracy" (Reichley 1986:801); that Catholicism "was associated with the absence of democracy or with limited or late democratic development" (Huntington 1991:75); and that it "appeared antithetical to democracy in pre-World War II Europe" (Lipset et al., quoted in Huntington 1991:75). Yet political Catholicism mediated by confessional parties proved to be a factor of mass incorporation and democratic consolidation.[5] No confessional party sought to impose a dominant religious identity on civil society. As Suzanne Berger notes (1987:128), "Paradoxically, despite the church's hostility to the state and its attempts to encapsulate Catholics in a world as impermeable as possible to the influences of secular and liberal society, the impact of this subcultural development was in many ways to consolidate and stabilize the political and social order."[6] The democratic evolution of the Catholic movement is all the more puzzling because the church accepted democracy far later: the Vatican ceased combat and silently began to tolerate modern democracy only in 1918, while official acceptance came only in the 1944 Christmas address of Pius XII (Horner 1987:34–35).

Through its focus on party formation, this book provides the key for understanding the paradox of the secular and democratic evolution of confessional parties. It underlines the elasticity of the relationship between religion and politics by pointing to the need of the newly formed confessional parties to deemphasize religion to protect their autonomy and safeguard their independence from the church. Confessional parties could do so only by redefining their identity in a way that could be controlled by themselves rather than the church. Catholicism remained part of the new identity because it ensured the unity of these socially heterogeneous parties. By reinterpreting Catholi-

[5] Thus Misra and Hicks's finding that the relationship between Catholic population size and unionization is contingent on Christian Democratic party strength (1994: 317) makes full sense —not, however, for ideological reasons (Christian Democratic parties being vehicles of the social gospel of the church), as they claim, but because of constraints associated with the way they were formed.

[6] This paradox is formulated in a different way by Scoppola (1982:15): "The Popular party . . . is not of parliamentary origin because it plunges the roots of the consensus it created in the richness of the associative and organizational tissue provided by the intransigent movement. But it surpasses the narrowness of the intransigents' views for whom the modern liberties and the party itself represented only instruments for the reconquest of the positions lost by the church; it accepts, moreover, the modern liberties and the institutions of the liberal state." Scoppola claims that somehow the liberal Catholic ideology blended harmoniously with the intransigent organization, but does not provide an adequate explanation for this surprising development.

cism as an increasingly general, vague, and secular concept mediated by them, by evolving from "Catholic parties" to "parties of Christian inspiration" (Vecchio 1987:7), confessional parties reduced the importance of religion for politics and society. This amounted to a process of secularization—and a particularly pernicious one because it was carried out from within the Catholic camp.[7]

As they moved away from the church, confessional parties embraced democratic politics: voters became these parties' paramount source of support and legitimacy. Hence confessional parties integrated the masses of newly enfranchised voters into the democratic systems they were originally supposed to subvert and reinforced the parliamentary democratic regimes of their respective countries.[8] Thus secularization, integration, and acceptance of democracy were not the result of an exogenously induced adaptation to a secularizing environment. They were rather a by-product of the choices made by the new parties in response to endogenous constraints that were built in in the process of their formation. In dealing with these constraints, confessional parties contributed to the secularization and democratization of their political and societal environment. Still, a systematic analysis of the conditions under which religious movements become democratic remains to be written.

This account helps unravel the puzzle of contemporary Christian Democratic parties, which retain a religious label and some awkward links to religion and the church but have become secular parties thriving in a secular environment—without, however, having evolved into typical conservative parties. Hence Richard Rose and Thomas Mackie's (1988:553–54) finding that despite declining church attendance Christian Democratic parties have been among the most likely of all parties to survive intact should come as no surprise.[9] The wider theoretical significance of this account is that political parties, far from being reactive organizations that adapt to an exogenously

[7] As the Liberal anticlerical attack and the experience of communist regimes suggest, an open attack against religion is more likely to reinforce popular religious devotion. On the contrary, a secularization from within such as that carried out by confessional parties can have more devastating effects for religion. Of course, this is still only a hypothesis and needs to be tested empirically.

[8] As Anderson (1988:378) has pointed out about Germany, "the Center party provided Catholics—just as the SPD had provided working-class Protestants—with a recognition and a validation they could not find in society at large."

[9] Van Kersbergen (1994:45) argues that "secularization might be a threat to the churches or to organised religion in general, but it is neither imperatively a danger for Christian values nor necessarily an obstacle to the enduring attractiveness of the Christian Democratic alternative." My account reaches the same conclusion by bypassing ideological factors such as the appeal of Christian values.

changing environment, shape this environment in decisive, if not always anticipated, ways.

Party and political identity formation interact in many ways. A set of choices initiated by the church led, through organization, collective action, and political participation, to the gradual emergence of a Catholic political identity—best expressed in the person of the lay Catholic activist. In turn, confessional parties reshaped this identity into a new party-oriented collective identity based on the elimination of the contradiction between secular and religious identities. Cleavage, identity, and party formation are therefore processes that need theoretically informed unpacking, require a close focus on agency, and entail the specification of the mechanisms of their production and interaction. Furthermore, understanding party formation is a prerequisite for explaining identity formation and party development.

Church and conservative political elites did not intend or desire the formation of confessional parties. Likewise, confessional party leaders did not initially plan or wish the secularization and democratization of their parties and their societies. How did rational actors end up with an outcome that went against their preferences? How do we explain these unintended and unanticipated outcomes? Where do these phenomena fit into social science theory?

Although unintended and contingent, the formation of confessional parties was no random accident. Although unplanned and undesired, the declericalization of confessional parties and their democratic transformation were not idiosyncratic occurrences. William Sewell (1992) has recently emphasized the role of events and contingency in history and has advocated their incorporation into theoretical accounts. Likewise, Herbert Kitschelt (1992:1028) has underlined the existence and theoretical significance of outcomes that were neither anticipated nor desired by any of the participants at the beginning of the process that produced them. I show that the formation of confessional parties is such an instance and, beyond that, suggest how such outcomes are in fact reached. The intrinsically contingent nature of political developments should not deter one from a systematic analysis of the variables that foreclose this contingency.

Finally, this book demonstrates that ideology can be a poor predictor of political action. An exclusive focus on the ideology of Catholic movements would have led to the prediction that democratic regimes would not last. Yet, contrary to what Skocpol (1979) has argued, the fact that ideology can sometimes be misleading does not establish the necessity of a structuralist approach and the omission of agency and intentionality. Outcomes are often a bad indicator of initial intentions: looking at the intentions of the church at the beginning of the process, one would have made the erroneous prediction that no confessional parties would emerge. Yet this constitutes no evidence of the insignificance of intentionality.[10] Quite the contrary. Intentionality is not predicated on outcomes. Unintended or undesired outcomes are frequent occurrences precisely because they are produced by the strategic interaction between actors under structural and institutional constraints. Intentionality is reflected in the choice (within given constraints) of triggering a specific process among many possible, rather than ensuring a particular outcome. The emergence of confessional parties can also be thought as a perverse effect, a class of phenomena analyzed particularly by Raymond Boudon.[11] Boudon (1982:5) defines as perverse effects the "individual and collective effects that result from the juxtaposition of individual behaviours and yet were not included in the actors' explicit objectives."[12]

To return to the opening question: what are Christian Democratic parties? I have suggested an initial developmental answer that incorporates party formation: these parties were formed as contingent by-products of the church's response to Liberal anticlerical attacks. Resulting from a formation process that succeeded against the intentions of the church and Conservative political elites, these parties emerged as antagonistic to both. As products of religious mobilization they were socially heterogeneous. Hence they acquired a catch-all nature and a centrist orientation (often regarded by their adversaries as opportunism), cultivated the art of mediation, developed a moderate outlook, and avoided sweeping or radical programs and policies. They relied on their confessional identity to keep their disparate social basis together, yet this identity clashed with their need to detach themselves from

[10] According to Skocpol (1979:17–18): "The logic of these [revolutionary] conflicts has not been controlled by any one class or group no matter how seemingly central in the revolutionary process. And the revolutionary conflicts have invariably given rise to outcomes neither fully foreseen nor intended by—nor perfectly serving the interests of—any of the particular groups involved. It simply will not do, therefore, to try to decipher the logic of the processes or outcomes of a social revolution by adopting the perspective or following the actions of any one class or elite organization—no matter how important its participatory role."

[11] This point has important theoretical implications. As Boudon (1982:7) remarks, "In the first case, the very notion of perverse effect implies the notion of action. A perverse effect can only occur in an analytic framework, in which the sociological subject, *homo sociologicus,* is thought to be moved by objectives he has in mind and the way he represents their eventual realisation to himself. There is thus a logical contradiction between the perverse effects paradigm and those paradigms in which *homo sociologicus* is always depicted as a creature moved by social forces exterior to him. There is, in other words, a fundamental incompatibility between this paradigm and the contemporary sociological model of a *homo sociologicus* whose actions would have no more reality than that of responses determined by social 'structures.' "

[12] Since the focus of this study has been on collective rather than individual actors, I deal with collective actor instead of individual actor behaviors. The formation of confessional parties can be considered as a perverse effect even though it was foreseeable (although not foreseen) by the actors who initiated the process. Boudon includes this class of effects in his typology.

religion and the church in order to survive autonomously and expand electorally. To solve this confessional dilemma, these parties moved in directions that shaped politics and society in important and unanticipated ways. They constructed an identity of their own, redefining its confessional nature in a way that did not discard Catholicism but secularized it, while embracing liberal democracy.

In many ways, Christian Democratic and Social Democratic parties are mirror images of each other. Both parties were initially formed to subvert liberal democracies; both evolved into mass parties and decided to participate in the electoral process after painful and divisive debates. Their decision had tremendous consequences: both parties integrated masses of newly enfranchised voters into existing liberal parliamentary regimes, and both were deradicalized in the process, becoming part of the very institutions they initially rejected. By transforming themselves, they transformed their political and societal environment in ways that were hardly anticipated: democracy in Europe was often expanded and consolidated by its enemies. This lesson should not be lost, especially among those studying the challenges facing democratic transition and consolidation in the contemporary world.

References

Agócs, Sándor. 1975. *"Germania Doceat!"* The *Volksverein,* the Model for Italian Catholic Action, 1905–1914. *Catholic Historical Review* 61, 1:31–47.

——. 1988. *The Troubled Origins of the Italian Catholic Labor Movement, 1878–1914.* Detroit: Wayne State University Press.

Agulhon, Maurice. 1970. *La république au village: Les populations du Var de la révolution à la Seconde République.* Paris: Plon.

——. 1981. *Marianne into Battle: Republican Imagery and Symbolism in France, 1789–1880.* Cambridge: Cambridge University Press.

Aldrich, John H. 1995. *Why Parties? The Origins and Transformation of Party Politics in America.* Chicago: University of Chicago Press.

Altermatt, Urs. 1991. *Katholizismus und Moderne. Zur Social-und Mentalitätgeschichte der Schweizer Katholiken im 19. und 20. Jahrhundert.* Zurich: Benziger.

Alzaga Villaamil, Oscar. 1973. *La primera democracia cristiana en España.* Esplugues de Llobregat: Editorial Ariel.

Ambrosoli, Luigi. 1958. *Il primo movimento democratico cristiano in Italia, 1897–1904.* Rome: Cinque Lune.

Ameye, Jacques. 1963. *La vie politique à Tourcoing sous la Troisième République.* La Madeleine: Impr. Silic.

Aminzade, Ronald. 1993. *Ballots and Barricades: Class Formation and Republican Politics in France, 1830–1871.* Princeton: Princeton University Press.

Anderson, Malcolm. 1974. *Conservative Politics in France.* London: George Allen & Unwin.

Anderson, Margaret Lavinia. 1981. *Windthorst: A Political Biography.* Oxford: Clarendon Press.

——. 1986. The Kulturkampf and the Course of German History. *Central European History* 19:82–115.

——. 1988. Interdenominationalism, Clericalism, Pluralism: The *Zentrumsstreit* and the Dilemma of Catholicism in Wilhelmine Germany. *Central European History* 21:350–78.

——. 1991. Piety and Politics: Recent Work on German Catholicism. *Journal of Modern History* 63:681–716.

——. 1992. Book Review of *Felix Porsch, 1853–1930: Politik für Katholische Interessen in Kaiserreich und Republik* by August Hermann Leugers-Scherzberg. *Catholic Historical Review* 78:316–17.

——. 1993. Voter, Junker, *Landrat*, Priest: The Old Authorities and the New Franchise in Imperial Germany. *American Historical Review* 98:1448–74.

Armengaud, André. 1961. *Les populations de l'Est-Aquitain au début de l'époque contemporaine: Recherches sur une région moins dévelopée (vers 1845-vers 1871)*. Paris: Mouton.

Arnal, Oscar L. 1985. *Ambivalent Alliance: The Catholic Church and the Action Française, 1899–1939*. Pittsburgh: University of Pittsburgh Press.

Aubert, Roger. 1952. *Le pontificat de Pie IX 1846–1878*. Paris: Bloud & Gay.

——. 1968. L'église et l'état en Belgique au XIXe siècle. *Res Publica* 10:9–31.

——. 1975. L'église catholique de la crise de 1848 à la première guerre mondiale. In R. Aubert, M. D. Knowles, and L. J. Rogier, eds., *Nouvelle histoire de l'église*. Paris: Editions du Seuil.

——. 1981. The Reform Work of Pius X. In Hubert Jedin and John Dolan, eds., *History of the Church*. Vol. 9. New York: Crossroad.

——. 1982. La notion de mouvement catholique: Les enseignements de l'histoire. In E. de Jonghe and L. Preneel, eds., *Théorie et langage du Mouvement Catholique; Problèmes d'historiographie*. Leuven: Universitaire Pers.

Auspitz, Katherine. 1982. *The Radical Bourgeoisie: The Ligue de l'Enseignement and the Origins of the Third Republic, 1866–1885*. Cambridge: Cambridge University Press.

Baal, Gérard. 1977. Combes et la "république des comités." *Revue d'histoire moderne et contemporaine* 24:260–85.

Bakvis, Herman. 1981. *Catholic Power in the Netherlands*. Kingston and Montreal: McGill-Queens University Press.

Barbier, Emmanuel. 1923. *Histoire du catholicisme libéral et du catholicisme social en France, 1870–1914*. 5 vols. Bordeaux: Imprimerie Cadoret.

Barnouw, Adriaan J. 1940a. *The Dutch: A Portrait Study of the People of Holland*. New York: Columbia University Press.

——. 1940b. *The Making of Modern Holland: A Short History*. New York: Norton.

Barral, Pierre. 1962. *Le département de l'Isère sous la Troisième République, 1870–1940. Histoire sociale et politique*. Paris: Armand Colin.

Bartels, Larry M. 1988. *Presidential Primaries and the Dynamics of Public Choice*. Princeton: Princeton University Press.

Bartolini, Stefano. 1993. I primi movimenti socialisti in Europa. Consolidamento organizativo e mobilitazione politica. *Rivista Italiana di scienza politica*. 23:217–81.

Bartolini, Stefano, and Peter Mair. 1990. *Identity, Competition, and Electoral Availability: The Stabilization of European Electorates, 1885–1985*. Cambridge: Cambridge University Press.

Baum, Gregory, and John Coleman. 1987. Editorial. *Concilium* 193:xvii-xxiv.

Beaufays, Ignace. 1934. Nos archevêques depuis 1830. In Camille Joset, ed., *Un siècle de l'église catholique en Belgique, 1830–1930*. Paris: Editions Jos. Vermaut.

Beaufays, Jean. 1973. *Les partis catholiques en Belgique et aux Pays-Bas, 1918–1958*. Brusells: Emile Bruyland.

Becqué, Maurice. 1956. *Le cardinal Dechamps*. 2 vols. Louvain: Bibliotheca Alphonsiana.

Belardinelli, Mario. 1979. *Movimento cattolico e questione communale dopo l'unità.* Rome: Edizioni Studium.

——. 1981. Per una storia della definizione di movimento cattolico. In Francesco Traniello and Giorgio Campanini, eds., *Dizionario storico del movimento cattolico in Italia, 1860–1980*. Vol. 1. Turin: Marietti.

Berger, Suzanne. 1987. Religious Transformation and the Future of Politics. In Charles S. Maier, ed., *Changing Boundaries of the Political: Essays on the Evolving Balance between the State and Society, Public and Private in Europe.* Cambridge: Cambridge University Press.

Bergounioux, Alain, and Bernard Manin. 1979. *La social-démocratie ou le compromis.* Paris: PUF.

Berman, Harold J. 1983. *Law and Revolution: The Formation of the Western Legal Tradition.* Cambridge, Mass.: Harvard University Press.

Berstein, Serge. 1980. *Histoire du parti Radical.* 2 vols. Paris: Presses de la Fondation Nationale des Sciences Politiques.

Bertocci, Phillip A. 1978. *Jules Simon: Republican Anticlericalism and Cultural Politics in France, 1848–1886.* Columbia: University of Missouri Press.

Bessières, Albert. 1924. *Pour l'unité des forces catholiques: L'Union Catholique.* Paris: J. de Gigord.

Beyme, Klaus von. 1985. *Political Parties in Western Democracies.* Aldershot: Gower.

Biagini, Eugenio F., and Alastair J. Reid. 1991. Currents of Radicalism, 1850–1914. In Eugenio F. Biagini and Alastair J. Reid, eds., *Currents of Radicalism: Popular Radicalism, Organised Labour and Party Politics in Britain, 1850–1914.* Cambridge: Cambridge University Press.

Billiet, Jaak, and Karel Dobbelaere. 1985. Vers une desinstitutionalisation du pilier chretien? In Liliane Voyé, Karel Dobbelaere, Jean Remy, and Jaak Billiet, eds., *La Belgique et ses Dieux: Eglises, mouvements religieux et laiques.* Louvain-la-Neuve: Cabay.

Billiet, Jaak, and Emmanuel Gerard. 1985. Eglise et politique: Les relations difficiles entre les organizations catholiques et leur parti politique avant 1940. In Liliane Voyé, Karel Dobbelaere, Jean Remy, and Jaak Billiet, eds., *La Belgique et ses Dieux: Eglises, mouvements religieux et laiques.* Louvain-la-Neuve: Cabay.

Binchy, D. A. 1941. *Church and State in Fascist Italy.* London: Oxford University Press.

Birnbaum, Pierre. 1991. Catholic Identity and Universal Suffrage: The French Experience. *Social Science Journal* 129:571–82.

——. 1993. *La France aux français: Histoire des haines nationalistes.* Paris: Editions du Seuil.

Blackbourn, David. 1975. The Political Alignment of the Centre Party in Wilhelmine Germany: A Study of the Party's Emergence in Nineteenth-Century Württemberg. *Historical Journal* 18:821–50.

——. 1978. The Problem of Democratization: German Catholics and the Role of the Centre Party. In Richard J. Evans, ed., *Society and Politics in Wilhelmine Germany.* London: Croom Helm.

——. 1980. *Class, Religion and Local Politics in Wilhelmine Germany: The Centre Party in Württemberg before 1914.* New Haven: Yale University Press.

——. 1991. The Catholic Church in Europe since the French Revolution: A Review Article. *Comparative Studies in Society and History* 33:778–90.

——. 1994. *Marpingen: Apparitions of the Virgin Mary in Nineteenth-Century Germany*. New York: Knopf.

Blasco, Pedro González, and Juan de Dios González-Anleo. 1993. Socioeconomic Issues and the Catholic Church in Spain. In Richard Gunther, ed., *Politics, Society, and Democracy: The Case of Spain*. Boulder: Westview Press.

Bled, Jean-Paul. 1988. *Les fondements du conservatisme Autrichien, 1859–1879*. Paris: Publications de la Sorbonne.

Bomier-Landowski, Alain. 1951. Les groupes parlementaires de l'Assemblée nationale et de la Chambre des députés de 1871 à 1940. In François Goguel and Georges Dupeux, eds., *Sociologie électorale. Esquisse d'un bilan, guide de recherches*. Paris: Armand Colin.

Bon, Frédéric. 1978. *Les élections en France: Histoire et sociologie*. Paris: Editions du Seuil.

Borne, Etienne. 1965. Le catholicisme. In René Rémond, ed., *Forces religieuses et attitudes politiques dans la France contemporaine*. Paris: Armand Colin.

Boswell, Jonathan. 1993. Catholicism, Christian Democrats and "Reformed Capitalism." In Colin Crouch and David Marquand, eds., *Ethics and Markets: Cooperation and Competition within Capitalist Economies*. Oxford: Blackwell.

Bosworth, William. 1962. *Catholicism and Crisis in Modern France: French Catholic Groups at the Threshold of the Fifth Republic*. Princeton: Princeton University Press.

Boudon, Raymond. 1982. *The Unintended Consequences of Social Action*. London: Macmillan.

——. 1995. *Le juste et le vrai: Etudes sur l'objectivité des valeurs et de la connaissance*. Paris: Fayard.

Boulange, Bruno. 1986. L'établissement de l'enseignement primaire catholique à Liège sous l'episcopat de Monseigneur Doutreloux, 1879–1901. *Revue belge d'histoire contemporaine* 17:309–38.

Boulard, Fernand. 1982. *Matériaux pour l'histoire religieuse du peuple français, XIXe–XXe siècles*. Vol. 1. Paris: Editions de l'Ecole des Hautes Etudes en Sciences Sociales; Presses de la Fondation Nationale des Sciences Politiques; Editions du Centre National de la Recherche Scientifique.

Boulard, Fernand, and Gerard Cholvy. 1992. *Matériaux pour l'histoire religieuse du peuple français, XIXe–XXe siècles*. Vol. 3. Paris: Editions de l'Ecole des Hautes Etudes en Sciences Sociales; Presses de la Fondation Nationale des Sciences Politiques; Editions du Centre National de la Recherche Scientifique.

Boulard, Fernand, and Yves-Marie Hilaire. 1987. *Matériaux pour l'histoire religieuse du peuple français, XIXe–XXe siècles*. Vol. 2. Paris: Editions de l'Ecole des Hautes Etudes en Sciences Sociales; Presses de la Fondation Nationale des Sciences Politiques; Editions du Centre National de la Recherche Scientifique.

Bourdieu, Pierre. 1987. What Makes a Social Class? On the Theoretical and Practical Existence of Groups. *Berkeley Journal of Sociology: A Critical Review* 32:1–17.

Boutry, Philippe, and Alain-René Michel. 1992. La religion. In Jean-François Sirinelli, ed., *Histoires des droites en France*. Vol. 3. Paris: Gallimard.

Bowman, William D. 1989. Priests, Parish, and Religious Practice: A Social History of Catholicism in the Archdiocese of Vienna, 1800–1870. Ph.D. dissertation, Johns Hopkins University.

Boy, Daniel, and Nonna Mayer. 1993. *The French Voter Decides*. Ann Arbor: University of Michigan Press.

Boyer, John W. 1981. *Political Radicalism in Late Imperial Vienna: Origins of the Christian Social Movement, 1848–1897*. Chicago: University of Chicago Press.

——. 1995. *Culture and Political Crisis in Vienna: Christian Socialism in Power, 1897–1918*. Chicago: University of Chicago Press.

Brachin, Pierre, and L. J. Rogier. 1974. *Histoire du catholicisme hollandais depuis le XVIe siècle*. Paris: Aubier Montaigne.

Brose, Eric Dorn. 1985. *Christian Labor and the Politics of Frustration in Imperial Germany*. Washington, D.C.: Catholic University of America Press.

Broughton, David. 1988. The Social Bases of European Conservative Parties. In Brian Girvin, ed., *The Transformation of Contemporary Conservatism*. London: Sage.

Brown, Marvin L., Jr. 1974. Catholic Legitimists in the Early Years of the Third French Republic. *Catholic Historical Review* 60:233–54.

Bruce, Steve. 1992. *Religion and Modernization: Sociologists and Historians Debate the Secularization Thesis*. Oxford: Clarendon Press.

Brunetta, Giuseppe. 1991. Il clero in Italia dal 1888 al 1989. *Polis* 5:423–49.

Byrnes, Robert F. 1950. The French Christian Democrats in the 1890's: Their Appearance and Their Failure. *Catholic Historical Review* 36:286–306.

Caciagli, Mario. 1992. Doomed to Govern? Christian Democracy in the Italian Political System. In Mario Caciagli et al., *DC: Christian Democracy in Europe*. Barcelona: ICPS.

Callot, Emile-François. 1978. *Le Mouvement Républicain Populaire: Origine, structure, doctrine, programme et action politique*. Paris: Marcel Rivivière et Cie.

Canavero, Alfredo. 1981. Elezioni. In Francesco Traniello and Giorgio Campanini, eds., *Dizionario storico del movimento cattolico in Italia, 1860–1980*. Vol. 1. Turin: Marietti.

Capéran, Louis. 1960. *Histoire contemporaine de la laicité française*. 3 vols. Paris: Librairie Marcel Rivière.

Carr, Raymond. 1980. *Modern Spain, 1875–1980*. Oxford: Oxford University Press.

Carrillo, Elisa A. 1992. Book Review of *" 'Proletariato di chiesa" per la Cristianità. La FACI tra curia romana e fascismo dalle origini alla Conziliazione* by Achille Erba. *Catholic Historical Review* 78:137–39.

Carton de Wiart, Henri. 1948. *Souvenirs politiques, 1878–1918*. Brussels: Desclée de Brouwer.

Casanova, José. 1994. The Catholic Church's Loss of Interest in Sponsoring Christian Democracy. Paper presented at the 1994 Annual Meeting of the American Political Science Association.

Castles, Francis G. 1994. On Religion and Public Policy: Does Catholicism Make a Difference? *European Journal of Political Research* 25:19–40.

Caulier-Mathy, N., and P. Gérin. 1979. Les sénateurs dans la province de Liège durant le régime censitaire, 1831–1893. *Tijdschrift voor Geschiedenis* 92:413–25.

Chaline, Nadine-Josette. 1981. Une nouvelle forme d'apostolat: Patronages et mouvements de jeunesse en Normandie fin XIXe début XXe siècle. In *Histoire religieuse de la Normandie*. Chambray: CLD.

——. 1985. *Des catholiques Normands sous la Troisième République: Crises, combats, renouveaux*. Le Coteau, Roanne: Horvath.

Chapman, Guy. 1962. *The Third Republic of France: The First Phase, 1871–1894*. New York: St. Martin's Press.

Charnay, Jean-Paul. 1964. *Les scrutins politiques en France: De 1815 à 1962*. Paris: Armand Colin.

Chaves, Mark, and David E. Cann. 1992. Regulation, Pluralism, and Religious Market Structure. *Rationality and Society* 4:272–90.

Chevallier, Jean Jacques, and Gérard Conac. 1991. *Histoire des institutions et des régimes politiques de la France de 1789 à nos jours*. Paris: Dalloz.

Cholvy, Gérard. 1982. Patronages et oeuvres de jeunesse dans la France contemporaine. *Revue d'histoire de l'église de la France* 68:235–54.

——. 1994. Sociologists, Historians and the Religious Evolution of France from the 18th Century to the Present. *Modern and Contemporary France* 2:257–65.

Cholvy, Gérard, and Yves-Marie Hilaire. 1985. *Histoire religieuse de la France contemporaine*. Vol. 1. Toulouse: Privat.

——. 1986. *Histoire religieuse de la France contemporaine*. Vol. 2. Toulouse: Privat.

Claeys van Haegendoren, Mieke. 1967. Party and Opposition Formation in Belgium. *Res Publica* 9:413–36.

Cleary, M. C. 1989. *Peasants, Politicians and Producers. The Organization of Agriculture in France since 1918*. Cambridge: Cambridge University Press.

Coleman, John A. 1978. *The Evolution of Dutch Catholicism, 1958–1974*. Berkeley: University of California Press.

Collin, Paul-Victor. 1961–63. Un homme d' état: Auguste Beernaert, 1829–1912. *Res Publica* 3:251–54.

Colloquio sul Movimento Cattolico Italiano. 1976. *Il movimento cattolico e la società italiana in cento anni di storia*. Rome: Edizioni di Storia e Letteratura; Instituto per le Ricerche di Storia Sociale e di Storia Religiosa.

Congar, Yves. 1967. *Priest and Layman*. London: Darton, Longman and Todd.

Congar, Yves, and F. Varillon. 1947. *Sacerdoce et laicat dans l'église*. Paris: Editions du Vitrail.

Coppa, Frank J. 1967. Giolitti and the Gentiloni Pact between Myth and Reality. *Catholic Historical Review* 53: 217–28.

Corbin, Alain. 1975. *Archaisme et modernité en Limousin au XIXe siècle, 1845–1880*. Paris: Editions Marcel Rivière et Cie.

Cordewiener, André. 1970. Attitudes des catholiques et de l'épiscopat devant les problèmes posés par l'organisation de leur presse à Bruxelles, 1831–1843. *Revue belge d'histoire contemporaine* 2:27–43.

Coutrot, Aline. 1965. Les mouvements confessionnels et la société politique. In René Rémond, ed., *Forces religieuses et attitudes politiques dans la France contemporaine*. Paris: Armand Colin.

Crew, David F. 1979. *Town in the Ruhr: A Social History of Bochum, 1860–1914*. New York: Columbia University Press.

Cunsolo, Ronald S. 1993. Nationalists and Catholics in Giolittian Italy: An Uneasy Collaboration. *Catholic Historical Review* 79:22–53.

Daalder, Hans. 1955. Parties and Politics in the Netherlands. *Political Studies* 3:1–16.

——. 1960. The Netherlands: Opposition in a Segmented Society. In Robert A. Dahl, ed., *Political Opposition in Western Democracies*. New Haven: Yale University Press.

D'Andrea, Giampaolo. 1980. Società religiosa e movimento cattolico a Potenza tra XIX e XX secolo. In Antonio Cestaro, ed., *Studi di storia sociale e religiosa: Scriti in onore di Gabrielle de Rosa*. Naples: Editrice Ferraro.

Dansette, Adrien. 1961. *Religious History of Modern France*. 2 vols. Freiburg: Herder.

Darbon, Michel. 1953. *Le conflit entre la droite et la gauche dans le catholicisme français, 1839–1953*. Toulouse: Privat.

De Brouwer, Alain. 1992. Le Parti Populaire Européen: Son idéntité et son nécéssaire élargissement. In Mario Caciagli et al., *DC: Christian Democracy in Europe*. Barcelona: ICPS.

De Kwaasteniet, Marjanne. 1990. *Denomination and Primary Education in the Netherlands, 1870–1984: A Spatial Diffusion Perspective*. Amsterdam: Koninklijk Nederlands Aardrijkskundig Genootschap.

Delbreil, Jean-Claude. 1990. *Centrisme et démocratie-chrétienne en France: Le Parti Démocrate Populaire des origines au M.R.P., 1919–1944*. Paris: Publications de la Sorbonne.

Delfosse, Pascale. 1979. La formation des familles politiques en Belgique, 1830–1914. *Res Publica* 21:465–95.

Delfosse, Pascale, and André-Paul Frognier. 1988. Etat libéral et formation des partis politiques en Belgique, 1830–1884. *Recherches sociologiques* 19:59–79.

Delumeau, Jean. 1979. *Le diocèse de Rennes*. Paris: Beauchesne.

De Maeyer, Jan. 1984. De Ultramontanen en de Gildenbeweging, 1875–1896: Het Aandeel van de *Confrérie de St.-Michel*. In Emiel Lamberts, ed., *De Kruistocht tegen het Liberalisme: Facetten van het Ultramontanisme in België in de 19e eeuw*. Leuven: Universitaire Pers.

De Meeus, Adrien. 1962. *History of the Belgians*. New York: Praeger.

De Montclos, Xavier. 1965. *Lavigerie, le Saint-Siège et l'église, de l'avènement de Pie IX à l'avènement de Léon XIII, 1846–1878*. Paris: Editions E. De Boccard.

De Moreau, P. E. 1929. *Histoire de l'église catholique en Belgique*. Brussels: Librairie Albert Dewit.

DeNardo, James. 1985. *Power in Numbers: The Political Strategy of Protest and Rebellion*. Princeton: Princeton University Press.

Denis, Michel. 1977. *Les royalistes de la Mayenne et le monde moderne, XIXe–XXe siècles*. Paris: C. Klincksieck.

———. 1992. 1815–1848. Que faire de la révolution française? In Jean-François Sirinelli, ed., *Histoires des droites en France*. Vol. 1. Paris: Gallimard.

Derivry, Daniel, and Mattei Dogan. 1971. Unité d'analyse et espace de référence en écologie politique: Le canton et le département français. *Revue française de science politique* 21:517–70.

De Rosa, Gabriele. 1969. *Il Partito Popolare Italiano*. Bari: Editori Laterza.

———. 1972. *Il movimento cattolico in Italia: Dalla restaurazione all'età giolittiana*. Bari: Editori Laterza.

———. 1977. *Luigi Sturzo*. Turin: Union Tipografico-editrice Torinese.

Desan, Suzanne. 1990. *Reclaiming the Sacred. Lay Religion and Popular Politics in Revolutionary France*. Ithaca: Cornell University Press.

Desaubliaux, Marc. 1986. *La fin du parti royaliste, 1889–1890*. Paris: Editions Royaliste.

Deschouwer, Kris. 1995. Book Review of *Christian Democracy in Europe: A Comparative Perspective*, David Hanley, ed. *Political Studies* 43:176–77.

De Swaan, Abram. 1988. *In Care of the State*. New York: Oxford University Press.

De Trannoy, Baron. 1905. *Jules Malou, 1810 à 1870*. Brussells: Librairie Albert Dewit.

De Winter, Lieven. 1992. Christian Democratic Parties in Belgium. In Mario Caciagli et al., *DC: Christian Democracy in Europe*. Barcelona: ICPS.

Diamant, Alfred. 1960. *Austrian Catholics and the First Republic: Democracy, Capitalism, and the Social Order, 1918–1934*. Princeton: Princeton University Press.

Dietrich, Donald J. 1992. Book Review of *Zwischen Kirche und Gesellschaft. Das*

Zentralkomitee der deutschen Katholiken, 1945–1970 by Thomas Grossmann. *Catholic Historical Review* 78:468–69.

Dondeyne, Albert. 1964. *Priest and Layman.* London: Sheed and Ward.

Donegani, Jean-Marie. 1993. *La liberté de choisir: Pluralisme religieux et pluralisme politique dans le catholicisme français contemporain.* Paris: Presses de la Fondation Nationale des Sciences Politiques.

Dougherty, M. Patricia. 1994. *L'Ami de la Religion et les evêques français sous le concordat, 1815–1850. Revue d'histoire ecclésiastique* 89:577–621.

Doyle, Peter. 1986. The Catholic Federation, 1906–1929. In W. J. Sheils and Diana Wood, eds., *Voluntary Religion.* Oxford: Blackwell.

Duggan, Christopher. 1994. *A Concise History of Italy.* Cambridge: Cambridge University Press.

Dupeux, Georges. 1962. *Aspects de l'histoire sociale et politique du Loir-et-Cher, 1848–1914.* Paris: Mouton.

——. 1991. La IIIe République, 1871–1914. In Georges Duby, ed., *Histoire de France.* Vol. 3. Paris: Larousse.

Durand, Jean-Dominique. 1995. *L'Europe de la démocratie chrétienne.* Brussels: Editions Complexe.

Duroselle, Jean-Baptiste. 1951. *Les débuts du catholicisme social en France, 1922–1870.* Paris: Presses Universitaires de France.

Duverger, Maurice. 1954. *Political Parties.* London: Methuen.

——. 1966. *Sociologie politique.* Paris: PUF.

Ebbinghaus, Bernhard. 1992. The Transformation of Cleavage Structures into Western European Trade Union Systems. Paper presented for a European Consortium for Political Research Workshop on Trade Unions and Politics, University of Limerick.

Edelstein, Melvin. 1993. La participation électorale des français, 1789–1870. *Revue d'histoire moderne et contemporaine* 40:629–42.

Edmundson, George. 1922. *History of Holland.* Cambridge: Cambridge University Press.

Einaudi, Mario, and François Goguel. 1952. *Christian Democracy in Italy and France.* South Bend: University of Notre Dame Press.

Eliassen, Kjell A., and Lars Svaasand. 1975. The Formation of Mass Political Organizations: An Analytical Framework. *Scandinavian Political Studies* 10:95–121.

Elster, Jon. 1986. Introduction. In Jon Elster, ed., *Rational Choice.* New York: New York University Press.

——. 1989. *Nuts and Bolts for the Social Sciences.* Cambridge: Cambridge University Press.

——. 1993. *Political Psychology.* Cambridge: Cambridge University Press.

Epstein, Klaus. 1971. *Matthias Erzberger and the Dilemma of German Democracy.* New York: Howard Fertig.

Erba, Achille. 1967. *L'esprit laique en Belgique sous le gouvernment libéral doctrinaire, 1857–1880: D'après les brochures politiques.* Louvain: Publications Universitaires de Louvain.

——. 1990. *Proletariato di chiesa per la cristianità: La FACI tra curia romana e fascismo dalle origini alla conziliazione.* Rome: Herder Editrice e Libreria.

Esping-Andersen, Gøsta. 1990. *The Three Worlds of Welfare Capitalism.* Princeton: Princeton University Press.

Evans, Ellen Lovell. 1981. *The German Center Party, 1870–1933: A Study in Political Catholicism*. Carbondale: Southern Illinois University Press.

——. 1984. Catholic Political Movements in Germany, Switzerland, and the Netherlands: Notes for a Comparative Approach. *Central European History* 17:91–120.

Evans, Richard. 1982. Religion and Society in Modern Germany. *European Studies Review* 12:249–88.

Falter, Rolf. 1986. De Kamerverkiezingen van 10 juni 1884. In Emiel Lamberts and Jacques Lory, eds., *1884: Un tournant politique en Belgique—De Machtswisseling van 1884 in Belgie*. Brussels: Publications des Facultés Universitaires Saint-Louis.

Faury, Jean. 1980. *Cléricalisme et anticléricalisme dans le Tarn, 1848–1900*. Toulouse: Service des Publications de l'Université de Toulouse-Le Mirail.

Fleet, Michael. 1993. Christian Democracy. In Joel Krieger, ed., *The Oxford Companion to the Politics of the World*. New York: Oxford University Press.

Fogarty, Michael P. 1957. *Christian Democracy in Western Europe, 1820–1953*. London: Routledge and Kegan Paul.

Fonzi, Fausto. 1950. Per una storia del movimento cattolico italiano, 1861–1919. *Rassegna storica del risorgimento* 37:140–50.

Ford, Caroline C. 1987. Religion and Rural Politics in Lower Brittany, 1890–1926. Ph.D. dissertation, University of Chicago.

——. 1993. Religion and Popular Culture in Modern Europe. *Journal of Modern History* 65:152–75.

Formigoni, Guido. 1988. *I cattolici-deputati, 1904–1918: Tradizione e riforme*. Rome: Edizioni Studium.

Fox, Renée C. 1982. Is Religion Important in Belgium? *Archives européenes de sociologie* 32:3–38.

France, Alan W. 1975. Kulturkampf in Austria: The Vaterland Circle and the Struggle over the Confessional Legislation of May, 1868. Ph.D. dissertation, Rice University.

Fulton, John. 1987. Religion and Politics in Gramsci: An Introduction. *Sociological Analysis* 48:197–216.

Gabbert, Mark A. 1978. The Limits of French Catholic Liberalism: Mgr Sibour and the Question of Ecclesiology. *French Historical Studies* 10:641–63.

Gadille, Jacques. 1967. *La pensée et l'action politique des évêques français au début de la IIIe République, 1870–1883*. 2 vols. Paris: Hachette.

——. 1974. Les milieux catholiques libéraux en France: Continuité et diversité d'une tradition. In Jacques Gadille, ed., *Les catholiques libéraux au XIXe siècle: Actes du Colloque international d'histoire religieuse de Grenoble, 1971*. Grenoble: Presses Universitaires de Grenoble.

Gaines, Jena M. 1993. Alsatian Catholics against the State, 1918–1925. *Contemporary European History* 2:207–24.

Gambasin, Angelo. 1966. L'Italie. In S. H. Scholl, ed., *150 ans de mouvement ouvrier chrétien en Europe de l'Ouest, 1789–1939*. Louvain: Editions Nauwelaerts.

——. 1969. *Gerarchia e laicato in Italia nel secondo ottocento*. Padova: Editrice Antenore.

Geddes, Barbara. 1991. A Game Theoretic Model of Reform in Latin American Democracies. *American Political Science Review* 85:371–92.

Geehr, Richard S. 1990. *Karl Lueger: Mayor of Fin de Siècle Vienna*. Detroit: Wayne State University Press.

Gellott, Laura S. 1987. *The Catholic Church and the Authoritarian Regime in Austria, 1933–1938*. New York: Garland.

——. 1988. Defending Catholic Interests in the Christian State: The Role of Catholic Action in Austria, 1933–1938. *Catholic Historical Review* 74:571–89.

Gerard, Emmanuel. 1981. *Documenten over de Katholieke Partijorganisatie in Belgie-Documents relatifs à l'organization du parti catholique belge, 1920–1922, 1931–1933*. Louvain: Editions Nauwelaerts.

Gerard, Emmanuel, and Mark Van den Wijngaert. 1982. *Van Katholieke Partij naar Kristelijke Volkpartij*. Brussels: IPOVO.

Gherardi, Gabriele. 1967. *I cattolici cercano un partito*. Bologna: Edizioni Dehoniane.

Gibson, Ralph. 1989. *A Social History of French Catholicism, 1789–1914*. London: Routledge.

——. 1991. Why Republicans and Catholics Couldn't Stand Each Other in the Nineteenth Century. In Frank Tallett and Nicholas Atkin, eds., *Religion, Society and Politics in France since 1789*. London: Hambledon Press.

Gill, Anthony. 1994. Rendering unto Caesar? Religious Competition and Church-State Relations in Latin America. *American Journal of Political Science* 38:403–25.

Giovannini, Claudio. 1981a. Il movimento cattolico nell giudizio politico-culturale delle forze non cattoliche. In Francesco Traniello and Giorgio Campanini, eds., *Dizionario storico del movimento cattolico in Italia, 1860–1980*. Vol. 1. Turin: Marietti.

——. 1981b. Lega Democratica Nazionale. In Francesco Traniello and Giorgio Campanini, eds., *Dizionario storico del movimento cattolico in Italia, 1860–1980*. Vol. 1. Turin: Marietti.

Gladdish, Ken. 1991. *Governing from the Center: Politics and Policy-Making in the Netherlands*. DeKalb: Northern Illinois University Press.

Godson, Roy, and Stephen Haseler. 1978. *"Eurocommunism": Implications for East and West*. New York: St. Martin's Press.

Goguel, François. 1958. *La politique des partis sous la IIIe République*. Paris: Editions du Seuil.

Gouault, Jacques. 1954. *Comment la France est devenue républicaine: Les élections générales et partielles à l'Assemblée nationale, 1870–1875*. Paris: Librairie Armand Colin.

Gould, Andrew C. 1994. Origins of the Liberal Dominance in Western Europe. Paper presented at the 1994 Annual Meeting of the American Political Science Association, New York, September 1–4, 1994.

Goyau, Georges. 1909. *L'Allemagne religieuse: Le Catholicisme, 1800–1870*. 4 vols. Paris: Perrin.

Gramsci, Antonio. 1978. *Selections from Political Writings, 1921–1926*. Translated and edited by Quintin Hoare. New York: International Publishers.

——. 1990. *Selections from Political Writings, 1910–1920*. Selected and edited by Quintin Hoare. Minneapolis: University of Minnesota Press.

——. 1995. *Further Selections from the Prison Notebooks*. Edited and selected by Derek Boothman. Minneapolis: University of Minnesota Press.

Grubb, Alan. 1977. The Dilemma of Liberal Catholics and Conservative Politics in the Early Third Republic. *Proceedings of the Western Society for French History* 4:368–77.

Gruman, Massia. 1964. Origines et naissance du parti independant, 1979–1884. *Cahiers bruxellois* 9:89–171.

Gulick, Charles. 1948. *From Habsburg to Hitler.* Berkeley: University of California Press.

Guyot de Mishaegen, G. 1946. *Le parti catholique belge. De 1830 à 1884*. Brussels: Maison Ferdinand Larcier.

Haag, Henri. 1953. The Political Ideas of Belgian Catholics, 1789–1914. In Joseph Moody, ed., *Church and Society: Catholic Social and Political Thought and Movements, 1789–1950*. New York: Arts, Inc.

Hales, E. E. Y. 1958. *The Catholic Church in the Modern World: A Survey from the French Revolution to the Present.* Garden City, N.Y.: Hanover House.

Hall, Basil. 1975. Alessandro Gavazzi: A Barnabite Friar and the Risorgimento. In Derek Baker, ed., *Church Society and Politics.* Oxford: Blackwell.

Hanf, Theodor. 1984. Un son de cloche! Essai sur confession et style politique en Allemagne. *Revue d'Allemagne* 16:266–80.

Hanley, David. 1994. Introduction: Christian Democracy as a Political Phenomenon. In David Hanley, ed., *Christian Democracy in Europe: A Comparative Perspective.* London: Pinter.

Hanson, Eric O. 1987. *The Catholic Church in World Politics.* Princeton: Princeton University Press.

Hardin, Russell. 1982. *Collective Action.* Baltimore: Johns Hopkins University Press.

Hart, Oliver. 1989. An Economist's Perspective on the Theory of the Firm. *Columbia Law Review* 89:1757–74.

Harvey, Anna L. 1995. The Legacy of Disfranchisement: Women in Electoral Politics, 1917–1932. Ph.D. dissertation, Princeton University.

Hatfield, Douglas W. 1981a. Kulturkampf: The Relationship of Church and State and the Failure of German Political Reform. *Journal of Church and State* 23:465–84.

——. 1981b. German Protestantism and the Kulturkampf. *Red River Valley Historical Journal of World History* 5:288–98.

Hattam, Victoria C. 1992. Institutions and Political Change: Working Class Formation in England and the United States, 1820–1896. In Sven Steinmo, Kathleen Thelen, and Frank Longstreth, eds., *Structuring Politics: Historical Institutionalism in Comparative Analysis.* Cambridge: Cambridge University Press.

Hauss, Charles, and David Rayside. 1978. The Development of New Parties. In Louis Maisel and Joseph Cooper, eds., *Political Parties: Development and Decay.* Beverly Hills: Sage.

Haynes, Jeff. 1994. *Religion in Third World Politics.* Boulder: Lynne Rienner.

Heinen, Ernst. 1993. *Katholizismus und Gesellschaft. Das Katholische Vereinswesen zwischen Revolution und Reaktion, 1848/9–1853/54*. Idstein: Schulz-Kirchner.

Henderson, John. 1986. Confraternities and the Church in Late Medieval Florence. In W. J. Sheils and Diana Wood, eds., *Voluntary Religion.* Oxford: Blackwell.

Hendon, David W. 1976. The Center Party and the Agrarian Interest in Germany, 1890–1914. Ph.D. dissertation, Emory University.

Hendrickx, Jean-Pierre. 1969. A propos de la démission d'Alphonse Nothomb de la présidence de "l'Association Constitutionnelle Conservatrice" de Bruxelles, le 21 Février 1892. *Revue belge d'histoire contemporaine* 1:48–86.

Hilaire, Yves-Marie. 1977. *Une chrétienté au XIXe siècle? La vie religieuse des populations du diocèse d'Arras, 1840–1914*. 2 vols. Villeneuve-d'Ascq: Publications de l'Université de Lille III.

——. 1982. Le mouvement catholique en France. In E. de Jonghe and L. Preneel, eds., *Théorie et langage du mouvement catholique: Problèmes d'historiographie*. Leuven: Universitaire Pers.

Hirschman, Albert O. 1970. *Exit, Voice, and Loyalty: Responses to Decline in Firms, Organizations, and States*. Cambridge, Mass.: Harvard University Press.

Hoffmann, Stanley. 1963. *In Search of France*. Cambridge, Mass.: Harvard University Press.

Horner, Franz. 1987. The Church and Christian Democracy. *Concilium* 193:27–36.

Hours, Joseph. 1952. Les origines d'une tradition politique: La formation en France de la doctrine de la démocratie chrétienne et des pouvoirs intermédiaires. In Robert Pelloux, ed., *Libéralisme, traditionalisme, décentralization: Contribution à l'histoire des idées politiques*. Paris: Armand Colin.

Houska, Joseph J. 1985. *Influencing Mass Political Behavior: Elites and Political Subcultures in the Netherlands and Austria*. Berkeley: Institute of International Studies.

Houtart, François. 1953. Les paroisses de Bruxelles, 1803–1951: Législation, délimitation, démographie, équipement. *Bulletin de l'Institut de recherches economiques et sociales de l'Université de Louvain* 19:671–48.

Howard, Edith Pratt. 1957. *Il Partito Popolare Italiano*. Florence: La Nueva Italia.

Huard, Raymond. 1982. *Le mouvement républicain en Bas-Languedoc*. Paris: Presses de la Fondation Nationale des Sciences Politiques.

Huber, Evelyn, Charles Ragin, and John D. Stephens. 1993. Social Democracy, Christian Democracy, Constitutional Structure, and the Welfare State. *American Journal of Sociology* 99:711–49.

Hunley, J. D. 1974. The Working Classes, Religion and Social Democracy in the Düsseldorf Area, 1867–78. *Societas* 4:131–49.

Huntington, Samuel P. 1991. *The Third Wave: Democratization in the Late Twentieth Century*. Norman: University of Oklahoma Press.

Hürten, Heinz. 1986. *Kurze Geschichte des Deutschen Katholizismus, 1800–1960*. Mainz: Matthias Grünewald.

Iannaccone, Laurence R. 1991. The Consequences of Religious Market Structure: Adam Smith and the Economics of Religion. *Rationality and Society* 3:156–77.

Irvine, William D. 1989a. Royalists, Mass Politics and the Boulanger Affair. *French History* 3:31–47.

——. 1989b. *The Boulanger Affair Reconsidered: Royalism, Boulangism, and the Origins of the Radical Right in France*. New York: Oxford University Press.

Irving, R. E. M. 1973. *Christian Democracy in France*. London: Allen & Unwin.

——. 1979. *The Christian Democratic Parties of Western Europe*. London: Allen & Unwin [for] the Royal Institute of International Affairs.

Iserloh, Erwin. 1977. Il movimento sociale cattolico in Germania dal 1870 al 1914. In Ettore Passerin d'Entrèves and Konrad Repgen, eds., *Il cattolicesimo politico e sociale in Italia e Germania dal 1870 al 1914*. Bologna: Il Mulino.

Jadoulle, J.-L. 1990. La démocratie chretiénne belge à ses origines: Parcours historique et éssai de definition. *Revue politique* 2:37–50.
Jemolo, A. C. 1960. *Church and State in Italy, 1850–1950*. Oxford: Blackwell.
Jenks, William Alexander. 1950. *The Austrian Electoral Reform of 1907*. New York: Columbia University Press.
——. 1965. *Austria under the Iron Ring, 1879–1893*. Charlottesville: University Press of Virginia.
Joly, Bertrand. 1983. Le parti royaliste et l'affaire Dreyfus, 1898–1900. *Revue historique* 546:311–64.
Jones, P. M. 1985. *Politics and Rural Society: The Southern Massif Central, c. 1750–1880*. Cambridge: Cambridge University Press.
Jones, Rosemary C., and K. W. Swart. 1976. Survey of Recent Historical Works on Belgium and the Netherlands Published in Dutch. *Acta Historiae Neerlandicae* 9:193–244.
Joyce, G. H. 1913. Church. *Catholic Encyclopedia*. 3:744–61.
Judt, Tony. 1979. *Socialism in Provence, 1871–1914: A Study in the Origins of the Modern French Left*. Cambridge: Cambridge University Press.
Katz, Richard S., Peter Mair, et al. 1992. The Membership of Political Parties in European Democracies, 1960–1990. *European Journal of Political Research* 22:329–45.
Katznelson, Ira. 1986. Working-Class Formation: Constructing Cases and Comparisons. In Ira Katznelson and Aristide R. Zolberg, eds., *Working Class Formation: Nineteenth-Century Patterns in Western Europe and the United States*. Princeton: Princeton University Press.
Kayser, Jacques. 1962. *Les grandes batailles du radicalisme, 1820–1901*. Paris: Marcel Rivière et C[ie.]
Keman, Hans. 1993. Theoretical Approaches to Social Democracy. *Journal of Theoretical Politics* 5:291–316.
Kirchheimer, Otto. 1966. The Catch-All Party. In Joseph LaPalombara and Myron Weiner, eds., *Political Parties and Political Development*. Princeton: Princeton University Press.
Kitschelt, Herbert. 1989. *The Logics of Party Formation: Ecological Politics in Belgium and West Germany*. Ithaca: Cornell University Press.
——. 1992. Political Regime Change: Structure and Process-Driven Explanations? *American Political Science Review* 86:1028–34.
——. 1994. *The Transformation of European Social Democracy*. Cambridge: Cambridge University Press.
Klemperer, Klemens von. 1972. *Ignaz Seipel: Christian Statesman in a Time of Crisis*. Princeton: Princeton University Press.
Koelble, Thomas A. 1991. *The Left Unraveled: Social Democracy and the New Left Challenge in Britain and West Germany*. Durham: Duke University Press.
——. 1992. Social Democracy between Structure and Choice: A Review Article. *Comparative Politics* 24:359–72.
——. 1995. The New Institutionalism in Political Science and Sociology: A Review Article. *Comparative Politics* 27:231–43.
Köhler, Oscar. 1981. The Development of Catholicism in Modern Society. In Hubert Jedin and John Dolan, eds., *History of the Church*. Vol. 9. New York: Crossroad.

Kossmann, Ernst Heinrich. 1978. *The Low Countries, 1780–1940*. Oxford: Clarendon Press.

Krasner, Stephen D. 1988. Sovereignty: An Institutional Perspective. *Comparative Political Studies* 21:66–94.

Kreuzer, Marcus. 1995. Democratization and Party Development: Elections, Parties and Democratic Consolidation in Interwar France and Germany. Unpublished manuscript.

Kselman, Thomas. 1988. Funeral Conflicts in Nineteenth Century France. *Comparative Studies in Society and History* 30:312–32.

Lagrée, Michel. 1980. Exilés dans leur patrie (1880–1920). In François Lebrun, ed., *Histoire des catholiqucs en France: Du XVe siècle à nos jours*. Paris: Privat.

Laitin, David. 1986. *Hegemony and Culture: Politics and Religious Change among the Yoruba*. Chicago: University of Chicago Press.

——. 1995. National Revivals and Violence. *Archives européennes de sociologie* 36:3–43.

Lalman, David, Joe Oppenheimer, and Piotr Swistak. 1993. Formal Rational Choice Theory: A Cumulative Science of Politics. In Ada W. Finifter, ed., *Political Science: The State of the Discipline II*. Washington, D.C.: American Political Science Association.

Lamberti, Marjorie. 1986. School Reform during the Kulturkampf. *Central European History* 19:63–81.

Lamberts, Emiel. 1984. Une offensive de Pie IX et des ultramontains radicaux contre la législation matrimoniale belge, 1875. *Revue d'histoire ecclésiastique* 79:50–78.

Lamberts, Emiel, and Jacques Lory, eds. 1986. *1884: Un tournant politique en Belgique—De Machtswisseling van 1884 in Belgie*. Brussels: Publications des Facultés Universitaires Saint-Louis.

Lancelot, Alain. 1968. *L'abstentionisme électoral en France*. Paris: Armand Colin.

Lane, J.-E., and S. O. Ersson. 1991. *Politics and Society in Western Europe*. London: Sage.

Lanfrey, André. 1991. L'épiscopat français et l'école de 1902 à 1914. *Revue d'histoire de l'église de la France* 78:371–84.

Langlois, Claude. 1980. Permanence, renouveau et affrontements (1830–1880). In François Lebrun, ed., *Histoire des catholiques en France: Du XVe siècle à nos jours*. Paris: Privat.

LaPalombara, Joseph, and Myron Weiner. 1990/1966. The Origin of Political Parties. In Peter Mair, ed., *The West European Party System*. Oxford: Oxford University Press.

Lapierre, Jean-Pie, and Philippe Levillain. 1992. Laicisation, union sacrée et apaisement, 1895–1926. In Jacques le Goff and René Rémond, eds., *Histoire de la France religieuse*. Paris: Editions du Seuil.

Larkin, Maurice. 1974. *Church and State after the Dreyfus Affair: The Separation Issue in France*. London: Macmillan.

Latreille, A., J. R. Palanque, E. Delaruelle, and R. Rémond. 1962. *Histoire du catholicisme en France*. Paris: Editions Spes.

Laury, Jacques. 1964. Un cas de déchristianization cléricale en Belgique: Le fléchissement de la pratique pascale consécutif à la guerre scolaire, 1879–1884. *Cahiers d'histoire Lyon* 9:111–13.

——. 1979. *Libéralisme et instruction primaire, 1842–1879: Introduction à l'étude de la lutte scolaire en Belgique.* Louvain: Nauwelaerts.

Layton-Henry, Zig. 1982. Introduction: Conservatism and Conservative Politics. In Zig Layton-Henry, ed., *Conservative Politics in Western Europe.* New York: St. Martin's Press.

Lebas, Colette. 1960. *L'union des catholiques et des libéraux de 1839 à 1847: Etude sur les pouvoirs éxecutif et législatif.* Louvain: Nauwelaerts.

Le Béguec, Gilles. 1992. Le parti. In Jean-François Sirinelli, ed., *Histoires des droites en France.* Vol. 2. Paris: Gallimard.

Le Béguec, Gilles, and Jacques Prévotat. 1992. 1898–1919: L'éveil à la modernité politique. In Jean-François Sirinelli, ed., *Histoires des droites en France.* Vol. 1. Paris: Gallimard.

Leblicq, Yvon. 1978. Les premières interventions de l'Association Constitutionnelle Conservatrice de Bruxelles dans les luttes electorales de la capitale, 1863–1868. *Revue belge d'histoire contemporaine* 9:215–59.

Lechner, Frank J. 1991. The Case against Secularization: A Rebuttal. *Social Forces* 69:1103–19.

Leonardi, Robert, and Douglas A. Wertman. 1989. *Italian Christian Democracy: The Politics of Dominance.* Houndmills and London: Macmillan.

Lepointe, Gabriel. 1960. *Les rapports de l'église et de l'état en France.* Paris: PUF.

Levi, Margaret. 1991. Are There Limits to Rationality? *Archives Européenes de sociologie* 32:130–41.

Levillain, Philippe. 1982. Le mouvement catholique en France, 1870–1926. In E. de Jonghe and L. Preneel, eds., *Théorie et langage du mouvement catholique: Problèmes d'historiographie.* Leuven: Universitaire Pers.

——. 1992. 1871–1898: Les droites en république. In Jean-François Sirinelli, ed., *Histoires des droites en France.* Vol. 1. Paris: Gallimard.

Levine, Daniel H. 1992. *Popular Voices in Latin American Catholicism.* Princeton: Princeton University Press.

Lidtke, Vernon L. 1986. Catholics and Politics in Nineteenth-Century Germany: A Comment. *Central European History* 19:116–22.

Lijphart, Arend. 1971. Comparative Politics and Comparative Method. *American Political Science Review* 65:682–93.

——. 1990/1981. Dimensions of Ideology in European Party Systems. In Peter Mair, ed., *The West European Party System.* Oxford: Oxford University Press.

Lill, Rudolf. 1977. L'associazionismo cattolico in Germania dal 1848 al 1914. In Ettore Passerin d'Entrèves and Konrad Repgen, eds., *Il cattolicesimo politico e sociale in Italia e Germania dal 1870 al 1914.* Bologna: Il Mulino.

——. 1981. The *Kulturkampf* in Prussia and the German Empire until 1878. In Hubert Jedin and John Dolan, eds., *History of the Church.* Vol. 9. New York: Crossroad.

Lipset, Seymour M. 1981/1961. *Political Man.* Baltimore: Johns Hopkins University Press.

Lipset, Seymour M., and Stein Rokkan. 1967. Cleavage Structures, Party Systems, and Voter Alignments: An Introduction. In S. M. Lipset and S. Rokkan, eds., *Party Systems and Voter Alignments: Cross-National Perspectives.* New York: Free Press.

Locke, Robert L. 1974. *French Legitimists and the Politics of Moral Order in the Early Third Republic.* Princeton: Princeton University Press.

Lönne, Karl-Egon. 1986. *Politischer Katholizismus im 19. und 20. Jahrhundert.* Frankfurt: Suhrkamp.

——. 1987. The Origins of Christian Democratic Parties in Germany, Italy and France after 1943–45. *Concilium* 193:3–13.

Lorwin, Val. 1960. Belgium: Religion, Class, and Language in National Politics. In Robert A. Dahl, ed., *Political Opposition in Western Democracies.* New Haven: Yale University Press.

——. 1971. Segmented Pluralism: Ideological Cleavages and Political Cohesion in the Smaller European Democracies. *Comparative Politics* 3:141–75.

Loth, Wilfried, ed. 1991. *Deutscher Katholizismus im Umbruch zur Moderne.* Stuttgart: W. Kohlhammer.

Loubère, Leon A. 1974. *Radicalism in Mediterranean France: Its Rise and Decline, 1848–1914.* Albany: State University of New York Press.

Lovie, Jacques. 1963. *La Savoie dans la vie française de 1860 à 1875.* Paris: Presses Universitaires de France.

Lubelski-Bernard, Nadine, ed. 1983. *Léopold II et le cabinet Frère-Orban (1878–1884): Correspondence entre le roi et ses ministres.* Leuven: Nauwelaerts.

Luebbert, Gregory M. 1991. *Liberalism, Fascism, or Social Democracy: Social Classes and the Political Origins of Regimes in Interwar Europe.* New York: Oxford University Press.

Luykx, Theo. 1969. *Politieke Geschiedenis van België van 1789 tot Heden.* Brussels: Elsevier.

Lynch, Edward A. 1993. *Latin America's Christian Democratic Parties: A Political Economy.* Westport, Conn.: Praeger.

Lyon, Margot. 1967. Christian-Democratic Parties and Politics. *Journal of Contemporary History* 2:69–89.

Mabille, Xavier. 1985. Partis politiques et électorat catholique: Développements depuis 1945. In Liliane Voyé, Karel Dobbelaere, Jean Remy, and Jaak Billiet, eds., *La Belgique et ses Dieux: Eglises, mouvements religieux et laiques.* Louvain-la-Neuve: Cabay.

Macartney, C. A. 1968. *The Habsburg Empire, 1790–1918.* London: Weidenfeld and Nicolson.

Mackie, Thomas T., and Richard Rose. 1991. *The International Almanac of Electoral History.* Washington, D.C.: Congressional Quarterly.

Maertens, P. 1991. Démocrates-chrétiens et conservateurs: Un rapprochement sous conditions. *La Revue politique* 2:47–65.

Maier, Hans. 1969. *Revolution and the Church: The Early History of Christian Democracy, 1789–1907.* Notre Dame: University of Notre Dame Press.

Mair, Peter. 1984. Party Politics in Contemporary Europe: A Challenge to Party? In Stefano Bartolini and Peter Mair, eds., *Party Politics in Contemporary Europe: A Challenge to Party?* London: Frank Cass.

——. 1993. Myths of Electoral Change and the Survival of Traditional Parties. *European Journal of Political Research* 24:121–33.

Malgeri, Francesco. 1969. *Gli atti dei congressi del Partito Popolare Italiano.* Brescia: Morcelliana.

——. 1981. Partito Popolare Italiano. In Francesco Traniello and Giorgio Campan-

ini, eds., *Dizionario storico del movimento cattolico in Italia, 1860–1980*. Vol. 1. Turin: Marietti.
Mann, Golo. 1968. *The History of Germany since 1789*. New York: Praeger.
Martin, Benjamin F., Jr. 1970. The Creation of the Action Libérale Populaire: An Example of Party Formation in Third Republic France. *French Historical Studies* 9:660–89.
Martin, Benjamin F. 1978. *Count Albert de Mun: Paladin of the Third Republic*. Chapel Hill: University of North Carolina Press.
Martin, David. 1978. *A General Theory of Secularization*. Oxford: Blackwell.
Martin, Philippe. 1994. Un éspace culturel en mouvement: Les confréries du Saintois du XVIIe au XIXe siècle. *Revue d'histoire moderne et contemporaine* 41:121–35.
Mavrogordatos, George Th. 1983. *Stillborn Republic: Social Coalitions and Party Strategies in Greece, 1922–1936*. Berkeley: University of California Press.
May, Anita Rasi. 1973. The Falloux Law, the Catholic Press, and the Bishops: Crisis of Authority in the French Church. *French Historical Studies* 8:77–94.
Mayeur, Françoise. 1992. L'éducation. In Jean-François Sirinelli, ed., *Histoires des droites en France*. Vol. 3. Paris: Gallimard.
Mayeur, Jean-Marie. 1962. Les congrès nationaux de la démocratie chrétienne à Lyon, 1896–1897–1898. *Revue d'histoire moderne et contemporaine* 9:171–206.
——. 1966. *La séparation de l'église et de l'état*. Paris: Julliard.
——. 1968. *Un prêtre démocrate, l'abbé Lemire, 1853–1928*. Paris: Casterman.
——. 1972. Catholicisme intransigeant, catholicisme social, démocratie chrétienne. *Annales: Economies, sociétés, civilisations* 27:483–99.
——. 1973. *Les débuts de la IIIe République, 1871–1898*. Paris: Editions du Seuil.
——. 1980. *Des partis catholiques à la démocratie chrétienne*. Paris: Armand Colin.
——. 1981. Movimento cattolico italiano e movimenti cattolici europei. In Francesco Traniello and Giorgio Campanini, eds., *Dizionario storico del movimento cattolico in Italia, 1860–1980*. Vol. 1. Turin: Marietti.
McLeod, Hugh. 1981. *Religion and the People of Western Europe, 1789–1970*. Oxford: Oxford University Press.
——. 1986. Building the "Catholic Ghetto": Catholic Organizations, 1870–1914. In W. J. Sheils and Diana Wood, eds., *Voluntary Religion*. Oxford: Blackwell.
McManners, John. 1972. *Church and State in France, 1870–1914*. London: SPCK.
McRae, Duncan, Jr. 1958. Religious and Socio-economic Factors in the French Vote, 1946–1956. *American Journal of Sociology* 64:290–98.
Mélot, Auguste. 1935. *Cinquante années de gouvernement parlementaire: 1884–1934*. Brussels: Les éditions Rex.
Ménager, Bernard. 1983. *La vie politique dans le département du Nord de 1851 à 1877*. Lille: Université Lille III.
——. 1992. 1848–1871: Autorité ou liberté. In Jean-François Sirinelli, ed., *Histoires des droites en France*. Vol. 1. Paris: Gallimard.
Mendershausen, Ralph René. 1973. German Political Catholicism, 1912–1919. Ph.D. dissertation, University of California, San Diego.
Menozzi, Daniele. 1983. The Case of Italy. *Concilium* 193:62–71.
Mény, Yves (with Andrew Knapp). 1993. *Government and Politics in Western Europe: Britain, France, Italy, Germany*. Oxford: Oxford University Press.
Mesliand, Claude. 1976. Gauche et droite dans les campagnes provençales sous la IIIe République. *Études rurales* 63–64:207–34.

Miccoli, Giovanni. 1973. La chiesa e il fascismo. In Guido Quazza, ed., *Fascismo e società italiana*. Turin: Einaudi.

Michelat, Guy, and Michel Simon. 1977. *Classe, religion et comportement politique*. Paris: Presses de la Fondation Nationale des Sciences Politiques.

Misra, Joya, and Alexander Hicks. 1994. Catholicism and Unionization in Affluent Postwar Democracies: Catholicism, Culture, Party, and Unionization. *American Sociological Review* 59:304–26.

Molette, Charles. 1968. *L'Association Catholique de la Jeunesse Française, 1886–1907: Une prise de conscience du laïcat catholique*. Paris: Armand Colin.

——. 1976. A.C.J.F. et la politique de 1907 à 1914. *Bulletin du Centre Régional d'Histoire Religieuse*. December.

Molony, John. 1977. *The Emergence of Political Catholicism in Italy: Partito Popolare, 1919–1926*. Totowa, N.J.: Rowman and Littlefield.

Moody, Joseph. 1953. From Old Regime to Democratic Society. In Joseph Moody, ed., *Church and Society: Catholic Social and Political Thought and Movements, 1789–1950*. New York: Arts, Inc.

Moore, Barrington, Jr. 1966. *Social Origins of Dictatorship and Democracy: Lord and Peasant in the Making of the Modern World*. Boston: Beacon Press.

Neitzel, Sarah C. 1987. *Priests and Journeymen: The German Catholic Gesellenverein and the Christian Social Movement in the Nineteenth Century*. Bonn: Kommissions-Verlag L. Röhrscheid.

Nipperdey, Thomas. 1988. *Religion im Umbruch. Deutschland, 1871–1918*. Munich: Beck.

——. 1992. *Réflexions sur l'histoire allemande*. Paris: Gallimard.

Noiret, Serge. 1994. Political Parties and the Political System in Belgium before Federalism, 1830–1980. *European History Quarterly*. 24:85–122.

O'Gara, James, ed. 1962. The Layman in the Church. New York: Herder.

Olson, Mancur. 1971. *The Logic of Collective Action: Public Goods and the Theory of Groups*. Cambridge, Mass: Harvard University Press.

Osa, Maryjane. 1992. Pastoral Mobilization and Symbolic Politics: The Catholic Church in Poland, 1918–1966. Ph.D. dissertation, University of Chicago.

Osgood, Samuel M. 1960. *French Royalism under the Third and Fourth Republics*. The Hague: Martinus Nijhoff.

Ozouf, Mona. 1963. *L'école: l'église et la république, 1871–1914*. Paris: Armand Colin.

Pace, Enzo. 1995. *L'unità dei cattolici in Italia: Origini e decadenza di un mito collectivo*. Milan: Guerini.

Papanek, Ernst. 1962. *The Austrian School Reform: Its Bases, Principles and Developments. The Twenty Years between the Two World Wars*. New York: Frederick Fell.

Papini, Roberto. 1993. Christianity and Democracy in Europe: The Christian Democratic Movement. In John Witte, Jr., ed., *Christianity and Democracy in Global Context*. Boulder: Westview Press.

Partin, Malcolm O. 1969. *Waldeck-Rousseau, Combes, and the Church: The Politics of Anticlericalism, 1899–1905*. Durham, N.C.: Duke University Press.

Passerin d'Entrèves, Ettore. 1981. Cattolici liberali. In Francesco Traniello and Giorgio Campanini, eds., *Dizionario storico del movimento cattolico in Italia, 1860–1980*. Vol. 1. Turin: Marietti.

Pasture, Patrick. 1996. Entre église et citoyen: Le PSC-CVP et sa base organisée. In

Wilfried Dewachter, Georges-Henri Dumont, Michel Dumoulin, Manu Gérard, Emiel Lamberts, Xavier Mabille, and Mark van den Wijngaert, eds., *Un parti dans l'histoire, 1945–1995: 50 ans du Parti Social Chrétien*. Louvain-la-Neuve: Duculot.

Paxton, Robert O. 1982. *Vichy France: Old Guard and New Order, 1940–1944*. New York: Columbia University Press.

Pazzaglia, Luciano. 1981. Movimento cattolico e questione scolastica. In Francesco Traniello and Giorgio Campanini, eds., *Dizionario storico del movimento cattolico in Italia, 1860–1980*. Vol. 1. Turin: Marietti.

Piepers, N. 1968. *"La Revue Générale" de 1865 à 1940: Essai d'analyse du contenu*. Louvain: Nauwelaerts.

Pierrard, Pierre. 1972. *Histoire de l'église catholique*. Paris: Desclée.

Pinard, Maurice. 1971. *The Rise of a Third Party: A Study in Crisis Politics*. Englewood Cliffs, N.J.: Prentice-Hall.

Pirenne, Henri. 1932. *Histoire de Belgique: De la révolution de 1830 à la guerre de 1914*. Vol. 7. Brussells: Maurice Lamertin.

Pisani-Ferry, Fresnette. 1965. *Le coup d'état manqué du 16 mai 1877*. Paris: Robert Laffont.

Pizzorno, Alessandro. 1970. An Introduction to the Theory of Political Participation. *Social Science Information* 9:29–61.

Plavsic, Wladimir S. 1968. L'église et la politique en Belgique. *Res Publica* 10:211–52.

Pluymers, Magda. 1984. *Le Catholique*, 1865–1869: Een Ultramontaanse Poging tot Radicalisering van de Katholieke Pers. In Emiel Lamberts, ed., *De Kruistocht Tegen het Liberalisme: Facetten van het Ultramontanisme in België in de 19e Eeuw*. Leuven: Universitaire Pers.

Poggi, Gianfranco. 1967. *Catholic Action in Italy: The Sociology of a Sponsored Organization*. Stanford: Stanford University Press.

Poulat, Emile. 1977. *Eglise contre bourgeoisie: Introduction au devenir du catholicisme actuel*. Paris: Casterman.

——. 1982. Le mouvement catholique et son développement structurel: Origines et préalables. In E. de Jonghe and L. Preneel, eds., *Théorie et langage du mouvement catholique: Problèmes d'historiographie*. Leuven: Universitaire Pers.

Poulet, Charles. 1944. *Histoire de l'église en France*. Paris: Beauchesne et fils.

Post, Harry. 1989. *Pillarization: An Analysis of Dutch and Belgian Society*. Aldershot: Avenbury.

Preneel, L. 1982. Mouvements catholiques et expériences des catholiques en Belgique: In E. de Jonghe and L. Preneel, eds., *Théorie et langage du mouvement catholique. Problèmes d'historiographie*. Leuven: Universitaire Pers.

Przeworski, Adam. 1985. *Capitalism and Social Democracy*. Cambridge: Cambridge University Press.

——. 1986. Some Problems in the Study of the Transition to Democracy. In Guillermo O'Donnell, Philippe C. Schmitter, and Laurence Whitehead, eds., *Transitions from Authoritarian Rule: Comparative Perspectives*. Baltimore: Johns Hopkins University Press.

——. 1990. *The State and the Economy under Capitalism*. Chur: Harwood Academic Publishers.

Przeworski, Adam, and John Sprague. 1986. *Paper Stones: A History of Electoral Socialism*. Chicago: University of Chicago Press.

Putnam, Robert D. 1993. *Making Democracy Work: Civic Traditions in Modern Italy*. Princeton: Princeton University Press.

Rahner, Karl, et al. 1968. *Obedience and the Church*. Washington, D.C.: Corpus Books.

Ravitch, Norman. 1990. *The Catholic Church and the French Nation, 1589–1989*. London: Routledge.

Raymond-Laurent, J. 1966. *Le Parti Démocrate Populaire, 1924–1944*. Le Mans: Imprimerie Commerciale.

Reddick, James Allen. 1950. A Typology of Anticlericalism in France under the Third Republic, 1871–1914. Ph.D. dissertation, University of Chicago.

Reichley, James A. 1986. Democracy and Religion. *PS: Political Science and Politics* 19:801–6.

Reinerman, Alan J. 1993. Book Review of *Il "Kulturkampf" in Italia e nei paesi di lingua tedesca*, ed. by Rudolf Lill and Francesco Traniello. *Catholic Historical Review* 79:761–63.

Rémond, René. 1964. *Les deux congrès ecclésiastiques de Reims et de Bourges, 1896–1900: Un témoignage sur la France*. Paris: Sirey.

——. 1965. Forces religieuses et partis politiques. In René Rémond, ed., *Forces religieuses et attitudes politiques dans la France contemporaine*. Paris: Armand Colin.

——. 1982. *Les droites en France*. Paris: Aubier Montaigne.

Remy, Jean, and Liliane Voyé. 1985. L'église catholique de Belgique et la transaction avec la modernité. In Liliane Voyé, Karel Dobbelaere, Jean Remy, and Jaak Billiet, eds., *La Belgique et ses Dieux: Eglises, mouvements religieux et laiques*. Louvain-la-Neuve: Cabay.

Remy, Jean, Liliane Voyé, Karel Dobbelaere, and Jaak Billiet. 1985. Synthèse et conclusion. In Liliane Voyé, Karel Dobbelaere, Jean Remy, and Jaak Billiet, eds., *La Belgique et ses Dieux: Eglises, mouvements religieux et laiques*. Louvain-la-Neuve: Cabay.

Rhodes, Anthony. 1973. *The Vatican in the Age of the Dictators, 1922–1945*. New York: Holt, Rinehart, and Winston.

Riker, William. 1986. *The Art of Political Manipulation*. New Haven: Yale University Press.

Ritter, Gerhard A. 1990. The Social Bases of the German Political Parties, 1867–1920. In Karl Rohe, ed., *Elections, Parties and Political Traditions: Social Foundations of German Parties and Party Systems, 1867–1987*. New York: Berg.

Rivet, Auguste. 1979. *La vie politique dans le département de la Haute-Loire de 1815 à 1974*. Le Puy: Cahiers de Haute-Loire.

Rogowski, Ronald. 1995. The Role of Theory and Anomaly in Social-Scientific Inference. *American Political Science Review* 89:467–70.

Rommen, Heinrich. 1950. *The State in Catholic Thought: A Treatise in Political Philosophy*. St. Louis: Herder.

Rose, Richard, and Thomas T. Mackie. 1988. Do Parties Persist or Fail? The Big Trade-off Facing Organizations. In Kay Lawson and Peter H. Merkl, eds., *When Parties Fail: Emerging Alternative Organizations*. Princeton: Princeton University Press.

Rosenstone, Steven J., and John Mark Hansen. 1993. *Mobilization, Participation, and Democracy in America*. New York: Macmillan.

Ross, Ronald J. 1976. *Beleaguered Tower: The Dilemma of Political Catholicism in Wilhelmine Germany*. Notre Dame: University of Notre Dame Press.
Rossi, Mario G. 1977. *Le origini del partito cattolico: Movimento cattolico e lotta di classe nell'Italia liberale*. Rome: Editori Riuniti.
Rovan, Joseph. 1956. *Le catholicisme politique en Allemagne*. Paris: Editions du Seuil.
Saint-Moulin, Léon de. 1967. Contribution à l'histoire de la déchristianization: La pratique religieuse à Seraing depuis 1830. *Annuaire d'histoire liégeoise* 33–127.
Sartori, Giovanni. 1990/1968. The Sociology of Parties: A Critical Review. In Peter Mair, ed., *The West European Party System*. Oxford: Oxford University Press.
——. 1990/1976. A Typology of Party Systems. In Peter Mair, ed., *The West European Party System*. Oxford: Oxford University Press.
Schapiro, Salwyn J. 1967. *Anticlericalism: Conflict between Church and State in France, Italy, and Spain*. Princeton: D. Van Nostrand.
Schattschneider, E. E. 1960. *The Semisovereign People: A Realist's View of Democracy in America*. New York: Holt, Rinehart, and Winston.
Schlesinger, J. A. 1984. On the Theory of Party Organization. *Journal of Politics* 46:369–400.
Schmitt, Karl. 1990. Religious Cleavages in the West German Party System: Persistence and Change, 1949–1987. In Karl Rohe, ed., *Elections, Parties and Political Traditions: Social Foundations of German Parties and Party Systems, 1867–1987*. New York: Berg.
Schneider, Michael. 1982. Religion and Labour Organization: The Christian Trade Unions in the Wilhelmine Empire. *European Studies Review* 12:345–69.
Schorske, Carl E. 1967. Politics in a New Key: An Austrian Triptych. *Journal of Modern History* 39:343–86.
Scoppola, Pietro. 1977. La Lega Democratica Nazionale. In Ettore Passerin d'Entrèves and Konrad Repgen, eds., *Il cattolicesimo politico e sociale in Italia e Germania dal 1870 al 1914*. Bologna: Il Mulino.
——. 1982. Le mouvement catholique en Italie: De 1919 à Vatican II. In E. de Jonghe and L. Preneel, eds., *Théorie et langage du mouvement catholique: Problèmes d'historiographie*. Leuven: Universitaire Pers.
Sedgwick, Alexander. 1965. *The Ralliement in French Politics, 1890–1898*. Cambridge, Mass.: Harvard University Press.
Sewell, William H., Jr. 1992. Three Temporalities: Toward an Eventful Sociology. Unpublished manuscript.
Sferza, Serenella. 1991. Organizational Forms and Strategies of Growth: The Case of the French Socialist Party. Paper presented at the Annual Meeting of the American Political Science Association, August 29-September 1, 1991, Washington, D.C.
Shefter, Martin. 1986. Trade Unions and Political Machines: The Organization and Disorganization of the American Working Class in the Late Nineteenth Century. In Ira Katznelson and Aristide R. Zolberg, eds., *Working Class Formation: Nineteenth-Century Patterns in Western Europe and the United States*. Princeton: Princeton University Press.
——. 1994. *Political Parties and the State: The American Historical Experience*. Princeton: Princeton University Press.
Shelley, Thomas J. 1990. Mutual Independence: Church and State in Belgium, 1825–1846. *Journal of Church and State* 32:49–63.

Siegfried, André. 1949. *Géographie électorale de l'Ardèche sous la IIIe République*. Paris: Armand Colin.

——. 1964/1913. *Tableau politique de la France de l'Ouest*. Paris: Armand Colin.

Simon, Alois. 1955. *Catholicisme et politique. Documents inédits, 1832–1909*. Wetteren: Editions Scaldis.

——. 1958. *Le parti catholique belge, 1830–1945*. Brussels: La Renaissance du Livre.

——. 1961. *Réunions des évêques de Belgique, 1868–1883: Procès-verbaux*. Louvain: Nauwelaerts.

——. 1966. Le Vatican. In S. H. Scholl, ed., *150 ans de mouvement ouvrier chrétien en Europe de l'Ouest, 1789–1939*. Louvain: Nauwelaerts.

Sinistrero, Vincenzo. 1967. Catholic Education in Italy. In James Michael Lee, ed., *Catholic Education in the Western World*. Notre Dame: University of Notre Dame Press.

Skocpol, Theda. 1979. *States and Social Revolutions: A Comparative Analysis of France, Russia, and China*. Cambridge: Cambridge University Press.

Skocpol, Theda, and Margaret Somers. 1980. The Uses of Comparative History in Macrosociological Inquiry. *Comparative Studies in Society and History* 22:174–97.

Smith, Helmut Walser. 1991. Nationalism and Religious Conflict in Germany, 1887–1914. Ph.D. dissertation, Yale University.

Soete, Jean-Luc. 1980. La résistance catholique face à la loi Van Humbeck dans l'arrondissement de Tournai, 1878–1884. *Revue belge d'histoire contemporaine* 11:119–69.

——. 1983. Evolution du catholicisme politique en Belgique de 1831 à 1884: La structuration des forces catholiques et la question du programme. *Tijdschrift voor Geschiedenis* 96:193–202.

——. 1984. L'ultramontanisme et la formation du parti catholique en Belgique de 1875 à 1884. In Emiel Lamberts, ed., *De Kruistocht tegen het Liberalisme: Facetten van het Ultramontanisme in België in de 19e Eeuw*. Leuven: Universitaire Pers.

——. 1986. Les catholiques et la question du programme, 1878–1884. In Emiel Lamberts and Jacques Lory, eds., *1884: Un tournant politique en Belgique—De Machtswisseling van 1884 in Belgie*. Brussels: Publications des Facultés Universitaires Saint-Louis.

——. 1990. Parti catholique et sociabilité en Belgique au XIXe siècle: Les cercles catholiques, 1863–1884. *Revue politique* 3:71–81.

Soltau, Roger H. 1965. *French Parties and Politics, 1871–1921*. New York: Russell and Russell.

Somers, Margaret R. 1994. The Narrative Constitution of Identity: A Relational and Network Approach. *Theory and Society* 23:605–49.

Southern, Gilbert Edwin, Jr. 1977. The Bavarian Kulturkampf: A Chapter in Government, Church, and Society in the Early Bismarckreich. Ph.D. dissertation, University of Massachusetts, Amherst.

Sperber, Jonathan. 1980. Social Change, Religious Practice and Political Development in a Catholic Region of Central Europe: Rhineland-Westphalia, 1830–1880. Ph.D. dissertation, University of Chicago.

——. 1982. Roman Catholic Religious Identity in Rhineland-Westphalia, 1800–70: Quantitative Examples and Some Political Implications. *Social History* 7:305–18.

——. 1986. Prussian State and Catholic Church. *Central European History* 19:45–62.

——. 1987. Book Review of *Kurze Geschichte des Deutschen Katholizismus, 1800–1960* by Heinz Hürten. *American Historical Review* 92:980–81.
Spohn, Willfried. 1991. Religion and Working-Class Formation in Imperial Germany, 1871–1914. *Politics and Society* 19:109–32.
Stengers, Jean. 1981. L'église en Belgique: Doctrine et pratique. In Hervé Hasquin, ed., *Histoire de la laicité: Principalement en Belgique et en France*. Brussels: Editions de l'Université de Bruxelles.
Stephens, John D. 1979. *The Transition from Capitalism to Socialism*. Urbana: University of Illinois Press.
Stinchcombe, Arthur L. 1965. Social Structure and Organization. In James G. March, *Handbook of Organizations*. Chicago: Rand McNally.
Suardo, Dino Secco. 1962. *I cattolici intransigenti*. Brescia: Morcelliana.
Suval, Stanley. 1985. *Electoral Politics in Imperial Germany*. Chapel Hill: University of North Carolina Press.
Tarrow, Sidney. 1975. Communism in Italy and France: Adaptation and Change. In Donald Blackmer and Sidney Tarrow, eds., *Communism in Italy and France*. Princeton: Princeton University Press.
——. 1994. *Power in Movement. Social Movements, Collective Action and Politics*. Cambridge: Cambridge University Press.
Tash, Robert C. 1991. *Dutch Pluralism. A Model in Tolerance for Developing Democracies*. New York: Peter Lang.
Taylor, A. J. P. 1948. *The Habsburg Monarchy, 1809–1918. A History of the Austrian Empire and Austria-Hungary*. London: Hamish Hamilton.
Taylor, Michael. 1993. Structure, Culture, and Action in the Explanation of Social Change. In William James Booth, Patrick James, and Hudson Meadwell, eds., *Politics and Rationality*. Cambridge: Cambridge University Press.
Terlinden, Charles. 1929. *Histoire de la Belgique contemporaine, 1830–1914*. 3 vols. Brussels: Albert Dewit.
——. 1934. Un siècle de relations diplomatiques belgo-vaticanes. In Camille Joset, ed., *Un siècle de l'église catholique en Belgique, 1830–1930*. Paris: Editions Jos. Vermaut.
Thelen, Kathleen, and Sven Steinmo. 1992. Historical Institutionalism in Comparative Politics. In Sven Steinmo, Kathleen Thelen, and Frank Longstreth, eds., *Structuring Politics. Historical Institutionalism in Comparative Analysis*. Cambridge: Cambridge University Press.
Tilly, Charles. 1986. *The Contentious French: Four Centuries of Popular Struggle*. Cambridge: Belknap Press of Harvard University Press.
Tocqueville, Alexis de. 1988/1835. *Democracy in America*. New York: Harper & Row.
Tramontin, Silvio. 1981a. Opera dei Congressi e dei Comitati Cattolici in Italia. In Francesco Traniello and Giorgio Campanini, eds., *Dizionario storico del movimento cattolico in Italia, 1860–1980*. Vol. 1. Turin: Marietti.
——. 1981b. Unione Economico-Sociale. In Francesco Traniello and Giorgio Campanini, eds., *Dizionario storico del movimento cattolico in Italia, 1860–1980*. Vol. 1. Turin: Marietti.
——. 1981c. Unione Elettorale. In Francesco Traniello and Giorgio Campanini, eds., *Dizionario storico del movimento cattolico in Italia, 1860–1980*. Vol. 1. Turin: Marietti.

——. 1981d. Unione Popolare. In Francesco Traniello and Giorgio Campanini, eds., *Dizionario storico del movimento cattolico in Italia, 1860–1980*. Vol. 1. Turin: Marietti.

Traniello, Francesco. 1981. Movimento cattolico e questioni nazionali. In Francesco Traniello and Giorgio Campanini, eds., *Dizionario storico del movimento cattolico in Italia, 1860–1980*. Vol. 1. Turin: Marietti.

——. 1982. Le mouvement catholique en Italie jusqu'à la première guerre mondiale: Problèmes de méthode et de définition. In E. de Jonghe and L. Preneel, eds., *Théorie et langage du mouvement catholique. Problèmes d'historiographie*. Leuven: Universitaire Pers.

Tsebelis, George. 1990. *Nested Games. Rational Choice in Comparative Politics*. Berkeley: University of California Press.

Urwin, Derek W. 1970. Social Cleavages and Political Parties in Belgium: Problems of Institutionalization. *Political Studies* 18:320–40.

Vaillancourt, Jean Guy. 1980. *Papal Power. A Study of Vatican Control over Lay Catholic Elites*. Berkeley: University of California Press.

Valenzuela, J. Samuel. 1979. Labor Movement Formation and Politics: The Chilean and French Cases in Comparative Perspective, 1850–1950. Ph.D. dissertation, Columbia University.

Vanden Berg, Frank. 1960. *Abraham Kuyper*. Grand Rapids: Eerdmans.

Van Eekeren, Wilhelmus Antonius Marie. 1956. The Catholic People's Party in the Netherlands. A Study of the Party's Origin, Unity, Organization and Policies. Ph.D. dissertation, Georgetown University.

Van Isacker, Karel. 1955. *Werkelijk en Wettelijk Land: De Katholieke Opinie Tegenover de Rechterzijde, 1863–1884*. Antwerp: Standaard-Boekhandel.

Van Kersbergen, Kees. 1994. The Distinctiveness of Christian Democracy. In David Hanley, ed., *Christian Democracy in Europe: A Comparative Perspective*. London: Pinter.

——. 1995. *Social Capitalism: A Study of Christian Democracy and the Welfare State*. London: Routledge.

Van Kessel, P. J. 1976. The Attitude of the Roman Curia to the French Revolution and Its Opposite Effects in the Southern and Northern Netherlands. *Acta Historiae Neerlandicae* 9:103–20.

Vaussard, Maurice. 1956. *Histoire de la démocratie chrétienne. France-Belgique-Italie*. Paris: Editions du Seuil.

Vecchio, Giorgio. 1979a. *La democrazia cristiana in Europa, 1891–1963*. Milan: Mursia.

——. 1979b. Interpretations of the Italian Popular Party and the Italian Catholic Movement. *Journal of Italian History* 2:52–74.

——. 1987. *Alla ricerca del partito. Cultura politica ed esperienze dei cattolici italiani nel primo novecento*. Brescia: Morcelliana.

——. 1988. *Politica e democrazia nelle riviste popolari, 1919–1926*. Rome: Edizioni Studium.

Verdier, Daniel. 1994. *Democracy and International Trade. Britain, France, and the United States, 1860–1990*. Princeton: Princeton University Press.

Verhoef, Jan. 1974. The Rise of National Political Parties in the Netherlands, 1888–1913. *International Journal of Politics* 4:207–21.

Verkade, Willem. 1965. *Democratic Parties in the Low Countries and Germany: Origins and Historical Developments*. Leiden: Universitaire Pers Leiden.

Verschave, Paul. 1910. *La Hollande politique. Un parti catholique en pays protestant.* Paris: Perrin et C[ie.]

Viance, Georges. 1930. *La Fédération Nationale Catholique.* Paris: Ernest Flammarion.

Vigier, Philippe. 1963. *La Seconde République dans la region Alpine: Etude politique et sociale.* Paris: Presses Universitaires de France.

——. 1972. Le parti républicain en 1870. In Jacques Viard, ed., *L'esprit républicain. Colloque d'Orleans, 4 et 5 septembre 1970.* Paris: Klincksieck.

Vismara Chiappa, Paola. 1982. Eglise et état en France au début du Ralliement: L'affaire des catéchismes électoraux d'après les archives Vaticanes. *Revue d'histoire de l'église de la France* 68:213–33.

Vlekke, Bernard M. 1945. *Evolution of the Dutch Nation.* New York: Roy Publishers.

Von der Dunk, Hermann. 1978. Conservatism in the Netherlands. *Journal of Contemporary History* 13:741–63.

Wallerstein, Michael. 1989. Union Organization in Advanced Industrial Democracies. *American Political Science Review* 83:481–501.

Wandruszka, Adam. 1977. Il cattolicesimo politico e sociale nell'Austria-Ungheria degli anni 1870–1914. In Ettore Passerin d'Entrèves and Konrad Repgen, eds., *Il cattolicesimo politico e sociale in Italia e Germania dal 1870 al 1914.* Bologna: Il Mulino.

Warner, Carolyn M. 1995. Party Strategies, Organizations and Societal Cleavages: Constructing the French and Italian Christian Democratic Political Parties, 1944–1958. Paper presented at the 53d Annual Meeting of the Midwest Political Science Association, Chicago.

Weber, Eugen. 1976. *Peasants into Frenchmen: The Modernization of Rural France, 1870–1914.* Stanford: Stanford University Press.

——. 1991. *My France. Politics, Culture, Myth.* Cambridge: Belknap Press of Harvard University Press.

Weber, Max. 1963. *The Sociology of Religion.* Boston: Beacon Press.

Webster, Richard A. 1960. *The Cross and the Fasces: Christian Democracy and Fascism in Italy.* Stanford: Stanford University Press.

Wettengel, Michael. 1989. *Die Revolution von 1848/49 im Rhein-Main-Raum: Politische Vereine und Revolutionsalltag im Grossherzogtum Hessen, Herzotgum Nassau und in der Frein Stadt Frankfurt.* Wiesbaden: Historische Kommission für Nassau.

White, Harrison C. 1992. *Identity and Control: A Structural Theory of Social Action.* Princeton: Princeton University Press.

Whyte, John Y. 1981. *Catholics in Western Democracies: A Study in Political Behaviour.* New York: St. Martin's Press.

Wilensky, H. 1981. Leftism, Catholicism, and Democratic Corporatism: The Role of Political Parties in Recent Welfare State Development. In P. Flora and A. J. Heidenheimer, eds., *The Development of Welfare States in Europe and America.* New Brunswick, N.J.: Transaction Books.

Wils, Lode. 1986. De Katholieke Partij in de 19e Eeuw: Organisatie, Programma en Aanhang. In Emiel Lamberts and Jacques Lory, eds., *1884: Un tournant politique en Belgique—De Machtswisseling van 1884 in Belgie.* Brussels: Publications des Facultés Universitaires Saint-Louis.

Wilson, Brian R. 1968. Religious Organization. In David L. Sills, ed., *International Encyclopedia of the Social Sciences.* New York: Macmillan and Free Press.

Windell, George G. 1954. *The Catholics and German Unity, 1866–1871*. Minneapolis: University of Minnesota Press.

Witte, Els. 1973. The Political Struggle for Power in and for the Main Belgian Towns during the Period 1830–1848. *Res Publica* 15:371–83.

Witte, Els, and Jan Craeybeckx. 1987. *La Belgique politique de 1830 à nos jours: Les tensions d'une démocratie bourgeoise*. Brussels: Editions Labor.

Woeste, Charles. 1927. *Mémoires pour servir à l'histoire contemporaine de la Belgique*. Vol. 1. Brussels: Librairie Albert Dewit.

——. 1933. *Mémoires pour servir à l'histoire contemporaine de la Belgique*. Vol. 2. Brussels: L'Edition Universelle.

Wolff, Richard J. 1979. The Makings of Christian Democracy: The Federazione Universitària Cattolica Italiana between Church and State, 1925–1943. Ph.D. dissertation, Columbia University.

Wolinetz, Steven B. 1979. The Transformation of Western European Party Systems Revisited. *Western European Politics* 2:4–28.

Wright, Gordon. 1964. *Rural Revolution in France: The Peasantry in the Twentieth Century*. Stanford: Stanford University Press.

Yonke, Eric John. 1990. The Emergence of a Roman Catholic Middle Class in Nineteenth-Century Germany: Catholic Associations in the Prussian Rhine Province, 1837–1876. Ph.D. dissertation, University of North Carolina, Chapel Hill.

——. 1994. The Catholic Subculture in Modern Germany: Recent Work in the Social History of Religion. *Catholic Historical Review* 80:534–45.

Zeender, John K. 1976. *The German Center Party, 1890–1906*. Philadelphia: American Philosophical Society.

——. 1984. Recent Literature on the German Center Party. *Catholic Historical Review* 70:428–41.

——. 1992. Ludwig Windthorst, 1812–1891. *History* 77:237–54.

Zeps, Michael Joseph. 1979. The Politics of Education in Austria: Church, State and the Reform of Education, 1765–1962. Ph.D. dissertation, Stanford University.

Zerbi, Piero. 1961. *Il movimento cattolico in Italia da Pio IX a Pio X. Linee di sviluppo*. Milan: Editrice Vita e Pensiero.

Zsigmond, László. 1970. A propos de la discussion sur la notion et l'interprétation de la démocratie chrétienne. *Etudes historiques*. Budapest: Akadémiai Kiadó.

Zucker, Stanley. 1984. Philipp Wassenburg and Political Catholicism in Nineteenth-Century Germany. *Catholic Historical Review* 70:14–27.

Subject Index

Action catholique générale des hommes, 162
Action française, 160n, 163, 176
Action libérale (AL), 156–57
Adler, Victor, 47
Albertario Davide, 41
Algemeenen Bond, 195
Alliance libérale populaire (ALP), 12, 96n, 107, 110, 114n, 148, 155n, 156–61, 166
Anschluss, 236
Anticlerical attacks, 171–74; and conservatives, 54–55; and education, 97; popular petitions against, 66, 124, 207; reaction of the church, 60–63; reaction of the lower clergy, 83; and religious mobilization, 97; Austria, 196–97; Belgium, 189; France, 122–23; Germany, 208–9, 212–14; Italy, 215–16; Netherlands, 193
Antirevolutionary party, 111; formation 193–94
Association catholique de la jeunesse belge, 184
Association catholique de la jeunesse française (ACJF), 37, 70n, 93, 129n, 130, 133, 134n, 154n
Association constitutionnelle conservatrice, 59, 188, 189, 190
Association of German Catholics, 185
Association of German Christian Peasant Associations, 215
Associazione della gioventù cattolica, 72n, 217n
Assumptionists, 33n, 130n, 154n, 155
Augustinusverein, 215
Aulike, Mathias, 91, 178
Au milieu des sollicitudes, 151
Azione cattolica. *See* Catholic Action

Bachem, Carl, 182
Bachem, Julius, 248, 252, 253
Barthou, Louis, 138
Bauernvereine, 179
Bayerische Patriotenpartei. *See* Patriot party (Bavaria)
Bazire, Henri, 114
Beernaert, Auguste, 191–92
Beust, Ferdinand, 197
Benedict XV, 186
Bismarck, Otto von, 7, 45, 105, 126, 204, 206n, 232, 236, 240, 252
Bissing, Ferdinand, 227
Bitter, Franz, 235, 237
Blanquart de Bailleul, Mgr, 119
Blome, Gustav, 88
Bonapartists, 121, 151
Boncompagni law, 216
Bonghi, Ruggero, 225
Bonnet, Louis, 158
Boselli cabinet, 180, 221
Boulanger, Georges, 54n, 140–41, 150, 165
Brandis, Ferdinand, 246
Bürgerministerium, 196

Cameroni, Agostino, 246
Cartel des Gauches, 162

Casati law, 216
Catch-allism, 237
Catholic Action: absence of, in Germany, 254; Austria, 183; Italy, 81, 102n, 181, 186, 218n, 220, 221, 225; as a strategy, 183–84, 187n
Catholic church. *See* Church
Catholic congresses: Austria, 178, 200, 201, 232; Florence, 69–70; Germany. *See* Katholikentag; Malines, 59, 71, 187, 188; Modena, 175, 225n
Catholic electoral coalitions: electoral success of, 93–108; formation of, 76–79; surprising success of, 103–5; Austria, 94, 200–202; Belgium, 94, 191–92; France, 153–60; Germany, 94–95, 210–12; Italy, 95, 219–21; Netherlands, 94, 219–21
Catholic mass organizations: absence of, in France, 128–31; and conservative leaders, 226–32; and conservative political space, 223–25; effects of their absence in France, 141–50; electoral success, 99–103; evolution of, 72–74; growth in France after 1905, 161–63; obstruction by the church, 176–81; political socialization of members, 72–73; recuperation by the church, 183–87; repression by the church, 175–76; structure and objectives of, 68–72
Catholic Merchants' Association, 215
Catholic Officials' Association, 215
Catholic parties. *See* Confessional parties
Catholic political identity, 4, 9, 18, 57, 87, 108–10, 142, 145, 167, 180, 188, 222, 225, 227, 247, 262
Catholic Workers Association, 215
Center, Centrum. *See* Zentrum
Cercles d'ouvriers catholiques, 129n, 130
Chambord, Count of, 45, 121, 139n, 140n
Christian Democracy, 1–5, 258–64
Christian Democratic parties, 1–3, 5–6; definition, 263–64; distinctiveness of, 116, 237
Christian Democratic phenomenon, 1–3, 257–64
Christian Social party, 46, 83, 94, 178, 184, 185, 227, 230, 237, 245, 249–51; formation, 199–203
Church, 28–36; alliances with Liberals, 167–71; preferences in France, 119–20; reluctance to form a confessional party, 73–74; response to the anticlerical attacks, 123–28; and rise of mass organizations, 174–87; strategies of. *See* Organizational strategy; Participation strategy
Clam-Martinic, Heinrich, 69
Clerustag, 175
Codex, 86
Collective action, problem of, 11
Combes, Emile, 158
Comité central catholique, 190
Comité central conservateur, 188
Comités justice-égalité, 130n, 154n
Comités scolaires, 191
Commune, 118
Comparative method, 14–16
Concordat: and strategy of recuperation, 184, 187; Austria, 184, 196; France, 118, 133; Germany, 186
Confessional dilemma, 241–48
Confessional parties: accounts of formation, 3–5, 18; and aconfessionality, 234–41; and church intervention, 237–41; consequences for conservatives, 111–12; consequences for the church, 44–51, 112, 182; and constraints of religion, 232–34; and democracy, 112–13, 258–61, 264; description, 51; distinctiveness of, 24–25; emergence of, 21–25, 109–10; importance of initial electoral victories, 107–8; as instruments of the church, 5; political legitimacy of, 7; and redefinition of Catholicism, 244–47; secularization of, 2, 222–23, 261, 261n; social heterogeneity of, 235–38; toleration by the church, 181–82; and World War I, 5, 15
  Austria. *See* Christian Social party
  Belgium. *See* Parti catholique Belge
  France: theories of absence of confessional party, 116–18. *See also* Alliance libérale populaire; Jeune République; Mouvement republicain populaire; Parti démocrate populaire;
  Germany. *See* Zentrum
  Italy. *See* Partito popolare italiano (PPI)
  Netherlands. *See* Antirevolutionary party; General League of Roman Catholic Electoral Associations
  Poland, 3n, 175n
  Slovakia, 3n, 175n
  Spain, 3n, 110n
Confraternities, 38, 42n, 64n
Conquista Popolare, 96
Conservative Association. *See* Association constitutionnelle conservatrice

Conservatives, 51–57; and Catholic leaders, 226–32; and the Catholic movement, 223–26; and electoral success, 99; strategy of, 58–60; and vote maximization, 27, 241; Belgium, 59, 188–92
France, 120–22; and elections, 144–50; and mass politics, 146–50; and the Republic, 139–41
Germany, 214
Italy, 219–20
Netherlands, 194–95
Constitution party, 196
Contingency, 262–63
Coppino law, 216n, 219
Cronenberg, Eduard, 39
Croix, La, 46n, 77n, 130n, 154n, 158

Dalla Torre, Count, 186, 220, 221
De Castelneau, Edouard, 162
Dechamps, Adolphe, 59, 177, 229
Dechamps, Victor, 40, 46, 189
Declericalization of confessional parties, 242–48; Austria, 249–51; Belgium, 349; France, 255; Germany, 251–54; Italy, 254–55; Netherlands, 249
De Gasperi, Alcide, 227
De la Ligne, Prince, 169
De la Rochefoucauld, Duke of, 121
De la Tour d' Auvergne, Mgr., 119
De Lettenhove, Kervyn, 59
De Mun, Albert, 6, 45, 110, 120, 129, 132, 140n, 144, 150, 152, 153, 156, 157
Denier des écoles catholiques, 190
De Savornin Lohman, A. F., 88, 195n
Dolfuss dictatorship, 185, 251
Dreyfus affair, 123, 155
Droite Constitutionnelle, 153–54, 156
Ducpétiaux, Edouard, 169, 205n
Dumortier, Barthélemy, 53, 98, 205n
Dupanloup, Félix, Mgr., 119
Dutch Reformed church, 111

Eichart, Franz, 97
Essentialism, 8–11
Etsi nos, 217

Fédération catholique et constitutionnelle, 155
Fédération des cercles catholiques, 77, 188–90, 225
Fédération des cercles catholiques et des associations constitutionnelles conservatrices, 190, 192
Fédération des républicains démocrates du Finistère (FRDF), 149
Fédération électorale, 154–56
Fédération nationale catholique (FNC), 76, 162, 176
Federation of Independents, 99, 191
Federazione tra le associazioni del clero italiano (FACI), 84n, 181
Fermo proposito, il, 86, 219
Ferry laws, 124
Franckenberg, Fred von, 230
Frankfurt assembly, 170
Franz Josef, 197, 198
Free Conservative party, 210, 214, 224
Freezing hypothesis, 20
Frère-Orban, Walther, 94, 103, 172, 173
Functionalism, 7–8

Gallarati Scotti, Tomaso, 92
Gambetta, Léon, 122, 158
Garnier, abbé, 154n, 255
Gaspari, Pietro, 248
Gayraud, Hippolyte, 142, 154n
Gemelli, Agostino, 248, 255
General League of Roman Catholic Electoral Associations, 177, 249; formation of, 194–95
Gentiloni pact, 77, 81, 95, 154, 181, 219, 220
German Nationals, 200
Gessmann, Albert, 233, 236
Gibier, Charles, 33, 65
Giolitti, Giovanni, 58, 107, 219n
Goblet law, 123
Goudeau, Bernard, 259
Grévy, Jules, 122
Gröber, Adolf, 243, 251
Gröbl, Dominic, 179
Grusha, Anton, 202

Harmel, Léon, 6
Hefele, Karl Joseph von, 178
Hertling, Georg, 88
Hitler, Adolf, 185, 187n
Hohenlohe, Prince, 208
Hohenwart club, 198
Hussarek, Max, 197

Ideology, role of, 19, 167, 262
Institutions, role of in party formation, 111

Jacobini note, 240
Jacobs, Victor, 91, 192, 227
Jacobs law, 192

Jednota, 175
Jeugdverbond voor Katholieke Aktie, 184
Jeune Garde Catholique, 190
Jeune République, 114n, 163n
Jeunesse agricole catholique (JAC), 102
Jolly, Julius, 207
Jörg, Joseph Edmund, 62, 84, 227, 236

Kanzelparagraph, 213
Kappeyne van de Coppello, Joannes, 193
Katholikentag, 205n, 227
Katholikenverein, 80n, 175
Katholische Fraktion, 203
Katholische Konservative Volkspartei, 203
Katholische Schulverein, 199
Katholische Union von Österreich, 184
Katholische Volkspartei (Baden), 207, 227
Katholische Volkspartei (Tyrol), 231
Katholische Volksverein, 185, 198, 212
Katholisch-Konservative Volksverein, 198, 224n
Katholisch-Patriotische Volksverein, 198, 224n
Kevelaer pilgrimage, 248
Kleindeutsche option, 204
Klostergesetz, 213
Klostersturm, 208
Kopp, Cardinal, 46, 252
Korum, Felix Michael, 239
Kulturkampf, 46, 143, 168, 179, 212–14, 231, 251; Austrian, 198
Kuyper, Abraham, 77, 87, 88, 193, 194, 222n, 225n

Lamennais, Felicité Robert de, 119, 132
Lamy, Etienne, 153–55, 232, 233
Lasker, Eduard, 104, 105
Lateran agreements, 186
Lavigerie, Charles Martial, 48
Lay Catholics, 86–93; in France, 143–44; as part of the church's structure, 30–31
League of French Women, 130
Le Chapelier law, 134
Lega Democratica Nazionale, 175
Legitimists, 121
Lemire, Jules Auguste, 40n, 85, 141, 142n, 148, 154n, 181, 233
Leo XIII, 43, 48, 49, 89, 151, 156
Leoverein, 185, 243
Liberal Catholics, 259
Liberals, 51, 106–7, 172–74; Austria, 196–99; Belgium, 4, 187–88; Germany, 207–8, 212–14; Italy, 215–16; Netherlands, 192–94

Lichtenstein, Alois, 199, 202
Lieber, Ernst, 245
Ligue de l'Enseignement, 130, 136
Lindau, Jacob, 227
Longinotti, Giovanni Maria, 81
Lower clergy, 82–86; as electoral agitators, 98–99; in France, 142–43; as part of the church's structure, 29–30
Lueger, Karl, 200–202, 227, 247n, 250

Mackay law, 195
MacMahon, Marshall, 122, 140n
Mahr, Friedrich, 41
Mainzer Verein, 213, 215
Mallinckrodt, Hermann von, 210
Malou, Jules, 51n, 53, 59, 71, 74, 188, 192, 229
Maria Theresa, 197
Maritain, Jacques, 244
May laws, 197–99
Mechanisms, explanation by, 16
Meda, Filipo, 47, 88, 92, 93n, 108n, 180, 181, 221, 225, 227
Melchers, Paulus, 178, 209
Mercier, Désiré-Joseph, 29
Merry del Val, Rafael, 70, 165
Miglioli, Guido, 89, 236
Mirari vos, 168
Missiroli, Mario, 247
Moabit affair, 208
Molet, Guy, 7
Montalembert, Charles de, 119, 224
Mouvement républicain populaire (MRP), 7, 115, 116, 162, 255
Müller, Eduard, 104
Murri, Romolo, 175, 180, 218, 236, 239
Mussolini, Benito, 50, 51n

National Liberals, 207, 211, 224, 253
Naudet, Paul, 154n, 163
Necchi, Vico, 259
Noncomparative perspective, 12–13
Non expedit, 180, 218, 219

Olgiati, Francesco, 71, 255
Opera dei congressi e dei comitati cattolici in Italia, 40, 70, 72, 92, 180, 181, 217, 218, 258n, 259
Oppersdorff, Hans Georg von, 244
Opportunists, 151, 153, 154
Organizational strategy: content of, 63–68; costs of, 27–28, 36–43; failure of, 74–76;

political effects of, 74; political project of, 66–68; summary of, 22–23
Austria, 197–98
Belgium, 187–89
France: absence of, 128–31; post-1905, 161–63
Germany, 205–8
Italy, 216–18
Netherlands, 192–93
Orleanists, 121

Paganuzzi, Giambattista, 93n, 205n, 217
Pan-Germans, 250
Paris, Count of, 121, 139n, 140n
Parti catholique Belge, 176–77, 191n, 236, 237, 243n, 249; formation, 191–92
Participation strategy: compared to the organizational strategy, 76; content of, 76; costs of, 43–44; and electoral process, 98–99; forms of, 77–78; objective of, 80; political effects of, 78–81; role of lay catholics in, 81; summary of, 23–24; unraveling of, 82–93; Austria, 198–202; Belgium, 189–91; France, 150–60; Germany, 209–11; Italy, 218–20; Netherlands, 193–94
Parti démocrate populaire (PDP), 114n, 163n, 255
Parti social chrétien–Christelijke Volkspartij (PSC-CVP), 247
Partito nazionale conservatore, 175
Partito popolare italiano (PPI): compared to socialists, 7; confessional priorities of, 234; declericalization of, 247–48, 254–55; electoral performance, 95–96, 100, 103–4, 106; formation of, 15, 81, 107, 182, 221; relations to church, 4, 51, 181, 186, 238, 240; social composition of, 236; and Sturzo, 85, 245
Party formation, 3n, 6, 12–14
Patriot party (Bavaria), 62, 173, 207, 208, 210, 224n, 228, 236
Patriot party (Netherlands), 169
Pascendi, 69
Pellizzo, Luigi, 82
Pfalzer Kurier, 209
Picard, François, 129
Pieni l'animo, 175
Piou, Jacques, 88, 153, 156–58
Pius IX, 48, 82, 197, 213
Pius X, 31, 69, 181
Pius XI, 183, 186
Pius XII, 260
Pius associations. *See* Piusverein
Piusverein, 80n, 132, 170
Poell, L. T. J., 82
Political identities, 3, 8–11, 20
Popolari. *See* Partito popolare italiano
Popular Catholic Union, 194, 195
Popular Union. *See* Unione popolare
Porsch, Felix, 46, 231, 251
Priests. *See* Lower clergy
Primordial identities, 8, 9
Programmisme, 80, 191
Progressives: France, 158n; Germany, 170
Promotrice, 217
Protestants, 3n, 203n, 206, 211, 214
Protestantverein, 209

Quanta Cura, 64

Radicals, 136, 158
Ralliement, 33, 150–53, 156, 226
Rampolla, Mariano, 146, 149, 152, 154
Rauscher, Joseph, 31n, 61, 68, 71, 170, 199
Reichensperger, August, 104, 204, 210, 211
Reichensperger, Peter, 59, 210, 236
Reichsvolksschulgesetz, 197
Republicans, 122n, 136–39
Rerum Novarum, 64
Rhenish Artisans' League, 215
RK Volkbond. *See* Popular Catholic Union
Roman Catholic Electoral Association of North Brabant, 193
Roman Catholic State Party (Roomsch-Katholieke Staatspartij–RKSP), 195
Rudigier, Franz, 82n, 197

Sacchetti, Giuseppe, 39, 73, 89, 231
Sandri, Bartolomeo, 71, 87, 259
Sapientiae Christianae, 48
Savigny, Karl von, 210
Scheicher, Josef, 40, 104
Schindler, Martin, 202
Schönborn, Franz, 202, 252
Schopen, Edmund, 248
Schöpfer, Aemilian, 231
Second empire, 118, 140
Secularization, of confessional parties, 2, 222–23, 261
Seipel, Ignaz, 85, 235, 250, 251
Separation Law, 158, 159n, 161
Seyfardt, Ludwig Friedrich, 104
Shaepman, Herman, 47, 177, 195, 229, 249

Sibour, Marie Dominique Auguste, 29, 30
Siccardi laws, 216
Sillon, 120, 163n, 175
Simon, Jules, 134
Social Democracy, 5, 256, 264; in Austria, 199, 203
Social Democrats, 253, 261n, 264
Socialist parties, 2, 6, 96, 102, 248
Socialists, 10, 75, 173
Société générale d'éducation et d'enseignement, 129
Society for Christian National Education, 193
Soest program, 99, 209, 211
Standen, 231, 237
Sterckx, Engelbert, 31n, 176, 187
Stillfried, Eduard, 91
Structuralist approaches, 17
Sturzo, Luigi, 5, 6, 47, 81, 95, 186, 220, 222, 243, 245, 246, 254, 255
Syllabus Errorum, 64, 86, 139, 217n, 258

Taaffe, Eduard, 198
Taine, Hippolyte, 35
Thun, Leo, 54, 63
Tories, 1

Union catholique de Belgique, 174, 188
Union des droites, 147
Unione economico-sociale, 89, 218n
Unione elettorale, 218n, 219, 220
Unione fra le donne cattoliche italiane, 218
Unione popolare, 175, 181, 186, 218n, 221
Unionism, 169, 187
Union nationale pour le redressement des griefs, 184, 191, 192
Unitas, 175
United Christians, 77, 200, 201
Urbi Arcano Dei, 36, 65n, 80n, 183

Van Humbeck law, 169, 189, 192
Van Poldersveldt, Dommer, 175
Vehementer Nos, 30
Verbandskatholizismus, 65
Vereine: Austria, 183, 185, 201; Germany, 206, 208, 209
Vereinskatholizismus, 65
Verhaegen, Arthur, 229
Veuillot, Eugène, 73, 119, 150
Vichy, 166
Vogelsang, Carl von, 198, 200n
Volksverein für das Katholische Deutschland, 45, 179, 185, 215, 218n, 243, 244, 251–53

Wacker, Theodor, 45, 253
Wackernell, Josef, 46
Waldeck-Rousseau, Pierre-Marie-René, 172n
Weiss, Albert Maria, 248
Westphalian Peasant League, 210
Wilhelm Wehrenpfennig, 106
William I, 168
Windthorst, Ludwig, 6, 18, 41, 46, 55, 59, 80, 88, 120, 185, 204, 212, 215, 227, 239, 240, 245, 248, 251
Woeste, Charles, 71, 103, 192, 229

Zentrum: and anticlericalism, 208; compared to the Zentrumsfraktion, 204; confessional priorities, 234–35; and conservative politicians, 80, 226; declericalization of, 241, 243–45, 248, 251–54; electoral performance of, 94–96, 102, 104, 106, 232n, 233; formation of, 59, 107, 210–15; and German Catholics, 261; internal conflict, 230, 253; legitimacy of, 7; as a model, 180–81, 195; political personnel of, 88, 102n, 231; social composition of, 236; relations to church, 178–79, 182, 185, 237–38, 240; uniqueness of, 12; and Windthorst, 18, 55n, 227
Zentrumsfraktion, 171, 175, 203, 204, 210
Zentrumsstreit, 253
Zollparlament, 206, 207

Author Index

Agócs, Sándor, 31n, 46, 72n, 86, 89, 90, 96, 176, 214, 215, 247n
Agulhon, Maurice, 135, 138, 145n
Aldrich, John H., 12, 27, 165, 257n
Ameye, Jacques, 127, 156, 160
Aminzade, Ronald, 122n, 134, 136n, 167
Anderson, Malcolm, 87, 121, 129n, 130n, 157n, 158, 164, 166
Anderson, Margaret Lavinia, 4n, 6, 7, 10, 22, 33, 41, 45, 46, 55, 59, 62, 79, 80, 94, 96, 96n, 98, 101n, 104–6, 170, 179, 185, 204, 205, 209, 210–15, 223, 227, 230–33, 235–42, 245, 248, 251, 252, 253n, 261n
Arnal, Oscar L., 33, 142n, 162n, 163, 183
Aubert, Roger, 15, 18n, 21n, 22, 30, 31, 42, 65, 67, 69, 84, 87, 89, 117n, 120, 128, 140, 150n, 168, 187, 188, 249, 259

Bakvis, Herman, 12, 47, 69, 82, 169, 175, 177, 195, 229
Barbier, Emmanuel, 73, 150
Barral, Pierre, 69n, 102, 129n, 142n, 144, 147, 152, 153, 156, 162n, 163
Bartolini, Stefano, 11n, 20n, 115
Baum, Gregory, 5n, 245
Beaufays, Jean, 47, 73–74, 103, 168, 177, 189, 191–93, 195, 240
Becqué, Maurice, 46, 125, 189
Belardinelli, Mario, 45, 69, 81, 180, 182, 219
Berger, Suzanne, 148, 161, 259, 260
Bessières, Albert, 33, 48, 65, 69, 71, 127–30, 132, 162
Beyme, Klaus von, 2n, 8, 67n
Billiet, Jaak, 5n, 37n, 86, 110, 184, 190n, 191n, 231, 244, 249, 255
Birnbaum, Pierre, 139, 166
Blackbourn, David, 7, 8, 22, 30–32, 46, 137, 178, 179, 233, 234, 237, 243, 248, 251, 252, 254
Bled, Jean-Paul, 54, 62, 68, 69, 71, 82n, 88, 90, 91, 170, 177, 178, 199, 246
Bon, Frédéric, 147, 148
Boswell, Jonathan, 2n, 223
Bosworth, William, 5, 9, 15, 34n, 38, 116, 130, 133, 144, 159–61, 183
Boudon, Raymond, 16, 17, 263
Boulange, Bruno, 71, 75, 87
Boulard, Fernand, 66, 117n, 124
Bourdieu, Pierre, 10, 108
Boutry, Philippe, 12, 20n, 114, 117, 128, 144, 157n, 161, 162
Boyer, John W., 32n, 40, 41, 46–48, 61, 69, 82n, 83, 84, 90, 94, 97, 100, 103, 104, 173, 175, 177, 178, 184, 200–202, 226, 227, 231, 233, 236, 247–50
Brachin, Pierre, 83, 193, 194, 249
Brose, Eric Dorn, 39, 211
Broughton, David, 4

Canavero, Alfredo, 90, 104
Capéran, Louis, 124, 125, 126n, 127n, 133, 165, 190n
Carrillo, Elisa A., 84n, 181
Carton de Wiart, Henri, 12, 94, 99, 189, 228
Casanova, José, 185, 186

Chaline, Nadine-Josette, 120, 129, 134n, 161
Chapman, Guy, 26, 33, 134n
Cholvy, Gérard, 66, 101n, 117n, 124, 128, 130, 132, 161, 162n
Coleman, John A., 5n, 67, 245
Congar, Yves, 30, 65n
Coppa, Frank J., 219n, 220n
Corbin, Alain, 128, 129n, 145n
Cordewiener, André, 87, 176
Cunsolo, Ronald S., 95, 100, 181, 226

Daalder, Hans, 66, 169, 177, 193
D'Andrea, Giampaolo, 70, 101n
Dansette, Adrien, 10, 30, 32n, 33, 42, 56, 68, 70, 101n, 118, 120, 125–27, 130, 131, 134n, 142, 144, 152, 155, 158, 160, 161, 164, 171, 224
De Kwaasteniet, Marjanne, 8, 169, 193
Delfosse, Pascale, 65n, 100, 168, 188, 191, 192, 228, 229
Delumeau, Jean, 58, 129n, 162
De Moreau, P. E, 97, 190, 249
DeNardo, James, 8n, 17
Denis, Michel, 55, 121, 157, 158n, 160, 224, 229, 231
De Rosa, Gabriele, 8, 36, 39, 45, 47, 48, 50, 58, 64n, 70–74, 78n, 81, 82n, 83, 90, 92, 94, 95, 104, 108n, 175, 180, 181, 205n, 216–21, 225, 240, 246
Desaubliaux, Marc, 121, 150
De Trannoy, Baron, 51–53, 59, 187
Dobbelaere, Karel, 37n, 255
Doyle, Peter, 88n, 110n, 131
Dupeux, Georges, 139, 148, 152
Durand, Jean-Dominique, 6, 8, 39, 73, 114, 117, 175n, 241, 245, 249
Duverger, Maurice, 4, 159

Ebbinghaus, Bernhard, 2n, 116
Einaudi, Mario, 51, 100, 106, 133, 240, 254
Eliassen, Kjell A., 13, 14
Elster, Jon, 16, 32
Epstein, Klaus, 88, 236, 253
Erba, Achille, 59, 84, 181
Esping-Andersen, Gøsta, 2n, 4
Evans, Ellen Lovell, 7, 169, 170, 212, 213, 232, 251
Evans, Richard, 127n, 128, 215

Falter, Rolf, 99, 101, 191
Faury, Jean, 32, 117n, 125, 132, 142, 143, 145, 146
Fogarty, Michael P., 6n, 215, 252
Ford, Caroline C., 7n, 12, 69, 116, 117n, 142, 145, 149, 164
Formigoni, Guido, 81, 88, 245, 246
France, Alan W., 54, 61, 66, 71, 75, 87, 94, 104, 106, 107, 178, 196–99, 216
Frognier, André-Paul, 65n, 100, 168–69, 188, 192, 200, 228–29
Fulton, John, 5n, 26, 80, 160n

Gabbert, Mark A., 29–30
Gadille, Jacques, 33, 45, 48, 49, 62, 120, 124, 125n, 129, 130n, 142–45, 147, 155
Gambasin, Angelo, 30, 48, 64–69, 71, 72, 87, 89, 92, 126, 131, 217, 221, 258, 259
Geehr, Richard S., 200, 201
Gellott, Laura S., 43, 183–85, 250
Gerard, Emmanuel, 5n, 86, 110, 184, 190n, 191n, 231, 244, 245, 249
Gherardi, Gabriele, 72, 175, 180, 246
Gibson, Ralph, 35, 39, 117n, 132, 135, 139, 167, 172
Gill, Anthony, 26n, 35n
Giovannini, Claudio, 7, 175, 218
Goguel, François, 51, 100, 106, 121, 124, 133, 137–39, 140n, 147, 152, 157n, 240, 254
Goyau, Georges, 85, 204, 205n, 207–9
Gramsci, Antonio, 5n, 7, 26, 34, 38, 62, 63, 80, 93, 95, 101n, 143, 160n, 182, 254
Guyot de Mishaegen, 12, 53, 56n, 59, 89, 91, 94, 97, 98, 103, 172, 174, 176, 177, 188–90, 205n, 225, 227, 228, 249

Hanley, David, 6, 223
Hansen, John Mark, 11n, 12, 53, 100
Hanson, Eric O., 5, 29
Hart, Oliver, 31n, 35
Hatfield, Douglas W., 3n, 211, 213n
Hicks, Alexander, 2n, 4, 6, 116, 260n
Hilaire, Yves-Marie, 33, 61, 101n, 117n, 128, 129n, 130, 132, 142, 143, 151, 153, 161–63, 171
Hoffmann, Stanley, 115, 134
Horner, Franz, 72, 176, 260
Houska, Joseph J., 4, 38, 67n, 100, 182, 223
Houtart, François, 41, 128
Howard, Edith Pratt, 84, 180, 181, 218n, 219, 221, 234, 239, 254
Huard, Raymond, 117n, 135, 136
Huber, Evelyn, 2n, 4, 116
Hunley, J. D., 102, 106n
Hürten, Heinz, 185, 205n, 254

Irvine, William D., 52, 53, 54n, 136, 137, 139, 140n, 143, 146–49
Irving, R. E. M., 5, 6, 8, 19n, 116, 120, 163
Iserloh, Erwin, 185, 215

Jadoulle, J.-L., 1n, 259
Jemolo, A. C., 39, 55n, 67, 69, 83, 86, 92, 176, 216, 219, 220, 238, 240
Jenks, William Alexander, 59, 172, 197, 199, 202
Jones, P. M., 98, 99, 105, 106, 137, 142, 148

Katznelson, Ira, 11, 72, 73n, 79
Kirchheimer, Otto, 35n, 223, 237
Kitschelt, Herbert, 6, 14, 17, 32n, 227n, 262
Klemperer, Klemens von, 85, 201, 236, 250
Koelble, Thomas A., 16, 32n
Köhler, Oscar, 65, 128–29
Kossmann, Ernst Heinrich, 10, 98n, 169, 177

Laitin, David, 9, 10, 11n, 15
Lamberts, Emiel, 40, 91, 149, 258
Lapierre, Jean-Pie, 120, 125, 127, 140n, 141, 144, 151, 157, 171
Larkin, Maurice, 130n, 155, 158, 165
Latreille A., 126n, 129n, 139, 163
Laury, Jacques, 35, 94, 107, 128, 149, 187, 189, 190
Le Béguec, Gilles, 114, 143, 144, 157, 166
Leblicq, Yvon, 53, 169
Leonardi, Robert, 4, 223
Levi, Margaret, 16, 26
Levillain, Philippe, 120, 125–27, 129, 132, 140n, 141, 144, 147, 151–53, 157, 171
Lijphart, Arend, 14, 115
Lill, Rudolf, 29, 108, 127, 132n, 205
Lipset, Seymour M., 3, 6, 7, 13, 20, 63, 115, 116, 257, 260
Locke, Robert L., 121, 149
Lönne, Karl-Egon, 6n, 163n
Lorwin, Val, 8, 38, 116, 236
Loubère, Leon A., 145, 160, 171
Luebbert, Gregory M., 14, 41, 49n, 94, 100, 116, 151n, 159
Lynch, Edward A., 3, 5, 96
Lyon, Margot, 4, 8

Macartney, C. A., 197, 198
Mackie, Thomas T., 3n, 261
Maier, Hans, 2n, 8, 14, 226–27
Mair, Peter, 11n, 20n, 100, 115
Malgeri, Francesco, 8, 81, 100, 104, 181, 221, 255
Mann, Golo, 12, 170
Martin, Benjamin F. Jr., 95, 96n, 110, 120, 129n, 144, 150n, 155–59, 163
Martin, David, 3n, 223n
May, Anita Rasi, 22, 36n, 119
Mayeur, Jean-Marie, 5n, 6n, 7, 9n, 30, 33, 40, 46n, 62n, 79, 84–87, 115, 116, 117n, 120–22, 126, 131, 136, 138, 139n, 141, 143, 148, 158, 161, 163, 178, 181, 187, 207, 211, 214n, 228, 233, 258n, 259
McLeod, Hugh, 12, 32, 47, 65, 101n
McManners, John, 44, 48, 77n, 79, 83, 142n, 145, 146, 148, 156, 160, 255
Mélot, Auguste, 4, 48, 59–62, 76, 77n, 82n, 233, 234, 239
Mendershausen, Ralph René, 81, 102, 185, 215, 226, 254
Michel, Alain-René, 12, 19n, 114, 117, 128, 144, 157n, 161, 162
Misra, Joya, 2n, 4, 6, 116, 260n
Molette, Charles, 37, 42, 70n, 88, 93, 119, 120, 129, 132, 134n, 155, 156
Molony, John, 5, 14, 37, 51, 65n, 71, 83, 88–89, 95–97, 181, 182, 186, 221, 234, 238, 239, 243, 246, 247, 255

Neitzel, Sarah C., 8, 71, 72
Nipperdey, Thomas, 1n, 8, 9n, 92, 235
Noiret, Serge, 7n, 17n, 176

Olson, Mancur, 11, 128
Osa, Maryjane, 175n, 183
Ozouf, Mona, 61, 124, 126n, 129, 150

Pace, Enzo, 9, 86
Papanek, Ernst, 75n, 199, 201
Partin, Malcolm O., 115, 123, 126, 129n, 130, 139, 140, 154, 156, 157, 172n, 173
Pasture, Patrick, 247, 249
Pirenne, Henri, 35, 42, 94, 103, 169, 172, 173, 192
Pizzorno, Alessandro, 4, 10, 36, 52, 79
Plavsic, Wladimir S., 71, 176
Poulat, Emile, 9, 96, 130, 132, 227, 246, 259n
Preneel, L., 80, 175, 177, 184, 190, 191
Prévotat, Jacques, 114, 143, 144, 157, 166
Przeworski, Adam, 5n, 9, 10, 11n, 15, 17, 67, 75, 106, 115, 232, 256

Ravitch, Norman, 64n, 121, 132n, 133, 176
Raymond-Laurent, J., 130, 142
Reinerman, Alan J., 96n, 216

Rémond, René, 40n, 54n, 121, 129n, 140n, 141, 143, 148, 160n, 166
Remy, Jean, 127, 184, 255n
Rhodes, Anthony, 8, 183, 185, 186
Rivet, Auguste, 51n, 52, 56, 99, 101, 103n, 135n, 136, 148, 149, 158n, 161, 162n, 163, 229
Rogier, L.J., 83, 193, 249
Rokkan, Stein, 3, 7, 13, 14, 20, 63, 115, 116, 257
Rommen, Heinrich, 8, 11
Rose, Richard, 3n, 261
Rosenstone, Steven J., 11n, 12, 53, 100
Ross, Ronald J., 45, 179, 180, 182, 205, 208, 212, 230, 232, 235, 237, 239, 241–44, 248, 252–54

Sartori, Giovanni, 7, 117, 163n
Schorske, Carl E., 22, 87, 197, 200, 201
Scoppola, Pietro, 36, 112, 218, 219, 260n
Sedgwick, Alexander, 120, 121, 127, 149, 151–55, 232, 233, 259n
Sewell, William H. Jr., 15, 110, 167, 262
Shefter, Martin, 49n, 52n
Siegfried, André, 9, 148n, 156
Simon, Alois, 26, 29, 48, 55, 61, 82, 83, 90, 100, 108, 176, 188, 190, 192
Simon, Michel, 169, 191, 228, 238
Skocpol, Theda, 12, 14, 262, 263
Smith, Helmut Walser, 168, 202, 248
Soete, Jean-Luc, 21, 56, 59, 65n, 72, 80, 100, 101, 144, 176, 190, 191, 228, 229, 236, 259n
Somers, Margaret R., 11, 14
Southern, Gilbert Edwin, Jr., 41, 66, 70n, 72, 82–84, 86, 92, 97, 98, 100, 102, 103, 106, 179, 204, 206, 210, 227n, 228–29, 236, 237
Sperber, Jonathan, 15, 54, 62, 66, 67, 72, 74, 83, 94, 97–102, 170, 171, 204, 205, 206, 210–215, 247, 248
Spohn, Willfried, 7, 127n, 168
Sprague, John, 5n, 9–11, 15, 75, 115, 256
Stengers, Jean, 77, 78, 237, 243n, 249
Stephens, John D., 2n, 4, 149
Suardo, Dino Secco, 21, 38, 42, 69, 76, 80 87, 90, 103, 104, 106, 107, 231, 259
Svaasand, Lars, 13, 14

Tarrow, Sidney, 35, 36, 107, 134
Tash, Robert C., 35, 42
Terlinden, Charles, 64, 168, 189, 191
Tramontin, Silvio, 67, 89, 92, 131, 217n, 218, 225
Traniello, Francesco, 18, 47, 51n, 65–67, 86, 109

Vaillancourt, Jean Guy, 29–31, 34, 36n, 42, 182, 186, 187n
Vanden Berg, Frank, 66, 77, 87, 88, 103, 193n, 194, 225n
Van Eekeren, Wilhelmus Antonius Marie, 177, 194, 229, 249
Van Isaker, Karel, 67, 78
Van Kersbergen, Kees, 1n, 2n, 4, 56, 116, 223n, 237, 247, 261n
Van Kessel, P. J., 169
Varillon, F., 30, 65n
Vecchio, Giorgio, 6, 42, 66, 71, 72n, 82n, 89n, 92, 93, 96, 104, 181, 186, 187, 225, 228, 234, 243n, 245, 248, 254, 258n, 259, 261
Verhoef, Jan, 100, 195
Verkade, Willem, 61, 187, 188, 193–95
Verschave, Paul, 80, 87
Viance, Georges, 76, 90, 128, 132, 162
Vigier, Philippe, 130, 145n
Vismara Chiappa, Paola, 33, 146

Wallerstein, Michael, 12, 32n
Wandruszka, Adam, 197, 198, 200
Weber, Eugen, 145n, 146, 159, 162
Webster, Richard A., 39, 41, 50, 57n, 175, 180, 217, 218, 220, 221, 240, 254
Wertman, Douglas A., 4, 223
Whyte, John Y., 4, 6n, 18n, 56, 78, 133, 168, 170, 178, 204, 211
Wilensky, H., 2n, 116
Windell, George G., 11, 44, 61, 62, 71, 74, 83–86, 97, 98, 104, 168, 170, 171, 173, 175, 178, 179, 204, 206–9, 212, 224, 227
Witte, Els, 4, 106n, 173
Woeste, Charles, 71, 103
Wolff, Richard J., 104, 186
Wolinetz, Steven B., 223, 256

Yonke, Eric John, 30, 35, 84, 91, 92, 100, 102, 103, 178, 179, 203n, 205n, 206, 214, 226

Zeender, John K., 5, 7, 55n, 59, 236, 239, 248
Zeps, Michael Joseph, 63, 65, 67, 170, 184, 197, 198, 200, 227, 230, 235, 237, 245, 246, 249, 250–51
Zerbi, Piero, 5, 35, 40, 72, 131, 258

The Wilder House Series in Politics, History, and Culture

Language and Power: Exploring Political Cultures in Indonesia
by Benedict R. O'G. Anderson
Bandits and Bureaucrats: The Ottoman Route to State Centralization
by Karen Barkey
Reclaiming the Sacred: Lay Religion and Popular Politics in Revolutionary France
by Suzanne Desan
Divided Nations: Class, Politics, and Nationalism in the Basque Country and Catalonia
by Juan Díez Medrano
Manufacturing Inequality: Gender Division in the French and British Metalworking Industries, 1914-1939
by Laura Lee Downs
State and Society in Medieval Europe: Gwynedd and Languedoc under Outside Rule
by James Given
New Voices in the Nation: Women and the Greek Resistance, 1941-1964
by Janet Hart
The Rise of Christian Democracy in Europe
by Stathis N. Kalyvas
The Presence of the Past: Chronicles, Politics, and Culture in Sinhala Life
by Steven Kemper
True France: The Wars over Cultural Identity, 1900–1945
by Herman Lebovics
Unsettled States, Disputed Lands: Britain and Ireland, France and Algeria, Israel and the West Bank–Gaza
by Ian S. Lustick
Communities of Grain: Rural Rebellion in Comparative Perspective
by Victor V. Magagna
Hausaland Divided: Colonialism and Independence in Nigeria and Niger
by William F. S. Miles
"We Ask for British Justice": Workers and Racial Difference in Late Imperial Britain
by Laura Tabili
Gifts, Favors, and Banquets: The Art of Social Relationships in China
by Mayfair Mei-hui Yang